The Transnational Codification of International Arbitration

The Transnational Codification of International Arbitration

Uniformisation under the Shadow of War and Commerce

By

Bruno Sousa Rodrigues

BRILL | NIJHOFF

LEIDEN | BOSTON

The Library of Congress Cataloging-in-Publication Data is available online at https://catalog.loc.gov
LC record available at https://lccn.loc.gov/2025933522

Typeface for the Latin, Greek, and Cyrillic scripts: "Brill". See and download: brill.com/brill-typeface.

ISBN 978-90-04-72898-1 (hardback)
ISBN 978-90-04-72899-8 (e-book)
DOI 10.1163/9789004728998

This book is printed on acid-free paper and produced in a sustainable manner.

Dedicated to Caetano

Contents

Acknowledgements

This book is the outcome of my doctoral research. Writing a thesis is often portrayed as a solitary activity. If this were true, I would not have been able to complete this work. The process of researching and writing is a roller coaster of emotions – peaks of excitement are followed by an abyss of frustration. The pace of work can be frantic, as well as sluggish. Always lurking above a PhD candidate's head is the fear of failure, and the weight of one's own disproportionate ambitions. I have the conviction that without the guidance and emotional support from others nothing of importance can ever be achieved. A first thought goes to Diego P. Fernández Arroyo, who, more than a supervisor, has been a mentor and a friend. His scholarly example, generosity and advice are an inspiration. I must also thank all the professors and teachers who have taught me valuable lessons along the way, nurturing my curiosity and shaping my understanding of the world. Then, always by my side with a word of encouragement and a gesture of kindness were my family and friends. Camila, my partner and in-house editor, my godmother Rosa, my family in Japan, my in-laws, the friends I have from Brazil and the ones I made in France – without them where would I be? Likewise, I must acknowledge the contribution of my late mother, Maria Luisa, whose memory will always remind me of the core values I uphold. A final thought goes to my recently born son Caetano, who in such little time has filled my life with so much joy and purpose. I know that the completion of this book is as much the achievement of all the extraordinary people in my life as it is mine. Thus, I record here my profound gratitude for their patience and continuous support.

Defined Terms

Abbreviation	Definition
AAA	American Arbitration Association
AALCC	African-Asian Legal Consultative Committee
BIT	Bilateral Investment Treaty
ECAFE	Economic Commission for Asia and the Far East
ECE	Economic Commission for Europe
ECOSOC	United Nations Economic and Social Council
Geneva regime	1923 Protocol on Arbitration Clauses and the 1927 Convention on the Execution of Foreign Arbitral Awards, jointly considered
IBA	International Bar Association
IBRD	International Bank for Reconstruction and Development
ICC	International Chamber of Commerce
ICCA	International Council for Commercial Arbitration
ICJ	International Court of Justice
ICSID	International Centre for the Settlement of Investment Disputes
IDI	Institut de Droit International
ILA	International Law Association
LCA	London Court of Arbitration
LCIA	London Court of International Arbitration
MIGA	Multilateral Investment Guarantee Agency
New York Convention	1958 United Nations Convention on the Recognition and Enforcement of Foreign Arbitral Awards
OECD	Organization for Economic Co-operation and Development
PCA	Permanent Court of Arbitration
PCIJ	Permanent Court of International Justice
SLC	Société de législation comparé
UN	United Nations
UNCITRAL	United Nations Commission on International Trade Law
UNGA	United Nations General Assembly
UNIDROIT	International Institute for the Unification of Private Law
Washington Convention	1965 Convention on the Settlement of Investment Disputes between States and Nationals of Other States
WWI	World War I
WWII	World War II

CHAPTER 1

Introduction

The title of this monograph may be the object of some surprise. One may wonder how the opposing forces of war and commerce helped shape the transnational codification of international arbitration. The author cannot but present his excuses for an eventual drift towards obscurity and pretentiousness, reaffirming in these introductory remarks that the intention was not to add confusion to the debate but to hopefully expand ever so slightly our understanding of the field. The reader will therefore find in this preamble the unboxing of many ideas animating this research and guiding its inquiry.

For quite some time, the author has been intrigued by the materiality of law and the agency of legal form.[1] Legal scholarship has dissected law under various lenses, analysing it in relation to nature and morals,[2] assessing its structure and function,[3] scrutinizing it as a social institution,[4] a rhetorical device,[5] a network of normative orders,[6] as well as contemplating its existence as the contingent output of what judges have had for breakfast.[7] Yet, it has been a

1 See Ralf Michaels, 'Post-Critical Private International Law: From Politics to Technique' in Diego P Fernández Arroyo and Horatia Muir Watt (eds), *Private International Law and Global Governance* (Oxford University Press 2014); Annelise Riles, 'A New Agenda for the Cultural Study of Law: Taking on the Technicalities' (2005) 53 Buffalo Law Review 973; Annelise Riles, 'Models and Documents: Artefacts of International Legal Knowledge' (1999) 48 The International and Comparative Law Quarterly.

2 See Hans Kelsen, 'Foundation of the Natural Law Doctrine' (1973) 2 Anglo-American Law Review 83; HLA Hart, 'Positivism and the Separation of Law and Morals' (1958) 71 Harvard Law Review 593.

3 See Noberto Bobbio, *De la structure à la fonction : nouveaux essais de théorie du droit* (Dalloz 2012).

4 See Roscoe Pound, 'Sociology of Law and Sociological Jurisprudence' (1943) 5 The University of Toronto Law Journal 1.

5 See Neil MacCormick, *Rhetoric and the Rule of Law: A Theory of Legal Reasoning* (Oxford University Press 2005).

6 See Mireille Delmas-Marty, *Le Pluralisme Ordonné* (Seuil 2005).

7 See Jerome Frank, *Law and the Modern Mind* (Stevens & Sons Limited 1949).

 | DOI:10.1163/9789004728998_002

more recent ethnographical gaze over law that has successfully placed its most prosaic elements at the centre of intellectual inquiry.[8]

One knows quite well that the everyday life of law and lawyers is populated by a myriad of legal documents, such as files, case reports, textbooks, and codes. Nevertheless, while those initiated in the secrets of law do routinely engage with these elements, the legal document as a material object fades away with its technical manipulation. The paper, the ink and even the words disappear as normative meaning emerges, for it is the regulatory content of the document that will matter most for the legal professional. In other terms, the legal document itself is nothing but the vector of normativity, and its material dimension as a physical artefact encoding legal technique through language is usually forgotten in the maze of legal hermeneutics.

This caveat is made to highlight that, confronted with several legal documents aiming at the codification of arbitral procedure (reports, questionnaires, sets of arbitration rules, draft legislation, model laws, treaties and so on), the author took the stance of looking at them precisely as physical objects. This regard was conducive to studying codification projects with a heightened attention to their production processes, the conditions allowing for their advancement or retreat, as well as their circulation in time and space.[9]

While this monograph certainly contemplates the importance of the normative meaning conveyed in these documents, all the codification projects surveyed by this monograph are seen as "fragile bridges of texts" between various agents.[10] In this regard, they serve as an entry point for the analysis of how

8 See Bruno Latour, *The Making of Law* (Polity Press 2010). For an overview of Latour's anthropology of law, see Frédéric Audren and Cédric Moreau de Bellaing, 'Bruno Latour's Legal Anthropology' in Reza Banakar and Max Travers (eds), *Law and Social Theory* (Hart Publishing 2013).

9 See Milton Santos, *Técnica, Espaço, Tempo* (Edusp 2013); Milton Santos, *A natureza do espaço: técnica e tempo, razão e emoção* (Edusp 2009).

10 Bruno Latour is the one who carved the expression. The following extract offers a most insightful illustration of how this approach can be implemented: "Why should we discuss all these sordid details, as if the ethnographer had the myopia of a paper-eating mouse or that of an ant? Because, even while we are following the slow fabrication of a file, we are not neglecting the intellectual and cognitive foundations of the law for one moment. If the observer is short-sighted, the law is procedural: it's an eye for an eye, a tooth for a tooth ... It's precisely because the law follows a procedure that we might be able to discover the different professions at the Council by stubbornly following our cardboard folders and by noting how they grow and fatten, how they fold and unfold, as well as by noting the cupboards, offices, corridors, cellars, armchairs or desks on which they are put in order to let them turn ripe." See Latour, *The Making of Law*, 83.

such agents have acted and reacted in relation to the organization of arbitral procedure.

With that in mind, the reader will hopefully find in this monograph some potential explanations for how the transnational codification of arbitration affected its authority in the division of labour structuring a globalized administration of justice. Against this background, the story unfolding in the following pages will be populated by public and private international lawyers connected through reports, working groups, professional networks, many of whom ambitioning to produce instruments for the codification of arbitration procedure in order to govern the use of force in international relations and global economic flows.

At this point, a few words on the term codification seem appropriate.[11] In this study, codification is used in reference to the compilation, systematization and uniformization of scattered legal technique, having as its main output a written normative instrument.[12] The particularity of such normative instrument is to reduce a diversity of practices into a single mould, while vesting it with an allure of universality.[13] Yet, one may also argue that codification is

---

11 The attention to codification is inspired by the contributions of Fernández-Arroyo. See Diego P Fernández Arroyo, 'La Codificación Del Derecho Internacional Privado En América Latina (Ambitos de Producción Jurídica y Orientaciones Metodológicas)' (Universidad Complutense de Madrid 1993).

12 The literature on the topic is vast, but some points of reference might be highlighted. See Reinhard Zimmermann, 'Codification' (2012) 8 European Review of Contract Law; Gabrielle Kaufmann-Kohler, 'Soft Law in International Arbitration: Codification and Normativity' (2010) 1 Journal of International Dispute Settlement 283; Catherine Kessedjian, 'Codification Du Droit Commercial International et Droit International Privé : De La Gouvernance Normative Pour Les Relations Économiques Transnationales', *in Collected Courses of the Hague Academy of International Law*, vol 300 (Martinus Nijhoff Publishers 2002); Georges Abi-Saab, 'Fragmentation or Unification: Concluding Remarks' (1999) 31 New York University Journal of International Law and Political Science 919; Kenneth S Carlston, 'Codification of International Arbitral Procedure' (1953) 47 American Journal of International Law 203; René David, 'The Methods of Unification' (1968) 16 American Journal of Comparative Law 13; Charles de Visscher, 'La Codification Du Droit International', *in Collected Courses of the Hague Academy of International Law*, vol 6 (Brill 1925); Johann Kaspar Bluntschli, *Le Droit International Codifié* (Guillaume et Cie, Éditeurs 1895).

13 Bourdieu notes the following: "The law, an intrinsically powerful discourse coupled with the physical means to impose compliance on others, can be seen as a quintessential instrument of normalization. As such, given time, it passes from the status of 'orthodoxy,' proper belief explicitly defining what ought to happen, to the status of 'doxa,' the immediate agreement elicited by that which is self-evident and normal. Indeed, doxa is a normalcy in which realization of the norm is so complete that the norm itself, as coercion, simply ceases to exist as such. [...] One cannot take complete account of this effect of naturalization without extending the analysis to include the most specific effect of

the quintessential expression of symbolic violence, for it cloaks the struggles underlying codification itself under the guise of a self-evident consensus.[14] And here is another element which this monograph puts on the spotlight: the conflicts for the codification of arbitral authority. In this regard, codification projects will often be analysed as trenches where allied forces may gather and opposing sides may clash.

No doubt some readers shall wonder about the relevance of this intellectual endeavour. The answer is simple: there is a gap in specialized literature on the influence of the transnational codification of international arbitration in relation to an equally transnational administration of justice. In the field of arbitration, certain chimeric notions of consent and party autonomy are quite prevalent to explain its operation and authority. Take the example, for instance, of Bruno Oppetit, who qualified arbitration as a type of private justice enjoying an autonomous legitimacy where "*l'adhésion volontaire du justiciable se substitue à l'effet d'autorité que connaît la justice publique.*"[15]

Curiously, many fail to see that the triumph of contractual freedom was the outcome of a long and fierce battle in legal theory. Resisting party autonomy in arbitration were those that insisted on the subordination of arbitral authority to national positive law,[16] as well as those that were not convinced by the

---

juridical formalization: the *vis formae*, the power of form, of which the ancients spoke. The shaping of practices through juridical formalization can succeed only to the extent that legal organization gives explicit form to a tendency already immanent within those practices. The rules which succeed are those which, as we say, regularize factual situations consonant with them. Even so, however, the movement from statistical regularity to legal rule represents a true social modification. By eliminating exceptions and the vagueness of uncertain groupings, and by imposing clear discontinuities and strict borders in the continuum of statistical limits, juridical formalization introduces into social relations a clarity and predictability. [...] By ordaining patterns that govern behaviour in practice, prior to any legal discourse, through the objectivity of a written rule or of an explicitly expressed regulation, formalization establishes the operation of what might be termed a homologation effect. The objectification of the practical code in the form of an explicit code permits different speakers to associate the same meaning with the same perceived sound and the same sound with the same conceived meaning. Similarly, the explicit statement of principles makes possible explicit verification of consensus concerning the principles of consensus or disagreement themselves. Although this process cannot be completely identified with axiomatization because the law contains zones of obscurity which are the very basis for legal commentary, homologation makes possible a form of rationalization comprehended, in Weber's terms, as predictability and calculability." See Pierre Bourdieu, 'The Force of Law: Towards a Sociology of the Juridical Field' (1987) 38 The Hastings Law Journal 805, 849.

14 See Pierre Bourdieu, *Choses Dites* (Les Éditions de Minuit, 1987), at 102–103.

15 See Bruno Oppetit, *Théorie de l'arbitrage* (Presses universitaires de France 1998), at 22.

16 FA Mann, 'Lex Facit Arbitrum' (1986) 2 Arbitration International 241.

existence of party autonomy itself. Notably, around the time when international commercial arbitration emerged, J-P Niboyet argued that "*l'autonomie de la volonté n'existe pas, et que, par suite, il ne saurait être question d'en faire la théorie.*"[17] Such a statement, under present conditions, would be perceived by the arbitral community as heretical. Although there are varying degrees of attachment to the dominant contractual outlook in arbitration,[18] even State courts now feel comfortable with the idea that "arbitration is a creature that owes its existence to the will of the parties alone."[19]

Taking a closer look at the *corpus* of knowledge exploring the history of arbitration, it is not unusual to find sweeping statements on its immemorial nature.[20] Some works venture into a more concrete analysis of empirical elements related to the development of arbitral procedure, but they persevere in disregarding the fluidity of transnational law. Hence, private and public forms of arbitration are often analysed as descriptively and normatively discrete. In concrete terms, some scholars will look at international commercial arbitration and investment-treaty arbitration as separate fields, implying that any overlap between the two is either accidental or inappropriate.[21]

More recently, however, an emerging thread of studies has produced an insightful socio-historical analysis of transnational dispute settlement, which has also been accompanied by a most welcome turn towards the sociology of arbitration.[22] Some of these works have focused on a precise and limited period of time,[23] while others have emphasized certain actors and forces for the expansion of arbitral authority. As fruitful as these studies have been, they

17 See JP Niboyet, 'La Théorie de l'autonomie de La Volonté' (1927) 16 Collected Courses of the Hague Academy of International Law 1, at 5.

18 For moderate and nuanced accounts of the role of party autonomy in arbitration, see Diego P Fernández Arroyo, 'Arbitrator's Procedural Powers: The Last Frontier of Party Autonomy?' in Franco Ferrari (ed), *Limits to party autonomy in international commercial arbitration* (JurisNet 2016); Giuditta Cordero-Moss, 'Limitations on Party Autonomy in International Commercial Arbitration' (2014) 372 Collected Courses of the Hague Academy of International Law 129.

19 See *Dell Computer Corp v Union des Consommateurs* 34 (Supreme Court of Canada) at para. 51.

20 See Gary B Born, *International Commercial Arbitration* (Kluwer law international 2021); Charles Jarrosson, *La Notion d'arbitrage* (LGDJ 1987).

21 See, for instance, Anthea Roberts, 'Clash of Paradigms: Actors and Analogies Shaping the Investment Treaty System' (2013) 107 American Journal of International Law 45.

22 See Emmanuel Gaillard, 'Sociology of International Arbitration' (2015) 31 Arbitration International 1.

23 See Michel Erpelding, Burkhard Hess and Hélène Ruiz Fabri (eds), *Peace Through Law: The Versailles Peace Treaty and Dispute Settlement After World War I* (Nomos Verlagsgesellschaft mbH & Co KG 2019).

have also laboured, as any intellectual endeavour does, under methodological constraints that have left certain avenues open for further exploration.

Notably, there seems to be a general disregard for the materiality and agency of encoded legal technique in the production of transnational arbitral authority, which has favoured an analysis of the role of professional and business interests in the advancement of arbitration. Hence, some have focused their narrative of the history of arbitration on its "grand old men," while others have stressed the role of merchant networks in its expansion.[24] There are also those who tried to take law more seriously, but centred their inquiry on rather abstract notions of legal consciousness.[25] Within this context, this monograph should not be read as an attempt to discard any of these contributions, but rather as an effort to complement the portrait that has been painted thus far.

The author should caution the reader that the main materials analysed in this research were archival documents recording the ebbs and flows in various transnational projects for the codification of arbitral procedure. Hence, scarce reference will be found to judicial decisions or to doctrinal exegesis of normative texts. This was intentional, for it is not the purpose of this monograph to produce a doctrinal analysis of arbitral procedure. As noted, the main drive guiding this work is to understand the materiality and agency of legal technique. In simpler terms, this monograph wishes to explain how certain pieces of paper came to encode arbitration procedure, structuring its authority in a broader transnational administration of justice.[26] In order to do so,

24 See Eduardo Silva Romero, Emmanuel Jollivet, Florian Grisel, 'Aux Origines de l'Arbitrage Commercial Contemporain: L'Emmergence de l'Arbitrage CCI (1920–1958)' (2016) 2 Revue de l'Arbitrage 403; Jérôme Sgard, 'A Tale of Three Cities: The Construction of International Commercial Arbitration' in Grégoire Mallard and Jérôme Sgard (eds), *Contractual Knowledge* (Cambridge University Press 2016); Yves Dezalay and Bryant G Garth, *Dealing in Virtue: International Commercial Arbitration and the Construction of a Transnational Legal Order* (University of Chicago Press 1996).

25 See Mikaël Schinazi, *The Three Ages of International Commercial Arbitration* (Cambridge University Press 2022).

26 Such an attention to the materiality of legal technique is very much informed by the contributions of Bruno Latour to the study of law. The following extract may assist the reader in further understanding what is mean by the materiality of legal technique: "Every case, at least in our countries of written law, is physically enveloped in a carton folder held together with elastic bands. Even though it is not attributed any place in legal theories, it is by moving through this palace while following this little animal that we are going to become acquainted with all the various functions of the Palais-Royal. If the ethnographer wants to achieve this unstable mix of proximity (that only a field study can obtain) and detachment (which allows him to avoid immediately attaching himself to concepts which have been worn out by much prolonged usage), then it is sufficient for him to substitute the grand talk about Law, Justice and Norms with a meticulous inquiry about files

this monograph produces a thick description of the transnational production processes of various codification instruments in international arbitration,[27] regardless of whether they were successfully implemented or just served as a stepping stone for yet another codification project.

In the pages to come, this monograph will survey a broad array of instruments and their legislative history, including, but not limited to, the 1899 and 1907 Hague Convention for the Pacific Settlement of International Disputes, the 1923 Protocol on Arbitration Clauses, the 1958 New York Convention on the Recognition and Enforcement of Foreign Arbitral Awards, and the UNCITRAL Arbitration Rules. Each of these codification projects represents a snapshot of a moment, but when displayed one after the other at the right speed they show a motion picture of a long history of the codification of arbitration procedure.[28]

The choice of materials that were analysed in this study was a challenging endeavour. Evidently, the author could not survey every document relevant to the history of international arbitration. The reader should be cautioned that, in general, this study made the choice to focus on projects of a global reach, leaving regional codification processes out of its scope. Similarly, emphasis was put on the codification of arbitration procedure *per se* rather than developments related to contiguous dispute settlement mechanisms. Notably, this monograph did not address the institution of mixed claims commissions. This was not an arbitrary decision. Despite its contribution to international adjudication, mixed claims commissions were bilateral initiatives of a limited geographical reach that often dealt with a large number of claims of a repetitive nature. In this respect, the practice of these bodies was closer to that of domestic courts than to that of international arbitral tribunals. An exception was made in relation to the Reparations Commission and the Mixed Arbitral Tribunals created by the Treaty of Versailles, for the institution of these bodies played a central role in the transnational governance of the economic effects of WWI – an element of undeniable global interest.

– grey, beige or yellow, thin or thick, easy or complex, old or new – and to see where they lead him. Yes, let us begin law at the beginning, that is to say at the stamps, elastic bands, paperclips and other office paraphernalia which are the indispensable tools of cases. Jurists always speak of texts, but rarely of their materiality. It is to this materiality that we must apply ourselves." See Latour, *The Making of Law*, at 71.

27 Attention to thick, as opposed to thin, descriptions, is borrowed from Geertz. See Clifford Geertz, 'Thick Description: Toward an Interpretive Theory of Culture', in *The interpretation of cultures: selected essays* (Basic Books 1973).

28 The notion of long history is borrowed from Braudel's emphasis on the *long durée*. See Fernand Braudel, *Les Ambitions de l'histoire* (Éditions de Fallois 1997), 191 ss.

Overall, some may criticize the approach undertaken by this study and wonder whether this qualifies as legal research. Such a question begs a straightforward answer. Indeed, for the ones holding on to a certain doctrinal method, pursuant to which the role of the legal researcher is to produce an exegesis of normative instruments and judicial decisions, it suffices to say that methodological pluralism is currently not just embraced but regarded as an inescapable intellectual paradigm.[29] Hence, doctrine no longer holds the monopoly over legal research, standing as one among many methods available in the menu offered to legal scholars.[30] Any attempt to produce a "pure" theory of law is now a vain ambition.[31]

There may also be those who question the relevance of a historical inquiry on the codification of international arbitration. The author is a firm believer that to adequately navigate the present and build the future, one must be curious about the past. Consequently, this study is an invitation to the arbitral community to further its reflection on the grounds upon which it has been founded. Moreover, this monograph hopes to add another piece to the broader puzzle regarding the transnationalisation of legal authority.

A final element in this introduction concerns the writing strategy followed in this monograph, which was a chronological one. The author does not wish to express with this choice that history must be told linearly, nor does he wish to amend the periodization of arbitration history.[32] In fact, faced with several moving parts throughout his research, the author preferred to follow a

29 Champeil-Desplats notes the following: "*La multiplicité même des revendications de la 'bonne' ou la 'vraie' méthode scientifique rend aujourd'hui intenable l'affirmation d'une méthodologie ou d'une méthode de la science au singulier. Il n'existe pas une méthode, ni une méthodologie mais des méthodes et des méthodologies concurrentes et compossibles. Celles-ci variant non seulement d'un champ de savoir à l'autre mais également au sein même d'un même champ de savoir et de ses sous-champs.* [...] *Le champ juridique n'échappe pas à cette diversité des chemins de la connaissance. La littérature juridique comprend des propositions méthodologiques, des sciences de la méthode ou, en d'autres termes, une pluralité de conceptions de la science de la méthode que se succèdent ou, le plus souvent, coexistent, voire se font concurrence dans des espace-temps détermines." Véronique Champeil-Desplats, Méthodologies Du Droit et Des Sciences Du Droit* (Dalloz 2022), 11–12.

30 See, for instance, Reza Banakar and Max Travers, *Theory and Method in Socio-Legal Research* (Hart Publishing 2005); Geoffrey Samuel, *Epistemology and Method in Law* (Routledge 2003).

31 Kelsen would certainly disagree with this statement, for whom "the science of law describes the legal norms created by acts of human behaviour and to be applied and obeyed by such acts; and thereby describes the norm-constituted relations between the facts determined by the norms." See Hans Kelsen, *Pure Theory of Law* (The lawbook exchange 2005), 71.

32 For some thoughts on the periodization of the history of international commercial arbitration, see Schinazi, *op.cit.*, at 26–27.

chronological approach in order to give some stability to the text. Concretely, the monograph is divided into four core chapters, the first one being a shorter methodology chapter and three subsequent ones consisting of larger substantive chapters.

The second chapter will present in more depth the epistemic and methodological underpinnings of this research. Notably, the reader will find further elements on the author's reflection on authority, transnational law, and the role of various types of conflicts in the process of codification of international arbitration.

The third chapter will address a certain metamorphosis of international arbitration taking place in the late 19th and early 20th centuries. A particular attention will be given to the emergence of a doctrine of procedural uniformity in the realm of international law, as well as to the production of a first soft codification instrument to govern interstate arbitral procedure. In addition, the chapter will analyse an early expansion in the scope of arbitral procedure towards transnational disputes.

The fourth chapter will cover the laboratory of transnational justice implemented in the interwar years. This is a most fruitful time for those interested in dispute settlement, for a series of codification projects would emerge and deeply influence the evolution of arbitral procedure in the transnational administration of justice. Elements addressed in this chapter are the engagement of the League of Nations with so-called private international arbitration, the role of arbitral procedure in the economic settlement of WWI, and the emerging role of private entities in the uniformization and transnationalisation of arbitral procedure.

The fifth chapter covers the cold war years, having as central themes of exploration the increasing concern related to arbitration involving States and private parties, as well as the circulation of arbitral knowledge between East and West. In these pages the reader will find an analysis of the relation between the International Law Commission's Model Rules on Arbitral Procedure, the UNIDROIT involvement with the theme of arbitration involving States and private parties, as well as a portrait of the birth of ICSID and of the United Nations arbitration framework.

Some final thoughts will be laid out in the sixth chapter as concluding remarks.

With this general scheme in mind, the author humbly wishes the reader a pleasurable reading.

CHAPTER 2

Methodological Remarks

The literature on legal authority tends to allocate great energy to understanding why some actors have the capacity to issue binding orders, an approach that is usually conducive to a discussion on the legitimacy of authority. This approach tends to overemphasize positive normativity and recognition as analytical frames for the study of legal authority, devoting a sustained effort to the study of obedience of State sanctioned rules. Consequently, the conflictive interactions underlying legal authority are shadowed in favour of an analysis of varied forms of consensus, often manifested in contractual theories of positive law.

This work proposes an analytic framework making a dual shift in relation to the study of legal authority. First, it moves from the perspective of consensus and legitimacy towards one of conflict over the ability to define "what is arbitration." That is to say, instead of explaining how international arbitration is able to produce transnationally binding norms, this study will focus its attention on the struggles underneath the emergence of arbitration as a legal procedure embedded in the transnational administration of justice. Second, the monograph adopts an archaeological approach to this analysis,[1] exploring the manifestation of these struggles through the study of the layers of material documents leading to the transnational codification of arbitral procedure. In this regard, various codification projects, tracing back to the 1870s, will be scrutinized in order to uncover the forces moving forward this historical process.

The next two sections of this chapter will flesh out this methodology. In a first moment, the reader will find a discussion of the cosmopolitan turn animating the monograph's embrace of transnational law as a framework of reference. A second part will then discuss authority beyond legitimacy, explaining the author's emphasis on a conflict-based method for the study of the codification of arbitral procedure.

1 See Michel Foucault, *L'archéologie Du Savoir* (Gallimard 1969); Michel Foucault and Colin Gordon, *Power/Knowledge: Selected Interviews and Other Writings, 1972–1977* (1st American ed, Pantheon Books 1980).

 | DOI:10.1163/9789004728998_003

1 Cosmopolitanism, Transnational Law and Arbitration

The social sciences have developed their corpus of knowledge by looking at the national society as their fundamental unit of reference – and the law under the aegis of legal positivism was no exception. Still, theoretical and practical considerations have raised serious doubts as to the pertinence of sticking to the "national outlook" in the study of human affairs. Second modernity has deeply disrupted the empirical foundations of this analytic approach, especially as power became increasingly mobile and symbolic,[2] leading many scholars to highlight the need to think the human experience through different lenses. Of particular interest is the scholarship calling for a cosmopolitan turn, which would consist of a methodological move away from the national outlook and towards a cosmopolitan one.[3] This analytic framework would abandon the study of exclusive identities operating under an either/or structure of reasoning, favouring inclusive identities operating under the rationality of both/and.

Obviously, this should not be read as a denial that the world is still one of States, nations, and territorial struggle. It is clear that themes connected to the defence of national interests, which seemed moribund throughout the past decades, have made a momentous comeback. Yet, even the conservative nationalism that has now resurfaced in response to the years of neoliberal hegemony can serve as evidence supporting a cosmopolitan methodology. Indeed, this resurgent nationalism cannot be properly understood without taking global and local dynamics into account, as this movement is coordinating itself at both dimensions.[4]

2 See Ulrich Beck, 'Varieties of Second Modernity and the Cosmopolitan Vision' (2016) 33 Theory, Culture & Society 257.

3 See Ulrich Beck, *The Cosmopolitan Vision* (Polity 2006); Ulrich Beck, 'Reframing Power in the Globalized World' (2008) 29 Organization Studies 793.

4 In 2018, Steve Bannon, a prominent American far-right activist and former national security advisor to the Trump administration, participated in Marine Le Pen's rally, the leader of the French far-right. In the occasion, Bannon stated the following: "You are part of a movement that is bigger than that of Italy, bigger than in Poland, bigger than in Hungary." See The Guardian, "Steve Bannon tells French far-right 'history is on our side,'" Available at: https://www.theguardian.com/us-news/2018/mar/10/steve-bannon-tells-french-far-right-history-is-on-our-side. Accessed on 6 August 2018). This extract is informative, as it demonstrates that, despite the national rhetoric, far-right political actors are well aware of the global dynamics at stake. Donald Trump's first presidential campaign made a similar move when it invited Nigel Farage, British politician and one of the main Brexit political supporters, to speak in one of his rallies. See BBC, "Donald Trump can beat polls, UKIP's Nigel Farage tells rally." Available at: https://www.bbc.co.uk/news/uk-politics-37177938. Accessed on 6 August 2018. These

One of the areas of human affairs where methodological nationalism has been most inadequate as a research framework is that of law. Perhaps the group of legal professionals that suffered the most with legal issues going transnational has been that of legal scholars. From the prevalent and comfortable definition of law as an order of concatenated norms enacted by a sovereign State, legal scholars saw themselves surrounded by a myriad of normative voices, institutions, and practices, becoming perplexed by a growing inability to sort out the legal from the non-legal.

By calling upon a cosmopolitan turn in law, the hope is to raise awareness of the idea that the provinces of law extend beyond national boundaries. Yet, a cosmopolitan turn also suggests that the borderless world proposed by liberalism is, at best, an utopian one. Life in second modernity takes place simultaneously at the level of *cosmos* and *polis*. Hence, these two dimensions cannot be neglected and have to be integrated in a research strategy that takes their interdependency seriously. As it will be seen below, this is the aim of this research when it decides to analyse conflicts over the transnational codification of arbitral procedure.

1.1 *Arbitration as Part of the Transnational Administration of Justice*

The term transnational law is usually attributed to Philip Jessup, who in 1956 published a seminal book entitled "Transnational Law."[5] The opening of this book frames a discussion on the insufficiency of the existing legal vocabulary to grasp awkward phenomena that would hardly fit in the dichotomy national/international law. Transnational law, thus, was a concept developed to investigate "law which regulates actions or events that transcend national frontiers," encompassing public and private law and "other rules which do not wholly fit into such standard categories."[6]

The notion got considerable traction and has given rise to an extensive body of literature discussing the most diverse aspects of the transnationalisation of law.[7] Indeed, it has been argued that lawyers have now formed transnational alliances, creating normative practices that cannot be confined to the geopolitical configuration of the world. In some cases, these transnational legal

---

formal and informal transnational alliances of far-right political actors are a trend in global politics, as can be seen in Italy, Hungary, Austria and Brazil.

5 See Philip C Jessup, *Transnational Law* (Yale University Press 1956).

6 See Jessup, *Transnational Law*, at 1.

7 See, for instance, Thomas Schultz, *Transnational Legality* (Oxford University Press 2014); Marcelo Neves, *Transconstitutionalism* (Hart Publishing 2013); Roger Cotterrell, 'What Is Transnational Law?' (2012) 37 Law & Social Inquiry 500; Fabrizio Cafaggi, 'New Foundations of Transnational Private Regulation' (2011) 38 Journal of Law and Society 20.

practices have been recognized by States and were conducive to investing certain actors with formal prerogatives concerning norm production.

Transnational law, therefore, is marked by the decentralization of norm-making, and by a correlative explosion of normative voices materialized in the most diverse types of documents. Positive law now faces the competition of guidelines, standard contracts and model laws, leading to a growing literature exploring the pluralism of legal sources.[8] It is, however, important to note that this normative pluralism was not followed by a complete surrender of States' control over means of coercion. Indeed, the de-centralization of normative production did not necessarily break up States' oligopoly of violence at the global stage, nor did it dismiss States' claim to the corresponding monopoly of violence within their territorial boundaries. Despite the emergence of informal, and very effective, mechanisms to obtain compliance, States have largely retained ultimate control over physical coercion. Even in arbitration, where current normative sources are now far from being state-centred, arbitral tribunals do not control the material means to enforce their awards.

That notwithstanding, in terms of enforcement, one observes a decreasing reliance on organized material force and an increasing reliance on symbolic and more diffuse forms of coercion. The global governance of "legitimate" violence, in which the transnational administration of justice is embedded, may be largely supervised by States and States' agencies, yet its operation has progressively evolved into a public-private partnership. That is to say that the transnational administration of justice outsources some of its services to private or hybrid private agencies, while keeping in the hands of States considerable amounts of control over material coercive devices. One of these hybrid agencies is that of transnational arbitration.

Arbitration functions as an organ of the transnational administration of justice, performing quintessential judicial tasks. Still, arbitration is not directly entrusted with the role of dispensing material violence. It can instruct litigants to conform to a certain behaviour by tapping on the symbolic capital with which it is endowed, or it can refer litigants back to the organs directly controlling means of material coercion. Its primary function is to control legal

8 For this reason, there is a growing body of legal scholarship exploring the fragmentation of law, legal pluralism and an emergent "global law." See, for instance, Benedict Kingsbury, Nico Krisch and Richard B Stewart, 'The Emergence of Global Administrative Law' (2005) 68 Law and Contemporary Problems 15; Andreas Fischer-Lescano and Gunther Teubner, 'Regime-Collisions: The Vain Search for Legal Unity in the Fragmentation of Global Law' (2004) 25 Michigan Journal of International Law 999; Martti Koskenniemi and Päivi Leino, 'Fragmentation of International Law? Postmodern Anxieties' (2002) 15 Leiden Journal of International Law 553.

facts and legal norms, being invested with diffused and organized sanctioning capabilities so as to properly discharge its duties.

It should be noted, however, that the term transnational arbitration is still a contentious one, with a large majority of scholars preferring to use the expression international arbitration. This seems to derive from an impulse to stick to the traditional dualism national law/international law, leading many of these scholars to embark in attempts, sometimes byzantine, to define what would characterize an arbitration as national or international.[9]

Diverse criteria and methods have been used in this definitional endeavour, with some scholars looking into the "nature" of the constitutive act of the arbitral proceedings in order to figure out whether these acts would be national or international.[10] Others have preferred to base their taxonomy upon the type of enforcement of arbitral awards, whether exclusively national or international. Finally, a few scholars have investigated the type of positive law applicable to the dispute, or to the procedure, in order to stamp the proceedings as national or international. All these efforts, because they are founded on the premise of exclusive identities ultimately underlined by the national outlook, always reach a point where considerable incongruencies appear in relation to the definition put forth.

The transnational approach, manifesting a cosmopolitan sensibility conscious of the global and local dynamics at stake in a globalizing world, has the advantage of escaping the false necessity of defining something as either national or international.[11] Indeed, it does not impute an essential nature to arbitration, rather it looks at the interdependency of the national and international dynamics in which arbitration is usually inserted.

A simple example may help illustrate the argument. Suppose, for instance, an *ad hoc* arbitration seated in Rio de Janeiro, involving two Brazilian companies, with an Arbitral Tribunal composed of Brazilian nationals applying Brazilian law. Suppose, however, that the losing party has assets in Spain. As Spain

---

9 For further discussion on the criteria for distinguishing national and international arbitration, see Florian Grisel, *L'arbitrage international ou le droit contre l'ordre juridique: application et création du droit en arbitrage international* (Fondation Varenne/LGDJ 2011) at 11–23.

10 See for instance, Pierre Mayer, 'L' autonomie de l'arbitre international dans l'appréciation de sa propre compétence' in Collected Courses of the Hague Academy of International Law, vol. 217 (Martinus Nijhoff Publishers 1989).

11 For a in depth discussion of false necessities in social theory, see Roberto Mangabeira Unger, *False Necessity: Anti-Necessitarian Social Theory in the Service of Radical Democracy* (Verso 2004).

is party to the Convention of New York on Recognition and Enforcement of Foreign Arbitral Awards, one may quickly realize that this seemingly domestic arbitration may go transnational, when one considers that, under Article 1 of that treaty, an eventual arbitral award rendered in a situation as described above may be enforced in Spain.[12]

Even still, the transnational framework is not sufficient to advance a comprehensive analysis of conflictive interactions for the control of legal norms and legal facts taking place within the field of arbitration, nor is it appropriate to the analysis of the emergent struggles in arbitration for the control of structuring legal ideas and professional legal assets. Accordingly, it is important to understand the dynamics of authority in arbitration.

1.2 *A Diachronic Perspective on Arbitration*

Socio-legal approaches to law have renewed their breath as a research method, for they point to the necessity of looking into not merely the sources of legal norms, but to social practices sustaining the life of these artefacts and the institutions that they animate. Paraphrasing Roscoe Pound, second modernity should have made ever clearer for scholars that it does not suffice to look at arbitration in books, but to understand it in action.[13]

Such an approach suggests shifting the analysis from static dimensions of the law towards its dynamic aspects. These assumptions imply that legal studies on arbitration should not have a defined normative instrument as its exclusive centre of attention. Evidently, the idea is not to deny the existence, or the importance, of legal norms to legal reality. Instead, the animating assumption is that "[t]he rule part of the law-institution is thus one *tool* part of the institution, one hugely developed part, one vital part to communication over space and time and variant personnel; but one vital tool-part and no more than that, and a tool part nowhere near so effective as it purports to be."[14]

---

12 Article I, paragraph I, provides the following: "This Convention shall apply to the recognition and enforcement of arbitral awards made in the territory of a State other than the State where the recognition and enforcement of such awards are sought, and arising out of differences between persons, whether physical or legal. It shall also apply to arbitral awards not considered as domestic awards in the State where their recognition and enforcement are sought." See United Nations, Convention on the Recognition and Enforcement of Foreign Arbitral Awards [Treaty Series, 1959, vol. 330].

13 See Roscoe Pound, 'Law in Books and Law in Action' (1910) 44 American Law Review 12.

14 See Karl N Llewellyn, 'Law and the Social Sciences – Especially Sociology' (1949) 62 Harvard Law Review 1286, at 1291.

It has been argued above that arbitration is an organ in the transnational administration of justice, one which operates the binary pair legal-illegal within a public-private legal space and that dispenses mostly symbolic forms of coercion. Yet, this legal institution is itself made of conflictive and coordinated interactions of a variety of agents. In particular, rather than manifesting some sort of spontaneous and customary *lex mercatoria*,[15] structures of arbitral authority have been crafted in transnational law through a series of initiatives involving both private and public actors over a prolonged period of time.

Indeed, the integration of arbitration in the transnational administration of justice was anything but spontaneous. This was a long process marked by intense struggles and lobbying before States (and their subnational entities), academia, international organizations, business and businesses alliances. This is not a novel insight,[16] but the current study aims at expanding, complementing and nuancing the literature in this regard. As already noted, there has not been a comprehensive study exploring the intertwined development of "public" and "private" arbitral forms or their mutual influence in the transnational codification of arbitral procedure.

Furthermore, in the struggle for the transnational codification of arbitral procedure, positive legal norms were only part of the story. This is a field of law that can easily disregard distinctions between official and non-official normative discourse, as demonstrated by the extensive use in arbitral proceedings of instruments such as the IBA Rules on the Taking of Evidence and the IBA Guidelines on Conflicts of Interest in Arbitral Proceedings.[17] One must not think that this is a recent phenomenon. Since the earliest stages of the codification of arbitral procedure, soft normative instruments have played a central role.

Concretely, the practice of arbitration operates under an intricate division of labour among public and private actors, with formal officials usually carrying the torch of positive law and informal agents whispering unofficial

---

15 For an articulation of the argument defending the existence of sort of a-national private international law governing arbitration, see Berthold Goldman, 'La lex mercatoria dans les contrats et l'arbitrage internationaux: réalité et perspectives' in Droit international privé: travaux du Comité français de droit international privé' (1980) Droit international privé: travaux du Comité français de droit international privé 221.

16 See Claire Lemercier and Jérôme Sgard, Arbitrage privé international et globalisation(s) (CNRS; Sciences Po 2015); Dezalay and Garth, *Dealing in Virtue*.

17 For further analysis on the deployment of unofficial normative discourse in arbitral practice, see Florian Grisel, 'Droit et Non-Droit Dans Les Sentence Arbitrales CCI: Une Perspective Historique' (2014) 25 ICC International Court of Arbitration Bulletin 13.

normative spells, both of which often find themselves in a constant struggle for the control of legal services, legal ideas, legal facts and legal norms.

Within this framework, rather than focusing on the exegesis of a static legal text, this monograph undertakes a diachronic investigation of codification projects that ambitioned to promote the uniformization of arbitration practice at both public and private international law contexts. These projects provide a privileged vantage point to look into the competing actors, ideas and interests at a given point, allowing for the analysis of the relative strength of each of these elements in the gradual evolution and transformation of arbitration as an institution of the transnational administration of justice.

2 Authority, Symbolic Struggle and Codification

Authority has always been a multifarious term in ordinary language, but specialized literature has traditionally treated it as a prerogative to command.[18] In second modernity, however, the understanding of the term has become more elusive than ever. The de-centralization of norm production and decision-making led to the disruption of traditional accounts of legal authority, usually founded upon the idea of sovereignty and consent. It is now unlikely that one would understand authority's role in any meaningful way by merely referring to legitimate ordering, regardless of whether such legitimacy builds upon state sovereignty or contractual freedom.

The roots of the notion of authority are Roman, as are of Roman origin its legal use and the confusion surrounding its deployment.[19] Albeit legal authority is referred routinely as a synonym of legitimate normative power, an operative notion of authority may be more meaningful if understood as a hierarchical relation rather than something to be possessed. Instead of looking at the prerogative to command, or the legitimate ability to issue binding norms, it might be more fruitful to study authority from the point of view of relational structures of subordination.

18 See, for instance, Max Weber, *Economy and Society* (University of California Press 1978).; Joseph Raz, *Between Authority and Interpretation: On the Theory of Law and Practical Reason* (Oxford University Press 2009).

19 In a very interesting study on authority, Hannah Arendt traces the origins of the concept of authority to ancient Rome, trying to demonstrate what authority never was rather than trying to state what it has become. In a sustained intellectual effort, she portrays Roman authority as a hierarchical relation sustained by past practices transmitted from one generation to the other through tradition and religion. Hannah Arendt, *Between Past and Future* (Viking Press 1961).

Certainly, this uneven distribution is based upon coercion, and it may be this coercive dimension that leads to the conflation of authority and power. Even still, the two concepts do not seem entirely reducible to one and the same thing.[20] The notion of authority is semantically charged with imagery referring to invisible dimensions of violence, while power alludes to an imagery of control based upon visible forms of force.[21] This semantic echo is not an ontological necessity, but it represents a compelling starting point for attempts to frame an idea of authority that can be of use at present time.

2.1 *The Adversarial Turn: Authority beyond Legitimate Power*

Authority and power convey a similar asymmetric relation of subordination under which an expectation of behaviour conformity is obtained by one agent at the expense of a subordinate. However, it can be argued that the expectations of obedience expressed by the two concepts are structured over different means of coercion. While power operates through the visible manipulation of coercive devices, authority obtains subordination through surreptitious coercive means.[22]

Notably, it could be said that, while power is primarily structured upon organized sanctions harming the subject in broad daylight, authority is structured upon diffuse sanctions harming the subject under the shadows of socialization. As a consequence, phenomena of power tend to be marked by the imperative mode, while the indicative may suffice to phenomena of authority. One may even argue that, while communication of power is achieved through commands and orders, communication of authority manifests itself in customs, compelling instructions and advice.[23] In any case, the picture drawn hardly allows one to portray authority as a relation of subordination based merely on consent, conviction or legitimacy.

The dichotomy of diffuse versus organized sanctions is an analytical framework that has been in use for quite some time,[24] serving to study different

20 See Arendt, *op. cit.*; Myriam Revault d'Allonnes, *Le pouvoir des commencements: essai sur l'autorité* (Éd du Seuil 2012); Alexandre Kojève, *La notion de l'autorité* (Gallimard 2004).

21 For a study on the semantic horizon of the term authority, see Paul Audi, 'Sémantique de l'autorité (quelques remarques)' (2002) 50 La lettre de l'enfance et de l'adolescence 15.

22 This argument is based on Bourdieu's insights on symbolic violence as the ability to hide capital imbalances under the cloak of a socially shared reality (*"méconnaissance"*). Here, the focus is centred on the coercive devices that allow the *méconnaissance* to happen. See Pierre Bourdieu, *Esquisse d'une théorie de la pratique: précédé de trois études d'ethnologie kabyle* (Librairie Droz 2015).

23 See Arendt, *op.cit.*, at 123.

24 See Ruwen Ogien, 'Sanctions diffuses: Sarcasmes, rires, mépris' (1990) 31 Revue Française de Sociologie 591; Alfred Radcliffe-Brown, *Structure and Function in Primitive Society*

manifestations of heteronomy. On the one hand, organized sanctions consist of compelling someone to take a certain course of action under the articulated, *ex ante*, threat of positive or negative coercion – this mode of sanctioning has been the preferred method deployed by modern law. On the other hand, diffuse sanctions relate to *ex post facto* juxtaposition of social reactions mobilized in support of, or as punishment to, a given social practice, which may manifest as laughter, applause, despise etc.

The use of the referred dichotomy is not done with the intent of emulating age-old sociological analysis of law and society, portraying legal norms as manifestations of organized sanctions and social norms as representations of diffuse sanctions. Instead, the idea is to shed light on the repertoire of coercive devices supporting legal authority. That said, one should not assume that the ideal typical relation of authority proposed is to be found in a rigid form in the world. As a theoretical model, this analytic framework is merely a tool serving to manage a wider and complex social reality. Relations of authority and power are fluid, with diffuse and organized sanctions being combined in a range of structures of control. Thus, notwithstanding the placement of authority and power at the extremes of a continuum of hierarchical relations that goes from diffuse to organized forms of coercion, the empirical reality will most likely consist of hybrid phenomena in a spectrum between the two.

The fluidity of authority has specifically become the object of study of an emerging body of literature in international legal theory, which now makes express reference to solid and liquid manifestations of authority in order to refer to these hybrid structures of power-authority.[25] The literature on the fluidity of authority seems to have developed under the direct influence of Hannah Arendt, subscribing to the theoretical and practical differences of authority and power advanced by her.[26] Nevertheless, this same literature seems to be too concerned with the idea of legitimacy as a source of authority. Within this approach, legitimacy and authority are conflated, and consensual legitimation is used as an explanatory device for the force of authority.[27] Pursuant to this

(The Free Press 1952); Émile Durkheim, *Les Règles de La Méthode Sociologique* (Champs Classiques 2010).

25 See Nico Krisch, 'Liquid Authority in Global Governance' (2017) 9 International Theory 237; Ole Jacob Sending, 'Recognition and Liquid Authority' (2017) 9 International Theory 311.

26 For an analysis inspired by Arendt's approach on the problem of authority in international law, see Ingo Venzke, 'Between Power and Persuasion: On International Institutions' Authority in Making Law' (2013) 4 Transnational Legal Theory 354.

27 For instance, Sending's work is particularly interesting as he explores the relational dimension of authority and its dynamics under the light of Bourdieu's sociology. However,

view, the subordination arising in relations of authority would be sustained by an assumed voluntary recognition of the ability to instruct.

This approach seems to echo the framework proposed by Max Weber to the study of domination, and to some extent Bourdieu's idea of "miscognition" (*méconnaissance*). In the Weberian model, power and domination would differ as a function of legitimacy. Domination, consisting of an order likely to obtain obedience, would manifest the deployment of means of coercion socially perceived as legitimate, while power would represent the crude ability to obtain obedience through violence, regardless of its legitimacy. In other words, domination would be the manifestation of voluntarily recognized authority.[28]

Within the Weberian model, consent plays a key role, as all three modes of power legitimation (charisma, tradition and rationality) depend on the subject's acceptance of the agent's supremacy. For Bourdieu, symbolic violence is fundamentally marked by its capacity to misrepresent a certain asymmetry of force, conducing the subordinates to a deceptive, but voluntary, recognition (or miscognition) of its position as an inferior.

Despite the insightfulness of these approaches, one may wonder whether it is always necessary to analyse authority under the lenses of legitimacy, consent or any type of volitional (mis)recognition.[29] In fact, it is argued here that the concept of authority can be of better theoretical use by shifting the analysis from the internal perceptions imputed to the subjects of authority towards the study of the social features supporting relations of authoritative subordination. In other words, it seems theoretically sound to give visibility to the structural dimension of authority instead of insisting upon the analytical mystification of violence under the idea of legitimacy or the guise of deceptively obtained recognition.

It is posited here that authority expresses an asymmetric relation structured on an uneven distribution of certain symbolic assets. It is this imbalance in

---

Sending's still attribute in his paper a very important role to recognition as source of authority, which is conducive to shadowing the adversarial dimension of authority in favour of a consensual approach. See Sending, 'Recognition and Liquid Authority.'

28 In Weber words, "[s]o far as it is not derived merely from fear or from motives of expediency, a willingness to submit to an order imposed by one man or a small group, always implies a belief in the legitimate authority (*Herr- schaftsgewalt*) of the source imposing it." See Weber, *op.cit.*, at 37.

29 For an account of the institutional conditions for the establishment of authority exploring beyond the questions related to legitimacy, see Andrei Marmor, 'An Institutional Conception of Authority' (2011) 39 Philosophy & Public Affairs 238. Even still, the author seems to be of the view that authority is founded in some loose form of consent. In this regard, see also Andrei Marmor, 'The Dilemma of Authority' (2011) 2 Jurisprudence 121.

symbolic capital that places one actor in the position of superiority capable of instructing and another in the role of subordinate expected to conform. Trespassing the limits of conformity created by the possession of certain symbolic assets generates a given coercive response upholding the *status quo*.

This coercive dimension of authority is prone to generating tensions, friction and resistance. Indeed, rather than consensual, social sanctions sustaining authority create latent struggles, and give rise to declared or undeclared conflicts over the possession, construction and reconstruction of the symbolic assets protected by the sanctions. This adversarial approach to authority suggests the analysis of struggles for the production and control of symbolic resources, for these are at the root of authoritative structures of subordination. Thus, instead of studying the reasons that may explain the dormant state of conflicts over authority (inquiries on recognition and legitimacy), it is fruitful to discuss the dynamics of this competition over time.

2.2 *The Authority of Arbitration and the Struggle for the Transnational Codification of Arbitral Procedure*

The authority of the law, *i.e.* its ability to subordinate, is underlined by a generalized conflict over the monopoly of being able to affirm what the law is.[30] Notwithstanding the state of this overarching conflict (dormant or alive), it is always possible to find piecemeal disputes for the exclusive control of legal assets, such as legislation, case law, doctrine and so on. These struggles obviously take place in an intellectual arena mobilizing legal discourse and opposes mostly actors with legal credentials and professional training.[31] In this respect, law serves simultaneously as the space where these struggles take place and as the technique deployed in the combat.

By evoking the authority of arbitration, one should bear in mind that such an authority has been construed as a legal one. Consequently, references to the authority of arbitration, or to arbitral authority, are to be understood as a special case of legal authority. Concretely, arbitral authority manifests itself in awards and orders produced by arbitral tribunals, as well as in the division of labour between State courts, arbitral tribunals and arbitral institutions.

30 See Pierre Bourdieu, 'The Force of Law: Towards a Sociology of the Juridical Field' (1987) 38 The Hastings Law Journal 805.

31 It is not the purpose of this research to conduct an ontology or genealogy of law as an autonomous or semi-autonomous social field. It is assumed, and this assumption seems to be a reasonable one, that there is a specialized area of life populated by lawyers, an exotic animal produced by Law Schools and Bar exams, speaking a discrete language and producing particular artefacts.

The struggle for the authority of arbitration follows a similar pattern to that of the law. That is to say, one finds conflicts for the soul of arbitration, with contending camps trying to affirm what arbitration is. Yet, piece-meal battles have always taken place, with the long march for the codification of arbitral procedure presenting itself as a most prominent one. Indeed, if the authority of arbitration finds expression in awards and orders produced by arbitral tribunals, these are nothing but the output of a procedure that has been transnationally codified and embedded in the transnational administration of justice.

Codexis a term that originally refers to wooden tablets covered with a medium for writing, such as paper or leather, bound together in book format.[32] Booklets collecting and recording laws in writing have been in existence for millennia, with a notable example being the case of the Roman XII Tables.[33] Even still, modern codification is an idea introduced by Jeremy Bentham, who envisioned it as a particular legislative process covering all at once an entire field of law in a systematic way.[34] In that sense, modern codification was associated with an ambition to produce legal unity, rationality and predictability, through a coherent and exhaustive body of rules recorded in one single written instrument. This ambition was sponsored by emerging Nation-states, for they identified codification as a means of promoting national unity and consolidating their aspiration for holding a monopoly over the production of law.

Given that the legal professional is broadly acquainted with this notion of codification, it may seem striking that one refers to the transnational codification of arbitration. Indeed, the field has never experienced the enactment of a normative instrument with such ambitions. Yet, once again it seems reasonable not to replicate in second modernity ideas that were questionably valid for modernity. Codification is still a strong force for legal development, one pushing forward the systematisation of law – albeit no longer through one single instrument exclusively sanctioned by the State. In second modernity, codification is a multi-tiered normative process, taking place simultaneously at the global and local level, through a series of hard and soft normative instruments. These instruments are concatenated to operate in a system-like form, but they are produced in instalments, enacted separately, and given varying degrees of State recognition.

---

32 See Reinhard Zimmerman, 'Codification' (2012) 8(4) European Review of Contract Law 367–399, at 370.

33 See Aldo Schiavone, *The Invention of Law in the West* (Harvard University Press, 2012), at 85 ss.

34 See Jeremy Bentham, *Papers relative to Codification and Public Instructions, including correspondence with the Russian Emperor and the Divers Constituted Authorities in the American United States* (J. M'Creery, 1817), 40 ss.

An insightful illustration of the argument relates to the division of labour between the various actors in arbitration, which has been implemented through certain codified legal obligations and jurisdictional prerogatives. One knows that contractual obligations can currently be used to impose on an arbitral tribunal the precedence of a Dispute Board's determination on legal facts and vice-versa. This feature, in whatever direction it runs, will structure a hierarchical relation between the two bodies with regards to legal cognition. Likewise, jurisdictional tools like *lis pendens* may be used to preclude litigants from looking for new venues for the settlement of their dispute, and devices such as *res judicata* and issue preclusion may foreclose further inquiry on a given matter.

The codification of the procedural tools discussed are achieved at different levels in order to advance a monopolistic agenda in a Bourdieusian sense, namely the control over what arbitration is. Assuredly, struggles for the monopoly of producing legal norms and for the hegemony over their interpretation are both part of the landscape of conflicts regarding the codification of arbitral procedure. However, these are merely the most external and visible dimensions of these conflicts. Underneath conflicts over norm production, one quickly finds struggles over cognitive, epistemic and professional prerogatives.

As noted, struggles over the codification of normative production are the most external and visible face of the topic under analysis. Clashes over the delimitation of the bodies entrusted with the ability to produce legal norms may entail adversarial interactions between States fostering their positive law, intergovernmental organizations advancing their normative regimes,[35] professional bodies marketing a profusion of norms,[36] and transnational corporations seeking normative emancipation through alleged self-sufficient contracts. In addition, one observes arbitral tribunals following an informal rule of *stare decisis*,[37] which reflects an attempt to extend adjudicators' normative authority over time and space. Interconnected to conflicts over norm production, one may observe interpretive clashes between arbitral tribunals and State judiciaries, which have a formal last say on matters of legal interpretation due to their prerogative of annulling and recognizing awards. Finally, one can

35 For instance, the UNIDROIT and its Principles on International Commercial Contracts or the UNCITRAL and its Arbitrations rules.

36 For instance, the Forms of Contract from the Fédération Internationale des Ingénieurs-Conseils (FIDIC) or the Rules on the Taking of Evidence issued by the International Bar Association (IBA).

37 See Diego P Fernández Arroyo, 'Private Adjudication without Precedent?' in Horatia Muir Watt and Diego P Fernández Arroyo (eds), *Private International Law and Global Governance* (Oxford University Press 2014).

identify struggles between doctrine and practice, with the latter attempting to control the former through commentary, scholarship, and training programs.

If one peels the onion related to the issues at stake in the codification of arbitral procedure, it is also possible to observe a variety of conflicts over the division of labour concerning legal cognition. The construction of a legal fact is a most important element in the life of legal professionals, and actors compete for determining who and how a fact can be ascertained from a legal standpoint. Struggles over legal cognition are not just manifested in clashes between the disparate views of judges and arbitrators on the factual dimension of a given legal dispute, but these are certainly a frequent example of such competition.

The conflicts over legal facts involving judges and arbitrators are currently mediated by positive law and tend to favour transnational arbitration. Indeed, arbitrators are attributed the prerogative of having an abstract last say on the determination of legal facts, for neither the 1958 New York Convention nor the 1965 Washington Convention provides for a jurisdiction of appeal. However, the inexistence of a formal jurisdiction of appeal does not entirely preclude courts and arbitral tribunals from clashing over facts. For instance, an application for annulment may exceptionally invite State courts to entertain a cognitive construction of the facts of the dispute. Part of the ambition of this study is to explain how this codified, but conflictive, division of labour came to be established.

Beyond the obvious struggle of judges and arbitrators over legal facts, one may find clashes over legal cognition between arbitrators and arbitral institutions, as these institutions have considerable control over the flow of disputes and awards in the province of arbitration. Despite the existence of *ad hoc* arbitration, international arbitration greatly operates in its institutional variant. Accordingly, institutions become *de facto* and *de jure* gatekeepers of arbitration. This is reflected, for instance, in the *prima facie* control of jurisdiction that arbitral institutions may perform concerning the factual existence of an arbitration agreement.[38] Also, a few arbitral institutions do provide for a control of arbitral awards, as is the case of the ICC.[39]

---

38 See, for instance, Article 6(4) of the 2021 ICC Arbitration Rules, which reads as follows: "In all cases referred to the Court under Article 6(3), the Court shall decide whether and to what extent the arbitration shall proceed. The arbitration shall proceed if and to the extent that the Court is *prima facie* satisfied that an arbitration agreement under the Rules may exist". Similarly, Article 36(3) of the ICSID Rules reads as follows: "The Secretary-General shall register the request unless he finds, on the basis of the information contained in the request, that the dispute is manifestly outside the jurisdiction of the Centre. He shall forthwith notify the parties of registration or refusal to register."

39 See Article 34 of the ICC Arbitration Rules, which read as follows: "Before signing the award, the arbitral tribunal shall submit it in draft form to the Court. The Court may lay

Moreover, the transnational administration of justice is populated by other bodies performing legal cognitive work, with some of them primarily created to control legal facts. This is the case, for instance, of Dispute Boards, which may or may not compete for the control of legal norms, but that are in charge of monitoring the factual performance of certain types of contracts.[40] These organs operate in an obligational space and, paradoxically, emerge out of an attempt of parties to a contract to enhance their control over the construction of legal facts. With a similar objective, once turned into litigants in arbitral proceedings, these parties employ a variety of experts, whose main task is to control cognition in relation to the construction of a certain legal fact.

Digging below legal normativity and cognition, the codification of arbitral procedure is also a terrain for struggles over legal epistemology. The competition in the realm of legal ideas is primarily articulated at the level of legal theory, catering for an audience of legal scholars and practicing lawyers who are academically oriented. Although legal theory is sometimes viewed as an arcane enterprise by practicing lawyers, epistemic conflicts have high and concrete stakes. Indeed, an epistemic monopoly allows the re-shuffling of professional legal activities, which may be conducive to a complete redistribution of symbolic and economic assets among lawyers, such as prestige, expertise, clients and lawyers' fees. Accordingly, theoretical conflicts may flow upwards to the practical dimension as a result of the shocks of the epistemic plates.

Most of these epistemic conflicts emulate the modern competition between private and public legal scholars for the primacy of determining what the law is. This structural hostility is usually translated into competing models of law and justice, which will serve as the basc for the dogmatic operation of legal technique. Despite the terminology portraying arbitration as a "transnational arbitral order,"[41] or as a dimension of "global governance,"[42] what is at stake is control of the epistemic legal grounds upon which arbitration is supposed to be built. In particular, the opposition concerning the "nature" of arbitration,

---

down modifications as to the form of the award and, without affecting the arbitral tribunal's liberty of decision, may also draw its attention to points of substance. No award shall be rendered by the arbitral tribunal until it has been approved by the Court as to its form."

40 On Dispute Boards, see Nael G Bunni, *The FIDIC Forms of Contract: The Fourth Edition of the Red Book, 1992, the 1996 Supplement, the 1999 Red Book, the 1999 Yellow Book, the 1999 Silver Book* (3rd ed, Blackwell Pub 2005), specially chapter 26.

41 See Emmanuel Gaillard, 'Aspects Philosophiques de l'arbitrage,' in *Collected Courses of the Hague Academy of International Law*, vol 329 (Martinus Nijhoff Publishers 2007).

42 See Walter Mattli and Thomas Dietz, *International Arbitration and Global Governance* (Oxford University Press 2014).

whether contractual or jurisdictional, has weighted greatly in the long march for the codification of arbitral procedure.

This delineation of how some of the professional, epistemic, and normative tensions have historically shaped transnational arbitral procedure gives a big picture of the subject-matter of this study. Now it is time to turn to the concrete historical data.

CHAPTER 3

Great Transformations

Just a few days before the assassination of Archduke Franz Ferdinand, delegates of business interests and government officials met in Paris for the sixth International Congress of Chambers of Commerce and Commercial and Industrial Associations. In their agenda, a central element of concern was the unification of procedural legislation governing arbitration involving citizens of different countries. On that 8 June 1914, at the premises of the *Sorbonne*,[1] none of the more than two thousand participants could yet imagine that the *Pax Britannica* was about to fall to pieces and that in a few years Europe would be completely devasted.[2]

At this moment, domestic arbitration was a burgeoning practice, with specialised literature on the subject dating back to the 18th century. Indeed, a Matthew Bacon had published a technical manual for arbitrators already in 1731.[3] The book compiled the practices of arbitration of his time in order to lay down "in a plain and easy Method, those Things which seem clear and uncontroverted in our Law Books, and which are chiefly necessary for an Arbitrator to have his Eye upon."[4]

Less than a century later, the number of manuals on arbitration had grown considerably. These publications privileged, more often than not, the transmission of technical knowledge on the ins and outs of the craft. In France, Pierre B. Boucher published a manual with precisely that purpose in 1806,[5] while the

1 See Louis Canon-Legrand and Emile Jottrand, 'Letter from the Comité Permanent – Invitation to the 6th Congress.'

2 The delegations present at the 6th Congress represented around thirty national governments, six cities, and six hundred and fifty chambers of commerce and industrial associations. See Comité Permanent des Congrès, 'Compte rendu du VIe Congrès International des Chambres de Commerce et des Associations Commerciales et Industrielles (Paris – 8, 9 et 10 Juin)' (Chambre de commerce de Paris 1914) Bulletin de la Chambre de commerce de Paris.

3 Matthew Bacon was an English lawyer admitted to the Inner Temple on 27 May 1726. See N. G. Jones, 'Bacon, Mathew (b. c. 1700, d. in or before 1757), Legal Writer'. Available at: <https://www.oxforddnb.com/view/10.1093/ref:odnb/9780198614128.001.0001/odnb-9780198614128-e-64033>.

4 Matthew Bacon, *The Compleat Arbitrator, or, The Law of Awards and Arbitraments* (Printed by E and R Nutt, and R Goslin (Assigns of Edward Sayer, Efq;) for John Worrall, at the Dove in Bell-Tard, near Lincoln's Inn 1731), at 2.

5 Pierre B Boucher, *Manuel Des Arbitres, Ou Traité Complet de l'arbitrage, Tant En Matière de Commerce Qu'en Matière Civile* (Arthur-Bertrand 1807).

 | DOI:10.1163/9789004728998_004

first edition of the famous "Russell on Arbitration" was published in England in 1849.[6]

By the second half of the 19th century, there were numerous new editions of "Russel on Arbitration,"[7] as well as the publication of John T. Morse's "The Law of Arbitration and Award."[8] This consistent editorial growth suggests a sustained interest within national legal communities for the acquisition and circulation of arbitral knowledge. Still, these were books targeting a domestic audience and centred on the municipal practice of arbitration.

Around 1870, when the award of the famous Alabama case was rendered,[9] international arbitration was still in its infancy, being almost inseparable from interstate disputes. Indeed, international arbitration was characterized as purely a State-to-State mechanism of dispute settlement, and throughout the second half of the 19th century it was perceived, first and foremost, as a procedural feature pertaining to public international law. Over time, however, its practice would leave the purview of public international lawyers and become a preserve of private international lawyers. This changing of the guard is marked by a long process that begins at the turn of the 20th century.

Although the first Hague Peace Conference of 1899 managed to create the Permanent Court of Arbitration (PCA), by 1907, when the second Hague Peace Conference was held, there was considerable discontentment with the institution. For many, the only way forward was judicialization. Unsuccessful attempts to create a permanent judicial body, a so-called Court of Arbitral Justice, had taken place at the Hague, but the judicialization trend would only come to fruition in the 20th century. When the Permanent Court of International Justice was created in the aftermath of the Great War,[10] and then with the proliferation of international courts following World War II, public international lawyers gradually shifted their attention away from arbitration.

---

6 Francis Russell, *A Treatise on the Power and Duty of an Arbitrator, and the Law of Submissions and Awards; with an Appendix of Forms, and of the Statutes Relating to Arbitration.* (T & J W Johnson 1849).

7 The book is still on print, now in its 24th edition. See David Sutton, Judith Gill and Matthew Gearing, *Russell on Arbitration* (24th edn, Sweet & Maxwell 2015).

8 John Morse, *The Law of Arbitration and Award* (Little, Brown, and Company 1872).

9 For a comprehensive analysis of the case, published at the time of the award's publication, see Carlos Calvo, 'Examen Des Trois Règles de Droit International Proposées Dans Le Traité de Washington: Mémoire Présenté à l'Institut de Droit International (Session de Genève 1874)' (1874) 6 Revue de droit international et de législation comparée 453.

10 For an analysis on the creation of the PCIJ, see Ole Spiermann, '"Who Attempts Too Much Does Nothing Well": The 1920 Advisory Committee of Jurists and the Statute of the Permanent Court of International Justice' (2002) 73 British Yearbook of International Law 187.

Conversely, developments like the adoption of the 1907 Convention respecting the Limitation of the Use of Force for the Collection of Contract Debts, which would become known as the Drago-Porter Convention, contributed to an inverse phenomenon in private international law. By extending the jurisdiction of international arbitration to cover the collection of contractual debt, that instrument laid out the foundations for a novel type of procedure. Notably, the settlement of disputes under the Drago-Porter Convention would be much closer to that of municipal disputes governed by private law, with the difference that they involved foreign creditors contending against a State.

From that starting point, it would not take long for private colours to be permanently embroidered on the cloak of international arbitration. This was done in great part by people gravitating around the International Congress of Chambers of Commerce and Commercial and Industrial Associations. Albeit the last of these congresses was the one held in Paris in 1914, the work performed by the participants in these events would be carried on by its successor institution, the International Chamber of Commerce.[11] Undeniably, the ICC and its International Court of Arbitration would for the first-time vest private forms of arbitral procedure with an institutional structure dedicated to its internationalisation.[12]

Within this framework, and unlike public international lawyers, private international lawyers would nurture a continuous interest in arbitral procedure for the governance of cross-border economic flows. The invention of "private international arbitration," as it was first called, was very much connected to international trade and comparative commercial law, which is made clear by its current name – "International Commercial Arbitration." If the mechanism was seen as a most useful tool for the administration of cross-border justice and the promotion of international trade, it would also serve as an opportunity to push forward the agenda concerning the uniformization of private international law.

This chapter will follow these many transformations of arbitration. In particular, it will survey the gradual emergence and early circulation of ideas aiming at the codification of arbitration practice under a uniform procedural framework. First, the chapter will explore the contribution of *Belle époque*

11 For a broad account on the creation of the International Chamber of Commerce, see George L Ridgeway, *Merchants of Peace: Twenty Years of Business Diplomacy through the International Chamber of Commerce, 1919–1938* (Columbia University Press 1938).

12 For a historical analysis on the creation of the International Court of Arbitration of the International Chamber of Commerce, see Lemercier and Sgard, *Arbitrage privé international et globalisation(s)*.

international lawyers to the creation of a doctrine of procedural uniformity in international arbitration, and their influence over the normative project of producing a code to record such uniform procedure (1). Then, the chapter will discuss how the interplay between war and economic interests laid the foundations for the settlement of cross-border contractual disputes through international arbitration procedure (2). Finally, the chapter will analyse the pre-war endorsement of business interests of a doctrine fostering arbitral uniformity and the role of these interests in the invention of a private international form of arbitral procedure (3).

1 Sowing the Seeds of Uniformity in International Arbitration

The first encounter between international arbitration and ideas of legal uniformity happened in the late 19th century, and it would take some years for this love story to blossom into a structured doctrine of arbitral uniformity. This first encounter was made possible probably by some combination of fortuitous chance and the prevailing spirit of a time. The period, as it is widely known, was one of increasing globalization due to disruptive changes in communications and transportation – a state of affairs that would be favourable to the brewing of new legal ideas and to the formation of a community of cosmopolitan-minded lawyers.[13] Regardless of why arbitration and uniformization were brought together, what can be stated with some certainty is that the two ideas first met at the crossroads of public and private international law around the year of 1870.

Two men are worthy of mention for their role in diffusing ideas of uniformity within international arbitration: Pasquale Stanislao Mancini and Tobias Michael Carel Asser. The two were prominent members of an embryonic global community of international lawyers and left their fingerprints in both the institutionalization of international arbitration and in the movement towards the uniformization of private international law.

In the 1870's, Mancini was an accomplished legal scholar and a known political figure involved in the Italian unification.[14] Mancini held professorships in

---

13 For an account of a participant observer, see René Demogue, *L'unification Internationale du Droit Privé* (Rousseau & Co, Editeurs 1927) 16.

14 For a profile of Mancini, see Vincent Genin, 'Pasquale S. Mancini: Du laboratoire juridique national à la fabrique du droit international' (2018) 130 Mélanges de l'École française de Rome – Italie et Méditerranée modernes et contemporaines. For an analysis of Mancini's political thought, see Giuseppe Grieco, 'A Legal Theory for the Nation State. Pasquale

international law in Naples and in Turin, and became notorious for his defence of the principle of nationality as the foundational stone of *jus gentium*.[15] After the unification of Italy, he occupied several offices at the highest levels of Italian government, such as that of Minister of Education (1862), Minister of Justice (1876–1878) and Minister of Foreign Affairs (1881–1885).

When they first met, Asser was certainly in the shadows of Mancini. A junior to the Italian professor, the Dutchmen would in due course shine a light of his own.[16] Along with his scholarship on civil and commercial law, T.M.C. Asser's practice in commercial and maritime law would give him notoriety in the banking and business community of Amsterdam.[17] Similarly to Mancini, Asser would also have a career in public service, acting as legal advisor to the Dutch Ministry of Foreign Affairs from 1875 to 1913. As a consequence, he was offered the opportunity to be involved "in virtually every treaty concluded by the Dutch government."[18] For his long years of public service, Asser would be appointed a member of the Council of State in 1893 – the highest body in the Dutch administration.

The importance of the two individuals for the current analysis relies on their direct and lasting role in the production of ideas of uniformity in international arbitration, as well as on their activism for the uniformization of international law generally. Even still, their individual efforts would not be possible without the concurrence of a broader network of people working under an emerging institutional framework devoted to the promotion of international law.

Since the 1830's, an intellectual infrastructure began to take shape and serve as an outlet to legal cosmopolitanism. Indeed, during that decade one sees the

---

Stanislao Mancini, Hegelianism and Piedmontese Liberalism after 1848' (2019) 24 Journal of Modern Italian Studies 266.

15 Mancini was exiled to Turin due to the purge taking place in Naples after the 1848 revolutionary wave – in which he had taken part. See Grieco, *op.cit.*, at 276.

16 Born in a family of lawyers and statesmen, he was awarded a doctorate degree in "*utiusque iuris*" (i.e., in both Roman and Canon law) from Leiden University in 1860. His doctoral thesis was written on Dutch constitutional law relating to foreign policy, suggesting that international concerns begin early in his legal career. In 1862, he was appointed a law professor at Athenaeum, an institution that would become the Municipal University of Amsterdam, and would teach classes on criminal procedure, civil, commercial and criminal law up until 1877. That year, Asser reduced his teaching load, becoming a part-time professor of commercial and private international law at the same institution – something that was probably done in order to allow him to reconcile his many interests and activities. For a detailed profile on Asser, see Geert de Baere and Alex Mills, 'T.M.C. Asser and Public and Private International Law: The Life and Legacy of "a Practical Legal Statesman"' (2011) Netherlands Yearbook of International Law 3.

17 See de Baere and Mills, *op.cit.*, at 25.

18 See de Baere and Mills, *op.cit.*, at 6.

growth of an interest for the study of both international and comparative law, which was expressed in the publication of books and in the foundation of specialized journals.[19] Efforts to coordinate and institutionalize the field followed suit, bringing together like-minded scholars and practitioners labouring in the traditions of conflict of laws and the law of nations.

Animated by a certain "*esprit d'internationalité*,"[20] the emerging community of international lawyers rallied together to equip their infant discipline with the tools necessary to advance shared intellectual, political and professional interests. The most immediate initiative taken was editorial, materialized in the foundation of several reviews devoted to the study of international law and to the indexation of international legal materials. For instance, the "*Revue de droit international et législation comparé*," founded in 1869, is usually referred to as the first brick in this intellectual infrastructure.[21]

The *Institut de Droit International* represents another layer of the edifice established for the promotion of international law. The IDI was meant to create a permanent intellectual space devoted to the study and development of international law, acting as a "Senate of jurists" in charge of conducting the preparatory works for the codification of international law.[22] Along with Gustave Rolin-Jaequemyns and Gustave Moynier, who were the instigators of the initiative to invite "the main international jurists" to a sort of "ecumenical legal-council,"[23] the founding members of the IDI were Pasquale Mancini (who was also the institute's first president), T.M.C. Asser, James Lorimer, Wladimir

19 In 1834, Joseph Story published the first edition of his famous "Commentaries on the Conflict of Laws, Foreign and Domestic." That same year, Jean Jacques Gaspard Foelix published the first number of the *Revue étrangère et française de législation, de jurisprudence et d'économie politique*. The journal was continuously published up until 1850 – although later rebranded as *Revue de droit français et étranger*. It served to rally individuals living mostly across Europe and sharing an interest for what could be now labelled comparative economic governance. Foelix himself would use the journal as an outlet for his very influential study entitled "Du conflit des lois de différentes nations, ou du droit international," published in 1840. See Jean Jacques Gaspard Foelix, 'Du Conflit des lois de différentes Nations, ou du droit international' (1840) 7 Revue étrangère et française de législation, de jurisprudence et d'économie politique 81.

20 The expression is found in Rolin-Jaequemyn's introduction to the first number of the journal. See Gustave Rolin-Jaequemyns, 'De l'étude de la législation comparée et du droit international' (1869) 1 Revue de droit international et de législation comparée 1, 17.

21 For a comprehensive analysis of the broader trend towards the professionalization of international law, see Martti Koskenniemi, *The Gentle Civilizer of Nations: The Rise and Fall of International Law 1870–1960* (Cambridge University Press 2001), chapter 1.

22 See Gustave Rolin-Jaequemyns, 'Communications relatives à l'Institut de Droit International' (1873) 5 Revue de droit international et de législation comparée 667.

23 See Institut de Droit International, *Annuaire: Tome 1/1877* (Schmidt Periodicals 1994), 12.

Besobrassof, Jean Gaspar Bluntschli, Augusto Pierantoni, Carlos Calvo and David Dudley Field.

The IDI concretely introduced a regular schedule of meetings and a constant workflow on cross-border legal matters. At its foundation, in 1873, the institute launched a collective work on two issues that would be of central importance for the future birth of a doctrine of procedural uniformity in international arbitration. On the one hand, the IDI produced a draft procedural code for international arbitration, which would have a lasting impact on the development of the craft (1.1). On the other hand, the IDI was a platform for the development and advocacy of a doctrine of uniform private international law (1.2).

1.1 *An Early Procedural Code for International Arbitration*

In 1873, the IDI created a working group to codify the practice of international arbitration under a uniform procedural framework. The group was composed of David Dudley Field, William Vernon Harcourt, Émile de Laveleye, Augusto Pierantoni and Levin Goldschmidt. The latter was appointed as rapporteur on the matter, which is especially interesting in light of his background. Goldschmidt was most famous for his expertise on commercial law, which granted him a seat at the Supreme Commercial Court of the German Confederation and an appointment to the commission in charge of preparing a draft of the German civil code.[24] In addition, he had acted as an arbitrator in the San Juan dispute between England and the United States,[25] a practical experience that may have qualified him for reporting on international arbitration.

Arbitration was then a trending topic that drew attention from all audiences in both specialised and non-specialized circles. Despite the growing continental drift that would gradually separate internationalists in the categories of public and private international lawyers, arbitration was a shared interest among the members of the two branches of the sister professions. These individuals were strongly committed to the peaceful settlement of interstate disputes, leading to a militant faith on the benefits of arbitration for world peace.

In line with the prevailing views of the time, the report submitted by Goldschmidt defined international arbitration as a mechanism for settling disputes between sovereign States. The definition was followed by an analytic effort to distinguish this type of arbitration from neighbouring types of dispute resolution, including arbitration involving private parties against states acting in

24 See Charles Lyon-Caen, 'Notice nécrologique sur M. Goldschmidt, décédé en 1897', *Annuaire de l'Institut de Droit International*, vol 17 (Imprimerie James Regame 1898).

25 See Lyon-Caen, *op.cit.*, at 328–329.

their private capacity – something that was considered merely a special case of domestic arbitration falling under the purview of municipal law.[26]

Given the inexistence of international judicial bodies at the time, Goldschmidt presented arbitration as the best alternative to fill that gap. Certainly, arbitration was not suited to deal with the vital interests of states nor could it settle large-scale conflicts, Goldschmidt contended,[27] but it could preclude the transformation of punctual and localized disputes into aggression and war.[28]

Overall, the IDI considered that a necessary step for the promotion of international arbitration was the formalization of its procedural framework, something that had not been done up until that point. Hence, given the novelty of the endeavour, Goldschmidt had no normative instrument or institutional experience to use as reference point. The main source of inspiration for his report was Roman law, which he found more adapted to govern international arbitration than domestic arbitral legislation. Under classic Roman law, Goldschmidt noted, arbitration was purely contractual. From his perspective, this model seemed quite appropriate for the governance of interstate disputes, a belief that resulted from a certain autarkical notion of sovereignty that is still prevalent in current times.

Some of the Roman solutions, however, were modulated by features taken from the emerging practice of international arbitration, as well as nuanced by the comparative analysis of municipal legislation governing arbitration and civil procedure. As a result of this eclectic methodology, the draft rules penned by Goldschmidt brought into life a mechanism that was at one time consent-based and also strongly influenced by the Romano-Canonical procedural tradition. It was also clear for him that international arbitration would be very much dependent on domestic law. In particular, he acknowledged that the conditions of validity of international arbitration agreements, especially in relation to powers of representation, would stem from municipal public law.[29]

---

26 See Levin Goldschmidt, 'Projet de règlement pour Tribunaux Arbitraux Internationaux présenté à l'Institut de Droit International (Session de Genève 1874)' (1874) 6 Revue de droit international et de législation comparée, at 421.

27 Goldschmidt notes the following: "*Et si l'on examine les exemples recueillis avec soin d'arbitrages internationaux à diverses époques, on verra qu'il s'agit de contestations qualifiées pour une sentence judiciaire, parce que le point litigieux était délimité avec précision et susceptible d'être décidé par les principes du droit. Tel est le cas, en particulier, dans les importants compromis Anglo-Américains sur les affaires de l'Alabama et de San Juan. Dans aucun de ces cas des intérêts vitaux des nations n'étaient en jeu.*" See Goldschmidt, *op.cit.*, at 424.

28 See Goldschmidt, *op.cit.*, at 424.

29 See Goldschmidt, *op.cit.*, at 430.

The structure of the normative regime proposed was divided into five parts, dealing respectively with the arbitration agreement, the constitution of the arbitral tribunal, the conduction of proceedings, the arbitral award and the possibility of challenging the award. Still, it should be noted, the adoption of a contractual model for international arbitration was conducive to the subsidiarity of this set of rules. In other terms, the arbitration agreement was granted a precedence over procedural regulation – an approach that gained currency and is now widespread in arbitration practice.

Goldschmidt's project unfolded the arbitration agreement into two types of contracts. On the one hand, there would be the agreement entered into by the parties submitting a dispute to arbitration (the *compromis* in his proposed terminology). On the other hand, there would be the agreement entered into by the litigants and the arbitrators establishing the tribunal's mandate. This bipartition was built upon the Roman distinction between *compromissum* and *receptum arbitri*. Most notably, the unjustified failure to perform the *receptum arbitri*, following the Roman tradition, could lead to the arbitrator's civil liability.[30]

At this point in time, it was unclear whether only existing disputes could be submitted to arbitration or whether it would be possible to provide in advance for the submission of supervening disputes. The solution proposed by Goldschmidt was once again taken from the Roman experience, which favoured the validity of arbitration clauses covering both actual and future disputes. Curiously, this proposition was in direct contradiction to the prevailing views in several domestic legal systems at the time, such as those of Germany and France.

Presented with this issue, members of the institute wondered how effective an arbitration agreement providing for the settlement of supervening disputes could be, as such arrangement was not endowed with a formal sanction against its violation. Mancini, siding with Goldschmidt, noted that the violation of an arbitration clause could be conducive to the denunciation of the treaty, and this had the potential to serve as an incentive to comply with the terms of the arbitration agreement.[31]

The exercise of institutional imagination emerging at the IDI is particularly interesting in relation to the constitution of the tribunal. Goldschmidt envisioned an arbitral tribunal composed of only two arbitrators, with each

30 See Goldschmidt, *op.cit.*, at 429–430.

31 Institut de Droit International, 'Procès verbal de la session de Genève, n. 2, séance du 1 septembre de 1874' (1874) 6 Revue de droit international et de législation comparée 589, at 590.

of them being nominated by a respective litigant. The decision of the tribunal, therefore, would have to be unanimous. An escape valve to safeguard the proceedings from a standoff in case the tribunal could not reach a unanimous decision was also contemplated, providing for the appointment of a third person to act as a "*surarbitre*." If agreement could not be reached on the appointment of this third person, or if the individual appointed could not take office, then the arbitration agreement would be deemed inoperative.[32]

The model proposed by Goldschmidt will certainly strike the 21st century reader as unusual, but it was also controversial to his fellow colleagues at the IDI in the year 1874. The provisions on the constitution of the tribunal generated much debate, with T.M.C. Asser leading the dissent against Goldschmidt's approach. Asser proposed an amendment establishing a three-member tribunal from the outset of proceedings. He noted that the whole mechanism proposed by Goldschmidt could lead to the failure of arbitration altogether, pointing to the fact that two arbitrators could always disagree on the appointment of a "*surarbitre*" whenever this proved necessary. Conversely, a tribunal composed of three members would allow the formation of a majority since the introduction of the claim, and the third arbitrator would be able to follow the proceedings in their entirety.

The amendment proposed by Asser also stipulated the method of appointment for the tribunal, with each party appointing one arbitrator, who would then together directly appoint the third arbitrator or designate another person to appoint the third arbitrator. Ultimately, Goldschmidt deferred to his opponent, and the institute adopted Asser's amendment unanimously.[33] In this three-member arbitral tribunal, a president would be selected among any of its members. It is noteworthy that the nomination process and the duties of the president under the IDI Rules were quite different from the ones performed by the presiding arbitrator under contemporary procedural frameworks. Notably, the president was then in charge only of directing the oral debates.[34]

The grounds envisioned by the IDI for the refusal of arbitrators provide a privileged vantage point to observe the type of society in which the "conscience of the civilized world" had emerged. Pursuant to Goldschmidt's project, being a

32 See Goldschmidt, *op.cit.*, at 431–433.

33 See Institut de Droit International, 'Procès verbal de la session de genève, n. 2, séance du 1 septembre de 1874', *op.cit.*, at 590.

34 See Institut de Droit International, 'Procès verbal de la session de Genève, n. 3, séance du 2 septembre de 1874' (1874) 6 Revue de droit international et de législation comparée 591, at 592.

woman or deaf were grounds upon which an arbitrator could be refused.[35] Conversely, the nomination of a monarch was met with deference, dispensing royals from the formalities established to commoners. In Goldschmidt's words, "[q]*uand on choisira des souverains mineurs ou du sexe féminin, ce sera le plus souvent en pleine connaissance de ces qualités, et si même il n'en était pas ainsi, encore serait-il difficile de les récuser*."[36] The final text adopted on the matter was slightly less anachronic, maintaining the privilege of monarchs but omitting *a priori* prohibitions pertaining to sex in relation to the office of arbitrators.[37]

Furthermore, the codification process at the IDI granted great discretion to the arbitral tribunal in the conduction of proceedings. This approach represented a frontal departure from the one taken by national legal systems at the time, which favoured the law of the forum as the law governing the procedure.[38] In particular, under the IDI framework the arbitral tribunal had the prerogative to decide the language of the proceedings, the organisation of hearings, and the submission of written statements. The tribunal, however, would be bound by a certain understanding of due process, being required, at minimum, to hear each party and allow them to produce evidence necessary to build their case.[39]

Another remarkable feature concerning the prerogatives of the arbitral tribunal was introduced by Mancini, who proposed to include the issuance of procedural orders among the express powers of arbitrators.[40] In this regard, one cannot but see the direct link connecting such a prevalent prerogative in contemporary arbitral procedural rules with the IDI project. Furthermore, the tribunal was also vested with the prerogative to nominate as many secretaries as it deemed appropriate for the administration of the proceedings.[41]

---

35 See Goldschmidt, *op.cit.*, at 434.

36 See Goldschmidt, *op.cit.*, at 435.

37 Pursuant to Article 4 of the IDI project, "*seront capables d'être nommés arbitres internationaux les souverains et chefs de gouvernement sans aucune restrictions, et toutes les personnes qui ont la capacité d'exercer les fonctions d'arbitres d'après la loi commune de leur pays.*" See Gustave Rolin-Jaequemyns, 'Procès verbal de la session de la Haye du 25 Au 31 août' (1875) 7 Revue de droit international et de législation comparée 273, at 278.

38 See Goldschmidt, *op.cit.*, at 437, 439 and 441.

39 See Goldschmidt, *op.cit.*, at 438–439.

40 See Institut de Droit International, 'Procès verbal de la session de Genève, n. 3, séance du 2 septembre de 1874', 6 *Revue de Droit International et de Législation Comparée* (1874) 591, at 593.

41 Article 15(4) of the arbitration rules adopted by the IDI read as follows: "*Sauf dispositions contraires du compromis, le tribunal arbitral a le droit:* [...] *De rendre des ordonnance de procédure (sur la direction du procès), faire administrer des preuves, et requérir, s'il le faut,*

Importantly, it seems that the invention of competence-competence in the realm of arbitration arises from the IDI Rules. Indeed, it was Goldschmidt who envisioned the need to provide for the prerogative of the arbitral tribunal to rule on its own jurisdiction.[42] In his report, Goldschmidt noted that a similar rule would be very controversial in the context of domestic arbitration, especially in Germany. Still, he argued that such prerogative was necessary to avoid the paralysation of proceedings – an issue that would be even more pressing in international arbitration given the absence of a forum to rule on jurisdictional issues.[43]

This proposal gave rise to a lively debate at the Geneva session of the IDI held in 1874. The discussion actively involved Mancini, Pierantoni, Asser, Esperson, de Parieu, de Holtzendorff and obviously Goldschmidt. The discussion revolved around the question of whether arbitrators would have an absolute prerogative to rule on their jurisdiction or whether this prerogative would be relative to certain subject matters. This unfolded into an inquiry on whether it would be necessary to provide for a recourse against the arbitrators' decision on jurisdiction. The debate was settled with a new formulation for that provision, which was adopted in the following terms:

> Les exceptions tirées de l'incapacité des arbitres doivent être présentées avant toute autre. Dans le silence des parties, toute contestation ultérieure est exclue, sauf en cas d'incapacité survenue postérieurement.

---

du tribunal compétent les actes judiciaires pour lesquels le tribunal arbitral n'es pas qualifié, notamment l'assermentation d'experts et de témoins." See Rolin-Jaequemyns, 'Procès verbal de la session de la Haye au 25 Au 31 Août' (n 117), at 280. See, also, Goldschmidt, *op.cit.*, at 437–438.

42 See §18 of Goldschmidt's project, which read as follows: "*Le Tribunal Arbitral est juge de sa compétence. Si l'exception d'incompétence n'est pas opposée au premier moment opportun ou si, l'exception opposée en temps utile ayant été repoussée par le tribunal arbitral, les parties passent outre sans faire de réserves, toute contestation ultérieure de la compétence est exclue.*" See Goldschmidt, *op.cit.*, at 440.

43 Goldschmidt states the following: "*L'opinion juste est constamment soutenue par la Cour suprême de commerce de Leipzig contre le tribunal suprême de Berlin. Le danger d'un excès de compétence ne justifie point une immixtion préjudicielle du tribunal officiel. Dans l'arbitrage international il y a cette raison de plus, qu'une procédure judiciaire préliminaire est impossible. On pourrait donc, par l'exception d'incompétence, paralyser entièrement l'action du tribunal arbitral. Il va de soi que le recours doit être ouvert pour excès. Reste à savoir si le tribunal arbitral serait autorisé à refuser la division pour le motif que l'exception d'incompétence aurait été soulevée ? Dans l'état actuel des moyens de recours, il y a pour la négative des raisons déterminantes.*" See Goldschmidt, *op.cit.*, at 440.

> Les arbitres doivent prononcer sur les exceptions tirées de l'incompétence du tribunal arbitral, sauf le recours réservé au §32(1), n°6, et conformément aux dispositions du compromis.
>
> Aucune voie de recours ne sera ouverte contre les jugements préliminaires sur la compétence, si ce n'est cumulativement avec le recours contre le jugement arbitral définitif.
>
> Dans le cas où le doute sur la compétence dépend de l'interprétation d'une clause du compromis, les parties sont censées avoir donné aux arbitres la faculté de trancher la question, sauf clause contraire.[44]

The rule adopted, in its second paragraph, enshrined that the prerogative to rule on jurisdictional matters did not preclude parties from challenging the award for an excess of jurisdiction before domestic courts. A division of labour between judicial courts and arbitral tribunals was already envisioned by the IDI, with the jurisdictional prerogatives of arbitrators being counterbalanced by the attribution of a final say on jurisdiction to municipal judges.

It was not only the decision on jurisdiction that could lead to an application for revision. The award was certainly final and binding for the parties, but it could be subject to *ex officio* corrections of clerical mistakes – and, upon request of one of the parties, it could even be supplemented with a ruling on litigious points not previously decided by the tribunal.[45] Furthermore, certain grounds could lead to annulment proceedings before domestic or, failing an agreement by the parties on the forum for annulment proceedings, before the Supreme Court of the seat of arbitration.[46]

The revision of arbitration awards led Goldschmidt to evoke the desirability of creating a higher and permanent international instance of appeal, while simultaneously contemplating the possibility of establishing *ad hoc* arbitration tribunals to deal with annulment proceedings.[47] In any event, the solution endorsed by the IDI Rules was understood as a pragmatic option, which emphasized the importance of the seat of arbitration. In a territorially rooted world where international travelling was much more limited, the seat was

44 The provision is conveyed in Article 14 of the arbitration rules adopted by the IDI. See Rolin-Jaequemyns, 'Procès verbal de la session de la Haye du 25 au 31 août', *op.cit.*, at 280. For the debate on this rule, see Institut de Droit International, 'Procès verbal de la session de Genève, n. 3, séance du 2 septembre de 1874', *op.cit*, at 592–593.

45 See Goldschmidt, *op.cit.*, at 445–446.

46 See Goldschmidt, *op.cit.*, at 447–448.

47 The parallel with the ICSID system seems striking.

perceived as an essential element for the tribunal's ability to render an impartial award.[48]

The actual grounds for challenging the award were greatly inspired by Roman sources with some modulation introduced by the European legal experience.[49] The guiding idea was to narrow the grounds of annulment to matters concerning the validity of the arbitration agreement, the constitution of the tribunal, excess of jurisdiction and violations of what was already portrayed as international law and human rights.[50]

The finality of the arbitral award gave rise to another animated discussion among the members of the IDI. On one side, Field, Bulmerincq and Westlake pleaded for the suppression of the sections governing the annulment of awards. On the other side, Pierantoni was the loudest voice defending the provisions as they were drafted by Goldschmidt. Some other members were sceptical that any such means of recourse could be organised or effective. In light of this controversy, Mancini proposed a solution that managed to get the unanimous support of all members, reducing the grounds for annulment to hypothesis of excess of jurisdiction, corruption, or error caused by the production of fraudulent documents.[51]

Counterclaims and decisions *ex aequo et bono* were not permitted under the IDI Rules, unless the parties agreed otherwise.[52] The tribunal should decide by absolute majority on the basis of international law, and deliberations ought

48 Goldschmidt, *op.cit.*, at 437.

49 The grounds for appeal covered the following circumstances: invalidity of the arbitration agreement, provided that the concerned party had raised objections to the validity of the agreement during the proceedings (§32(1)); existence of a valid but inoperative arbitration agreement (§32(2)); defects related to the deliberation of the arbitral tribunal (§32(3)); lack of motivation when the arbitration agreement provided for a motivated decision (§32(4)); failure to afford one of the parties the right to present its arguments (§32(5)); excess of power (§32(6)); rulings *ultra petita* (§32(7)); violation of procedural rules established by the parties, or by the tribunal itself (§32(8)); immoral or prohibited acts ordered by the tribunal (§32(9)); a situation in which, prior to the decision, any member of the tribunal received an advantage or the promise of an advantage from one of the parties (§32(11)); a situation in which it could be established that the tribunal erred due to fraudulent actions of one of the litigants (§32(11)). See Goldschmidt, *op.cit.*, at 447–449.

50 See Goldschmidt, *op.cit.*, at 451.

51 The exact terms proposed by Mancini were the following ones: "*La sentence arbitrale est nulle en cas de compromis nul, ou d'excès de pouvoir, ou de corruption prouvée d'un des arbitres, si elle a entraîné la majorité, ou d'erreur essentielle causée par la production de faux documents. Le compromis déterminera devant quelles personnes ou facultés de droit ou corps constitué sera porté le recours en nullité et dans que délai.*" Institut de Droit International, *Procès verbal de la session de Genève, n. 3, séance du 2 septembre de 1874*, at 596.

52 See Goldschmidt, *op.cit.*, at 442.

to take place behind closed doors with the presence of all the members of the tribunal. The refusal of members of the tribunal to sign the award would not preclude its issuance as long as the majority of the tribunal signed it and declared that a minority refused to sign the decision. Still, failure to reach an absolute majority would make the arbitration agreement inoperative.[53]

Curiously, the report submitted by Goldschmidt did not provide for a default rule on the obligation to motivate the award, even if motivation was considered convenient.[54] This was another issue that generated debate among the members of the IDI. In light of Esperson's suggestion to include an opt-out provision on motivation,[55] Mancini suggested a formula that made its way into the final text adopted.[56] Pursuant to Mancini's proposition, the award was required to be reasoned, written and signed by at least the majority of the tribunal.[57]

After concluding the work on the codification of arbitration procedure, the IDI kept advocating in favour of international arbitration. In 1877, it adopted a resolution recommending states to insert an arbitration clause for the settlement of disputes concerning the interpretation and application of treaties. Furthermore, the same resolution proposed a model clause to be adopted alongside the arbitration agreement, which read as follows:

> Si les États contractants ne sont pas tombés d'accord préalablement sur d'autres dispositions touchant la procédure à suivre devant le tribunal arbitral, il y a lieu d'appliquer le Règlement consacré par l'Institut dans sa session de la Haye, le 28 août 1875.[58]

The drafting of the IDI Rules consists of a first blueprint for the codification of arbitral procedure within the context of interstate disputes. This would

53 See Goldschmidt, *op.cit.*, at 444.

54 See Goldschmidt, *op.cit.*, at 445.

55 See Institut de Droit International, 'Procès verbal de la session de genève, n. 1, séance du 31août de 1874' (1874) 6 Revue de droit international et de législation comparée 585, footnote 2, at 587.

56 Institut de Droit International, *Procès verbal de la session de Genève, n. 3, séance du 2 septembre de 1874*, at 595.

57 Article 23 of the rules adopted read as follows: "*La sentence arbitrale doit être redigée par écrit, et contenit un exposé des motifs, sauf dispense stipulée par le compromis. Elle doit être signé par chacun des members du tribunal arbitral. Si une minorité refuse de signer, la signature de la majorité suffit, avec declaration écrite que la minorité a refusé de signer.*" Rolin-Jaequemyns, *Procès verbal de la session de la Haye du 25 au 31 août*, at 281.

58 See Institut de Droit International, "Arbitrage international. – Clause compromissoire. – Résolution votée en séance du 12 septembre 1877" *in Annuaire: Tome 2/1878* (Schmidt Periodicals 1994), at 160.

constitute an important legacy for the future expansion and transnationalisation of arbitral authority.

1.2 *The Institut de droit International and the Uniformization of Private International Law*

The idea to promote the uniformization of private international law had not yet been coupled with the procedural uniformization of international arbitration in the early 1870s. Still, in a few years, a yet to be born practice of international commercial arbitration would be greatly influenced by the doctrine of uniformity in private international law. Notably, many of the ideas animating the transnational codification of private forms of arbitral procedure have been borrowed from debates on the uniformization of private international law.

The quest for the uniformization of private international law emerged within the scholarly tradition devoted to the study of conflict of laws, a branch of legal scholarship that usually trace its origins to the writings of the glossators and to the statutist school.[59] Faced with the expansion of globalization in the second half of the 19th century, especially in connection to commercial matters, many in the field of conflict of laws had been preaching in favor of the legislative unification of segments of private law, such as commercial law, and for the uniformization of legal regimes governing conflict of laws.

In the early 1860s, some scattered bilateral treaties had been adopted with that objective. France, for instance, had entered into a treaty with the Kingdom of Sardinia in 1860 with the purpose of implementing the mutual recognition and enforcement of decisions of their respective supreme courts.[60] Notably, one would be justified in wondering whether Pasquale Mancini was involved in these negotiations, as he was living in Turin at the time and was a tutor of the crown prince. Asser, for his part, had been publicly advocating for the uniformization of legislation on the circulation of judicial decisions as early as 1869.[61]

Asser was most likely behind the initiative taken by the government of the Netherlands in 1874 to issue a call for the adoption of uniform rules on the enforcement of judicial decisions.[62] The Dutch initiative, however, did

59 For a brief historical overview of private international law, see Alex Mills, 'The Private History of International Law' (2006) 55 The international and comparative law quarterly 1.

60 See France and Sardaigne, 'Déclaration relative à l'exécution réciproque des décrets et jugements des Cours suprêmes selon la forme du droit,' 11 September 1860.

61 See TMC Asser, 'De l'effet ou de l'exécution des jugements rendus à l'étranger en matière civile et commerciale' (1869) 1 Revue de droit international et de législation comparée 82.

62 For the entire call issued by the Dutch government, see United States Department of State, 'Papers Relating to the Foreign Relations of the United States, with the Annual

not come to fruition. Similarly, from 1882 to 1885, in his capacity as the Italian Minister of Foreign Affairs, Mancini tried to relaunch the uniformization efforts – an initiative that ultimately failed despite Mancini's prestige and the weight of his office.[63]

In 1889, South American countries concluded a series of treaties governing, *inter alia*, the harmonization of civil procedure and private international law. Even if the Treaties of Montevideo came to have a rather limited territorial coverage, as they were only ratified by Argentina, Bolivia, Paraguay, Peru and Uruguay, the event brought new energy to the movement for the uniformization of private international law.[64]

At the other side of the Atlantic, certainly inspired by the achievement of South American jurists, T.M.C. Asser was finally able to mobilize forces for the organization of the first two Hague Conferences on Private International Law.[65] Presiding the conferences held in 1893 and 1894, Asser was instrumental for the adoption of the 1896 Hague Convention on Civil Procedure.[66]

Figures like Asser and Mancini laboured both in the universes of theory and practice, producing material results and lasting contributions to the doctrine of uniformity in private international law. Their ability to navigate through the world of diplomacy, law and commerce, and their close ties to their respective governments, would prove essential to the success of the movement for the uniformization of private international law. Since its inception, the doctrine of uniform private international law would not have endured without governmental support.

Even still, all these concrete outcomes were preceded by a sustained and collective reflection on the strategies for and limits of the uniformization of private international law. This preparatory work was also led by Mancini and Asser – and it was consistently conducted within the framework of the IDI. Notably, the activities of the first commission of the IDI were devoted to the

---

Message of the President Transmitted to Congress December 5, 1899' 789–793. Available at: <http://digital.library.wisc.edu/1711.dl/FRUS.FRUS1899> accessed 3 April 2020. For an analysis of Asser's influence over the Dutch initiative, see De Baere and Mills, *op.cit.*, at 21.

63 See Kurt Lipstein, 'One Hundred Years of Hague Conferences on Private International Law' (1993) 42 The International and Comparative Law Quarterly 553, at 554–557.

64 For an analysis of the codification of private international law in South America, see Fernández Arroyo, *op.cit.*, at 112 ss; Haroldo Valladão, 'Le droit international privé des états américains' in *Collected Courses of the Hague Academy of International Law*, vol 81 (Martinus Nijhoff Publishers 1952), at 98 ss; Wyndham Bewes, 'The Treaties of Montevideo' (1920) 6 Transactions of the Grotius Society 59.

65 Se de Baere and Mills, *op.cit.*, at 22.

66 See TMC Asser, 'Les projets de Convention de la Haye pour le Droit International Privé' (1901) 33 Revue de droit international et de législation comparée.

uniformization of private international law, constituting a central forum for the development of a transnational doctrine of uniform private international law. The commission was composed of the most prominent specialists at the time and had as its rapporteurs Mancini and Asser.[67] Each man produced a report with a different emphasis. Mancini focused his attention on a general theory of uniform private international law (1.2.1), while Asser analysed the practical uniformization of civil procedure (1.2.2).

1.2.1 Mancini's Report to the 1st Commission of the IDI

Pasquale Mancini had been working on the unification of rules governing conflict of laws since the 1860s. Entrusted by the Italian government with the task of studying the potential for uniformization endeavours between Italy and France already in 1861,[68] his report to the IDI builds upon this previous work on uniformization while drawing heavily from his theoretical formulations on *jus gentium*.

The scholarship of the Neapolitan jurist is marked by a certain methodological eclecticism and a predilection for theoretical inquiry.[69] Mancini viewed law as inseparable from justice, leading him to engage in a quest for a universal and transcendental theory of natural law. His goal was to produce a theoretical contribution standing midway between the liberal and conservative conceptions of justice of his time. Furthermore, through the reassembly of Hegelian ideas, Mancini's views on international law tried to reconcile national independence and individual autonomy under a principle of nationality.[70] His

67 The 1st commission was composed of T.M.C Asser, Johan Bluntschli, Carl Ludwig Von Bar, Chales Brocher, Esperson, P. Fiore, Beach Lawrence, Laurent, Pasquale Mancini, Massé and John Westlake.

68 See Pasquale Mancini, 'De l'utilité de rendre obligatoires pour tous les Etats, sous la forme d'un ou de plusieurs Traités internationaux, un certain nombre de règles générales du droit international privé pour assurer la décision uniforme des conflits entre les différentes législations civiles et criminelles' (1874) 1 Journal de Droit International Privé 221, at 236–237.

69 Mancini's ideas echoed the contributions of Pasquale Liberatore, his former professor, Pellegrino Rossi and Vicco's historicism read through the lenses of Gian Domenico Romagnosi – an Italian scholar who postulated for the progressive development of society towards constitutional freedom through historical processes that could be channelled by legal science. See Grieco, *op.cit.*, at 371–372.

70 For some of Mancini's thoughts on Hegel, see Pasquale Mancini, *Della vocazione del nostro secolo per la riforma e la codificazione del diritto delle genti, e per l'ordinamento di una giustizia internazionale: discorso per la inaugurazione degli studi nella universitá di Roma, pronunziato nel 2 novembre 1874* (Stabilimento Civelli 1874), at 35–36.

ambition was to foster the coordination of both municipal and international politics,[71] channelling these two dialectic forces of history towards the fulfilment of human potential.[72] Mancini moved in the world of law and politics animated by those convictions.

The tensions between oracular illumination and political will as central elements for the production of law, *i.e.* between *ius* and *lex*, is embedded in the ancient genesis of this distinctive social field that is law.[73] At the 19th century, especially in the aftermath of the French revolution, one sees the re-emergence of legislation as the primary tool of the jurist – and the French civil code was the poster child of this project.

With the gradual triumph of codified positive legislation as the central source of law, many scholars labouring in the tradition of conflict of laws felt compelled to portray their discipline as yet another "department of national law which arises from the fact there are in the world different territorial jurisdictions possessing different laws."[74] The reaction to this state of affairs was best encapsulated by Savigny and his historical school of jurisprudence, for whom law was the historical product emerging out of the shared values of a community as vocalized by trained jurists.[75]

---

71 See Grieco, *op.cit.*, at 287.

72 Mancini states the following: "*Egli è ben vero che più tardi, trasportati dalle tendenze del secolo, vennero altri pensatori a sublimare il concetto dello Stato, così appellando non più qualunque associazione politica di uomini retti da un comune governo, ma (se vogliamo attenerci alle parole di una delle più alte sommità della filosofia alemanna) 'a la realtà stessa della morale idea, lo spirito morale che si manifesta ed appalesa come sostanziale volontà, che pensa e conosce sé stesso, ed esegue quanto conosce; che la sua immediata esistenza ne' costumi, nella coscienza, e nell'attività dell' individuo … il ragionevole in sé e per sé, lo svolgimento di Dio nel mondo, cioè dell'idea, di questa reale divinità.' Sotto la panteistica pompa di queste parole a noi basta riconoscere, che in tal nuovo aspetto lo Stato non è opera di arte, né di consenso: ed implica già come suo principio di vita la idea di nazionalità, la quale per necessità lo antecede. Infatti la Nazionalità che liberamente si costituisce all'interno, ed è possesso della sua piena autonomia ne' rapporti esterni, non si differenzia dallo Stato raffigurato nel concetto Hegeliano, ed allora (a parte la questione di ortodossia filosofica) la scelta tra i due punti di partenza si risolve in una semplice questione di precedenza logica.*" Pasquale Mancini, *Della nazionalità come fondamento del dritto delle genti: prelezione al corso di dritto internazionale e marittimo pronunziata nella R. Università di Torino* (Tipografia Eredi Botta 1851), at 48–49.

73 See Schiavone, *op.cit.*, at 74–84.

74 See John Westlake, *A Treatise on Private International Law* (William Maxwell & Son 1880), at 1. The same approach is taken by Foelix already in the 1840s. See Foelix, *op.cit.*

75 Savigny expresses these ideas as follows: "*Les vues que je viens d'exposer sur la possibilité et les avantages qu'il y aurait à régler d'un commun accord la collision des droit locaux se trouvent en grande partie réalisées par les traités conclus à ce sujet entre différents États,*

Mancini's report to the IDI, echoing his aforementioned methodological eclecticism, made an effort to reconcile the ideas of *ius* and *lex*, mediating the clash between historicists who saw law as a preserve of jurists and positivists who favoured an understanding of law as the province of the legislator. Mancini postulated that, while political autonomy was conducive to the primacy of legislation within a territory, such autonomy would neither be absolute nor unfettered. For him, national legislators were not authorized to enact norms that were unjust. Hence, Mancini was quite reticent in relation to the idea of a unified civil code for the world, but he believed that a set of universal legal rules were discoverable through reason and could limit the scope of national law.

Using the register of natural law theory, Mancini's report to the IDI shows great awareness of the interplay between global and local legal dynamics, as well as of historical contingencies in the formation of a legal tradition.[76]

---

surtout entre États voisin, où les cas de collision sont les plus fréquents. Les jurisconsultes recommandent et appellent de tous leur vœux ces espèces de traités, et nous en avons depuis longtemps des exemples. Mais il ne faut pas croire que là où les traités existent ils établissent un droit positif tout nouveau, et changent complément l'état de choses antérieur. Presque toujours ils ne sont que l'expression de cette communauté de droit dont j'ai parlé plus haut, et dès lors un acheminement à sa reconnaissance toujours plus complète." See Carl Von Savigny, *Traité de droit romain*, vol 8 (2nd edn, Librairie de Firmin Didot Frères, Fils et Cie 1860), at 33. A reading of Savigny's concept of law as oracular finds support in Halpérin, who argues that "[*e*]*n partant d'un droit fondé sur l'esprit des peuples, Savigny aboutissait à une communauté intellectuelle d'idées juridiques, avec le risque de divergences entre juristes dans l'interprétation d'un droit devenu 'savant.'*" See Jean-Louis Halpérin, *Entre nationalisme juridique et communauté de Droit* (PUF 1999), at 62. For another insightful analysis of Savigny's thought, see Hermann Kantorowicz, 'Savigny and the Historical School of Law' (1937) 53 The Law Quarterly Review 326.

76 The tension is expressed as follows in Mancini's report: "*Si l'on examine attentivement l'origine du Droit dans toute société humaine, on y constate le concours de deux éléments très distincts, qui ont contribué à sa naissance et à son développement graduel. Le premier consiste en une série de lois générales révélées par la raison de l'homme, dépendantes des conditions générales de la nature humaine, et qui ne changent et ne peuvent changer selon les temps et les pays.* [...] *Ce patrimoine de règles universelles peut augmenter avec l'expérience, avec nos connaissances et avec les progrès de la civilisation. Mais ces additions progressives ont-elles aussi un caractère d'universalité, parce que les nouvelles règles comme les anciennes sont applicables, non pas à telle ou telle nation, mais à la société humaine dans tous les pays et sur toute la surface du globe. Ce droit naturel, universel et constant, postulat de la raison, est l'essence et pour ainsi dire l'esprit vivifiant de toutes les législations particulières des différents peuples, et comme la base sur laquelle chacun d'eux élève son édifice national. Mais à côté de ces lois générales qui régissent toute l'espèce humaine, on*

In addition, he draws from and reworks Savigny's concept of *jus gentium*, expressly refusing any role to comity and sovereign discretion in the production of international law.[77] Rather, he argues that international law would be a global order coordinating national legal regimes through general principles of justice inherent to humankind.[78] Echoing Savigny, this international order would be based on a sort of oracular and exoteric type of legal knowledge accessible to the jurist.

Within this framework, ethnic and local idiosyncrasies could be expressed in domestic legislation, as long as they did not violate general principles of justice. Accordingly, the limits of national legislative autonomy would be defined by a group of enlightened few charged with the task of discovering the content

---

voit s'élever au sein de chaque peuple et de chaque nationalité, par une évolution également nécessaire, une autre catégorie de règles, de préceptes et de défenses qui sont le résultat local et caractéristique de chaque pays. On a déjà observé que le climat et la température, avec l'action incessante de leur influence physique, modifient. Dans les différents peuples les degrés de sensibilité, les tendances, les forces actives, les moyens de dominer la nature, et même les besoins et les conditions de leur satisfaction. La nature du pays, montagne ou plaine, baigné par des rivières ou par la mer, détermine le genre de vie et la direction du développement national, aussi bien que les produits du sol." See Mancini, *De l'utilité*, at 224–225.

77 Mancini expresses this idea in the following terms: *"Cette fausse idée d'une concession libre et non obligatoire, de la part d'une souveraineté, quant à l'admission d'une loi étrangère, fut, à notre avis, le principal obstacle à la formation d'une doctrine scientifique du Droit international privé. En effet, de cet ordre d'idées que la condition civile des individus hors de leur patrie et la force reconnue aux lois étrangères ne dérivaient que d'une concession généreuse et spontanée, on tirait logiquement deux conséquences : l'une, que la souveraineté, dont émane la concession, avait le droit de déterminer, selon son bon plaisir, les limites et les conditions de cette admission (limites et conditions toujours justes quant'il s'agissait d'une concession gratuite, et d'une restriction volontaire de son pouvoir législatif), l'autre, que dans une matière tout à fait discrétionnelle et arbitraire, il n'y avait pas lieu à rechercher des principes spéculatifs et rationnels de droit international privé ; de sorte que ceux qui raisonnaient ainsi réduisaient cette science à une étude des textes positifs et des législations comparées, ou tout au plus à une appréciation expérimentale des résultats des différents codes. Mais dans ces derniers temps la doctrine de la comitas, a non seulement perdu son ancienne faveur, mais a été de plus l'objet de réfutations sévères et victorieuses."* See Mancini, *De l'utilité*, at 229.

78 In this respect, Mancini argues the following: *"Mais la puissance de faire des lois n'implique pas celle de dicter des lois injustes et blessantes pour la communauté de droit, qui découle des nécessités humaines et civiles et des devoirs internationaux imposés par le lien de la société générale existant entre tous les peuples. Le principe de l'indépendance d'un État ne peut pas être exagéré jusqu'au point d'autoriser la violation des droits d'un autre État ; l'indépendance mutuelle des États n'est ni plus ni moins que l'inviolable liberté mutuelle des individus ; or, l'on n'a pas la liberté de porter atteinte au droit des autres, ni la liberté d'être injuste."* See Mancini, *De l'utilité*, at 228.

of those principles. It would be up to these oracles of law the role of codifying such norms in international instruments that would ultimately advance legislative uniformity. In other terms, uniformity would be achieved with the codification of international law through treaties adopted between sovereign States, but the contents of these codification instruments would be a manifestation of oracular justice rather than sovereign will.[79]

Besides this theoretical discussion, Mancini's report to the IDI goes through some practical ideas for the unification of private international law. Most of his propositions, he acknowledged, did not stray away from traditional solutions proposed by the statutist school. Although Mancini considers that tradition to be based on a convoluted and mostly incorrect theory, he was also convinced that many of their insights were valid. If solutions were similar, the theory advanced by Mancini is however quite distinct. He believed that his theory corrected mistakes and refined the conceptual tools available for the analysis of conflict of laws. In this respect, Mancini's theory rejects the domestication of conflict of laws, presenting it as a true branch of international law.[80]

At its core, his doctrine of uniformity is permeated by a dialectical tension between individualism and collectivism. This tension is translated into the dichotomy between private and public order. Public law governed relations of the public order, consisting of a territorialized legal regime qualified as a valid limitation to an individual's freedom. For Mancini, public law would represent a sort of expropriation of individual rights for the sake of individuals themselves.[81] Private law, for its part, would govern relations of the private order. Still, not all private law could be qualified similarly. On the one hand, there

79 See Mancini, *De l'utilité*, at 285.

80 See Mancini, *De l'utilité*, at 297–298.

81 Mancini advances the argument as follows: "*Dans ce territoire la volonté nationale établit la constitution, l'organisation des pouvoirs publics, l'étendue et les limites de leur exercice, les rapports avec les individus, quels qu'ils soient habitant le territoire, les règles générales de leur action politique, enfin, les défense et prescriptions jugées nécessaires à la propriété de la vie sociale. L'ensemble de ces lois constitue précisément ce que l'on appelle le droit public d'un État contre ses ennemies intérieurs et extérieurs, et même pour garantir à tous les habitants la paisible jouissance de leurs droits. On voit avec raison dans cette institution une espèce d'expropriation légitime que l'État fait d'une partie de la liberté personnelle des individus protégés par lui. Nous disons expropriation et non cession, pour ne pas tomber dans l'erreur reprochée à l'auteur du contrat social, car nous considérons l'état social non comme volontaire et conventionnel, mais comme une nécessité pour l'homme. Nous considérons donc comme nécessaires aussi les rapports essentiels de l'ordre public, les conditions qui la constituent, enfin les sacrifices individuels exigés pour l'établissement d'un pouvoir public*

would be a so-called "necessary part," related to personal status and familial relations. On the other hand, there would be a "voluntary part," which would be essentially contractual. This taxonomy does not yet use the terms disposable and non-disposable rights, but it seems to lay the seeds for the development of such concepts. Accordingly, the necessary part of private law was defined as a legal emanation of the individual's nationality, and it could not be disposed of or renounced. The voluntary part of private law, however, would be disposable and could be governed by any law chosen by the individual.[82]

In due course, both the exception of public order and the dichotomy between disposable and non-disposable rights would become foundational ideas for the organization of international arbitration. Notably, they were largely used to establish the boundaries for the work of arbitrators, as well as for the division of labour between state courts (the ultimate guardians of public order) and arbitral tribunals (the keepers of contractual autonomy).

1.2.2 Asser's Report to the 1st Commission of the IDI

The report submitted by Asser to the 1st commission of the IDI focused on the circulation of judicial decisions and its corresponding liberalization. His report is divided in the following four parts: competence and jurisdiction; "*cautio judicatum solvi*" and legal aid; the administration of evidence; and the enforcement of foreign judicial decisions. In line with his practical mind, Asser seeks to find a minimum common denominator for the international codification of these issues, which would be translated in treaty rules replacing domestic law.

Besides the necessity of giving uniformity to rules on jurisdiction, such a treaty would be an occasion to promote the uniformization of some rules governing conflict of laws of a civil and commercial nature. This could be achieved, he notes, in order to avoid having the courts of the place of enforcement feeling compelled to apply a different law to the merits than the one adopted by the

---

fort, tutélaire et imposant, que l'on appelle souveraineté ou gouvernement." See Mancini, *De l'utilité*, at 295–296.

82 This idea is originally presented as follows: "*Un examen attentif conduit néanmoins à distinguer dans le droit privé de l'individu étranger deux parties, l'une nécessaire, l'autre volontaire. Nous appelons partie nécessaire les lois qui régissent l'état personnel, l'ordre et les rapports de famille. En effet, il ne dépend pas de la volonté de l'homme d'altérer ou de modifier cette partie nécessaire. Personne ne peut renoncer à l'état et aux rapports de famille qui lui sont attribuées par la loi de sa patrie. L'état des personnes et de la famille constitue un ensemble d'attributs et de qualités qui ne sont pas propres à toute personne humaine, mais à l'individu appartenant à une nationalité déterminée.*" See Mancini, *De l'utilité*, at 294.

courts that originally rendered the decision, something that could ultimately put in jeopardy the uniform regime of judicial enforcement.[83] Moreover, the negotiation of a similar treaty would be an opportunity to foster the equal treatment of residents and non-residents before national courts.[84]

From a methodological standpoint, Asser's report is representative of a somewhat similar ambition to that of Mancini. Asser seemingly strives for the reconciliation of legislated rules enshrined in positive instruments with norms produced by scholars and courts. Still, differently from the Neapolitan jurist, the Dutchman has a stronger conviction on the primacy of legislation over other sources of law.[85] For instance, he refuses to grant judges the discretion to rule on an open-textured clause of *ordre public*, postulating a rather formalistic exception pursuant to which only violations of positive public law could be conducive to refusing to grant enforcement to foreign judicial decisions.[86]

In terms of content, the report first addresses the distribution of jurisdiction, focusing exclusively on territorial questions. The underlying idea informing his propositions is that the uniformization of rules on territorial jurisdiction should reflect, as much as possible, uniform rules on the law applicable to the dispute.[87] The report praises the treaty concluded between

83 Asser's argument is as follows: "*Enfin, last not least, il semble de toute nécessité que les États, qui s'entendent sur l'exécution réciproque des jugements, adoptent en même temps des règles uniformes pour servir de base à la solution des conflits de législations civile et commerciale.* [...] *Mais, ce qui doit être évité, c'est que le juge étranger soit obligé par la loi de son pays d'appliquer une autre loi que celle qui eût régi le cas d'après la loi du lieu où l'exécution est demandée.*" See TMC Asser, 'Rapport de M. Asser sur la procédure civile' (1875) Revue de droit international et de législation comparée 37, at 587.

84 According to Asser, the outcomes of his proposals were the following ones: "*La réforme qu'on s'efforce d'accomplir par rapport à l'exécution des jugements étrangers, si utile et si bienfaisante en elle-même, aurait encore pour conséquence, comme on voit, de faire un grand progrès à tout le droit international privé. Car, si cette réforme est accompagnée des garanties que nous jugeons nécessaires, on aura obtenu en même temps l'adoption de règles uniformes concernant la compétence et concernant la décision des conflits de lois. D'un autre côté l'influence de cette réforme se fera sentir à l'égard de plusieurs dispositions actuellement en vigueur, qui ont pour but d'accorder aux régnicoles une protection exceptionnelle vis-à-vis des forains, et qu'on tâche de justifier en s'appuyant sur l'impossibilité ou la difficulté d'exécuter les jugements à l'étranger.*" See Asser, *Rapport sur la procédure civile*, at 591.

85 This is well illustrated by the following extract: "*Si l'on réussit, le droit international privé sera entré dans une ère nouvelle: parmi les sources de ce droit, l'autorité des livres et des arrêts aura fait place, en grande partie du moins, au droit codifié. Et ce droit codifié sera le fruit des études scientifiques des plusieurs siècles.*" See Asser, *Rapport sur la procédure civile*, at 591.

86 See Asser, *Rapport sur la procédure civile*, at 589–590.

87 See Asser, *Rapport sur la procédure civile*, at 370.

France and Switzerland in 1869 on jurisdiction and enforcement of court decisions,[88] analysing its implementation with the goal of exploring the obstacles to the multilateral uniformization of the regime governing the circulation of court decisions.

Furthermore, Asser's report analyses in great detail the uniformization of evidentiary procedural rules. Notably, the report discusses the law applicable to the production of different types of evidence, pointing to the convenience of having an international treaty governing the matters so as to promote clarity and certainty. The solutions he puts forth tended to portray the means of proof as greatly connected to the merits of a dispute, despite the fact that many of his contemporaries were more inclined to place evidentiary matters within the exclusive purview of the law of the forum. Asser notes that the approach of his opposers was built on the assumption that the production of evidence aims merely at convincing the judge, disregarding the adversarial nature of civil procedure and the relative effects of the judicial civil decision. These two elements, Asser believed, would militate in favour of mitigating the oversight of the *lex fori* regarding evidentiary issues.[89]

The report also devotes great attention to the practical problems emerging from the conduct of proceedings involving a foreign element, which lead to the analysis of issues pertaining to the notification of non-residents and the use of rogatory letters for the performance of certain procedural acts. Notably, Asser observes the informality under which rogatory letters were used, suggesting the necessity of a mandatory international framework to operate this mechanism.[90]

The final part of Asser's report is devoted to a discussion on the formalization and uniformization of a regime of exequatur, which followed a brief description of the three approaches in force at the time. In this respect, Asser first pointed that some states only granted exequatur after a full review of the merits of the dispute. Still, he also noted the existence of an opposite model, which granted an exequatur without any review of the merits, provided there was reciprocity and certain formal conditions were met. In between the two models, there was also a hybrid exequatur regime. This approach encompassed a dual system for enforcement of foreign court rulings, one for cases involving

88 See the *Convention Franco-Suisse relative à la compétence judiciaire et à l'exécution des jugements en matière civile* dated 15 June 1869. This document was the outcome of a long process of maturation, and it was preceded by the *Traité entre la France et la Suisse concernant les rapports de justice et de police* dated 18 July 1828.

89 See Asser, *Rapport sur la procédure civile*, at 575–576.

90 See Asser, *Rapport sur la procédure civile*, at 583–584.

nationals and another for cases involving non-nationals. Notably, the enforcement against nationals of the forum would be subject to a full revision of the merits of the dispute, while enforcement of decisions against non-nationals would be granted without review.[91]

In light of this reality, the report suggests replacing this multiplicity of enforcement mechanisms by a uniform regime enacted through an international treaty and inspired by the second model – which was actually adopted by Italy, Germany and Austria at the time. Asser was an advocate of the liberalization of the international regime of exequatur, advancing the argument that the courts of the place where enforcement was sought should abstain from reviewing the merits of the dispute and should merely conduct a formal analysis of foreign court's decisions. This formal analysis should be centred mostly on the jurisdiction of the foreign court, an assessment that ought to be governed by both the law of the place where enforcement was sought and the law of the place where the decision was rendered. In addition, some minimum due process safeguards should be provided as conditions for enforcement, such as guarantees on procedural delays and defendants' rights. These ideas would later gain traction in relation to the enforcement of foreign arbitral awards, with Asser's report serving as a sort of early roadmap for future generations to follow.

Beyond the proposals conveyed in the report, it is also interesting to observe the contribution given by Asser related to the work methods for the uniformization of private international law. In particular, he took the initiative to ask the members of the IDI to answer a questionnaire with a number of items on comparative legislation relevant to private international law.[92] His

---

91 See Asser, *Rapport sur la procédure civile*, at 585.

92 Asser's survey was formulated as follows: "*Quelles sont les dispositions des lois et des traités, en vigueur dans votre pays, concernant les parties suivantes du Droit international privé? I. – Droit civil. 1. La qualité de national, l'acquisition et la perte de la nationalité et l'influence de ce changement de nationalité sur la condition de la femme et des enfants mineurs. 2. Le droit des étrangers, l'état et la capacité des personnes, les rapports de famille et les droits et obligations qui en découlent. 3. Les successions, en tant ab intestat qu'ex testamento, – par rapport aux personnes successibles, aux conditions requises pour la validité intrinsèque des dispositions testamentaires, etc. (au point de vue du droit international). 4. Les mariages de nationaux à l'étranger et les mariages d'étrangers dans les pays. 5. L'effet des divorces, – prononcés régulièrement à l'étranger, – dans les pays dont la législation ne les admet pas. 6. La législation qui, en cas de conflit de lois, doit régir les biens meubles et les biens immeubles. 7. Celle qui régit la forme des actes entre vifs et des testaments.* II. – *Procédure civile. 1. La base et les limites de la compétence des tribunaux ratione personae, tant en général que par rapport à la nationalité des parties. 2. Les dispositions exceptionnelles du droit de procédure à*

questionnaire was composed of twelve questions, divided into two sections, and the members of the institute were asked to answer the questions in light of the legislation in force in their home states. The first section contained seven questions and pertained to substantive issues of private law, such as the capacity of aliens, the effects of divorce, the law governing the form of contracts and so on. The second section listed five questions and focused on questions of civil procedure, such as the scope of territorial jurisdiction, the enforcement of foreign judicial decisions etc. The answers to this questionnaire were compiled and summarized by Asser, being later published as a supplement of his report.[93]

It is not clear when the use of questionnaires made its way into uniformization endeavours, but the style of questions posed by Asser had the ambition to be objective. This becomes even clearer if one compares his questionnaire with the one proposed by Charles Brocher to the members of the IDI that same year. Brocher's questionnaire concerned the uniformization of criminal legislation, but the formulation of questions is conducive to subjective and prescriptive answers.[94] Asser's use of questionnaires echoes a practical concern. It seemingly aims at asserting the treatment given by positive legislation in regard to private international law, producing data that lends itself easily to an instrumental comparative analysis pinpointing the convergences and divergences in national legislation. Asser's approach is certainly a forerunner of the

l'égard des étrangers, comme : la caution judicatum solvi, l'assistance judiciaire gratuite, etc. 3. Les formalités prescrites à l'égard des assignations en justice et autres exploits à signifier à des personnes domiciliées ou résidant à l'étranger, et les délais de comparution à l'égard de ces personnes. 4. Les règles de droit international concernant les moyens de préuve et les commissions rogatoires. 5. L'exécution des jugements étrangers." See TMC Asser, 'Questionnaire de mars 1875' (1875) 7 Revue de droit international et de législation comparée 592.

93 See TMC Asser, 'Rapport supplémentaire, par M. Asser: résumé des réponses au questionnaire de mars 1875' (1875) 7 Revue de droit international et de législation comparée 593.

94 Compare, for instance, the following first three questions taken from Brocher's questionnaire with Asser's questionnaire presented above: "*1. La nature du droit pénal et les considérations théoriques qui lui servent de principes dirigeants, ne conduisent-elles pas à faire prédominer tel principe de compétence sur les autres? 2. Serait-il possible, dans l'état actuel des choses, de s'arrêter exclusivement à l'un de ces principes? 3. De quelle manière convient-il de les combiner et lequel doit finir par l'emporter sur les autres?*" For all the questions in Brocher's questionnaire, see Charles Brocher, 'Propositions de M. Ch. Brocher relatives à un questionnaire se rapportant aux conflits de législations en droit pénal' (1875) 7 Revue de droit international et de législation comparée 416.

similar practice followed by UNCITRAL, which uses surveys in order to collect data on the state of positive law regarding matters under its purview.[95]

2 In the Shadows of War

The practice of international arbitration was unquestionably born as an interstate concern, one that was greatly advanced by international lawyers sharing a pacifist outlook on foreign affairs. In a certain way, international arbitration would be the mirror image of war, projecting itself as the best alternative for the settlement of interstate disputes through peaceful means. As it will be seen throughout this study, the long shadows of war will often serve as catalyst for many procedural developments in international arbitration.

Two early developments attributable to the interplay between war and arbitration emerge in the context of the Hague Peace Conferences of 1899 and 1907. Each of these intergovernmental initiatives introduced procedural innovations that profoundly influenced the practice of arbitration and the place of its authority for global governance.

The first Hague Conference is at the root of the Permanent Court of Arbitration, comprising both an institutional platform and a procedural set of rules that would serve as a focal point for the future transnational codification of arbitral procedure. Indeed, the PCA Rules would constitute an authoritative procedural template for any future endeavours dealing with the uniformization of arbitration practice through codification. In addition, the PCA as an intergovernmental organization would serve as the first international custodian of arbitral memory, knowledge and technique,[96] as well as a model for future intergovernmental arbitral institutions like ICSID.

---

95 For an example of this practice, see UNCITRAL Secretariat, 'Report on the Survey Relating to the Legislative Implementation of the Convention on the Recognition and Enforcement of Foreign Arbitral Awards' (United Nations Commission on International Trade Law 2008) A/CN.9/656.

96 Article 22 of the 1899 Convention for the pacific settlement of international disputes provides as follows: "[…] The Signatory Powers undertake to communicate to the International Bureau at The Hague a duly certified copy of any conditions of arbitration arrived at between them, and of any award concerning them delivered by special Tribunals. They undertake also to communicate to the Bureau the Laws, Regulations, and documents eventually showing the execution of the awards given by the Court." See Charles I Bevans (ed), '1899 Convention for the Pacific Settlement of International Disputes', *Treaties and other international agreements of the United States of America, Multilateral 1776–1917*, vol 1 (Department of State Publication 1968), at 237–238.

The second Hague Conference, for its part, promoted a subtle but fundamental change in the place of arbitral authority for global governance. Through the adoption of the 1907 "Convention respecting the Limitation of Employment of Force for Recovery of Contract Debts", known as Drago-Porter Convention, arbitration procedure was extended to the collection of international contractual debts. These claims were once settled through armed force and had been the source of numerous international incidents.[97] In the 1900's, the impact of such innovation was limited, but it created the conditions for a profound transfiguration of arbitral procedure, one that would only be completed a few years later. Indeed, it is posited here that the Drago-Porter Convention laid the groundwork for the birth of a transnational form of arbitral procedure.

This section will first address the creation of the PCA and its procedural framework in 1899 (2.1), and then it will analyse the extension of arbitral procedure to the vindication of international contractual wrongs at the Hague Peace Conference of 1907 (2.2).

2.1 *An Alternative to War: the Creation of the Permanent Court of Arbitration*

An imperial rescript was circulated at the weekly reception of the Russian Foreign Office on 24 August 1898.[98] The document conveyed an invitation issued by Tzar Nicholas II with the clearly stated aim of halting an escalating arms race. Indeed, the Hague Peace Conference of 1899 came to work extensively on the laws governing warfare and arms proliferation, but it would be best remembered more than one hundred years later for the adoption of the 1899 "Convention on the Peaceful Settlement of International Disputes." This document has brought to life the first institution devoted to the international administration of arbitral procedure, as well as the first State-endorsed procedural code to operate this mechanism of dispute settlement.

The third commission of the conference was the one entrusted with the mandate to work on the peaceful settlement of international disputes, meeting from 23 May to 25 July 1899.[99] Although its efforts covered commissions of inquiry and mediation, the articles on arbitration were widely seen as the

97 For an overview on the process leading towards the prohibition of the use of force in international relations, see Oona Hathaway and Scott J Shapiro, *The Internationalists: How a Radical Plan to Outlaw War Remade the World* (Simon & Schuster Paperbacks 2017).

98 See Stephen Barcroft, 'The Hague Peace Conference of 1899' (1989) 3(1) Irish Studies in International Affairs 55, at 57.

99 For the records of the third commission's work, James Brown Scott, *The Proceedings of The Hague Peace Conference: The Conference of 1899* (Oxford University Press 1920) 581.

core of its mandate.[100] Similarly to the views espoused by Goldschimidt in his report to the IDI twenty-five years earlier, international arbitration was yet again presented as a cornerstone for the maintenance of international peace and as a remedy for the inexistence of international courts.

Much of the heavy lifting at the third commission was performed by an "examination committee," composed of T.M.C. Asser, Édouard Descamps, Paul d'Estournelles, Frederick William Holls, Heinrich Lammasch, Fyodor Martens, Édouard Odier and Philipp Zorn. Édouard Descamps is certainly a name to be retained, as he acted both as president of the examination committee and as rapporteur on the work of the third commission before the plenary session of the conference.

The work performed at the Hague was no longer done in a vacuum nor would it start from zero, with Chevalier Descamps formally acknowledging the importance of the IDI Rules.[101] It was also through Descamps that the work of the *Conférence interparlamentaire* on arbitration would come to penetrate the institutional design of a soon to be created "court of arbitration."[102] The *Conférence interparlamentaire* was an institution gathering members of parliament from Europe and the United States, having being created in 1888 to strengthen peaceful relations amongst nations and to promote arbitration as a means of settling interstate disputes.[103]

Descamps, who was a Belgium Senator and former president of the *Conférence interparlamentaire,* was the leading author of a study commissioned by that body on the organization of a permanent court of arbitration.[104] Upon request of the delegate of Luxembourg (Eyschen), who raised awareness to

100 See Brown Scott, *The Proceedings of The Hague Peace Conference of 1899, op.cit.*, at 595.

101 Descamps noted that "[t]he Institute of International Law long ago understood the inconveniences resulting from the present state of affairs and formulated regulations concerning arbitral procedure which are of the greatest interest." See Brown Scott, *The Proceedings of The Hague Peace Conference of 1899, op.cit.*, at 600.

102 This institution still exists and is now named Interparliamentary Union in English (and *Union Interparlamentaire* in French).

103 The first resolution adopted at its 1889 session read as follows: "*Les membres de la conférence interparlementaire recommandent de nouveau, et avec insistance, à tous les gouvernements civilisés la conclusion de traités par lesquels, sans porter atteinte à leur indépendance et sans admettre aucune ingérence dans ce qui touche à leur constitution intérieure, ces gouvernement s'engageraient à soumettre à l'arbitrage le règlement de tous les différends qui peuvent surgir entre eux.*" See 'Procès verbal de la Conférence Interparlementaire de juin 1889,' at 11–12.

104 The study was published in 1895 with an annexed project for the creation of such an institution. See Édouard Descamps, *Essai sur l'organisation de l'arbitrage International: Mémoire aux Puissance* (E Guyot 1896).

a "most interesting work on arbitration,"[105] Descamp's study was circulated amongst the members of the third commission at the outset of its activities. Although the essay was not reproduced on the official records of the conference, the document is most likely that same essay published by Descamps on behalf of the *Conférence interparlamentaire.*

It must be noted that the creation of a permanent court of arbitration was not originally tabled for discussion in 1899. The matter surfaced through the contribution of Julian Pauncefote, the first delegate of the UK. In the first meeting of the third commission, Pauncefote remarked that a mere procedural codification of arbitration was insufficient to accomplish the "great cause" that brought them together, and argued that it would be "absolutely necessary to organise a permanent international tribunal which may be able to assemble at once upon the request of the disputing parties."[106] This proposition was met with some scepticism, and Constantino Nigra, the Italian delegate, moved to first address procedural codification leaving the eventual establishment of a permanent court to the end of discussions.[107]

Despite the initial hesitations, the committee of examination was entrusted with the task of working on a draft for the creation of a permanent institution overseeing international arbitration. This work was performed on the basis of projects submitted by the British, Russian and American delegations. In particular, the British proposal was used as a working document, but amendments were made to accommodate elements of the American and Russian submissions.[108]

In relation to the convention itself and to the codification of arbitration procedure, the committee of examination used two Russian submissions as working documents, i.e., an "Outline for the preparation of a draft convention to be concluded by the Powers participating in the Hague Conference" and a "Draft arbitral code." Martens was the leading figure of the Russian delegation, not simply for being its first delegate but also for his worldwide prestige as an international lawyer. Accordingly, his views in general, and on arbitration in particular, were highly regarded and very influential.[109]

105 See Brown Scott, *The Proceedings of The Hague Peace Conference of 1899*, *op.cit.*, at 581.
106 See Brown Scott, *The Proceedings of The Hague Peace Conference of 1899*, *op.cit.*, at 584.
107 See Brown Scott, *The Proceedings of The Hague Peace Conference of 1899*, *op.cit.*, at 584.
108 See Brown Scott, *The Proceedings of The Hague Peace Conference of 1899*, *op.cit.*, at 597.
109 The weight of Marten's prestige can be illustrated by an exchange he had with Frederick Holls on the finality of arbitration awards. Indeed, before objecting to one of Martens' arguments, Holls felt the need to make the following statement: "I cannot forbear to express, at the outset, the great reluctance and hesitation with which I find myself in disagreement, on a question of such great importance, with the gentleman who may

The procedural codification of international arbitration was also marked by great many contributions of T.M.C. Asser. Serving as the living memory of the work performed by the IDI on the codification of arbitral procedure, Asser was a very active member of both the committee of examination and the third commission. It was upon his suggestion, for instance, that a provision on third-party intervention was included in the draft articles.

More importantly, it was under the terms proposed by Asser that the very controversial issue of challenging arbitral awards came to be settled. There was an opt-out rule on revision in a first draft produced by the committee of examination, establishing as a ground for revision the "discovery of some new fact which is of a nature to exercise a decisive influence upon the award."[110] This rule was supported by a slight majority of the members at the committee of examination, a group that was led by the American delegate Frederick Holls. Quoting Lincoln, Holls was of the view that nothing could be settled until it was properly settled.[111] Nevertheless, many felt that the finality of arbitration awards was essential for the success of international arbitration. Martens was perhaps the most vocal supporter of this opinion, making a forceful and solemn address against the inclusion of a revision mechanism. In particular, he argued that "[t]he end of arbitration is to terminate the controversy absolutely" and that "[t]his idea of rehearing is the most fatal blow which could be struck against the idea of arbitration."[112] Martens advocated that "[t]o preserve peace he would have all disputes cut short by some radical means."[113]

---

perhaps be called the most eminent representative in the entire world of the idea of arbitration, the president of the one tribunal of arbitration which is sitting at present, our most honourable colleague from Russia, Mr. Martens." See Brown Scott, *The Proceedings of The Hague Peace Conference: The Conference of 1899*, *op.cit.*, at 620.

110 The text of the first draft read as follows: "Unless stipulated to the contrary in the *compromis*, revision of the arbitral award may be demanded of the tribunal which rendered it, but only on the ground of the discovery of some new fact which is of a nature to exercise a decisive influence upon the award and which, at the time the tribunal entered its decree, was unknown to the tribunal and to the party demanding revision. Proceedings for revision can only be instituted by a decision of the tribunal expressly recording the existence of the new fact, recognising in it the character described in the preceding paragraph, and declaring the demand admissible on this ground. No demand for revision can be received unless it is formulated within three months following the notification of the award." See Brown Scott, *The Proceedings of The Hague Peace Conference: The Conference of 1899*, *op.cit.*, at 617.

111 See Brown Scott, *The Proceedings of The Hague Peace Conference of 1899*, *op.cit*, 621.

112 See Brown Scott, *The Proceedings of The Hague Peace Conference: The Conference of 1899*, *op.cit.*, at 619.

113 See Brown Scott, *The Proceedings of The Hague Peace Conference: The Conference of 1899*, *op.cit.*, at 624.

The IDI had been confronted with a somewhat similar controversy in the early 1870s. At that moment, the inclusion of an annulment mechanism in the final text of the IDI Rules had also generated debate, and the matter was only settled upon Mancini's suggestion to narrow the grounds of annulment to the hypothesis of excess of jurisdiction, corruption and error caused by the use of fraudulent documents.[114]

At the Hague, it was T.M.C. Asser who would be in charge of promoting a conciliatory position in relation to the diametrically opposed views on the finality of arbitration awards. Asser advocated for a rule that does "not imply a right of revision as a natural consequence in every arbitration case, but it allows the parties to reserve this right expressly and, if they do, it fixes the rules and procedure to be followed."[115] The text proposed by Asser was still based on the vague notion of "new fact which is of a nature to exercise a decisive influence upon the award," but it essentially reverted the logic of the original provision. The new rule would convey an opt-in mechanism aiming at the middle ground between the two opposing camps. Asser did not believe that the matter could be decided pursuing "radical measures" as those evoked by Martens.[116] Rather, Asser repeatedly called for compromise, which ultimately convinced all delegations to support his opt-in rule.[117]

These individualized contributions should not overshadow the fact that the PCA framework was produced by many hands, as a considerable number of issues generated great controversy. The appointment of arbitrators, for instance, gave rise to a long debate on the influence litigants could exert over arbitrators. The framework proposed, and later adopted, envisioned a five-member tribunal,[118] where four of these arbitrators would be appointed

114 See Institut de Droit International, 'Procès verbal de la session de Genève, n. 3, séance du 2 septembre de 1874,' *op.cit.*, at 596.

115 See Brown Scott, *The Proceedings of The Hague Peace Conference of 1899*, *op.cit.*, at 618.

116 See Brown Scott, *The Proceedings of The Hague Peace Conference of 1899*, *op.cit.*, at 624.

117 Asser intervention was recorded as follows: "Mr. Asser recalls the remark made by one of the previous speakers, 'Radical measures are the best.' This may be so in a parliament, where the majority rules, but in an assembly like this, which may be termed an international parliament, we are often called upon to reach a compromise. That is the aim of his proposal. He has taken into account all the good reasons put forward by both sides. The partisans of revision will find their wishes met by an article that determines the procedure to be followed in a second hearing and designates it as a practical means within the reach of all the States. The partisans of no revision also will be satisfied by the exclusion of revision unless there is a special clause in the *compromis*. If the *compromis* contains nothing on the subject, the arbitral award will be irrevocable". See Brown Scott, *The Proceedings of The Hague Peace Conference of 1899*, *op.cit.*, at 624.

118 See Articles 24 and 32 of the 1899 Convention, in Bevans, *op.cit.*, at 238, 240.

by the litigants – Claimant and Respondent would each appoint two arbitrators. Then, these party-appointed arbitrators would choose the "umpire," who would act *ex officio* as president of the tribunal.[119]

Some members of the third commission were of the view that party-appointed arbitrators could be considered agents of the government responsible for their appointment, especially regarding the selection of the umpire. The debate revolved around the eventual prerogative of litigants to challenge the umpire that had been jointly chosen by the arbitrators. Bildt, the delegate of Norway and Sweden, pushed for including in the convention a formal right to refuse the umpire, as he was particularly concerned with an eventual arbitrator who "publicly expressed an opinion on the dispute, which is submitted to him, thus laying himself open to rejection."[120] Resistance to the proposition came from all sides. Édouard Descamps considered "dangerous in practice to establish a general right of approval,"[121] while Martens thought that Bildt's proposal contained "a principle contrary to established practice, sanctioned by time and experience."[122]

Asser suggested an alternative look on the matter, analysing it from two distinctive perspectives. In a first moment, prior to the constitution of the tribunal, Asser was of the view that party-appointed arbitrators could be qualified as agents of the government. For this reason, governments should be allowed to directly influence the selection of the umpire. Even still, as soon as the tribunal was constituted, he defended the position that all arbitrators ought to act as independent judges.[123] In the end, most members of the third commission felt that the inclusion of a formal right of refusal could hamper the development of international arbitration, but this debate demonstrates how fundamental elements of arbitral procedure, such as the independence and impartiality of arbitrators, were not yet clearly delineated.

The motivation of arbitration awards was another issue that greatly occupied the minds of the members of the third commission. The Russian project did not require the tribunal to provide reasons for its decision, but Philipp Zorn, the first delegate of Germany, did not share this view and proposed an

119 See Article 34 of the convention of the 1899 Convention in Bevans, *op.cit.*, at 240. As presented above, a similar rule existed in the IDI draft articles on arbitration procedure. See also Institut de Droit International, 'Procès verbal de la session de Genève, n. 3, séance du 2 septembre de 1874,' *op.cit.*, at 592.

120 See Brown Scott, *The Proceedings of The Hague Peace Conference of 1899*, *op.cit.*, at 611.

121 See Brown Scott, *The Proceedings of The Hague Peace Conference of 1899*, *op.cit.*, at 611.

122 See Brown Scott, *The Proceedings of The Hague Peace Conference of 1899*, *op.cit.*, at 612.

123 See Brown Scott, *The Proceedings of The Hague Peace Conference of 1899*, *op.cit.*, at 655.

amendment including the formulation "must state reasons."[124] The opposition to motivation was led by Martens, who noted that "as regards the obligation to give reasons on which the award is based, he can accept this requirement as a jurisconsult, but as a practical man he must reject it."[125] In particular, the Russian jurist felt that secrecy could shield arbitrators from undue external interference.[126] Many delegates claimed that the force of the award lied with its motivation, while Léon Bourgeois, the president of the third commission and a member of the French delegation, highlighted that the provision did not create any specific form under which such motivation had to be given. Accordingly, Bourgeois observed that the "tribunal will be at liberty to formulate the reasons briefly or at length as it may see fit,"[127] settling the debate on motivation.

In the context of this discussion, a parallel issue had emerged as a result of Nigra's proposition to include the possibility of issuing dissenting votes.[128] The idea did not find much support – the majority followed the views expressed by Édouard Descamps, for whom dissenting opinions "would give the appearance of there being two judgments and of laying the dissent arbitrators before public opinion."[129] In particular, Descamps believed that "dissenting arbitrators are allowed to state their dissent, but it would not be safe to go further than that." The final version of the text of the provision on arbitral awards was conveyed in Article 52 of the convention, providing that the award had to be written, signed by all members of the tribunal and state the reasons for its adoption.

The provision on litigants' representation before the arbitral tribunal gave rise to another animated exchange. This time, the focus of attention was the problem of double-hatting. Seth Low, one of the delegates of the United States, asked whether "members of the Permanent Court, who are not members of the special tribunal, shall be permitted to serve as delegates, special agents, counsel, or advocates before the special tribunal."[130] Descamps, on behalf of the committee of examination, advanced a proposal expressly prohibiting

124 See Brown Scott, *The Proceedings of The Hague Peace Conference of 1899*, *op.cit.*, at 740.

125 See Brown Scott, *The Proceedings of The Hague Peace Conference of 1899*, *op.cit.*, at 615.

126 Martens noted the following: "If the arbitrators in a large arbitral tribunal agree in recognizing the wrongs committed by their own Government, they may in all good conscience concur in the award of the majority; but if they are forced to give the reasons for this award and thus to criticize the policy and measures of their Government, they will find it impossible to sign the award, and the operation of arbitration will thus be impeded." See Brown Scott, *The Proceedings of The Hague Peace Conference of 1899*, *op.cit.*, at 615.

127 See Brown Scott, *The Proceedings of The Hague Peace Conference of 1899*, *op.cit.*, at 616.

128 See Brown Scott, *The Proceedings of The Hague Peace Conference of 1899*, *op.cit.*, at 615.

129 See Brown Scott, *The Proceedings of The Hague Peace Conference of 1899*, *op.cit.*, at 616.

130 See Brown Scott, *The Proceedings of The Hague Peace Conference of 1899*, *op.cit.*, at 668.

double-hatting.[131] Asser, for his turn, was of the view that the rule should be more restrictive, while Frederick Holls pushed even further than Asser. To shield arbitrators from compromising their authority,[132] the American delegate subscribed to the maxim "once a judge always a judge."[133] Accordingly, even former arbitrators who had left office should be barred from appearing as counsel in arbitral proceedings. All this discussion, however, did not produce concrete results, and Article 37 came to life without providing any restrictions on double-hating.

Perhaps the most controversial debate arising in 1899 pertained to the "nature" of claims that could be submitted to arbitration. The first draft produced by the committee of examination reserved recourse to arbitration to legal disputes that did not affect the "vital interests or national honour" of states.[134] Conversely, international arbitration would cover "pecuniary claims for unlawful injuries" and "controversies relating to the interpretation of certain conventions."[135] This discussion took place within a broader debate on the possibility of establishing a general obligation to arbitrate certain types of interstate disputes, and it was suggested that pecuniary claims and hermeneutic questions could fall under said compulsory jurisdiction. The German delegation, however, was particularly opposed to the creation of any obligation regarding jurisdiction. A compromise solution was thus adopted, pursuant to which the voluntary submission to arbitration would be retained while allowing arbitral tribunals to rule on all types of case whether legal or political.[136]

The debate on "obligatory arbitration," as the issue was known at the time, would again resurface in relation to the introduction of a provision meant to impose a symbolic obligation on contracting parties to remind states at the brink of a serious conflict that the permanent court of arbitration was open to settle their dispute.[137] Some delegations, particularly those of the Balkan States, feared that this was a backdoor for political interference that unduly

131 His proposal read as follows: "No member of the Court may during the exercise of his functions as a member of an Arbitral Tribunal accept a designation as special agent or advocate before another arbitral tribunal." See Brown Scott, *The Proceedings of The Hague Peace Conference of 1899*, *op.cit.*, at 675.

132 See Brown Scott, *The Proceedings of The Hague Peace Conference of 1899*, *op.cit.*, at 675–676.

133 See Brown Scott, *The Proceedings of The Hague Peace Conference of 1899*, *op.cit.*, at 675.

134 See Brown Scott, *The Proceedings of The Hague Peace Conference of 1899*, *op.cit.*, at 596.

135 See Brown Scott, *The Proceedings of The Hague Peace Conference of 1899*, *op.cit.*, at 596.

136 See Brown Scott, *The Proceedings of The Hague Peace Conference of 1899*, *op.cit.*, at 237. See also Article 21 of the 1899 Convention, in Bevans, *op.cit.*, at 237.

137 See Article 27 of the 1899, in Bevans, *op.cit.*, at 239.

favoured the "great powers" to the detriment of smaller states. Others, like Frederick Holls, felt that such a provision was central to the convention, and failure to include it could turn arbitration into "dead letter."[138] Veljkovitch, the delegate for Serbia, then claimed that the best way to grant the convention moral authority was to embrace "obligatory arbitration." This made the discussion turn full circle, with Philipp Zorn highlighting that the German government was opposed to that idea and that "[t]o proceed in this important matter without sufficient experience would seem to be a dangerous thing and might lead to discord rather than to harmony."[139] However, the creation of a symbolic obligation to arbitrate was sponsored by the French delegation, and Léon Bourgeois made a personal effort to see it approved. It was only after a passionate address by him that resistance was overcome, and the provision was adopted.[140]

Despite the collegiality of the Hague Peace Conference of 1899, it should be remarked that quite many relevant procedural developments were introduced without any particular opposition or discussion. For instance, there was no significant debate on entrusting the tribunal with wide discretion regarding the conduct of proceedings. The rule in question concretely granted arbitrators the prerogative to organize proceedings as they saw fit, including to decide on the form and time of oral arguments (if any), as well as administer the formalities for the production of evidence.[141]

Similarly, the provision governing the validity of the arbitration agreement did not raise much interest. The final text was a variation of the Russian

138 See Brown Scott, *The Proceedings of The Hague Peace Conference of 1899*, *op.cit.*, at 661.

139 See Brown Scott, *The Proceedings of The Hague Peace Conference of 1899*, *op.cit.*, at 659.

140 Among other things, Bourgeois argued the following: "Yesterday in the committee of examination I said to our colleagues on the opposite side: Every time in the history of the world that a tribunal has been instituted and that a thoughtful and impartial decision has thus been enabled to rise above the clash of interests and passions, has it not been another guaranty to the weak against the abuses of force? It will be the same, gentlemen, between nations as between men. International institutions, like this one, will be the guaranty of the weak against the strong. In the clashes of force, when it is a question of soldiers of flesh and steel, there are great and small, weak and strong. When it is a question of piling up swords on both sides of the scales, one side can be heavier and the other lighter. But when it is a question of weighing rights, there is no longer any inequality, and the rights of the smallest and weakest weigh just as much on the scales as the rights of the greatest. This is the sentiment which has inspired our work, and in carrying it out we have had the weak especially in mind. May they understand our motives and respond to our hope by joining in the efforts we are making to govern the future of mankind in ever-increasing measure by the principles of law." See Brown Scott, *The Proceedings of The Hague Peace Conference of 1899*, *op.cit.*, at 664.

141 See Brown Scott, *The Proceedings of The Hague Peace Conference of 1899*, *op.cit.*, at 615.

draft,[142] which was the result of a slight adaption produced at the committee of examination. In this regard, Édouard Descamps and T.M.C. Asser gave an important contribution to the final version of this article, refining the language and omitting a duty originally envisioned to submit the Parties to the arbitral award "without appeal."[143] That said, the essential elements of the Russian proposal remained, pursuant to which the arbitration agreement would consist of a special (written) agreement signed by the litigants, defining the object of the dispute and the scope of arbitrators' powers. Likewise, an implicit duty to accept the arbitral award in good faith was endorsed.[144]

The provision on arbitration agreements was remarkably silent on the selection of the seat or the language of proceedings. In general, matters pertaining to the seat of arbitration were not perceived as problematic, with the Hague being retained as the default seat under the convention. There was only some brief discussion on the need to clarify that the default rule would not override party choice, as well as on the distinction between the arbitral tribunal and the permanent court of arbitration. The situation described suggests that the seat of arbitration was not yet perceived as an autonomous legal category, being conflated with the place of hearings. This seems to be the view expressed by Asser's cautionary suggestion to include the disclaimer that "the place of session can only be altered by the tribunal with the assent of the parties."[145]

It is also remarkable to note that a provision on what would be later labelled competence-competence did not generate much interest. The rule in question is basically a reproduction taken from the Russian draft arbitral code, with

---

142 Article 2 of the Russian draft read as follows: "The interested States, having accepted arbitration, sign a special act (*compromis*) in which the questions submitted to the decision of the arbitrator are clearly defined as well as all of the facts and legal points involved therein, and in which is found a formal confirmation of the agreement of the two contracting Powers to submit in good faith and without appeal to the arbitral decision which is to be rendered." See Brown Scott, *The Proceedings of The Hague Peace Conference of 1899*, *op.cit.*, at 801.

143 See Brown Scott, *The Proceedings of The Hague Peace Conference of 1899*, *op.cit.*, at 732–733.

144 Compare Article 2 of the Russian draft with Article 30 produced by the committee of examination and adopted unanimously by the third commission. Article 30, which would become Article 31 of the 1899 convention, conveyed the following rule: "The Powers which have recourse to arbitration sign a special act (*compromis*), in which are clearly defined the subject of the dispute and the extent of the arbitrators' powers. This act implies an engagement of the parties to submit in good faith to the arbitral award." See Brown Scott, *The Proceedings of The Hague Peace Conference of 1899*, *op.cit.*, at 611.

145 See Brown Scott, *The Proceedings of The Hague Peace Conference of 1899*, *op.cit.*, at 608. The suggestion was accepted and is part of Article 25 of the 1899 Convention. See Bevans, *op.cit.*, at 238.

minor linguistic adaptations.[146] Nevertheless, from the brief exchanges related to this provision,[147] one notes that the scope of competence-competence was very much unclear. For instance, Asser wondered whether the provision should expand the jurisdiction of arbitrators beyond the strict terms of the arbitration agreement, but the prevailing view, voiced by Édouard Descamps, was that it would be "difficult to introduce such a provision into an act as general in character as that which we are preparing."[148] This lack of debate on arbitrators prerogative to rule on their own jurisdiction, an invention seemingly attributable to Goldschmidt and the IDI, is quite remarkable. Importantly, as it will be seen in this study, future codifiers like Georges Scelle and Aron Broches would engage with the PCA procedural regime as the source of the rule on competence-competence in international arbitration.

2.2 *From Public to Private International Arbitration: the Use of Arbitration for the Collection of International Debt*

The Russian delegation laid before the 1899 Peace Conference a proposal of "obligatory arbitration" that was quite controversial, aiming at entrusting arbitrators with exclusive jurisdiction over pecuniary international claims. The proposal was greatly resisted, as has been seen above, especially by Germany. The subject resurfaced in the 1907 Peace Conference and was once again defeated as a result of German opposition. In fact, the Drago-Porter Convention was adopted against this background, for this instrument was the outcome of a different take on the idea of compulsory arbitral jurisdiction.[149]

---

146 The rule enshrined in Article 48 of the convention reads as follows: "The Tribunal is authorized to declare its competence in interpreting the *compromis* as well as the other treaties that may be invoked in the matter, and in applying the principles of international law." Compare this provision with Article 18 of the Russian draft, which read as follows: "The arbitral tribunal alone is authorized to determine its competence in interpreting the clauses of the *compromis*, and according to the principles of international law as well as the provisions of special treaties which may be invoked in the case." See Brown Scott, *The Proceedings of The Hague Peace Conference of 1899*, *op.cit.*, at 803.

147 See Brown Scott, *The Proceedings of The Hague Peace Conference of 1899*, *op.cit.*, at 614.

148 See Brown Scott, *The Proceedings of The Hague Peace Conference of 1899*, *op.cit.*, at 739.

149 The core of the treaty is established in its article 1, which read as follows: "The Contracting Powers agree not to have recourse to armed force for the recovery of contract debts claimed from the Government of one country by the Government of other country as being due to its nationals. This undertaking is, however, not applicable when the debtor State refuses or neglects to reply to an offer of arbitration, or, after accepting the offer, prevents any *compromis* from being agreed on, or, after the arbitration, fails to submit to the award." Charles I Bevans, 'Convention Respecting the Limitation of Employment of Force for the Recovery of Contract Debts', *Treaties and other international agreements of the*

Upon the proposal of General Horace Porter, a member of the American delegation, the issue of the forcible collection of contractual debt was introduced in the agenda of the first commission.[150] In an address in support of his proposition, General Porter made the following remarks:

> There exists a general and growing belief that the use of armed force for the collection of a contractual debt from a debtor nation, unless it is restrained by some general international agreement, may become the most prolific source of conflicts, or may at least occasion peaceful blockades, threats of hostilities, or rumours of warlike intentions well adapted to the disturbance of commerce, the unfavourable depression of markets and the creation of a feeling of uneasiness, and thus disturb not only the countries interested in the quarrel, but even those who are strangers to it. [...] The case most frequently in evidence is that of a capitalist or speculator who, depriving his own country of his service and money, goes to make an adventure in a foreign land with the sole object of increasing his private fortune. If he gains millions, he will not divide his profits with his government; but if he loses, he will go to it to demand that war be made to secure him the sums which he pretends are due him and which are often enormously exaggerated. The onerous conditions imposed on the loan prove that the lender recognises the greatness of the risk which he runs. Very often he buys on the market at a low-price certificates of indebtedness issued by the debtor state in question, and demands that

United States of America, Multilateral 1776–1917, vol 1 (Department of State Publication 1968), at 614.

150 The proposition read as follows: "For the purpose of avoiding between nations armed conflicts of a purely pecuniary origin, arising from contract debts which are claimed from the Government of one country by the Government of another country as due to its subjects or citizens, and in order to guarantee that all contract debts of this nature which it may have been impossible to settle amicably through the diplomatic channel shall be submitted to arbitration, it is agreed that there cannot be recourse to coercive measures, involving the employment of military or naval forces for the recovery of such contract debts, until an offer of arbitration has been made by the claimant and refused or not answered by the debtor State, or until arbitration has taken place and the debtor State has failed to comply with the award made. It is further agreed that such arbitration shall conform, as to its procedure, to Chapter III of the Convention for the pacific settlement of international disputes, adopted at The Hague, and that it shall determine the justice and the amount of the debt, the time and manner of its settlement and the guaranty to be given, if there is occasion, while payment is delayed." See James Brown Scott, *The Proceedings of The Hague Peace Conference: The Conference of 1907, Plenary Meetings of the Conference*, vol 1 (Oxford University Press 1920), at 548.

> they be paid to him at par. In fact, in the game which he plays, he counts on putting into practice the principle of 'Heads, I win; tails, you lose.[151]

The 1907 Drago-Porter Convention is certainly one of the ancestors of ISDS, and much of the debate at the second Hague Peace Conference was related to the protection of foreign investors. Notably, the words extracted from Porter's discourse in 1907 are still of current interest, as similar concerns may still be articulated in relation to the present form of ISDS. The allusion made by General Porter to the opportunistic speculator who buys bonds at a low price and seeks to collect at a par value evokes the persisting problems pertaining to investment-treaty arbitration of sovereign bonds.[152]

The Porter proposal was prompted by the Venezuelan crisis of 1902–03. The crisis was a textbook example of the deployment of armed forces for the settlement of the most mundane pecuniary disputes – a practice that would become known as gunboat diplomacy.[153] Around that time, Venezuela had been subject to a decade of revolutionary upheaval, which had inflicted considerable damage to foreign interests in the country. More specifically, there was outstanding debt owed to a number of international creditors. In order to force a settlement for the harm suffered by its nationals, the United Kingdom and Germany (joined by Italy at a later stage) conducted a military campaign along the Venezuelan shore, capturing vessels, bombarding some of its forts and ultimately imposing a naval blockade on the South American country. Retorsion followed suit, with the arrest of more than two hundred nationals of Britain and Germany who were residing in Caracas.[154]

As the conflict escalated, the Venezuelan government asked Washington to transmit an offer to arbitrate the dispute, to no avail at first. The offer was received by the European nations on 13 December 1902, the same day that Puerto Cabello was attacked. However, both Germans and the British would end up accepting to submit the dispute to arbitration, allegedly, as legend goes, due to an ultimatum issued by President Theodore Roosevelt.[155]

151 See William Hull, *The Two Hague Conferences and Their Contribution to International Law* (Ginn & Company 1908), at 352–353.

152 See, for instance, Michael Waibel, 'Opening Pandora's Box: Sovereign Bonds in International Arbitration' (2007) 101 The American Journal of International Law 711.

153 For an analysis of the crisis, see Nancy Mitchell, 'The Height of the German Challenge: The Venezuela Blockade, 1902–03' (1996) 20 Diplomatic History 185.

154 See Mitchell, *op.cit*, at 196.

155 See Mitchell, *op.cit.*, at 197–198.

The European aggression generated great concern, especially among countries in the region. In the face of the crisis, Luis Drago, then Argentinean minister of foreign affairs, transmitted to the American government a diplomatic letter dated 29 December 1902. This dispatch drew the fundamental contours of his policy on forcible collection of debt – the famous Drago doctrine. In the letter, Drago stressed the principle of sovereign equality in international law, affirming that "the summary and immediate collection at a given moment, by means of force, would occasion nothing less than the ruin of the weakest nations, and the absorption of their governments, together with all the functions inherent in them, by the mighty of the earth."[156] The Drago doctrine echoed at the third Pan-American Conference, held in Rio de Janeiro.[157] The issue of forcible collection of sovereign debt led the delegations in Rio de Janeiro to adopt a resolution recommending the referral of the matter to the Hague Peace Conference of 1907, so as to work on "means tending to diminish between nations conflicts having an exclusively pecuniary origin."[158] And so it was done by General Horace Porter.

Even if the Drago doctrine aimed at outlawing the use of force for the collection of sovereign debt,[159] the Porter proposal on the forcible collection of debt did not go as far as that. Drago himself, a member of the Argentinean delegation at the Hague, made it known that the project was not ambitious enough, stressing his particular concern over an indirect endorsement of the use of force.[160] Albeit arbitral authority was on route to become a mandatory

156 See Luis M Drago., 'Señor Luis M. Drago, Minister of Foreign Relations of the Argentine Republic, to Señor Martin Garcia Mérou, Minister of the Argentine Republic to the United States' (29 December 1902). Available at: https://history.state.gov/historicaldocuments/frus1903/d2. Accessed on 13 August 2020.

157 See Curtis Wilgus, 'The Third International American Conference at Rio de Janeiro, 1906' (1932) 12 The Hispanic American Historical Review 420.

158 See George Winfield Scott, 'Hague Convention Restricting the Use of Force to Recover on Contract Claims' (1908) 2 The American Journal of International Law 78, 86.

159 For a more detailed account of the doctrine, see Luis M Drago, 'State Loans in Their Relation to International Policy' (1907) 1 The American Journal of International Law 692.

160 Drago was particularly preoccupied with the extent to which armed force could be deployed under the Porter proposal. This is most clear in the following extract: "But there is reason to inquire how far coercive measures of this kind would go. According to John Basset Moore, the eminent American jurist, Secretary of State Blaine, in taking up the recovery of certain debts from Venezuela in 1881, proposed to the French Government that the United States should take possession of the custom houses of the South American Republic at La Guayra and Puerto Cabello, and put its agents in charge to collect the customs, which would then be distributed *pro rata* among the various creditors, charging the debtor country ten per cent additional. The same methods of recovery were later commended by Secretary of State Frelinghuysen. There is a way of understanding

mechanism for the vindication of contractual claims against states, a number of exceptions included in the instrument created a subsidiary right to resort to armed force.

In reality, the international order at the turn of the 20th century tended to see the use of armed force as an inevitable, if not normal, feature of international politics. Carl von Clausewitz encapsulated this view in his famous formulation that "war is a mere continuation of politics by other means." Accordingly, whenever a debtor government refused an offer to arbitrate, failed to cooperate for the establishment of the *compromis* or violated the terms of the arbitral award, the creditor state would be authorized to deploy armed forces to compel the debtor state to comply with its obligations. This residual right to deploy force raised concerns among Latin American States. For instance, the Colombian delegation highlighted that the document presupposed an imbalance of power favouring the powerful to the detriment of the weak. Santiago Pérez Triana, the Colombian delegate, argued that, while a powerful creditor would be able to collect the debt through the use of force, when "a creditor is weak in military resources as compared with a great military power which cannot pay its debts, the right of forcible collection would become ridiculous."[161]

More controversial than the subsidiary authorization on the use of force granted by the Porter proposal was the scope of disputes covered by the concept of "contractual debt." The expression had been considered ambiguous by some, and delegations were particularly wary of granting arbitral tribunals direct jurisdiction over individual claims against sovereign states. Furthermore, there was vocal opposition against placing "public debt" under the purview of international arbitrators.[162] It was again Luis Drago who most eloquently expressed such concerns. Distinguishing obligations stemming from actions of the State in its private capacity (*acta jure gestionis*) from those obligations born out of State's public capacity (*acta jure imperii*), Drago advocated for the

---

the application of coercive measures which might give rise to controversies and even to conflicts. Would the European or American nations without distinction be authorised to conduct the custom houses of a debtor country in this way; or, on the contrary, would the system of Blaine and Frelinghuysen be followed, according to which this function would devolve solely upon the United States? I ask the question simply to show how difficult it is to define and regulate in advance the employment of force, and how much more preferable it would be to leave each case to be settled according to the circumstances and necessities of the moment." See Brown Scott, *The Proceedings of The Hague Peace Conference: The Conference of 1907, Plenary Meetings of the Conference, op.cit.*, at 553.

161 See Hull, *op.cit.*, at 364.

162 See James Brown Scott, *The Proceedings of The Hague Peace Conference: The Conference of 1907, Meetings of the First Commission*, vol 2 (Oxford University Press 1921), at 558.

exclusion of sovereign debt from the roll of claims that could be submitted to international arbitration.

The carve-out of sovereign bonds from the ordinary law of contracts would be due to the fact that these debt instruments constituted "an act of sovereignty such as no private individual can exercise."[163] In sum, the act of issuing sovereign bonds would represent a "positive manifestation of sovereignty,"[164] which would consequently make it immune from both domestic and international jurisdictions.[165] Moreover, Drago was of the view that, even in relation to "private" state debt, recourse to arbitration had to be conditioned to the exhaustion of local remedies and that sovereign debt should be excluded from the roll of claims that could be submitted to arbitration.

Curiously, Drago's position was objected in its entirety at the conference by the Brazilian delegation. Ruy Barbosa, the first delegate of Brazil, was of the view that sovereign debt was not a political act but rather an ordinary act subject to private law. Accordingly, he argued that no exception to the arbitrability of sovereign debt should be established, nor should the possibility of using armed forces as a mechanism of enforcement be foreclosed.[166]

At first, the matter was considered unimportant by General Porter, but the issue kept stirring controversy.[167] The mere contemplation of an international jurisdiction bringing together private parties and states seemed inappropriate. In light of the debate, Martens wondered whether the project attempted to create a dispute mechanism extending beyond diplomatic protection.[168] General Porter's answer endorsed the commonly held understanding that international arbitration was very much a state-to-state ordeal, and accordingly "the

163 See Brown Scott, *The Proceedings of The Hague Peace Conference: The Conference of 1907, Meetings of the First Commission*, *op.cit.*, at 557.

164 See Hull, *op.cit.*, at 360.

165 See Brown Scott, *The Proceedings of The Hague Peace Conference: The Conference of 1907, Meetings of the First Commission*, *op.cit.*, at 558.

166 See Brown Scott, *The Proceedings of The Hague Peace Conference: The Conference of 1907, Plenary Meetings of the Conference*, *op.cit.*, at 551. Barbosa advanced his argument in the following terms: "But, truly, the theory once consolidated in law that states in borrowing contract no coercitive obligation whatever, that is to say, that their creditors are entirely disarmed towards them, can anyone believe that there would still be capitalists foolish enough to intrust their wealth to such privileged beings?" In Hull, *op.cit.*, at 361.

167 In Brown Scott, *The Proceedings of The Hague Peace Conference: The Conference of 1907, Meetings of the First Commission*, *op.cit.*, at 557.

168 In Brown Scott, *The Proceedings of The Hague Peace Conference: The Conference of 1907, Plenary Meetings of the Conference*, *op.cit.*, at 559.

application of the rule was intended to be restricted absolutely to the intervention of a government on behalf of its citizens, and not of the citizens themselves."[169]

The Swiss delegation was also very reluctant to accept the Porter proposal. From their perspective, the project covered much more than state to state affairs, extending arbitral jurisdiction over individual claims governed by private municipal law. This was of particular concern to Switzerland, as it considered that the submission of contractual disputes to international arbitration could lead to an encroachment on the jurisdiction of its domestic courts.[170]

After considerable amendments, with a most notable contribution from Luis Drago, the instrument was finalized and gave rise to the Drago-Porter Convention as it came to be known. This treaty encapsulated yet another transformation of the procedural framework governing arbitration, formally entrusting arbitrators with authority over disputes that one would now call international investment disputes. Certainly, this authority was bound by the exhaustion of local remedies and the operation of diplomatic protection. Even still, the Drago-Porter Convention did place the grey zone of "contractual debt" involving private parties and governments firmly within the province of arbitral procedure, which was the result of a fortuitous encounter between economic interests and the ambition to curb the use of force in international affairs. In this regard, the codification of arbitral jurisdiction concerning international contractual disputes created an important bridge over the growing gap separating the crafts of public and private international lawyers.

3 Uniform Commercial Law and Private International Arbitration

The uniformization of commercial law has long been treated as a self-evident truth in academic circles, especially in light of its "inherent international

169 In Hull, *op.cit.*, at 369.

170 The objections advanced by Mr. Carlin, the Swiss delegate, read as follows: "The cases of conflicts viewed in the proposition of the United States of America do not have their direct origin between States, but arise from private claims of individual parties. By their very nature, these claims are submitted to the jurisdiction of the requested State and to this jurisdiction only. But the Swiss courts offer to foreigners the same guaranties of impartiality that they vouchsafe their nationals. The Confederation can, therefore, not approve of a proposition that might result in invalidating decisions of the national courts upon matters of private law coming exclusively within their jurisdiction by deferring them to an arbitral court." In Brown Scott, *The Proceedings of The Hague Peace Conference: The Conference of 1907, Meetings of the First Commission*, *op.cit.*, at 559.

nature."[171] In an article published in 1880, Asser laid an action plan for the uniformization of private international law,[172] while in 1886 he then published a roadmap for the uniformization of commercial law.[173]

The academic support for the uniformization of commercial law would echo in ministerial cabinets due to the free transit that people like Asser and Mancini enjoyed with their home governments. This has led some states to entertain a sustained engagement with the idea of uniform commercial law. Belgium, in particular, decided to promote this agenda already in 1880, organizing an expert forum to debate challenges to the uniformization of commercial legislation – an event that became known as the "Antwerp Congress."[174]

The political support for the uniformization of commercial legislation, however, was not entirely unanimous. For instance, during the Antwerp Congress, jurists from codified legal systems did not hesitate to support it, but English lawyers would come to regard such an endeavour with great scepticism. This set of contrasting attitudes reflected the broader divide between codified and

171 See Mancini, 'De l'utilité de rendre obligatoires pour tous les Etats, sous la forme d'un ou de plusieurs Traités internationaux, un certain nombre de règles générales du droit international privé pour assurer la décision uniforme des conflits entre les différentes législations civiles et criminelles,' *op.cit.*, at 226–227.

172 See TMC Asser, 'Droit international privé et droit uniforme' (1880) 12 Revue de droit international et de législation comparée 5.

173 See TMC Asser, 'Le droit commercial uniforme' (1886) 18 Revue de droit international et de législation comparée 5.

174 Alphonse Rivier quotes the report substantiating the initiative of the Belgium government, which read as follows: "*Dans le cours de ces dernières années, on a vu, pour la première fois dans l'histoires du monde, des actes internationaux régler d'une manière uniforme des questions d'administration et de législation intérieure.* [...] *On n'en pourrait imaginer de plus important que l'unification des lois du commerce. Les relations commerciales sont aujourd'hui avant tout internationales, elles le deviennent de plus en plus, et quel essor nouveau ne prendraient-elles pas si elles étaient débarrassées des entraves, des difficultés, des incertitudes et des frais qui résultent de la diversité des législations?*[...] *Ce sera une œuvre de longue durée, qui doit être préparé mûrement; mais, dès à présent, l'unité pourrait être obtenue sans difficultés sérieuses pour quelques-unes des parties du droit commercial, notamment pour la lettre de change, le contrat de transport et le droit maritime.*" The same report advocated a piecemeal approach to uniformization, which would progressively advance unification. This work method would become a trademark in transnational uniformization of commercial law. See Alphonse Rivier, 'Notice: congrès international de droit commercial à Anvers' (1885) XVIII Revue de droit international et de législation comparée 161, at 161–162. For another account of the congress, see Alfred de Courcy, *Congrès international de droit commercial tenu à Anvers en 1885* (F. Pichon, Successeur, Imprimeur – Éditeur, 1885).

common law legal practice in Europe, which proved to be an important obstacle for uniformization initiatives.[175]

In addition to academic and government-led initiatives, business interests were also persuaded by the importance of uniform commercial law. In the early 1900's, chambers of commerce mostly from the North Atlantic would inscribe the uniformization of commercial legislation at the heart of their concerted advocacy initiatives. These efforts would take the form of regular international congresses, the first of which was launched by the *Fédération des Associations Commerciales et Industrielles de Belgique.* The city of Liège was chosen to host, in 1905, the first session of the International Congress of Chambers of Commerce and Industrial Associations, a date and place seemingly selected due to the overlap with the Universal Exposition that would be held that same year in that same city.[176]

The International Congress of Chambers of Commerce was regularly held from 1905 to 1914. The analysis of the records of these events shows that all of its sessions devoted considerable attention to the uniformization of commercial legislation. More interesting, however, was their contribution to the invention of a private form of international arbitration and to a corresponding doctrine of uniformity. The next two sub-sections will analyse this phenomenon, first addressing how exactly chambers of commerce contributed to the transformation of international arbitration into "private international arbitration" (3.1), and then exploring the early efforts of chambers of commerce for the promotion of uniformity in the field of private international arbitration (3.2).

---

175 Thomas Barclay, reporting on the congress, gives testimony of the divide in the following terms: "'The Congress at Antwerp brought out this difference very clearly. 'You English seem to think it negotiating to grant us your gracious permission to adopt your laws *telles quelles*,' exclaimed an exasperated Frenchman, in reply to an Englishman who thought he had given a sufficient reason for his dissent in saying that a proposal different from English law. But we have come here to make compromises in the interest of harmony. If we were all to make reservations where our laws differed, the results of this Congress would simply be that we agreed where we were already at one, and reserved all points we had come here to discuss.' I am afraid this is a true picture, but in pleading guilty we must ask the enlightened foreigner to remember that we old-fashioned English have no code of laws yet, and that the principles of our law still lie hidden in the bosoms of our great lawyers, who do not seem to think very highly of systems which would lower the standard of intelligence necessary for discovering the sense and sequence of our beautiful case law." Thomas Barclay, 'The Antwerp Congress and the Assimilation of Mercantile Law' (1886) 2 Law Quarterly Review 66, at 67–68.

176 See Comité Permanent des Congrès, *Compte rendu du Ie Congrès international des Chambres de commerce et des Associations commerciales et industrielles (Liège – 7, 8 et 9 Septembre 1905)'* (Imprimerie Dequesne-Masquillier & Fils 1905), at 7–9.

3.1 *The Procedural Turn in Business Diplomacy*

The way through which international arbitration evolved from a procedure devoted to settle interstate disputes to a procedure with jurisdiction over international contractual debt has been discussed above. Despite this change, it is undeniable that international arbitration was still largely seen by international lawyers as a state-to-state type of procedure in the early 20th century. Conversely, arbitration of "private" disputes would tend to be portrayed as essentially domestic, even when it involved governments acting as a merchant or when it involved parties coming from different jurisdictions.[177] The first involvement of business associations with arbitration took place against this background, and its only over time that greater emphasis is put on arbitration as a procedural mechanism for the settlement of private international disputes.

At the 1905 edition of the International Congress of Chambers of Commerce, the dominant view amongst the participants was the one portraying international arbitration as an interstate mechanism of dispute settlement. Accordingly, discussions were allusive of world peace, evoking arbitration once again as an alternative to war.[178] Arbitration was not originally part of the program of the event, but it was put up for discussion upon the proposal of the Pittsburgh Chamber of Commerce, which placed it as the twelfth item in a fifteen-item agenda. One could imagine that the last-minute inclusion of international arbitration in the order of business, and its position as one of the last matters to be discussed, was reflective of some disinterest for arbitral practice. This, however, was not the case.

At the opening of the 1905 congress, a certain Hubert Brunard moved to inverse the order of business, proposing to address international arbitration as the first item in the agenda. It was the aftermath of the Russo-Japanese war and international arbitration was presented as a great avenue for the promotion of peace and commerce. As a consequence, the first resolution adopted at that inaugural International Congress of Chambers of Commerce highlighted the tragedy of war for both humankind and for businesses, calling for the use of international arbitration as a means for the peaceful settlement of disputes between nations.[179]

177 See Goldschmidt, *op.cit.*, at 422.

178 See Comité Permanent des Congrès, Compte rendu du Ie Congrès,' *op.cit.*, at 3–4 and 19.

179 The resolution adopted read as follows: "*Considérant que la guerre paralyse et entrave le commerce et l'industrie, non seulement des belligérants, mais de toutes les nations; Considérant qu'elle entraîne la mort ou l'incapacité d'innombrables travailleurs et qu'elle est*

A shift of attention, however, was already noticeable at the second edition of the event, held in Milan in 1906. This time, under the heading "international arbitration," the final resolution curiously called for the implementation of coordinated efforts for the promotion of uniform legislation on arbitration and for a mild liberalization of municipal regimes governing the enforcement of foreign arbitral awards.[180] This certainly did not concern interstate disputes nor world peace, but it testified to the gradual semantic drift of the term international arbitration to cover also disputes of a fundamental private character carrying some level of internationality.

This approach was further explored in the fourth session of the congress, held in London in 1910. Then, the problem of cross-border recognition of arbitration agreements and the issue of enforcement of foreign arbitral awards led to extensive debates. Businesspeople were no longer interested in international arbitration merely as an alternative to war. Now, they began to engage with international arbitration also as an alternative to commercial courts. In particular, the participants of the 1910 congress had before them a study prepared by Charles Charleton, entitled "Enforcement of Judgment and Arbitration Awards Pronounced in Foreign Countries." Charleton, a former chairman of the London Chamber of Commerce, deployed a comparative method to survey the arbitration regime of more than thirty countries. His study highlighted the great diversity of attitudes towards arbitration,[181] stressing specially that a great number of countries refused to recognize arbitration agreements or to enforce foreign arbitral awards.

---

une cause de souffrances, de misères et de pertes incalculables; Le Congrès International des Chambres de commerce et des Associations commerciales et industrielles, Se permet d'appuyer, auprès des États et Gouvernements, les propositions de M. Bartholdt à la 13e Conférence interparlementaire pour l'Arbitrage international, tendant à l'extension des attributions de juridiction de la Cour arbitrale de la Haye et à la constitution d'un Congrès ou Parlement international." See Comité Permanent des Congrès, Compte rendu du Ie Congrès,' *op.cit.*, at 20.

180 The resolution reads as follows: "*Le Congrès engage ses adhérents à travailler avec ardeur à la propagande nécessaire pour obtenir en tous pays, dans la mesure du possible, une législation uniforme. Le Congrès engage aussi ses adhérents à tâcher d'obtenir une exception en faveur des décisions arbitrales et des amiables compositions (si elle n'existe déjà) de la part des Gouvernements qui jugent nécessaire de réviser, quant au fond, les jugements étrangers et subordonnent leur autorisation d'exécution à l'octroi de la réciprocité.*" See Louis Canon-Legrand and Emile Jottrand, 'Letter from the Comité Permanent – Actes and Resolutions of the Congress of Milan and Prague', 30 November 1908, at 8.

181 See John Ball Osborne, John L Griffiths and William Phillips, 'Fourth Congress of Chambers of Commerce' in *Daily Consular and Trade Reports* (Bureau of Manufacturers, Department of Commerce and Labor 1916), at 852.

The unfolding debate during that congress led to the adoption of a declaration promoting the recognition of arbitration agreements and the enforcement of arbitral awards on the basis of reciprocity. The prevalent view was that States with similar legislation on arbitration and with reciprocal confidence in their judiciaries should enter into bilateral or plurilateral treaties harmonizing their approach to the matter.[182] This strategy was essentially a pragmatic one resulting from a shared understanding that a universal treaty on arbitration procedure would be a difficult goal to pursue.

It was also during the 1910 congress that some began to note the emergence of a sense of community among the attendants of these regular events, which in turn was conducive to the uniformization of commercial practices and to the unification of the law on international trade. The American delegation to the congress, reporting back to its hierarchy, described the phenomenon as follows:

> Delegates who have attended the previous congresses stated that they notice at each successive meeting a greater feeling of solidarity, which perhaps indicates that the time is not very far distant when there will be a uniformity of practice in all the civilized countries in matters affecting international trade and commerce, as it is realized that local customs and usages must give way to broader conventions.[183]

Transcending the gap between public and private international arbitration, a most interesting discussion took place at the 1912 edition of the International Congress of Chambers of Commerce. Held in Boston, this was the first time the congress was organized outside Europe, counting with an expressive presence of American business interests. Under the ambitious rubric of "arbitral jurisdiction over all matters,"[184] the attendants gathered in Boston addressed the possibility of establishing a universal arbitral jurisdiction. The topic was discussed based on a report submitted by Max Apt, the "syndic" of the "*Die ältesten der kaufmannschaft von berlin*." His arguments referred to the Hague Conventions of 1899 and 1907, which provided for arbitration as a mechanism of dispute settlement between States, claiming that "[w]hile thus great progress

182 See Osborne, Griffiths and Phillips, *op.cit.*, at 853.

183 See Osborne, Griffiths and Phillips, *op.cit.*, at 855.

184 See Comité Permanent des Congrès, *Fifth International Congress of Chambers of Commerce and Commercial and Industrial Associations (Boston – 24, 25, 26 September 1912)* (Boston Chamber of Commerce 1912), at 16.

may be recorded in the domain of international law of nations the same cannot be said in respect of international personal legal rights."[185]

Max Apt was particularly concerned with the settlement of disputes between private parties and States, as he highlighted that sovereign immunity would be an obstacle to redressing wrongs in foreign courts while the lack of neutrality could preclude claimants from recovering damages caused by States in municipal courts. In addition, referring to a study conducted by his institution, Apt argued that "the existing lack of legal protection withheld a number of firms from entering in business relations with foreign States."[186] While it is now difficult to assess the empirical soundness of Apt's claims, as one has no access to the data used to substantiate his arguments, it is interesting to realize that this type of instrumental argument was already part of the public debate on arbitration. Even more interesting is to note the longevity of such rhetoric device, for arguments associating increases in investments with the implementation of arbitration are often replayed more than a 100 years later in discussions on the advantages of arbitration for economic prosperity.

The ideas advanced by Apt, and the discussion that ensued on the creation of an international court of arbitration, demonstrate that the establishment of an arbitral jurisdiction to settle what is now called investor-state disputes was already in contemplation in 1912. In reality, some concrete steps were underway towards that objective, as "the formation of a court for private suits against foreign States belongs to the organizing tasks of the Third Hague Conference."[187] Albeit these efforts were halted by the war, the interest for the creation of such forum was definitely on the radar.

Furthermore, the records of the 1912 congress testify to the emerging ambition of detaching commercial adjudication from the purview of states. For instance, Robert S. Fraser, a councilman of the London Chamber of Commerce, advanced the view that "commerce is the subject of no State and it is the sovereign of all."[188] The same Fraser highlighted that both the International Law Association and the British Board of Trade were also engaged with the

185 See Comité Permanent des Congrès, *Fifth International Congress of Chambers of Commerce and Commercial and Industrial Associations*, *op.cit.*, at 158.

186 See Comité Permanent des Congrès, *Fifth International Congress of Chambers of Commerce and Commercial and Industrial Associations*, *op.cit.*, at 158.

187 See Comité Permanent des Congrès, *Fifth International Congress of Chambers of Commerce and Commercial and Industrial Associations*, *op.cit.*, at 160.

188 See Comité Permanent des Congrès, *Fifth International Congress of Chambers of Commerce and Commercial and Industrial Associations*, *op.cit.*, at 162.

uniformization of commercial arbitration.[189] This is yet another evidence of the existing synergies and converging agendas amongst different stakeholders.

Despite the adoption of a resolution supporting the future creation of a court of arbitration with the widest jurisdiction possible,[190] the proposition was met with scepticism by some participants of the congress. The Calvo and Drago doctrines were popular, and it was noted that the IDI, in its Hamburg session held in 1891, had concluded that disputes between States and private parties should fall within the jurisdiction of regular courts.[191]

In addition, there was no unanimity on the urgency or desirability of such universal arbitral jurisdiction. In this respect, the reservations made by Lawrence V. Benet are especially informative. Benet, who was the representative of the American Chamber of Commerce of Paris, noted that in his thirty years of experience in business relations with the most diverse types of governments he had only experienced two minor cases of "uncollectible claims." The same Bennet also highlighted that a universal arbitral jurisdiction could represent a threat to individuals, for "it is hardly conceivable, if the right be given to individuals to summon governments before such a court, that governments should not enjoy a corresponding right to summon individuals or corporation before the same tribunal."[192] From Benet's point of view, a more modest,

189 Fraser's comments were as follow: "I have the honour to be a member of the International Law Association which met in London two years since and in Paris this last Whitsuntide and on both occasions this important subject [arbitration] was dealt with and pressed forward. Then again consequent upon the agitation for this movement in the British Board of Trade, a very active inquiry is proceeding with a view to concerted steps for establishing standardised courts in all parts of the world, the awards of which will be enforceable wherever compliance therewith is required." See Comité Permanent des Congrès, *Fifth International Congress of Chambers of Commerce and Commercial and Industrial Associations*, *op.cit.*, at 161.

190 The resolution adopted on the matter read as follows: "The Congress affirms its desire to see convene, as soon as possible, official international conferences which will assure between nations the existence of arbitral jurisdiction conceived in the widest sense of the term, and of a nature to assure an equitable solution of all international disputes either between individuals of different States or between the States themselves. The Congress declares its adherence to the principle of a combination of nations, when and where possible to endeavour to prevent the atrocities of war." See Comité Permanent des Congrès, *Fifth International Congress of Chambers of Commerce and Commercial and Industrial Associations*, *op.cit.*, at 16.

191 See Comité Permanent des Congrès, *Fifth International Congress of Chambers of Commerce and Commercial and Industrial Associations*, *op.cit.*, at 162.

192 See Comité Permanent des Congrès, *Fifth International Congress of Chambers of Commerce and Commercial and Industrial Associations*, *op.cit.*, at 170. The pertinence of the remark is all the more impressive one hundred years later, as the unilateral right of investors to initiate investment arbitration proceedings has become the target of growing criticism.

yet more tenable project, would be the creation of a court of commercial arbitration instead of a universal arbitral jurisdiction as the one proposed by Max Apt.

3.2 *The Quest for Uniformity in Private International Arbitration*

There is an element of particular interest in the agenda of the 1914 edition of International Congress of Chambers of Commerce, held in Paris. Item three of the program put forth a discussion on the unification of legislation governing arbitration involving citizens of different countries.[193] The reports submitted to the congress to substantiate the debate on the matter are very informative and enlightening. First, contrary to the current dominant idea that international commercial arbitration is a creature of autarkical contracts, these reports consider the uniformization of arbitral legislation to be of great importance for the success of arbitration. Second, these documents show that the deployment of model arbitration clauses emerged very early as a technique of procedural uniformization – it is possible to find numerous references to model arbitration clauses such as those of the Grain Syndicate of Paris, the International Publishers Association and the International Cotton Federation.

Roberto Pozzi, an Italian lawyer who represented the International Cotton Federation, was entrusted with the task of presenting a general report on the unification of arbitral legislation.[194] It was also Pozzi who suggested the inclusion

193 The original title of item 3 was the following: "*De l'unification des législations relatives à la procédure d'arbitrage pour régler les litiges entre citoyens de pays différents.*"

194 The General Report presented by Pozzi was submitted to the Congress in Italian, English, German and French. This research has consulted both Italian and English versions of the report, keeping always in mind that the Italian version was the original one, while the other versions were translations of it. It is important to note that, while for the most part the English version of the report can be used without much problem, it does contain a few translation errors. For instance, the translator refers to "private international right" while the Italian version speaks of "*diritto privato internazionale*" (compare pages 14 of the Italian and English versions). Clearly Pozzi was referring to private international law in the original version, not to rights. More serious, however, is the error contained in page 15 of the English version, which reads as follows: "3.rd The recognition of the sentences of arbiters pronounced in one country, in all countries with the simple formality of a judgment on the form and as to the merit". The Italian version, however, is phrased differently: "*3º Il riconoscimento delle sentenze degli arbitri pronunciate in paese in tutti gli altri paesi, con la semplice formalità di un giudizio sulla forma e non sul merito.*" Comparing both versions, the English version does not make it clear that Pozzi was advocating for awards to be recognized after a mere judgement on its form and not on its merit. That said, this research has preferred to quote the English version rather than the Italian version for the convenience of the reader – but it has always made sure that the content in the English version was in line with the content of the Italian version. See both

of the topic in the agenda of the Paris congress – and he would become in due course a very important actor for the codification of arbitration procedure.

Pozzi believed that "private international arbitration," as he refers to the emerging practice that would become known as international commercial arbitration, could not flourish within a fragmented legislative framework governing the recognition of arbitration agreements and the enforcement of arbitral awards. He had before him six reports presented respectively by Charles Bernheimer on behalf of the New York Chamber of Commerce, by Bartolomé Amengual on behalf of the Chamber of Commerce of Barcelona, by Max Leclerc on behalf of the Chamber of Commerce of Paris, by Sailly and Duché on behalf of the French Chamber of Commerce and Industry of Brussels, a report submitted by the Berlin Chamber of Commerce and a final one he himself authored on behalf of the International Cotton Federation.

Pozzi was very much concerned that the American report, which advocated for the creation of a private arbitral jurisdiction relying exclusively on moral sanctions, could harm the development of private international arbitration. Albeit moral sanctions were relevant and in line with the practices of many chambers of commerce and industrial federations, he considered the legal enforceability of arbitration awards as one of its strongest features. Moral sanctions, such as censure, expulsion or shaming, would be only alternatives to the absence of legal sanctions. From Pozzi's perspective, when it comes to arbitration involving parties from different countries, symbolic coercion manipulated by chambers of commerce would always remain of secondary importance in relation to material coercion organized by law.[195]

Furthermore, in a very nuanced language, Pozzi contends that the creation of an international arbitral forum under the private authority of a federative organism reuniting all existing arbitral institutions would deprive arbitration of its authority based on expertise. Given that such arbitral federation would be entrusted with a multiplicity of questions of the most diverse economic nature, this body would certainly not be able to mobilize the necessary expertise to decide on each and every single case. Worse, from Pozzi's perspective, the American proposal would harm arbitration's expert allure without amassing any extra authority. In his words, these adjudicators would be endowed with "generic and not specific competency as regards commercial matters"

Roberto Pozzi, Summary Notes on the Theme of Private International Arbitration (International Congress of Chambers of Commerce and of the Industrial Associations 1914); Note Riassuntive Sul Tema Dell'arbitrato Privato Internazionale (International Congress of Chambers of Commerce and of the Industrial Associations 1914).

195 See Pozzi, Summary Notes, *op.cit*, at 13.

and "would come to acquire the quality and authority of true judges of private election and who in confrontation with public judges would not even present that guarantee of absolute independence and autonomy which in every land constitutes the patrimony and prestige of the magistracy."[196]

Within this framework, Pozzi identifies three problems that ought to be addressed to vest arbitration with legal authority, i.e., the validity of arbitration agreements, the right of foreigners to act as arbitrators, and the extraterritorial effects of arbitral awards. Pozzi does not devote much attention to the first and the second issues, conceding that in general most States have already recognized arbitration agreement as valid and that most courts were inclined to allow foreigners to act as arbitrators. However, the third problem led him to engage in a more detailed analysis of the extra-territorial effects of judgements in general.

Pozzi's report notes that both legal practice and legal scholarship have tended to advocate in favour of the circulation of judgments beyond national borders. He paid special attention to the principle of reciprocity on the matters of recognition of foreign judgment, stressing its successful adoption by Italy in its procedural code of 1865 and by the contracting parties to the Montevideo Treaty of 1889. In a similar vein, the report acknowledged that the Hague Convention of 1894 and 1905 had also affirmed this principle on the matter of circulation of judgments.

Although the wide recognition of judgments under the principle of reciprocity could have been set as a goal to be pursued, Pozzi was convinced that such objective could only be achieved gradually. Even still, the recognition of the extra-territorial effects of arbitral awards seemed to him as perfectly ripe for international codification. This ripeness was attested by the fact that the circulation of arbitral awards under the principle of reciprocity was being subscribed even by France, which was perceived as the country where legal nationalism was most vivid.[197] In addition, differently from the circulation of judicial decisions, the enforcement of arbitral awards would not put in jeopardy a certain "national sentiment."[198]

The ideas espoused by Pozzi, especially the one on the relevance of legal enforcement, were shared by a great number of participants in the 1914 congress. This is evidenced in other reports submitted, such as those presented on

---

196 See Pozzi, Summary Notes, *op.cit.*, at 12.

197 See Pozzi, Summary Notes, *op.cit.*, at 17.

198 Max Leclerc, 'De l'unification des législations relatives à la procédure d'arbitrage pour régler les litiges entre citoyens de pays différents' (1914) Bulletin de la Chambre de commerce de Paris 776.

behalf of the French Chamber of Commerce and Industry of Brussels, and the Chamber of Commerce of Paris.[199] Indeed, the report submitted by Sailly and Duché provides an insightful reading for both the priority given to the unification of arbitration law in the agenda of business diplomacy, as well as for the clarity of its action plan.[200]

Echoing the commonly held view that arbitration should be a central element of commercial justice, and that the great diversity of arbitration legislation harmed its proper functioning, the Franco-Belgian report suggested a three-dimensional plan for an overarching unification of the procedural framework governing private arbitration. The first dimension focused on the unification of domestic legislations on private arbitration. The second dimension aimed at the unification of procedural rules of the various bodies administering arbitration. Finally, the third dimension was concerned with the unification of the international regime for the enforcement of arbitral awards, proposing the adoption of an international treaty on the matter.

A similar approach was followed in the report submitted by Max Leclerc,[201] which was presented on behalf of the Paris Chamber of Commerce.[202] It should be noted, preliminarily, that this document came to substantiate the

199 In total, 7 reports were submitted on item 3, being consolidated in a general report produced by Roberto Pozzi.

200 The plan is clearly laid out in the following terms: "*Nous estimons donc en résumé: Qu'il est indispensable d'unifier: 1° Les divers Codes de commerce et les divers Codes de procédure commerciale. 2° Les règlements des Organismes d'arbitrage, soit officiels, soit privés, car il ne faudrait pas retomber dans l'errement des différences de règlements qui compliquerait les choses bien autrement que les différences de législations, puisque ces règlements seraient multiples pour chaque pays, alors que la loi est unique. 3° Qu'une Convention soit conclue entre tous les états, pour rendre partout exécutoires, les jugements arbitraux rendu dans l'un d'eux. Les Chambres de Commerce ne peuvent pas seules, malgré leur bonne volonté, arriver à ce résultat ; elles ne peuvent que préparer le travail. Il appartient donc, croyons-nous, au Congrès, de nommer une Commission de Commerçants et de Jurisconsultes, chargée de réunir tous les éléments propres à l'étude de cette question.*" Sailly and Duché, 'Rapport en réponse à la 3e question de l'orde du jour du congrès: De l'unification des législation relatives à la procédure d'arbitrage pour régler les litiges entre citoyens de pays différents – Presenté au nom de la Chambre française de commerce et d'industrie de Bruxelles.' (Publications du VIe Congrès Internationaux des Chambres des Commerce et des Associations Commerciales et industriales 1914), at 14–15.

201 Max Leclerc was member of the Paris Chamber of Commerce from 1913 to 1920, and also sat at the board of the *Banque de France*. He had a background in political science and his career was tied to the publishing business, notably to the publishing house of Armand Colin – who was also his father-in-law. Curiously, Max Leclerc has been more recognized for the contribution he has given to the study of geography in France. See Les directeurs, 'Nécrologie: Max Leclerc 1864–1932' (1932) 41 Annales de Géographie 337.

202 See Leclerc, *op.cit.*

final resolution adopted on the unification of arbitral legislation. Notably, the report calls for the establishment of an expert committee to work on a preliminary draft convention on arbitration between nationals of different countries, a draft which should be later submitted to a diplomatic conference organized for the purpose of adopting an international convention on the matter.[203]

Leclerc's report is also informative and insightful in relation to the state of the practice of private international arbitration in 1914, especially regarding disputes concerning the markets of cotton, grains and books. Max Leclerc recognizes that there was a burgeoning arbitration movement at the level of private institutions, which emerged quite spontaneously. Yet, he noted that this spontaneity was a precarious strategy and, at best, provisional. In his view, the organization of arbitration on an exclusively private basis, relying on professional and moral sanctions was insufficient. The Leclerc report expressly subscribed to Pozzi's arguments, attributing great weight to the cross-border enforcement of arbitral awards and to the necessity of promoting a liberal approach to their circulation. In sum, it clearly stated that arbitral practice should strive to gain access to official States' recognition concerning the validity of arbitration agreements and the enforcement of arbitral awards.[204]

At the plenary of the Paris Congress, a long discussion ensued on the conditions for the *exequatur* of foreign arbitral awards – a debate that was won by the partisans of a liberal approach on the matter.[205] The resolution adopted pointed towards four avenues for concerted action concerning such liberalization, which were the following: *i*) the international recognition of the validity of arbitration agreements; *ii*) the right of foreigners to be arbitrators; *iii*) the international enforcement of arbitral awards;[206] and *iv*) the unification of arbitration procedure.[207]

---

203 The method proposed was inspired by other unification initiatives, such as the ones on labour protection and literary property. The draft resolution contained in Leclerc's report was adopted with very minor additions by the final resolution of the 6th Congress on the unification of arbitration law.

204 See Leclerc, *op.cit.*, at 770, 774.

205 See Comité Permanent des Congrès, 'Compte rendu du VIe Congrès international des Chambres de Commerce et des Associations commerciales et industrielles (Paris – 8, 9 et 10 Juin)' (1914) 21 Bulletin de la Chambre de Commerce de Paris 966, at 985.

206 See Comité Permanent des Congrès, 'Compte Rendu du VIe Congrès,' *op.cit.*, at 985.

207 The complete text of the resolution read as follows: "11. *Unification des législations relatives à la procédure d'arbitrage pour régler les litiges entre les citoyens de pays différents. Le Congrès, Considérant: Que, pour régler les différends en matière commerciale ou industrielle, principalement dans les relations internationales, la nécessité s'impose d'une procédure*

The 1914 congress demonstrates a certain competition between common law and civil law jurisdictions for the control of arbitration practice – a competition that would unfold throughout the 20th century. More important, however, was the significant clash of views on the fundamental contours of arbitral authority in relation to the administration of justice, expressed in the contrasting positions of Roberto Pozzi and Charles L. Bernheimer. Indeed, the opposition between the two men goes beyond the civil law/common law dichotomy, standing as an early iteration of the divide between those that wanted to vest

rapide et peu coûteuse; Que, par conséquent, des mesures doivent être prises pour mettre à la disposition des commerçants et industriels de tous les pays les organisations nécessaire au fonctionnement de l'arbitrage dans le contestations entre citoyens de nations différentes et que, à cet effet, il y a lieu de s'inspirer des précédents fournis par le règlement d'arbitrage de la Fédération internationale cotonnière et par celui du Congrès international des éditeurs, en tenant compte aussi des importants résultats de l'enquête proposé par la Chambre de Commerce de Berlin et de l'avant-projet de règlement rédigé par la Chambre de Commerce de New-York, c'est-à-dire d'organiser des collèges internationaux d'arbitres pour chaque profession ou groupe de professions similaires ; Considérant, en outre, d'après les rapports de la Fédération internationale cotonnière, de la Chambre de Commerce de Paris, de la Société pour la défense du Commerce et de l'industrie de Marseille et d'autres Associations ; Que la reconnaissance, par tous les États, de la validité de la clause compromissoire insérée dans les contrats entre commerçants et industriels s'impose comme l'une des conditions essentielles à la réalisation de l'arbitrage international dans les litiges qui naissent des transactions entre commerçants de pays différents ; Qu'il est également nécessaire que, dans tous les États, le législateur admette les étrangers à remplir les fonctions d'arbitre ; Et qu'il accorde force exécutoire aux sentences arbitrales étrangères, sans exiger un nouveau jugement sur le fond ; – mais sous réserve que l'autorité compétente vérifiera si les règles de la procédure ont été observées et si la sentence est rendue en conformité du droit public international et du droit public interne du pays dans lequel force exécutoire est demandée ; Enfin que même la forme des jugements arbitraux soit unifiée, autant que possible, au sujet du nombre des arbitres, du dépôt et de la ratification des sentences, des moyens d'appel, etc., Émet le vœu : Que les Chambres de Commerce et Associations commerciales et industrielles réunies dans les respectives Fédérations ou liées par des rapports fédératifs organisent des collèges d'arbitres internationaux par profession ou groupe de professions similaires ; Décide : Que le Comité permanent des Congrès convoquera une Conférence technique internationale formée de représentants des Chambres de Commerce, des Fédérations et des Associations commerciales et industrielles, assistés de jurisconsultes des divers pays représentés au Congrès, à l'effet d'élaborer un avant-projet de Convention internationale sur la procédure d'arbitrage pour régler les litiges entre citoyens de pays différents ; Et qu'ensuite le Comité permanent saisira de cet avant-projet le Gouvernement de la République française et la priera d'inviter les autres États à une Conférence diplomatique internationale, qui aura pour mission d'établir, sur la base de l'avant-projet élaboré par la Conférence technique, une Convention international sur la procédure d'arbitrage pour régler les litiges entre citoyens de pays différents." See Comité Permanent des Congrès, 'Compte Rendu du VIe Congrès,' *op.cit.*, at 993–994.

arbitration with jurisdictional authority and those that wanted to promote arbitration as an equitable mechanism of dispute settlement grounded on a contractual logic.

In order to understand this clash, it is necessary to take a closer look at the report submitted by Charles Bernheimer on behalf of the New York Chamber of Commerce. This document contained a set of procedural rules to govern private international arbitration, pursuant to which the practice of arbitration was to be operated on the basis of professional sanctions. This mechanism was built upon the assumption of a continuous membership of stakeholders to a certain trading association, which was a scheme reminiscent of guild regulation. The enforcement mechanism envisioned by Bernheimer, giving rise to so much controversy, would essentially amount to exclusion from trade and a type of contractual asset seizure.[208]

The draft rules produced by the New York Chamber of Commerce were developed by a committee chaired by Charles Bernheimer himself with the assistance of Julius Henry Cohen.[209] The project aimed at promoting the practice of arbitration beyond the auspices of the State, relying heavily on the value of comity between chambers of commerce. In his report, Bernheimer suggests that merchant associations of "recognized standing" should trust each other, giving "full credit and faith" to judgments passed under their purview in the same way that a "judgment of a court of record is given full faith and credit by the international treaties of nations."[210] This approach, claimed Bernheimer,

208 Article IV of Bernheimer's project, governing enforcement, read as follows: "Where legal proceedings are not practical, the Chamber, Board, Association or Exchange in the district of the residence of the party against whom the award is made, shall endeavour to enforce the award in the following manner: It shall first bring to the attention of the party against whom the award is made the fact of the award. If he shall fail to comply therewith, it shall prefer a complaint against him to any organized trade association of which he is a member, and shall follow up such charges to the full extent of its power. A monthly Bulletin should be published under the auspices of all the Chambers in which should be given a resumé of such decisions as shall have been rendered by the tribunals of the various Chambers, and in which shall be published a list of the awards made, together with results of such awards." Article VII provided for the seizure of assets in the following terms: "If the controversy involves merchandise, the tribunal of the place at which the merchandise is located may sell it, under suitable rules and regulations established for the government of such sales, and full credit for the proceeds of such sale shall be given to the party entitled thereto." For both provisions, see Charles L Bernheimer, 'International Arbitration of Individual Commercial Disputes' (Chamber of Commerce of the State of New York 1914), at 8.

209 See Bernheimer, *op.cit.*, at 6.

210 See Bernheimer, *op.cit.*, at 9.

bypassed legal technicalities, resting on a "universal base, – the base of commercial honour, integrity and credit that is itself the base of all commerce."[211]

As a consequence, the American report does not address at all the issue of unification of arbitration legislation and treats legal enforcement as a fortuitous situation. The idea that "[n]o honourable merchant would fail to avail himself of the tribunal so selected upon any technical legal ground unless he could adequately defend himself upon moral grounds"[212] may seem somewhat naïve, but it reflected a particular understanding of arbitration as an alternative dispute resolution mechanism when compared to courts.

It seems clear that Bernheimer's approach is based on a polar-opposite view of arbitration than the one advanced by Pozzi. On the one hand, Bernheimer advocates for a trust-based model that would exist in parallel and independently from the State administration of justice. In blunt terms, Berheimer pushes for an entirely private system of adjudication. On the other hand, Pozzi advocated for a coercion-based model that would be embedded in the existing administration of justice, postulating a division of labour between judges and arbitrators.

In the middle of the way, one finds the report submitted by Leclerc, on behalf of the Paris Chamber of Commerce. Even if Leclerc agrees with Pozzi's views on the importance of legal enforcement of arbitration awards, he also exhorts the creation of a "college" of arbitrators for each professional group and insists that expert knowledge is of paramount importance to arbitral practice.[213] That said, the arbitrator, to Leclerc, would essentially be a judge of facts deciding on the basis of equity.

Part of the explanation to the contrasting projects advanced in 1914 at the Paris Congress may stem from the professional affiliations of the leading figures behind these projects. Pozzi was an Italian lawyer, while Bernheimer and Leclerc had not received legal training. At this early stage of development, the interest of the business community in relation to international arbitration was not always mediated by lawyers. This also suggests that internal divisions in the legal profession were of a lesser significance in these debates than they could have been if the table of negotiations were filled with lawyers from different jurisdictions.

In any event, all the intellectual work done on the uniformization of arbitration practice throughout the six sessions of the International Congresses of Chambers of Commerce was halted by the World War I. Nevertheless, the

211 See Bernheimer, *op.cit.*, at 2–3.

212 See Bernheimer, *op.cit.*, at 2–3.

213 Comité Permanent des Congrès, 'Compte Rendu du VIe Congrès,' *op.cit.*, at 993.

knowledge and the networks created were not entirely lost. Most of the resolutions adopted on arbitration, including the one on the creation of an arbitration court, would resurface through the initiative of the International Chamber of Commerce in the aftermath of the war.

Moreover, American business interests would continue to lobby for private international arbitration during the war years. In 1915, American states were invited by the government of the United States to the First Pan-American Financial Conference. The meeting had as its central tasks both the promotion of uniform commercial legislation, as well as "the extension of the process of arbitration for the adjustment of commercial disputes."[214]

A concrete outcome resulting from this conference was the creation of an "International High Commission on Uniform Legislation" entrusted with the mission of developing uniformization activities. This body had as one of its early achievements the adoption of the arbitration agreements between the Chamber of Commerce of the United States with several chambers of commerce from south American countries, such as Argentina, Uruguay, Ecuador, Panama and Guatemala.[215]

---

214 John Basset Moore, 'Pan-American Financial Conferences and the Inter-American High Commission' (1920) 14 The American Journal of International Law 343, at 344.

215 See Moore, *op.cit.*, 350.

CHAPTER 4

The Promises of the Interwar Years

One knows that arbitral tribunals are essentially *ad hoc*, even when they operate under institutional rules. Each tribunal is constituted *ex post facto* and vanishes once its mandate is exhausted. This means that arbitral procedure is organized around a transient body with a mostly retrospective mandate, while the judiciary functions as a permanent jurisdiction entrusted with both retrospective concerns over the dispute at hand and prospective concerns over the systemic regulation of legal relations.

Even still, the progressive codification of transnational arbitral authority has gradually blurred these lines, embedding arbitral authority in the transnational administration of justice, and producing a division of labour between arbitral tribunals and municipal courts in the governance of cross-border disputes. The terms and the boundaries of this transnational division of labour were first sketched in the interwar years, comprising both a public and a private international law dimension. Indeed, the period in question gave rise to an exponential process of codification of arbitral authority and the uniformization of its practice.

It is remarkable to note the parallel dynamics concerning the codification of arbitral authority in public and private international law. The most outstanding of these developments are certainly the League of Nations' normative instruments adopted in relation to arbitration and security, as well as its work on what was then called private international arbitration. Notably, the advent of the League of Nations represented a dislocation in the custodianship of arbitral technique, shadowing the already decaying Permanent Court of Arbitration. Such custodianship, materialised in initiatives on the formalisation of arbitral knowledge and the preservation of arbitral memory, was undertaken by the many different bodies of the League – and it moved beyond the public and private divide in international law. In terms of the preservation of arbitral memory, the Assembly of the League adopted a resolution at its Ninth Session that read as follows:

> The Assembly,
>
> Recognising the importance of the documentation which the Secretariat of the League of Nations has begun to collect concerning treaties of judicial settlement, arbitration and conciliation, and of the maps and graphs which it contemplates establishing:

 | DOI:10.1163/9789004728998_005

> Requests the Secretary-General to be so good as to invite the Governments of States Members or non-Members of the League of Nations to communicate to the Secretariat the text:
>
> (i) Of those treaties for the pacific settlement of disputes which are now in force and which were concluded prior to the establishment of the League of Nations and which have not been registered;
>
> (ii) Of such arbitral awards affecting them as may be rendered in the future, with the exception of judgments of the Permanent Court of International Justice and of the Permanent Court of Arbitration and of special tribunals such as the Mixed Arbitral Tribunals.[1]

The first decade of existence of the League was particularly fruitful for the codification of arbitral procedure. The echoes of the war, the urgency of European reconstruction and the ebbs and flows in European politics would be important factors in some of these developments. Still, the defining contours of the normative production undertaken at the League would be indelibly marked by the participation of a growing legal technocracy, which would comfortably circulate within the halls of the Wilson Palace in Geneva. This gave rise to a series of procedural codes adopted with the ambition of promoting the harmonization of private and public arbitration.

The period covered by this chapter was also marked by great optimism towards the potential of vesting arbitrators with authority to govern war and peace. Arbitration was a central piece in the settlement of reparation payments, as well as in an emerging system of collective security. At the eve of the horrors of World War II, many still imagined that arbitral authority could guide the world towards the dream of perpetual peace. Within this framework, the economic settlement of the Great War was used as a laboratory for experiments concerning the division of labour between international and national jurisdictions over disputes at the intersection of public and private international law. Once again, the long shadows of war would blur disciplinary lines, producing a fertile soil for the transnational expansion of arbitral authority and the codification of its procedure.

---

1 See 'Resolution with regard to the Revision of the Systematic Survey of Arbitration Conventions and Treaties of Mutual Security deposited with the League of Nations, prepared by the Legal Section of the Secretariat' (1928) 63 Official Journal of the League of Nations, Special Supplement 19. This resolution was advanced by René Cassin on behalf of the French delegation. See René Cassin, 'Annex 8, A.I/6.1928: Revision of the Systematic Survey of Arbitration Conventions and Treaties of mutual Security Prepared by the Secretariat' (1928) 67 League of Nations Official Journal, Special Supplement 123.

Arbitration was also on the rise with regards to commercial disputes of a cross-border character, which generated many efforts towards the procedural codification of the nascent field of international commercial arbitration. Similarly, some of these initiatives gravitated around the League of Nations, but a great number of them transcended the purview of the League. Accordingly, one observes the proliferation of procedural codes designed and adopted by private entities.

As one can already note, the interwar years were marked by a series of codification endeavours, which would channel the future of arbitration. In order to account for such phenomena, this chapter will proceed as follows. In a first moment, it will analyse the engagement of the League of Nations with private international arbitration, which gave birth to an early transnational procedural framework governing the authority of arbitration involving private parties from different countries (1). In a second moment, the chapter will explore the role attributed to arbitration in the economic settlement of World War I, so as to highlight how procedural knowledge of international arbitration would circulate between public and private settings, promoting the hybridization of these adjudicative forms already in the 1920s (2). Finally, the third section of this chapter will address the emerging role of private entities in the uniformization and transnationalisation of arbitral authority (3).

1 Private International Arbitration before the League of Nations

Some fifteen years after the adoption of the Convention on the Execution of Foreign Arbitral Awards, which was negotiated within the League of Nations and opened for signature on 26 September 1927, Arthur Nussbaum considered the Geneva normative regime on private international arbitration as a failure due to the "congenital infirmities" of arbitral authority.[2] Notably, he felt that "the looseness of arbitral proceedings and the relative lack of authority in the arbitrators create an atmosphere which invites evasion and frustrating tricks on the part of recalcitrant parties," which was only made worse by the "absence or uncertainty of effective judicial compulsion in the international field."[3]

From his perspective, the only remedy to cure such infirmities was to produce an ever more uniform procedure and to vest arbitrators with an ever more coercive authority. Indeed, the future of arbitration was seemingly dependent

2 See Arthur Nussbaum, 'Treaties on Commercial Arbitration: A Test of International Private-Law Legislation' (1942) 56 Columbia Law Review 219, at 240.

3 See Nussbaum, *Treaties*, at 240.

on State sponsored codification of what was then called private international arbitration, and this code ought to be capable of overcoming the common law and civil law idiosyncrasies.[4] Such ambitions had guided, and would guide, much of the transnational codification of private forms of arbitral procedure throughout the 20th century.

Nussbaum's bleak analysis at the dawn of the 1940's contrasts with the optimism of the early 1920's, when the League of Nations first engaged with the codification of private international arbitration. The normative regime that emerged from this endeavour was made of the following two instruments: the Protocol on the Validity of Arbitration Clauses, adopted in Geneva by the Assembly of the League of Nations on 24 September 1923; and the 1927 Convention on the Execution of Foreign Arbitral Awards.

Despite its ambiguous practical effects, the Geneva regime epitomizes the ongoing debates and correlation of forces existing in the field of private international arbitration at the time. Notably, the processes to produce these normative instruments consisted of a concerted effort to codify arbitral procedure and to establish a clear division of labour between arbitral tribunals and municipal courts. For this reason, these attempts to promote the legislative unification of arbitration law help to understand the gradual construction, expansion and transnationalisation of arbitral authority The next sections will first analyse how the standardization of contractual relations has impacted the production of the 1923 Protocol (1.1), and then it will explore how the Hague Conference on Private International Law influenced the division of labour between arbitral tribunals and municipal courts enshrined in the Convention of 1927 (1.2).

1.1 *The Expansion of Arbitral Authority through Standard Clauses*

Received wisdom on the history of arbitration tends to portray the 1923 Protocol on the Validity of Arbitration Clauses as a mere prelude to the more encumbering and pressing task that was the promotion of a uniform regime for the enforcement of foreign arbitral awards. Certainly, the judicial enforcement of arbitral awards would be of central importance for the transnationalisation of arbitral authority. Still, the 1923 Protocol on the Validity of Arbitration Clauses

4 Nussbaum manifests the following view: "Undoubtedly, the civil-law view was embodied in the Geneva Protocol, as far as arbitration agreements are concerned. Thus, under an agreement, the parties are unconditionally bound to turn to the arbitrators for the prosecution of their rights, and this obligation of the parties must be unconditionally respected by the courts. The English quibbling on this point is all the more puzzling since England would have been the main beneficiary of the treaty had they not failed for unforeseen reasons." See Nussbaum, *Treaties*, at 242.

played a larger role in this process than it is usually assumed, one that mirrored the main strategy for the expansion of private international arbitration.

When the League of Nations began its work on arbitration clauses, one ought to bear in mind that the issue at stake was not exactly the legalization of arbitral agreements *per se*. At the time, there was not much controversy concerning the validity of standalone arbitration agreements (*compromis*) or the legality of arbitration in general. The preparatory works of the Protocol make it clear that the attention of the League was exclusively focused on the validity of arbitration clauses (*clause compromissoire*) – and the title of the Protocol itself is no mere accident. The importance of promoting the validity of these clauses, as it was noted within the League, lied on the fact that this was "the typical method by which people commonly seek to secure commercial arbitration."[5]

Understanding the difference between a *compromis* and an arbitration clause is not an arcane or byzantine endeavour. Rather, these two instruments had distinctive mechanics, leading to very different legal realities. A standalone arbitration agreement was a backward-looking contractual instrument that submitted a delimited set of existing disputes to arbitration. In contrast, an arbitration clause was a forward-looking contractual instrument, which would submit a supervening and undefined set of disputes to arbitration.

The validity of arbitration clauses had a long career of controversy, and these debates were not limited to private international law circles. In 1870, when the IDI's was working on the codification of procedural rules for international arbitration, the problem had already emerged. As seen elsewhere in this study, the IDI Rules took a favourable view regarding the validity of arbitration clauses[6] – and this would ultimately lead the IDI to draft its own model arbitration clause to be inserted in future treaties.[7]

In the 1920s, during the League's work on the matter, there was a vivid fear within national legal communities that arbitration clauses could generate

---

5 In Frank Douglas MacKinnon and others, 'Sub-Committee on Arbitration Clauses: Report on the Session Held in London, July 1922' (1922) 3 League of Nations Official Journal 1410, at 1411.

6 See Goldschmid, *op.cit.*, at 429–430.

7 On 12 September, at its Zurich session, the IDI adopted the following resolution: "*L'Institut de Droit International: Recommande avec instance d'insérer dans les futurs traités internationaux une clause compromissoire, stipulant le recours à la voie de l'arbitrage en cas de contestation sur l'interprétation et l'application de ces traités. L'Institut propose en même temps, en considération de la difficulté que les parties pourront avoir à s'entendre préalablement sur la procédure à suivre, l'addition, à la clause compromissoire, de la disposition qui suit : 'Si les États contractants ne sont pas tombés d'accord préalablement sur d'autres dispositions touchant la procédure à suivre devant le tribunal arbitral, il y a lieu d'appliquer le Règlement consacré par l'Institut dans sa session de La Haye, le 28 août 1875.*" See Institut de Droit International, *Annuaire: Tome 2/1877* (Schmidt Periodicals Gmbh 1994), at 160.

problems to the weak contractual party in asymmetric contractual relations. The example of France is illuminating in this regard.[8] Although the 1843 Prunier decision is often presented as a case in point for French distrust of arbitration,[9] the protection of weaker contractual parties was a central concern for the direction taken by *Cour de Cassation* in that case.

It should be noted that Prunier did not outlaw arbitration clauses *per se*, rather it restricted its usage. Concretely, the holding of the decision enshrined that arbitration clauses ought to be given the same treatment as standalone arbitration agreements (*compromis*), which meant that these clauses had to provide the name of arbitrators that would sit in the tribunal as well as the precise object of the dispute to be resolved through arbitration. In Prunier, the *Cour de Cassation* aimed at shielding weaker parties from unfavourable terms being inserted as a result of an asymmetric contractual relation. In essence, the now infamous decision established that arbitration agreements had to be the result of a fair and balanced contractual negotiation in order to be upheld.[10]

---

8 On the ongoing French debate at the time, see Georges Cohendy, 'La clause compromissoire au point de vue du droit interne' (1923) 52 Bulletin de la Société de Legislation Comparée 347; Emmanuel Gounot, 'La clause compromissoire dans les relations commerciales internationales' (1923) 52 Bulletin de la Société de Legislation Comparée 354; Joseph Hamel, 'La clause compromissoire dans le rapports de commerce internationaux' (1923) 18 Revue de Droit International Privé 721; Joseph Hamel, 'La clause compromissoire dans les rapports de commerce internatioaux' (1924) 19 Revue de Droit International Privé 15; René Hoffher, 'Discussion sur la validité de la clause compromissoire au groupe lyonnais de la Société de Législation Comparée' (1923) 52 Bulletin de la Société de Legislation Comparée 345; Maurice Picard, 'La clause compromissoire et l'arbitrage dans les rapports internationaux' (1923) 50 Journal du Droit International 508.

9 See, for instance, Carine Jallamion, 'La jurisprudence francaise et l'arbitrage de 1843 a 1958: De la defaveur a la faveur jusqu'a l'avenement de l'arbitrage international (Partie I)' [2015] Revue de l'arbitrage 739; Mikaël Schinazi, 'The Three Ages of International Commercial Arbitration : Between Renewal and Anxiety' (Sciences Po 2019), at 125–130.

10 This is very clear in the following passage of the decision: "*Attendu que l'obligation de nommer des arbitres lors des compromis a pour but d'éviter les incidents et les procès sur la composition d'un tribunal arbitral, et principalement de mettre les citoyens en garde contre leur propre irréflexion, qui les porterait à souscrire avec trop de légèreté et d'imprévoyance à des arbitrages futurs, sans être certains d'avoir pour juges volontaires des personnes capables et dignes de leur confiance;–Que, dans l'espèce actuelle, l'importance et la nécessité des prescriptions de l'art. 1006 ressortait avec clarté de la position même que les assureurs prétendent faire à leurs assurés, pour la décision de tous leurs différends;–Qu'en effet, la compagnie l'Alliance, dont le siège principal est à Paris, et qui étend ses opérations sur toute la France, veut, à l'aide de l'art. 15 de sa police, forcer les assurés, quel que soit leur domicile, quelque considérable ou léger que soit le dommage éprouvé, de constituer à Paris, où, peut-être, le plus grand nombre n'ont aucune relation d'affaires, et ne connaissent même personne loin du lieu où les sinistres se sont effectués, et où le préjudice qu'ils ont causé peut seulement être vérifié et apprécié, un tribunal arbitral qui les jugerait souverainement.*" In 'Compagnie

In France, the legislative overturn of Prunier was often seen as an immediate threat to weaker contractual parties, and there was fear that arbitration clauses would charter the same waters of unilateral forum selection clauses.[11] For the partisans of this approach, an all-encompassing validity of arbitration clauses meant that stronger parties would always be able to impose unfavourable arbitration agreements to weaker ones.

Furthermore, there was considerable concern among the French legal community that the dissemination of an arbitral system relying on standard arbitration clauses could hamper the judicial development of commercial case law. Interestingly, this has been an issue that has re-emerged in international commercial dispute settlement, for municipal commercial courts have been attempting to seize back a share of territory long lost to arbitration under this banner.[12]

L'Alliance v. Prunier, Cour de Cassation (Chambre Civile), 10 July 1843' [1992] Revue de l'arbitrage 399, at 404.

11 This fear was expressed in the following terms by Georges Cohendy: "*Toutes les fois que des relations se noueront entre contractants de puissance inégale (contractants d'assurance, de transports, d'éditions, contrat entre une petite ou moyenne maison et une grosse firme, etc.), ce sera le plus fort qui imposera sa loi au plus faible ; il désignera des arbitres de préférence dans la ville où il a ses relations.* [...] *Et cette crainte est si peu vaine que déjà, aujourd'hui, dans une mesure infiniment plus réduite, elle se réalise grâce aux clauses attributives de juridictions; en fait, le petit négociant est toujours distrait de son tribunal local au profit du tribunal de la grosse firme, éloigné où sa defense est difficile et coûteuse.*" See Cohendy, *op. cit.*, 351–352.

12 Lord Thomas expressed the following views: "The effect of the diminishing number of appeals compounds the problem that arises from the diversion of more claims from the courts to arbitration. It reduces the potential for the courts to develop and explain the law. This consequence provides fertile ground for transforming the common law from a living instrument into, as Lord Toulson put it in a different context, "an ossuary". Here lies the irony. As I have explained reform was effected to promote the use of London as a centre for dispute resolution largely based on contracts based on the common law as developed in the Commercial Courts of London. However, the consequence has been the undermining of the means through which much of the common law's strength – its 'excellence' was developed – a danger not merely to those engaged in dispute resolution in London, but more importantly to the development of the common law as the framework to underpin the international markets, trade and commerce." See Lord Thomas of Cwmgiedd, 'Bailii Lecture 2016: Developing Commercial Law through the Courts: Rebalancing the Relationship between the Courts and Arbitration' (London, 9 March 2016) 9–10. Available at: <https://www.judiciary.uk/announcements/speech-by-the-lord-chief-justice-the-bailii-lecture-2016/>. Accessed on 24 October 2020.

The ambition to ensure State oversight over commercial disputes was not an exclusive feature of French legal circles. In the early 20th century, another relevant forum for commercial transactions shared a similar reticence over arbitration agreements. Across the common law pond, American courts were very much inclined to uphold the revocability of arbitration agreements in favour of municipal courts. Back then, it was understood that "either party has been accorded the legal power to repudiate his arbitration agreement and to maintain a lawsuit in the courts in breach thereof."[13] This American approach was tied to a line of English precedents, of which the Vynior's case from 1609 and Kill v. Hollister from 1764 are the early sources.[14] In England, these precedents were overturned through the adoption of the 1889 arbitration act, but in the United States their echoes were still well heard in the first decades of the 20th century.[15]

The Protocol of 1923, therefore, must be understood as an essential step for the expansion of arbitral authority and yet as another expression of a phenomenon that was at the time called the "standardization of modern economic development."[16] Indeed, the Protocol would give transnational effect to boilerplate arbitral clauses, and these clauses would ultimately become the source

13 See Wesley A Sturges, 'Commercial Arbitration in the United States of America' in Arthur Nussbaum (ed), *International Yearbook on Civil and Commercial Arbitration* (Oxford University Press 1928), at 165.

14 See Sturges, *op.cit.*, at 165–166.

15 For instance, in 1915, the United States District Court for the Southern District of New York made the following statement: "Whatever form of statement the rule takes, the foregoing citations show that it always amounts to the same thing, viz.: The courts will scarcely permit any other body of men to even partially perform judicial work, and will never permit the absorption of all the business growing out of disputes over a contract by any body of arbitrators, unless compelled to such action by statute. [...] Neither the Legislature of New York nor the Congress has seen fit thus to modernize the ideas of the judges of their respective jurisdictions." See United States District Court for the Southern District of New York, 'United States Asphalt Refining Co. v. Trinidad Lake Petroleum Co. Limited, 222F 1006, Nos. 58–115, 58–121', at 1010–1011.

16 Nussbaum offers an interesting account of arbitration development as part of such standardization: "Agreements to arbitrate are promoted by the various trade and commercial associations by advocating the inclusion of standard arbitration clauses in contracts. The use of such clauses may be considered as one of the symptoms of the 'standardization' of modern economic development – that is, an effort in the interest of economy, to reduce the same types of transactions to standard forms; in this manner the systematic development of standard clauses forms a parallel to technical standardization." See Arthur Nussbaum, 'Problems of International Arbitration' in Arthur Nussbaum (ed), *International Yearbook on Civil and Commecial Arbitration* (Oxford University Presss 1928) 3.

of the authority of arbitral institutions over arbitration proceedings. In sum, when the League was entrusted with the task of framing the international normative regime on arbitration clauses, at stake was the future of institutional arbitration and its strategy of expanding through standardized arbitration clauses.

The model of an autarkical type of institutional arbitration gradually emerged as an alternative to the so-called "national system of international arbitral tribunals."[17] This former model was championed by the United Kingdom, which promoted an arbitral procedure entirely grounded on municipal law and strictly overseen by courts. A problem, however, was quickly identified by non-English lawyers: such national system of international arbitral tribunals favoured the jurisdiction of the largest trading nations – and especially that of England.[18]

Two versions of this autarkical, or non-state, type of institutional arbitration were advanced in the early 1920s. On the one hand, there was a type of private multilateralism fostered under the ICC procedural framework, which imagined its court of arbitration as a world forum for private international arbitration. On the other hand, there was a private bilateralism, most notably advocated by the United States Chamber of Commerce, through the promotion of a network of bilateral arbitration arrangements with its Latin American counterparts.

The ICC and the US Chamber of Commerce, like most arbitration institutions, sought to extend the reach of its procedural authority using model arbitration clauses to be inserted in commercial contracts. These clauses served to incorporate institutional procedural rules to any contract, producing a multi-layered source for the prerogatives of arbitrators and institutions. The first model ICC arbitration clause is quite interesting for its brevity, reading as follows:

> *Les parties contractantes s'engagent à recourir à un arbitrage rendu conformément au règlement d'arbitrage de la Chambre de commerce*

---

17 See Nussbaum, *Problems*, at 2.

18 This fear is expressed in a report presented to the section of the city of Lyon of the *Société de Législation Comparé* in the following terms: "*Et alors je crains fort que la clause compromissoire, une fois reconnue, ne serve le plus souvent à imposer systématiquement aux commerçants des pays acheteurs l'arbitrage des chambres corporatives des certains pays vendeurs, faisant en fait la loi du contrat ; que, par exemple, la clause 'Arbitrage à Londres, aux conditions et usages de Londres, et avec renonciation au droit d'appel' ne devienne une clause de style dans tous les marchés des négociants de Londres, comme le sont aujourd'hui dans les factures de la plupart des commerçants les clauses attributives de juridiction.*" See Gounot, *op.cit*, at 360.

> *internationale, pour le règlement de tous litiges relatifs à l'interprétation ou à l'exécution du présent contrat.*[19]

The work of the League of Nations on arbitration clauses was not immune to such developments. Notably, it had been prompted "in consequence of judicial decisions in certain countries tending to undermine the validity of commercial arbitration clauses," which had "aroused great interest in the commercial world."[20] More, it was felt that the inclusion of arbitration on the agenda of the Economic Committee of the League of Nations would be of "great practical value" in avoiding litigation and as a means of promoting "commercial honesty."[21]

A subcommittee was then created under the direct purview of the Economic Committee of the League, and under the ultimate authority of the League's Council. The mandate of the subcommittee, which was chaired by Francis Douglas MacKinnon (a British official),[22] was to produce a study of arbitration agreements in commercial contracts entered by residents of different countries with the aim of promoting such arrangements.[23] The work done by the group chaired by McKinnon was finalized with great speed and led to the adoption of a report that would leave a strong mark in the future 1923 Protocol. Indeed, after only two sessions held on 3 and 4 July 1922, the work had been concluded, and the expediency would have been the result of "sympathetic cordiality which we mutually discovered from the outset of our deliberations."[24]

The report was essentially a piece of comparative legislation, singling-out France for its alleged exceptionalism on the treatment of arbitration clauses.[25] The comparative exercise was based on the expertise of the members of the subcommittee and on a few national reports circulated prior to their meeting. Notably, the subcommittee had before itself a report on English law prepared by F.D. MacKinnon, one on French law prepared by Percerou, another

19 In Gounot, *op.cit.*, at 360.

20 See M Wallenberg and MD Serruys, 'Provisional Economic and Financial Committee, Report on the Session of the Committee Held at Geneva in September 1922, and Submitted to the Council on September 16th, 1922, Annex 421a, A.73.1922.II.' (1922) 3 League of Nations Official Journal 1212, at 1404.

21 See Wallenberg and Serruys, *op.cit.*, at 1403–1404.

22 The other members of the subcommittee were the following ones: Prof. Gilbert Gidel from France; Mr. Ernst Meyer from Denmark; the Hon. Kan-Ichi Kayama from Japan; Dr. J. Novak from Czechoslovakia; and Dr. M. Friedeberg from Germany. See MacKinnon and others (n 299).

23 See MacKinnon and others, *op.cit.*, at 1411.

24 See MacKinnon and others, *op.cit.*, at 1411.

25 See MacKinnon and others, *op.cit.*, at 1412.

on Danish law prepared by Meyer, one on Swedish law prepared by Meyer and Stiernsted, and a translated extract of Japanese arbitral legislation prepared by Kan-ichi Kayama. The sub-committee's comparative analysis reached the conclusion that there was great variety in the ways through which arbitration was governed, practiced, enforced, as well as varying degrees of popularity of arbitration as a mechanism of dispute settlement.[26]

Interestingly, the propositions advanced by the subcommittee relied heavily on ethical considerations. Rather than some individualistic notion of party autonomy, these jurists were concerned with *pacta sunt servanda* and good faith. The two concepts, so it was argued, required the preservation of the bargain reached by the parties to the contract, and militated in favour of the validity of arbitration clauses. The underlying reasoning was that whenever citizens of different States had agreed upon arbitration as the method of settling their disputes, domestic courts ought to uphold the "sanctity of the contract."[27] In sum, for the members of the subcommittee, national sovereignty could not be used as an excuse to "private immorality and dishonour of the citizen."[28]

The 1923 Protocol itself came to be a very succinct document.[29] It comprised a total of eight articles and only four of these dealt concretely with the validity and enforcement of arbitration agreements.[30] Notably, its Article 1 settled the debate on the validity of arbitral clauses and the possibility of submitting a host of indeterminate and supervening disputes to arbitration through those clauses. The provision read as follows:

---

26 See MacKinnon and others, *op.cit.*, at 1411.

27 The report reads as follows: "If Courts of law are concerned in upholding the sanctity of contract, the Court in A ought to prevent its citizen from prosecuting his action in violation to his promise. But if the Court in A must disregard his promise, either because the national law treats a '*clause compromissoire*' as invalid, or provides (as we understand is the case in Italy) that arbitrators must be citizens of A, the technicalities of the national law of A are upheld, but the sanctity of contract is sadly flouted, and the citizen of A is assisted in his personal breach of faith." See MacKinnon and others, *op.cit.*, at 1413.

28 See MacKinnon and others, *op.cit.*, at 1413.

29 The final text of the Protocol was adopted by the Assembly of the League of Nations on the 24 September 1923. For the full text of the instrument, in both English and French, see Secretary-General, 'Protocol on Arbitration Clauses, Note by the Secretary-General' (1924) 5 League of Nations Official Journal 235.

30 One of the interesting ancillary provisions of the protocol consists of a reserve of right in relation to colonial possessions of signatories, conveyed in its Article 8. Accordingly, Contracting Parties were allowed to subtract their colonial possessions from the territorial scope of the Protocol. See Secretary-General, *Note*, at 237.

> Each of the Contracting States recognises the validity of an agreement whether relating to existing or future differences between parties subject respectively to the jurisdiction of different Contracting States by which the parties to a contract agree to submit to arbitration all or any differences that may arise in connection with such contract relating to commercial matters or to any other matter capable of settlement by arbitration, whether or not the arbitration is to take place in a country whose jurisdiction none of the parties is subject.
>
> Each of the Contracting States reserves the right to limit the obligation mentioned above to contracts which are considered commercial under its national law. Any Contracting State which avails itself of this right will notify the Secretary-General of the League of Nations, in order that the other Contracting State may be so informed.[31]

At this point in time, the doctrine of separability was not yet envisioned as such, but the terms of the Protocol opened the way for such development. When the Protocol recognizes the validity of "agreements relating to [...] future disputes," it abolishes the practical distinction of a *compromis* and an arbitration clause. Both mechanisms were granted the same legal effects. Conversely, it would not take long for lawyers to realize that if a *compromis* and an arbitration clause were essentially the same thing, it would not be too farfetched to argue that arbitration clauses should be seen as an autonomous agreement separable from the underlying contract just as much as a *compromis* had been.

In addition, it must be noted that the Protocol relied on a so-called "diversity-of-citizenship" rule in order to exclude pure domestic matters from the purview of international law.[32] In addition, a vague rule on arbitrability was introduced as a way to give some flexibility to the implementation of the instrument, extending its scope beyond purely commercial matters whenever this was considered acceptable in a given jurisdiction.

Albeit not a central concern at the time, party autonomy did make its way into the Protocol. Pursuant to its Article 2, arbitral procedure would be governed by "the will of the parties," but also by the "law of the country in whose territory the arbitration takes place."[33] Certainly, the Protocol did not go as

31 See Secretary-General, *Note*, at 236.

32 See Giorgio Balladore Pallieri, 'L'arbitrage privé dans les rapports internationaux', in *Collected Courses of the Hague Academy of International Law*, vol. 51 (Brill 1935) 386; Nussbaum, *Treaties*, at 235.

33 See Secretary-General, *Note*, at 236.

far as dismissing the oversight of municipal jurisdictions altogether, but it withdrew arbitration procedure from the exclusive purview of municipal law. In other terms, arbitration could now be governed both by contractual provisions and the procedural framework of the seat.

A combined analysis of Articles 1 and 2 demonstrate that the Protocol envisioned a potential conflict between the law of the place of enforcement and that of the seat of arbitration. It was noted at the time, that the law of the place of enforcement was to be given preference in relation to matters of arbitrability,[34] while the law of the seat was the one competent to govern all other dimensions of the arbitral procedure – including the validity of the arbitration agreement.[35]

Another innovation of the Protocol relates to the principle of competence-competence. Article 4 laid out an express rule governing the stay of judicial proceedings in favour of arbitration. If seized, municipal courts retained only a *prima facie* jurisdiction over the existence and validity of the arbitration agreement, otherwise referring the parties to arbitration.[36] Comparing the corresponding provisions in the IDI Rules and the PCA Rules, which focused on the prerogative of arbitrators to rule on their jurisdiction, with the one in the 1923 Protocol, one realizes that competence-competence was gradually becoming

34 On the law applicable to arbitrability, Balladore explains the following: "*Il se dégage assez clairement de l'expression employé par le Protocole que chacun des États contractants ne s'engage qu'à reconnaître les compromis relatifs à des litiges qui, suivant sa législation, peuvent être soumis à l'arbitrage. Le Protocole n'impose aucune obligation aux États contractants d'appliquer un droit étranger ; bien plus, lorsqu'il leur accorde la faculté de restreindre leur engagement aux seules matières commerciales, il dit expressément que chaque État détermine suivant sons droit national si la matière est de nature commerciale.*" See Balladore Pallieri, *op.cit.*, at 386–387.

35 On the law governing the procedure, Balladore was of the following view: "*Par conséquent, lorsque l'article 2 du Protocole statue que l'arbitrage est réglé par la volonté des Parties et par la loi du pays où l'arbitrage a lieu, il statue sans possibilité de controverse que cette même loi a qualité pour régler le compromis et tout l'arbitrage. L'article 2 du Protocole énonce donc une règle de rattachement, et même une règle de rattachement différent de celle en vigueur dans tous les Etats. Aux compromis réglés par le Protocole, les Étas contractants doivent appliquer la loi du lieu de l'arbitrage, et non pas la loi qui serait compétente selon leurs règles internes de droit international privé.*" See Balladore Pallieri, *op.cit.*, at 388–389.

36 Article 4 reads as follows: "Tribunals of the Contracting Parties which, on being seized of a dispute regarding a contract between persons to whom Article I applies, recognise the existence in the contract of an arbitration agreement, whether referring to present or future differences, which is valid and capable of being put into force, shall, on the application of any of the parties, refer such parties to the decision of the arbitrators." See Secretary-General, *Note,* at 236.

an important mechanism through which codifiers would regulate the division of labour between courts and arbitral tribunals.

In fact, this approach to competence-competence would generate great pushback in the years that followed the adoption of the Protocol. This was the case of England, were many felt that the League of Nations departed from the English tradition on the matter.[37] Curiously, one of the central figures in the preparation of the Protocol would lead the charges against it. In 1927, Frank Douglas MacKinnon, former chairman of the subcommittee of experts that laid the basis of the Protocol, would propose "that the 1924 Act be amended to provide that a stay of action should be granted only were 'the court is satisfied that there is a real dispute to be determined by arbitrators.'"[38]

1.2 *At the Crossroads of Geneva and the Hague: an Emerging Transnational Division of Labour between Courts and Arbitral Tribunals*

It would have been too difficult of a task to accomplish in 1923. This was the commonly held view in the League of Nations on the legislative unification of the enforcement of foreign of arbitral awards. There was too much inconsistency across jurisdictions; there was no clear position on whether awards had to be motivated or not; what were to be the common grounds to set awards aside? In sum, the time was not ripe to engage with the topic.[39]

This is, indeed, the reason why the 1923 Protocol only paid lip service to the importance of enforcing arbitral awards, failing to lay down any binding rule on the matter. Its Article 3 was framed in a curious way, providing that Contracting Parties "undertake that arbitral awards made in its own territory under the preceding articles shall be enforced by its authorities in accordance with the provisions of its national laws." Albeit the provision could be thought to impose an international obligation concerning the enforcement of awards made within the territory of the Contracting Parties, it was clear that States retained their discretion to enforce foreign arbitral awards pursuant to their own domestic criteria.

The adjournment, however, would not last long and less than five years later a foundational instrument brought to life a brand-new transnational division of labour between courts and arbitral tribunals. The enactment of the 1927 Geneva Convention on the Execution of Foreign Arbitral Awards followed a

37 See Nussbaum, *Treaties*, at 224.

38 See Frank Douglas MacKinnon, 'Report of Committee on the Law of Arbitration' (1927) Cmd. Papers 2817, no. 43.; Nussbaum, *Treaties*, at 224.

39 See MacKinnon and others, *op.cit.*, at 1413.

tortuous path, starting in the Hague and ending in Geneva. Notably, many of its fundamental terms owe much to the work of the Fifth Hague Conference on Private International Law, that same network of private international law scholars first launched by T.M.C. Asser.[40]

The year was 1925 and international lawyers were summoned to the Hague to discuss, *inter alia*, a model bilateral treaty to govern the circulation of judgments and arbitral awards. Ideas would travel from the Hague to Geneva in the suitcases of people like Jules Basdevant and Dionizio Anzilotti, two men who took part in the discussions at the Hague,[41] and that would become leading figures in the drafting of the future arbitration treaty within the League of Nations.[42]

The second commission of the Fifth Hague Conference had been entrusted with the task of working on the enforcement of foreign arbitral awards.[43] As debates began, the delegations were soon divided between those approaching arbitral awards from a jurisdictional perspective and those delegations adopting a contractual approach to the issue under analysis. This divide expressed the longstanding competition for the definition of the "legal nature" of foreign arbitral awards. On one side, some considered arbitral awards as purely contractual animals. On the other side, there were those that saw arbitral awards as jurisdictional acts similar to court judgments. In the early 1920s, so it was thought, the contractual theory of arbitration had become dominant, and important voices writing on comparative law proclaimed that "an arbitral award should be treated in accordance with principles of contract, and not judgement."[44]

40 For an overview of the work of the Hague Conference in the interwar years, see Milorad Straznicky, 'Les Conferences de Droit International Privé Depuis La Fin de La Guerre Mondiale', in *Collected Courses of the Hague Academy of International Law*, vol. 44 (Brill 1933). For a general overview of the Hague Conference, see Dieter Martiny, 'Hague Conference on Private International Law', in *Max Planck Encyclopedia of Public International Law* (Oxford University Press 2009).

41 The two men were respectively part of the French and Italian delegations to the Hague Conference. See Conférence de la Haye de Droit International Privé, *Actes de la cinquième session, tenue du 12 Octobre au 7 Novembre 1925* (Imprimerie Nationale 1926), at 9–11.

42 For the role played by Anzilotti and Basdevant in the drafting of the 1927 Convention, see Dionisio Anzilotti, 'Draft Protocol on the Execution of Foreign Arbitral Awards, Report of the Committee of Legal Experts and Text of Its Draft, Annex 969, A.11.1927 II. [C.2341927 II.]' (1927) 8 League of Nations Official Journal 890; Dionisio Anzilotti, 'Meeting of Legal Experts to Consider the Execution of Arbitral Awards, Report by the Chairman, Appendix 2' (1927) 8 League of Nations Official Journal 582.

43 This was done in a single session held on 22 October 1925. See Conférence de la Haye de Droit International Privé, *op.cit.*, at 139.

44 See Nussbaum, *Problems*, at 8.

Echoes of the debate on the jurisdictional or contractual nature of arbitral awards can still be found in many books exploring the "theoretical" or "philosophical" grounds of arbitration.[45] Evidently, this is a clash over the soul of arbitration, that is to say, is arbitration supposed to be a jurisdictional mechanism embedded in the public administration of justice or an equitable mechanism founded on autarkical contractual relations?

Even still, the debate in the interwar years had more to do with technical efforts towards legislative unification rather than to inquiries on the foundations of arbitration. Back then, it was felt that the contractual and jurisdictional theories were conducive to quite different effects, especially when it came to their enforcement abroad. If arbitral awards were purely contractual, a foreign arbitral award would be able to enjoy the same binding force granted to any other type of foreign contract. However, if arbitral awards were of a jurisdictional nature, then foreign arbitral decisions would not be binding unless some sort of exequatur was granted.

French arbitral practice provides an illustrative example of the contractual theory. In France, up until the 1920's, a so-called Merlin's theory had become the dominant account on the nature of arbitral awards.[46] The formulation of the theory dated back to 1820 and laid out quite curious conclusions. Pursuant to Merlin's theory, arbitrators acted as mere agents of the parties, for which reason awards would consist of an act performed within the confines of such contractual relation of representation. In other terms, the arbitral award itself was strictly construed as contract entered by the parties through their agents.

At the other side of the divide stood Italian arbitral practice, which emphasized the jurisdictional role of arbitration. Italian law at the time had given extensive oversight to courts over arbitral tribunals, requiring the confirmation of arbitral awards by State courts in order to vest them with executory force. Accordingly, absent such confirmation, it was considered that "the award is not legally valid and has no effect; and it represents no executory acts and has no binding power."[47]

Considering this, Italian doctrine at the time often portrayed the office of the arbitrator as related to that of judges. Different views certainly existed as to

---

45 See Emmanuel Gaillard, 'Aspects Philosophiques de l'arbitrage', *Collected Courses of the Hague Academy of International Law*, vol 329 (Martinus Nijhoff Publishers 2007); Charles Jarrosson, *La Notion d'arbitrage* (LGDJ 1987); Oppetit, *op.cit.*; Jan Paulsson, *The Idea of Arbitration* (Oxford University Press 2013); Jacqueline Rubellin-Devichi, *L'arbitrage: Nature Juridique, Droit Interne et Droit International Privé* (LGDJ 1964).

46 See Nussbaum, *Problems*, at 8.

47 Tulio Ascarelli, 'Arbitration under Italian Law' in Arthur Nussbaum (ed), *International Yearbook on Civil and Commercial Arbitration* (Oxford University Press 1928), at 85.

the details of the division of labour between courts and arbitral tribunals, but the common premise in Italian doctrinal debates seemed to be that arbitral tribunals were embedded in the jurisdictional functions performed by the State. Within this framework, arbitrators were either considered to have delegated jurisdiction stemming from legislation or were regarded as auxiliary organs in the performance of jurisdictional acts by courts themselves.[48]

48 Ascarelli is very pedagogical in summarizing the Italian doctrinal debates on the powers of arbitrators: "The varying opinions may be summarized in three groups: the theory of judgment (teoria giurisdizionalista), among the most prominent exponents of which are Mortara, Bonfante, Galante, Fedozzi, Zanobini, Galgano, and others; the theory of the non-binding arbitral award, (teoriaprivatista) represented, among others, by Chiovenda, Rocco and Calamandrei; and finally an intermediary theory, represented by Carnelutti. The representatives of the first theory hold that arbitrators are really and properly judges, who derive their power from the law on the basis of the arbitration agreement (Mortara). The will of the parties is a means of the selection, not, however, the source of the juridical power of the arbitrators. The order for enforcement issued by the court is merely a confirmation of the award rendered by the arbitrators; it has, however, the characteristics of a juridical act (Zanobini) and its chief purpose is that of rendering the award executory after an examination which is intended to prevent the arbitrator from entering a domain withdrawn from the competence of the parties by reasons of public policy. Arbitration implies, therefore, an agreement upon competency (prorogatiofori) and this justifies the limitations for the conclusion of an agreement to arbitrate, prescribed by law. The exponents of the theory of non-binding arbitral awards, – which theory appears to be gaining ground in recent writings (Calamandrei, Scaduto) – hold, on the other hand, that an arbitral award, in itself, and without the order of court, represents no executory act and has no binding power whatsoever. This consideration alone, aside from the facts that the arbitrators are prohibited from the means of coercion exercised by the courts, and that the selection of the arbitrator is left to the will of the parties, allows the conclusion that in arbitral procedure only the order of the court confirming the award is an act of jurisdiction. The arbitrators, as private individuals, merely collect and prepare the facts and the law; such preparation takes place under certain guarantees and with the observation of certain prescribed forms; and the data is then acquired by the state which formulates its order on the basis of the arbitrators' findings (Chiovenda). Arbitrations, therefore, should be regarded as instances wherein the contents of a court judgment have been prepared privately. Such cases are possible because of the division of the work of the court in regard to judgments; one aspect of this work is the concrete order based on the abstract will of the legislator, which is the law; the other aspect is the logical process whereby the court arrives at its decision. Only the first aspect involves jurisdictional elements and is dependent upon sovereign power; the second aspect of the work may be exercised without such power and thus referred to private individuals (Calamandrei). It is, therefore, justified to describe a judgment as a composite act, whereby the private act contributes the logical, and the public act the jurisdictional part (Chiovenda). Some authors concede that awards may have the nature of a judgment when rendered under laws which pronounce them binding, if not executory (Calamandrei). Carnelutti, who has more suggested than developed

The many complications related to the enforcement of foreign arbitral awards puzzled those present at the Hague in 1925, and the problems connected to the status of the awards were of particular concern. Viktor Merz, a Swiss judge who was presiding the work of the second commission, proposed a mechanism at the seat for the confirmation of awards to cope with some of these difficulties. His idea was to allow the cross-border recognition and enforcement of arbitral awards if they had been confirmed as enforceable at the seat. Pursuant to this system, it was argued, there would be no confusion on the nationality of the decision nor on its legal status.[49]

The proposal likely echoed the Italian approach to the enforcement of awards and, if adopted, would have had the practical consequence of vesting arbitral awards with the same status of a court ruling. The proposition, however, found great resistance. It was a commonly held view that the seat was not to be granted so much say over the destiny of an arbitral award, as the place of arbitration could have been chosen incidentally.[50]

An alternative model prevailed in the Hague, one that relied on courts of the place of enforcement instead of those of the seat for the control of the legality of arbitral awards. Within this framework, judges at the place of enforcement would have to investigate whether certain conditions were met prior to granting a foreign arbitral award executory force. These conditions were the following ones: the award should be *res judicata* at the seat; it should not violate

---

an intermediate theory, was guided by these latter considerations. He concedes that the arbitration agreement in Italian law has a positive as well as a negative procedural effect, since from it arises the authority of the court to complete the award by granting the order for enforcement. It is, therefore, justified to describe the act as composite, in the sense of a judgment composed of two unequal parts (award, and order for enforcement) and rendered by a composite organ (arbitrators and judge)." See Ascarelli, *op.cit*, at 87–88.

49 Merz's idea was expressed under the following terms: "*M. le Président constate les divergences sérieuses qui se manifestent ici. Il n'y a pas de difficulté pour admettre les décisions qui ne constituent pas de véritables sentences arbitrales ou celles qui ont été prévues par la législation du pays auquel est soumis l'arbitrage ; elles peuvent être assimilées à des jugements. Mais il en est autrement quand la législation ne prévoit pas l'arbitrage et quand il n'est même pas possible de connaître la nationalité du compromis. On ne pourrait englober ces décisions arbitrales dans le traité qu'en prévoyant des conditions spéciales' auxquelles on ne peut songer. Il estime qu'on ne pourrait assimiler aux jugements que les décisions arbitrales qui pourraient être "nationalisées" et qui remplaceraient, en excluant la juridiction ordinaire d'un pays, des jugements rendus dans ce pays. Il suffirait peut-être de demander une attestation déclarant que, dans le pays où la sentence arbitrale à été rendue, elle a force exécutoire ou force de chose jugée.*" In Conférence de la Haye de Droit International Privé, *op.cit*, at 140–141.

50 In particular, the Swedish delegation voiced this concern. Conférence de la Haye de Droit International Privé, *op.cit.*, at 140.

jurisdictional rules or public order in the place of enforcement; and, in the case of default rulings, the award should comply with due process rules of the seat.[51]

It should be noted that the Hague model did not formally promote a double exequatur mechanism. Even still, by treating arbitral awards as jurisdictional acts, it created an incentive for the implementation of a mechanism of recognition at the seat. In other terms, a foreign arbitral award confirmed at the seat would enjoy a clear advantage from non-confirmed ones, for the former would presumably meet most of the enforcement criteria related to the seat. Consequently, there was an unintended push towards the double exequatur system, introducing the well-known mechanism in which awards would be controlled both at the seat and at the place of enforcement. These ideas and this debate, as it will be seen, would resurge in Geneva.

In 1926, about one year after the conclusion of the Fifth Hague Conference, the League of Nations re-engaged with the discussion concerning the enforcement of foreign arbitral awards. The decision to include the item in its agenda was done in order to foster "the spread of commercial arbitration."[52]

---

51 This is the result of a combined reading of Articles I, II and IV of the model treaty produced by the Hague Conference. Article I read as follows: "*L'autorité des décisions judiciaires, rendues en matière civile ou en matière commerciale dans l'un des Etats contractants, sera reconnue dans l'autre État si elles réunissent les conditions suivantes: 1°. Que, pour le litige en question, les règles de compétence judiciaire internationales, admises par le droit de l'Etat dans lequel la décision est invoquée, n'excluent pas la juridiction de l'autre État; 2°. Que la reconnaissance de la décision ne soit pas contraire à l'ordre public ou aux principes du droit public de l'État où la décision est invoquée; 3°. Que d'après la loi de l'Etat où la décision a été rendue, elle soit passée en force de chose jugée; 4°. Qu'en cas de jugement par défaut, la partie ait été déclarée défaillante conformément à la loi du pays où le jugement a été rendu et aux dispositions des traités en vigueur entre les États contractants. L'examen à faire par les autorités de l'État où la décision est invoquée, se borne aux conditions énumérées dans l'alinéa 1er, nos. 1–4. Ces autorités doivent examiner d'office, si ces conditions sont remplies." Article* II *reads as follows : "Les décisions judiciaires rendues dans un des États contractants peuvent être mises à exécution dans l'autre État après avoir été déclarées exécutoires. L'exequatur est accordé si la décision est exécutoire dans l'État où elle a été rendue et si elle remplit les conditions énumérées dans l'article I, alinéa 1, n°s. 1–4. L'alinéa 2 de cet article s'applique à l'examen à faire par les autorités de l'État où l'exécution est demandée." Article* IV *read as follows: "Les sentences arbitrales rendues dans l'un des États contractants et y ayant la même autorité que les décisions judiciaires seront reconnues et déclarées exécutoires dans l'autre État, si elles satisfont aux prescriptions des articles précédents, en tant qu'elles sont applicables. Il en est de même pour les transactions judiciaires.*" See Conférence de la Haye de Droit International Privé, *op.cit.*, at 193.

52 In a report presented to the Council on 7 September 1926, the Economic Committee noted the following: "You will remember that, on the occasion of the Assembly of 1923, a Protocol was opened for signature by the various States for recognising the validity of

In addition, the work on the enforcement of foreign arbitral awards was perceived as the logical and necessary continuation of the Protocol of 1923. This would leave an indelible mark in the 1927 Convention, for it was framed in a way to make sure that the two instruments, Protocol and Convention, were parts of a single normative framework for the governance of arbitral proceedings involving parties from different contracting States.

The intertextuality of the two texts is clearly seen in Articles 6 and 8 of the Convention, which respectively established that the Convention was open only to Parties to the Protocol and that the denunciation of the Protocol entailed the denunciation of the Convention.[53] The Protocol and Convention were so close-knit that States interested in limiting the scope of the instrument on enforcement would have to make a reservation to that effect under the terms of the Protocol of 1923, as no clause on reservation was provided under the Convention – something of particular importance for any potential State seeking to take advantage of the dichotomy established between civil and commercial arbitration by the Protocol.[54]

The Convention of 1927 would be produced in the lapse of one year,[55] and a great number of experts came to be invited to contribute to the draft instrument. The preliminary work was performed by a "Committee of Jurists,"

arbitration agreements in contracts, especially in commercial contracts. This Protocol, which was ratified by a considerable number of States, has already largely contributed to the spread of commercial arbitration. It does not make provision, however, for the execution of arbitral awards rendered abroad. You will realise the practical importance of this question and the desirability of endeavouring by means of a further international agreement to ensure in the future the execution of such awards also. I am happy to note that the investigations of the Economic Committee on this subject have already enabled it to achieve certain results. The Committee recommends that we should authorise it to convene a meeting of expert jurists with whose help it hopes to succeed in preparing a draft international agreement. The general form of such a draft is outlined in its report." See Émile Vandervelde, 'Work of the Economic Committee during Its Nineteenth and Twentieth Sessions, Annex 905, C.521(I).1926.II.' (1926) 7 League of Nations Official Journal 1358, at 1359.

53 See Draft submitted to the Assembly, in League of Nations Secretariat, 'Opening for Signature of a Protocol Relating to the Execution of Foreign Arbitral Awards, Report of the Secretariat, Annex 2, A.II/3/1927' (1927) 56 League of Nations Official Journal, Special Supplement 70, at 73–74.

54 See Anzilotti, *Draft*, at 891.

55 The final text of the Convention was adopted and opened to signature by the Assembly under a resolution dated 26 September 1927. See League of Nations, 'Opening of a Convention Relating to the Execution of Foreign Arbitral Awards' (1927) 11 Resolutions and recommendations adopted by the Assembly during its Eight Ordinary Session – September 5th to 27th, 1927, League of Nations Official Journal, Supplement 15.

chaired by Dionizio Anzilotti, and functioning under the Economic Committee of the League – a body that operated within the purview of the Council of the League.[56] The group was composed of legal scholars, representatives of business interests and state officials.[57]

The final text of the Convention would then be prepared by the Assembly of the League based on the work done by the Committee of Jurists. It was a so-called "Sub-committee of experts" labouring under the purview of the Second Committee of the Assembly of the League that would produce the text as it was adopted. The experts assembled for this task did not act in their individual capacity, but as delegates of member States of the League.[58]

Surely the final text itself was penned by Jules Basdevant, who had been appointed the rapporteur of the Sub-committee of experts,[59] but much of the conceptual heavy lifting had already been done by the working group chaired by Anzilotti. Interestingly, the two men had similar profiles and similar careers.[60] Both, in fact, would become known for their expertise in public international law and would come to be international judges – Anzilotti at the PCIJ and Basdevant at the ICJ. One should note that the disciplinary barriers at the time seemed much more fluid than what is usually portrayed. Anzilotti

56 See Anzilotti, *Meeting*, at 582.

57 Besides Anzilotti, the members of the Committee of Jurists were the following ones: Jules Basdevant, who was a Law Professor in Paris at the time; Benjamin H. Conner, a lawyer and President of the American Chamber of Commerce in France; Vaclav Hora, a Law Professor in Prague; H. Claughton Scott, a King's Counsel; Erich Volkmar, a Privy Counsellor and Ministerial Counsellor in the German Ministry of Justice; G. Walker, a Law Professor in Vienna, who would later be replaced by Marc Leitmaier, an Austrian government official; and René Arnaud, who was a the time Assistant Secretary-General of the International Chamber of Commerce, but who would only attend the first preparatory meeting of the working group and then disappear from the records.

58 In terms of people involved, some of the individuals had already participated in the work led by Anzilotti. This was the case of Jules Basdevant (France), Marc Leitmaier (Austria), H. Claughton Scott, K.C. (Great Britain), Erich Volkmar (Germany) and Vaclav Hora (Czechoslovakia). However, other experts joined at this stage. These new members were Wladimir Molloff (Bulgaria), Holger Andersen (Denmark), Oskar Opik (Estonia), Sir Edward Maynard des Champs Chamber, K.C.I.E. (India), Nobumi Ito (Japan), Joseph Limpurg (Netherlands), Szymon Rundstein (Poland), Walther Burckhardt (Switzerland), and Vittorio Scialoja (Italy).

59 See League of Nations Secretariat, 'Sub-Committee of Jurists to Study the Question of the Execution of Foreign Arbitral Awards, Annex 2b., A.II/14/1927' (1927) 56 League of Nations Official Journal, Special Supplement 88.

60 On Basdevant's profile, see Georges Berlia, 'Le président Jules Basdevant' (1968) 33 Politique étrangère 5. On Anzilotti's profile, see Antonio Tanca, 'Dionisio Anzilotti (1867–1950) Biographical Note with Bibliography' (1992) 3 European Journal of International Law 156.

FIGURE 1 League of Nations, Geneva, meeting of the Committee of Jurists, 1927. Seating, from left to right, H. Conner, Volkmar, Anzilotti, Basdevant. Standing, from left to right, Vaclav Hora, Claugthon Scott, Gustav Walker, René Arnaud and others. Gallica, Rol, 116007.

was very comfortable writing on private international law,[61] while Basdevant, despite seemingly more at home in relation to public international law and State to State arbitration, demonstrated a sustained interest regarding the private aspects of international adjudication.[62]

Behind the scenes, the adoption of the 1927 Convention was based on the fundamental assumption that a multilateral instrument promoting legal uniformization could not go as much in detail as domestic law or a bilateral treaty. It was accepted that the document produced by the League would have to be general enough to accommodate the multitude of private

61 See Dionisio Anzilotti, *Scritti di diritto internazionale privato* (CEDAM 1960).

62 See, for instance, Jules Basdevant, 'Études sur quelques conflits de lois dans les arbitrages internationaux de la première moitié du XIXe siècle' (1906) 2 Revue de Droit International Privé et de Droit Pénal International 861; Jules Basdevant, 'Conflits de nationalité dans les arbitrages vénézuéliens de 1903–1905' (1909) 5 Revue de Droit International Privé et de Droit Pénal International 41.

international law approaches in both the seat of the arbitration and the place of enforcement.[63]

It is for this reason that the League decided to drop any plans to work on the legislative unification of the enforcement of foreign arbitral awards, favouring a more modest ambition. Rather than replacing the municipal law of Contracting Parties, the 1927 Convention established a minimum common denominator to govern the enforcement of foreign arbitral awards. Accordingly, the preparatory works of the instrument make it clear that its aim was to outline "a few formulae which would be wide and elastic enough to fit all cases."[64]

When the Committee of Jurists chaired by Anzilotti was first seized of the topic, it held a series of meetings from 27 to 29 January 1927. In these meetings, however, none of the members felt ready to deal with such a difficult project without "previous individual investigation."[65] Each member took up the responsibility to conduct their own research on the subject, which would then be sent for compilation and coordination by the Secretariat.[66] And so it was done.

Three months later, on 28 March 1927, the Anzilotti committee met again to produce their final deliberation. Two of its original members did not take part in the meeting. This was the case of G. Walker, an Austrian professor who was replaced by an Austrian government official called Marc Leitemeier, and René Arnaud who was the Deputy Secretary-General of the ICC.

The absence of Arnaud's is particularly intriguing, as no replacement was sent to the meeting. This is also a point of interest considering the centrality often attributed to the ICC in the drafting of the Convention by recent literature on the history of commercial arbitration. For instance, Schinazi, echoing the work of Lermecier and Sgard,[67] has argued that "the 1927 convention was chiefly the work of the International Chamber of Commerce."[68] Similarly, Kronke considers that "the Geneva instruments [...] were principally creatures of the International Chamber of Commerce."[69] Even still, no ICC representative

63 The Committee of Jurists considered that "a collective agreement on this subject must take all possible precautions." See Anzilotti, *Draft*, at 893–895.

64 See Anzilotti, *Meeting*, at 583.

65 See Anzilotti, *Meeting*, at 583.

66 See Anzilotti, *Meeting*, at 583.

67 See Lemercier and Sgard, *op.cit.*, at 106–112.

68 See Schinazi, *op.cit.*, at 205.

69 See Herbert Kronke, 'The Role of Private International Law: UNIDROIT and the Geneva Conventions on Arbitration' in Hélène Ruiz Fabri, Burkhard Hess and Michel Erpelding (eds), in *Peace Through Law: The Versailles Peace Treaty and Dispute Settlement After World War I* (Nomos Verlagsgesellschaft mbH & Co KG 2019), at 188.

took part in the actual drafting of the Convention, despite the fact that they had been given this opportunity. Furthermore, one finds only one direct reference to ICC arbitration practice in the actual preparatory works of the Convention – and this was done in the context of a discussion on the role of the seat in enforcement proceedings.[70]

Clearly influential, but rather neglected by specialized literature, were the people and the ideas gravitating around the Fifth Hague Conference held in 1925. Indeed, the Hague's shadows had been cast since the very reengagement of the League with the problem of enforcement of foreign arbitral awards, becoming central to the definition of the next steps to be taken in Geneva.[71]

Notably, the League of Nations mandated the Anzilotti committee to work on the enforcement of foreign arbitral awards presenting them with a document expressly inspired by the work done by the Fifth Hague Conference on Private International Law.[72] It was clear at the League that the Hague Conference could not be ignored and that it was bound to impact numerous aspects of the discussions in Geneva. This is most clear in the following extract from the report of the Anzilotti committee:

> The object of the Protocol is to ensure the recognition and execution of such awards in the Contracting States. In practice, the principal interest

70 The Committee of Jurists noted that an "award will often be made in a third country by an arbitrator who is of different nationality from either of the parties notably this is a practice of the International Chamber of Commerce," which would make it pointless to require the decision to be enforceable at the seat. See Anzilotti, *Draft*, at 892.

71 Indeed, already in March 1926, in a report presented by the Economic Committee to the Council, the following was noted: "The Committee is disposed to think that the task of finding such a solution, difficult and complicated as it must be in any case, in view of the different legal systems and procedure prevailing in the various countries, would only be rendered more difficult by attempting, as was done at the Conference on International Private Law held at The Hague in October 1925, to deal at the same time with the wider question of the mutual enforcement of judicial decisions which raises issues of a different nature. But the Hague Conference itself appears to have had in view the question of the execution of arbitral awards independently of the larger question of judgments, apparently with the desire to respond to the wishes of the commercial world which were strongly expressed at the International Chamber of Commerce. The Committee propose for the present, therefore, to confine their attention strictly to the specific question of providing better means for enforcing arbitral awards of a nature falling within the scope of the Protocol on Commercial Arbitration and given in the territory of a State party to that Protocol within the territories of the other participating States." See Émile Vandervelde, 'Work of the Economic Committee during Its Eighteenth Session, Annex 847' (1926) 7 League of Nations Official Journal 540, 568.

72 See Anzilotti, *Meeting*, 582.

> lies in the execution, but it has seemed necessary also to make special provision for recognition, in conformity with the practice of most modern Conventions on the enforcement of foreign judgments, and the scheme elaborated at the Fifth Conference of Private International Law.[73]

One sees in this extract that the notion of recognition travelled directly from the Hague to Geneva as a tribute paid to the work on the unification of private international law. This was not the only overlap between the model treaty produced at the Hague and the Convention adopted in Geneva.

A most important dimension of the interplay between Geneva and the Hague concerns the division of labour between courts and arbitral tribunals. Both the model treaty elaborated by the Fifth Hague Conference and the 1927 Convention sponsored by the League aimed at foreclosing a retrial on the merits, grounding the analysis of enforcement on formal aspects related to due process and substantial issues connected to public policy. This concretely granted arbitral tribunals an almost exclusive authority over the production of legal facts. Such cognitive authority, if not completely unbound as it was subject to a procedural control by municipal courts, would place arbitral cognition beyond the reach of a double degree of jurisdiction.

In addition, similarly to the model treaty drafted by the Fifth Hague Conference, the Convention of 1927 vested domestic judges with oversight over the arbitral manipulation of legal norms. Notably, the normative authority of arbitral tribunals would be kept under a tight leash given that the courts invited to enforce or recognize an arbitral award were given the prerogative to refuse recognition and enforcement if the submission to arbitration was invalid under the relevant applicable law,[74] if the dispute was not arbitrable under the law of the place where it is being relied upon,[75] if the tribunal was not properly constituted under the relevant applicable law,[76] if the arbitral award was not final at the seat,[77] and in case the arbitral award violates public policy of the place where it is being relied upon.[78]

The administration of arbitral procedure was also placed under the potential watch of municipal courts. It was understood that courts were to be

73 See Anzilotti, *Draft*, at 892.

74 See Article 1(a) of the 1927 Convention.

75 See Article 1(b) of the 1927 Convention.

76 See Article 1(c) of the 1927 Convention.

77 See Article 1(d) of the 1927 Convention.

78 See Article 1(e) of the 1927 Convention.

equipped with "large discretionary powers which it ought to use to ensure that the rights of the defendant party are respected in an equitable manner."[79] Notably, judges were granted a discretionary prerogative to refuse recognition and enforcement in the face of violations of due process,[80] and if the award itself was *infra, extra* or *ultra petita*.[81]

Although many of the terms established in 1927 Convention for the relation between courts and arbitral tribunals were evocative of the work done at the Hague, the League also introduced quite a few innovations for the regulation of arbitral awards. Differently from the Hague Conference, that dealt jointly with the cross-border enforcement of arbitral awards and court judgments, the work in Geneva was exclusively focused on the enforcement of arbitral awards. This allowed for a much more detailed treatment of procedural issues specific to arbitration, such as arbitrability and the validity of arbitration agreements.

In some other instances, the League would formally recognize its incompetence to deal with certain matters and would defer the issue to the appreciation of the Hague Conference. This was the case of a discussion on the law governing the arbitration agreement. The German delegation had suggested setting the law of the seat as the default applicable law to arbitration agreements, but the Assembly of the League rejected this idea on the basis that "no definition could be given in a simple formula" and that this topic would be "rather a matter for The Hague Conference on Private International Law."[82]

In other aspects, the League of Nations would make a conscious effort to depart from the Hague model, as was the case of the role of the seat over the life of the arbitral award. In this regard, and although the Geneva framework passed into history as one implementing an intricate system of double exequatur,[83] one finds in the preparatory works of the 1927 Convention an express intent to abandon the mechanism of double exequatur indirectly promoted by the Hague model.

---

79 See Anzilotti, *Draft*, at 893.

80 See Article 2(b) of the 1927 Convention.

81 See Article 2(c) of the 1927 Convention.

82 On the German proposition, see League of Nations Secretariat, *Report*, at 77. On the solution adopted, see Marc Leitmaier, 'Opening of a Convention Relating to the Execution of Foreign Arbitral Awards, Annex 2a., A.II/23/1927' (1927) 56 League of Nations Official Journal, Special Supplement 81, 83.

83 See, for instance, the views expressed by Dana H. Freyer and Hamid G. Gharavi, 'Finality and Enforceability of Foreign Arbitral Awards: From "Double Exequatur" to the Enforcement of Annulled Awards: A Suggested Path to Uniformity Amidst Diversity' (1998) 13 ICSID Review 101.

Notably, there was an attempt to loosen up the control of the seat over the award by replacing the term *res judicata* employed by the model treaty produced in the Hague with a more flexible concept of finality. This deviation caused resistance among certain delegations, especially that of the Netherlands, which considered the model produced at the Hague more expedient and in line with legal certainty.[84] One may be justified in wondering to what extent this Dutch resistance manifested an early example of the competition between the various *loci* for the control over the production of transnational legal rules. In any event, the Dutch view did not prevail and when the 1927 Convention saw the light of day the concept of finality was favoured over that of *res judicata.*

One must note, however, that this specific deviation from the Hague regime was of limited effect. At the time, it was already foreseeable that finality was not essentially different from *res judicata,* meaning simply "the exhaustion of the arbitral machinery at the country in which it is set in motion before relying on the award in another country."[85] Furthermore, the seat kept considerable authority over the destiny of the award, for finality would be appraised from the perspective of the law of the seat and enforcement ought to be refused in case the award had been annulled at the seat.[86] Similarly, the purview over the notion of arbitrability introduced by the Convention had also been attributed to the law of the seat.[87]

All in all, the codification efforts led by the League of Nations in relation to the enforcement of foreign arbitration awards were very much indebted to the Fifth Hague Conference on Private International law. Indeed, even the novelties introduced by the Convention of 1927, including some of its express deviations for the model treaty espoused by the Fifth Hague Conference, were always in a constant dialogue with the solutions retained at the Hague.

2 Mobilizing Arbitration for the Administration of War and Peace

Belle époque international lawyers had diligently deposited much hope on the authority of arbitration and arbitrators for the peaceful settlement of

84 See League of Nations Secretariat, *Sub-Committee,* at 75–76.
85 See Anzilotti, *Draft,* at 893–894.
86 See Article 2(a) of the 1927 Convention.
87 In this respect, it was noted that "the Committee has wished to emphasise that this law [of the seat] must be considered, and not to call in question the principle that the subject-matter of the award must be also arbitrable under the law governing the arbitration proceedings" See Anzilotti, *Draft,* at 892.

international disputes. The creation of the PCA, previously discussed, equipped the field of international arbitration with an important bureaucratic infrastructure and an all-encompassing procedural framework to govern its activities. However, the push towards embedding arbitral authority in the governance of war and peace would come to a sudden halt with the war of 1914–1918 and would only resurface in the interwar years.

Indeed, the reconstruction efforts in the aftermath of World War I were underlined by two important developments for the transnational expansion and codification of arbitral authority. On the one hand, arbitral procedure was made a central part of the legal mechanism created to administer the economic settlement of the war (2.1). On the other hand, international lawyers devoted much time and energy to the codification of a coercive and compulsory type of arbitration governing collective security, which, despite its concrete failure, was supposed to prevent a future war (2.2).

2.1 *The Economic Settlement of World War I*

The peace treaties following World War I provided for the liability of the Central Powers in respect of war damages.[88] The economic settlement of the war was administered under a two-tiered framework comprising the Reparations Commission and several Mixed Arbitral Tribunals. Both institutions were early experiments in international adjudication and transnationalism more broadly,[89] greatly blurring the jurisdictional boundaries between public and private international law.

The Reparations Commission was created to govern State-to-State relations concerning reparation payments. The body was given an official format with the entry into force of the Treaty of Versailles on 10 January 1920, but its *de facto*

88 For instance, Article 231 of the Treaty of Versailles read as follows: "The Allied and Associated Governments affirm and Germany accepts the responsibility of Germany and her allies for causing all the loss and damage to which the Allied and Associated Governments and their nationals have been subjected as a consequence of the war imposed upon them by the aggression of Germany and her allies." See Allied Powers, Associated Powers and Germany, 'Treaty of Peace with Germany (Treaty of Versailles)', *Treaties and other international agreements of the United States of America 1776–1949: Multilateral, 1918–1930*, vol 2 (Department of State Publication 1969).

89 For a recent multi-dimensional analysis of the dispute settlement landscape following World War I, see Michel Erpelding, Burkhard Hess and Hélène Ruiz Fabri (eds), *Peace Through Law: The Versailles Peace Treaty and Dispute Settlement After World War I* (Nomos Verlagsgesellschaft mbH & Co KG 2019). For a broader study on experiments in international adjudication, see Ignacio de la Rasilla and Jorge E Viñuales (eds), *Experiments in International Adjudication: Historical Accounts* (1st edn, Cambridge University Press 2019).

creation can be traced back to the Peace Conference of 1919.[90] The Reparations Commission was originally an inter-allied organ charged with the liquidation of damages caused by Germany and its allies during the war.[91] Gradually, however, it came to transform itself in a mechanism for the oversight of the war's economic settlement.[92] This is made clear in one of the Commission's report, which described the organ's mandate in the following terms:

> *La tâche principale de la Commission des Réparations, instituée par la Partie* VIII *du Traité de Versailles, consiste dans l'application de cette Partie du Traité; il est fort probable, et d'ailleurs naturel, que les multiples autres devoirs qui incombent à la Commission aient passé inaperçus du public. La Commission est chargée, en outre, de l'application des clauses de réparations du Traité de Saint-Germain conclu avec l'Autriche, du Traité de Trianon conclu avec la Hongrie et, bien que dans une moindre mesure, du Traité de Neuilly conclu avec la Bulgarie; il lui incombe encore en vertu de chacun de ces Traités un grand nombre de taches d'ordre financier ou administratif dont quelques-unes sont délicates et complexes et dont l'ensemble a absorbé une grande partie de son temps et de son travail. Le rôle de la Commission*

---

90 See, for instance, the description given by the Commission of its origins: "*Officiellement, la Commission des Réparations entra en fonctions le 10 janvier 1920, date de la ratification du Traité de Versailles. En réalité, son histoire remonte à plusieurs mois auparavant, au moment de la création, par la Conférence de la Paix, du Comité d'Organisation de la Commission des Réparations. Au début, les Membres de ce Comité furent pris dans le personnel des diverses Délégations à la Conférence de la Paix, sous la présidence de M. Loucheur, Ministre des régions libérées. La composition de ce Comité fut peu à peu modifié, jusqu'au moment où sa constitution devint en fait presque identique à celle de la Commission des Réparations à sa création.*" Secrétaire Général de la Commission des réparations, *Rapport sur les travaux de la Commission des réparations de 1920 à 1922, Tome 1* (F Alcan 1923), at 5–6.

91 Halpérin notes, in particular, that the "*question of fixing the amount of reparations was delegated to the Reparation Commission, as the Allied Governments were not able to find an agreement about an achieved process of evaluation or lump sum.*" See Jean-Louis Halpérin, 'Article 231 of the Versailles Treaty and Reparations: The Reparation Commission as a Place for Dispute Settlement?' in Hélène Ruiz Fabri, Burkhard Hess and Michel Erpelding (eds), *Peace Through Law: The Versailles Peace Treaty and Dispute Settlement After World War I* (Nomos Verlagsgesellschaft mbH & Co KG 2019), at 197.

92 It should be noted that the Treaty of Neuilly created a commission to administer the settlement of war reparations in relation to Bulgaria, usually referred to as the International Commission at Sofia. The Reparations Commission and the International Commission at Sofia entered into an agreement in order to coordinate their work. See Secrétaire Général de la Commission des réparations, *Rapport sur les travaux de la Commission des réparations de 1920 à 1922, Tome 2* (F Alcan 1923), at 313 and ss.

> *n'est d'ailleurs pas limité aux travaux qui lui ont été confiés expressément par les Traités. En effet, comme elle est le seul organisme interallié qui ait été institué pour une longue durée par les Traités de paix, il a paru expédient aux Gouvernements de la charger de temps à autre d'étudier et de résoudre plusieurs questions qui, sans rentrer, à proprement parler, dans ses attributions, touchent de près à son rôle principal. C'est ainsi que les Puissances alliées lui ont confié l'exécution de celles des clauses financières des Traités de paix que ces Traités ne lui avaient pas déjà expressément attribuées. Elle a de même accepté, à la demande des Puissances alliés, d'assurer la vente et la dispersion des stocks considérables de matériel de guerre allemand, militaire, naval et aéronautique remis par l'Allemagne aux Commissions de contrôle pour être détruit ou rendu inutilisable. Elle a dû se tenir en contact plus ou moins étroit avec les autres organismes chargés de l'application du Traité, principalement avec la Conférence des Ambassadeurs, la Haute Commission Interalliée des Territoires Rhénans et les diverses Commissions de contrôle. En diverses occasions, il lui a fallu se préoccuper des répercussions que pouvait avoir sur la situation économique et financière de l'Allemagne, et par suite les réparations, l'exécution des dispositions des clauses économiques du Traité de Paix, notamment de celles relatives au règlement des dettes privés d'avant-guerre concernant la mise sous séquestre de la propriété privée.*[93]

The Treaty of Versailles in its Part VIII, Annex II, laid out the institutional structure for the Reparation Commission. Reading its 23 paragraphs, one learns that the governments of the United States, the United Kingdom, France, Italy, Japan, Belgium and the Serb-Croat-Slovene State could nominate one delegate and one assistant delegate to represent them in the Commission's proceedings. One learns further that the Reparation Commission sat in divisions of five members and that four of these seats would always be occupied by representatives of the United States, the United Kingdom, France, and Italy. The fifth seat would be usually reserved to Belgium, or exceptionally would be occupied by delegates representing Japan or the Serb-Croat-Slovene State in the very strict cases defined by the instrument.[94] Although Germany was not represented at

93 See Commission des Réparations, *Rapport sur les Travaux de la Commission des Réparations de 1920 à 1922, Tome 1* (Libraire Félix Alcan, 1923), at 1–2.

94 See Treaty of Versailles Allied Powers, Associated Powers and Germany, *op.cit*, Part VIII, Annex II, paragraph 2.

the Reparations Commission, Article 233 of the Treaty of Versailles provided for its right to be heard.

The mandate entrusted to the delegates seating at the Reparations Commission was imminently political,[95] having first and foremost the task of defending the interests of the Allied powers.[96] Even still, it was also considered that the body ought to perform a somewhat independent judicial role, administering the disputes concerning reparations, as well as controlling the interpretation of the reparation clauses in the peace treaties under its purview.[97] It will be seen below that this judicial role came to be delegated to arbitral tribunals, which were called to control the interpretation of the reparation clauses in the treaty.

The proceedings of the Reparation Commission were not subject to any procedural formality, and the body was called to be "guided by justice, equity and good faith."[98] German failure to meet its obligations would allow the organ to "forthwith give notice of such default to each of the interested Powers and make recommendations as to the action to be taken in consequence of such default."[99] In such a scenario, Allied and Associated Powers would have the ability to resort to "economic and financial prohibitions and reprisals and in general such other measures as the respective Governments may determine to be necessary in the circumstances."[100]

The Mixed Arbitral Tribunals, for their part, were created by the "Economic Clauses" of the peace treaties. In the case of the Treaty of Versailles, these

95 Halpérin highlights that if delegates "did not agree with the instructions of their governments they had logically to resign." See Halpérin, *Article 231*, at 200.

96 It was acknowledged that "*la Commission des Réparations est chargée de sauvegarder les intérêt respectifs des diverses Puissances représentées.*" See Secrétaire Général de la Commission des réparations, *Tome 1*, at 7.

97 This was expressed by the Reparations Commission in the following terms: "*Elle doit, en outre, jusqu'à un certain point, remplir un rôle de juge entre les Alliés d'une part et les Puissances ex-ennemies d'autre part ; en particulier, elle a dû prononcer en pleine indépendance une sentence sur des questions telles que celle du montant des dommages dont l'Allemagne est responsable, questions qui ont une répercussion considérable, non seulement sur les intérêts financiers, mais aussi sur les intérêts politiques de toutes les Puissances directement intéressées et sur la situation économique du monde entier. La Commission est chargée, en outre, de remplir un rôle d'ordre judiciaire particulièrement difficile et délicat. Elle a pouvoir d'interpréter souverainement les dispositions du Traité contenues dans la partie relative aux Réparations.*" See Secrétaire Général de la Commission des réparations, *Tome 1*, at 7.

98 See Allied Powers, Associated Powers and Germany, *op.cit.*, Part VIII, Annex II, paragraph 11.

99 See Allied Powers, Associated Powers and Germany, *op.cit*, Part VIII, Annex II, paragraph 17.

100 See Allied Powers, Associated Powers and Germany, *op.cit.*, Part VIII, Annex II, paragraph 18.

clauses were laid out in its Part x, from Article 264 to 312, bestowing upon individuals a direct claim against Germany for damages suffered in relation to the war.[101] In order to operationalize this mechanism, each Allied and Associated Power was granted the ability to create an arbitral body to deal with their national's claims against the German government.

The jurisdiction of theses tribunals encompassed, among others, outstanding debt not settled through the mechanism of clearing offices,[102] as well as restitution and compensation concerning property rights in enemy territory.[103] Furthermore, Mixed Arbitral Tribunals had supervisory jurisdiction over enemy national courts, which included the prerogative to overturn decisions from these courts.[104] This is certainly a most interesting feature when it comes to the division of labour between courts and arbitral tribunals, for it may characterize a unique instance in which arbitral authority was given precedence over judicial authority in the application of law.

The creation of Mixed Arbitral Tribunals has been credited to the mistrust war victors had of the national courts of defeated powers in relation to their commitment to the implementation of the peace treaties.[105] It is estimated that around 36 Mixed Arbitral Tribunals were established following the war,

101 The Treaty of Versailles, Part x, Article 297, letter *e* read as follows: "The nationals of Allied and Associated Powers shall be entitled to compensation in respect of damage or injury inflicted upon their property, rights or interests, including any company or association in which they are interested, in German territory as it existed on August 1, 1914, by the application either of the exceptional war measures or measures of transfer mentioned in paragraphs 1 and 3 of the Annex hereto. The claims made in this respect by such nationals shall be investigated, and the total of the compensation shall be determined by the Mixed Arbitral Tribunal provided for in Section vi or by an Arbitrator appointed by that Tribunal. This compensation shall be borne by Germany, and may be charged upon the property of German nationals within the territory or under the control of the claimant's State. This property may be constituted as a pledge for enemy liabilities under the conditions fixed by paragraph 4 of the Annex hereto. The payment of this compensation may be made by the Allied or Associated State, and the amount will be debited to Germany." See Allied Powers, Associated Powers and Germany, *op.cit.*

102 See Allied Powers, Associated Powers and Germany, *op.cit.*, Article 296, Annex, paragraph 16.

103 See Allied Powers, Associated Powers and Germany, *op.cit.*, Article 297.

104 See Allied Powers, Associated Powers and Germany, *op.cit.*, Articles 296 and 305.

105 Marta Requejo Isidro and Burkhard Hess, 'International Adjudication of Private Rights: The Mixed Arbitral Tribunals in the Peace Treaties of 1919–1922', *Peace Through Law: The Versailles Peace Treaty and Dispute Settlement After World War I* (Nomos Verlagsgesellschaft mbH & Co KG 2019), at 242.

with some 70,000 cases being tried by these bodies. The Franco-German Mixed Arbitral Tribunal alone dealt with more than 23,000 cases.[106]

Despite the ambition of being "neutral," at least in relation to domestic courts, observers at the time were concerned with the impartiality of Mixed Arbitral Tribunals.[107] In hindsight, the concerns were most likely justified, but recent literature attribute the partiality of Mixed Arbitral Tribunals less to bad faith of its members and more to the way they were structured.[108] For instance, the language of proceedings was usually that of the Allied powers, something that would privilege the nationals of the war victors.[109] Similarly, the seat of these tribunals was often the capital city of one of the concerned Allied powers – and the tribunals established by Belgium, Romania and Greece were seated in Paris.[110]

Both Mixed Arbitral Tribunals and the Reparation Commission would be disbanded by the so-called Young Plan.[111] The plan aimed at giving a final response to the problem of war reparations and was brought to life by Owen D. Young – someone who actually had been very much involved in the promotion of private international arbitration at the ICC. Interestingly, the central role played by people gravitating around the ICC in the economic settlement of the war seems of relevance to understand the place of arbitral procedure in the administration of reparation payments. Notably, this specific instance of ICC's influence in relation to the transnationalisation of arbitral authority has been somewhat neglected by specialized literature on the history of arbitration.

Two individuals are particularly important in this regard, i.e., Young himself and Étienne Clémentel. Young and Clémentel were certainly no strangers to each other, and both were well versed in the ongoing debates on reparations and arbitration. As it will be seen below, Young was a key player all throughout

106 See Requejo Isidro and Hess, *op.cit.*, at 247.

107 See Rudolf Blühdorn, 'Le fonctionnement et la Jurisprudence des Tribunaux Arbitraux Mixtes créés par les traités de Paris', in *Collected Courses of the Hague Academy of International Law*, vol. 41 (Brill 1932), at 171.

108 It has been argued that "partiality was not the result of bad faith but rather the natural consequence of the origin and training of arbitrators, who were more easily convinced by arguments presented from a familiar point of view – the one corresponding to their nationality or to their national law." See Requejo Isidro and Hess, *op.cit.*, 257.

109 It is noted that: "Finally, the question of the language of the process was considered key to the inequality of the parties. According to section 8, the VPT itself foresaw the election by the Allied Power among French, English, Italian or Japanese, except if otherwise agreed." See Requejo Isidro and Hess, *op.cit.*, at 257.

110 See Blühdorn, *op.cit.*, at 178.

111 See Requejo Isidro and Hess, *op.cit.*, at 252.

the resolution of the crisis concerning German reparation payments. Clémentel, for his part, would be a leading French negotiator of the agreements that brought the occupation of the Ruhr to an end through the implementation of a first plan to restore reparation payments – a settlement that came to be known as the Dawes plan. The two men were colleagues at the ICC Council and were likely privy to the work of the ICC Financial Committee towards a business settlement of reparations.[112] Clémentel, for instance, had spoken in 1923 on behalf of the ICC in favour of the reestablishment of international trade relations through the closure of the "hateful book of war."[113]

In addition, one knows that the two men were actively involved in the process of codification of private international arbitration. Owen D. Young had taken a prominent role in the creation of the ICC Arbitration Court,[114] and was a longstanding supporter of commercial arbitration in general. Étienne Clémentel would be a leading voice in the French Senate advocating for the reform of the French legislation on arbitration law.[115]

The interplay of German reparations and commercial interests is all the more remarkable considering that one of the plans to re-establish reparation payments promoted the transfer of all German railways, once controlled by the Reich, to a private company created under the terms of that plan.[116] Similarly, all plans implemented to solve the reparations crisis relied heavily on international loans operated by American banks, especially JP Morgan & Co, which would grant Germany fresh money for the specific purpose of paying back some of its war debt.

Indeed, the financialization of war debt would produce a highly sensitive connection between public and private international law, one which would heavily rely on arbitral authority for the transnational governance of these economic relations. This is corroborated by a contemporary of the crisis, for whom "[t]he replacement, at the London conference, of sanctions by provisions for

112 Viz Ridgeway, *op.cit.*, at 183.

113 During the Second Congress of the ICC, held in Rome on 18 March 1923, Étienne Clémentel, president of the ICC at the time, urged the presents to "close the hateful book of war." See Ridgeway, *op.cit.*, at 169.

114 Ridgeway, *op.cit.*, at 321–323.

115 See Schinazi, *op.cit.*, at 77–78.

116 The company would accommodate foreign interests in the board of directors, but the majority of its directors were to be German. Interestingly, it was provided that disputes between the company and the Reich would be under the authority of a special German court, but upon appeal some of these disputes could be heard by an international arbitral tribunal. See Carl Bergmann, *The History of Reparations* (E Benn 1927), at 258.

arbitration, completed the transformation of the reparations contract from a political settlement guaranteed by military coercion to a commercial contract with an arbitration clause."[117]

Considering the foregoing, the next two sections will dive in more detail on the contribution of the economic settlement of World War I to the codification of arbitral procedure and the transnational expansion of its authority.

2.1.1 The Place of Arbitration in the Settlement of Germany's Reparation Payments

When French and Belgium soldiers marched over the Ruhr valley on that 11 January 1923, the infant multi-lateral system of international law was brought to an early stress test. The military move was triggered by outstanding German reparation payments, giving rise to a two-year occupation of the Ruhr. The League of Nations was an early-born and force was unliterally used as an enforcement mechanism to the great dismay of many.

The 1919 Peace Conferences had been unable to reach an agreement on the optimal level of reparation payments. In fact, German liability was only liquidated in April 1921 by the Reparations Commission, being set at a total of 132 billion gold marks.[118] That same year, a schedule of payments, known as the London Schedule, structured German war obligations on three categories of debt instruments, i.e., A Bonds, B Bonds and C Bonds.[119] As noted above, this financialization of war debt would make the issue as much of a commercial concern as a political one.

Already in the summer of 1922 it was clear that Germany would be unable to service its debt. The German economy was in a state of chaos and the depreciation of its currency was rampant. While Germany attributed its economic

---

117 See Ridgeway, *op.cit.*, at 190.

118 It is argued that the amount was a compromise reflecting "the lowest amount that public opinion in continental receiver states would tolerate." See Sally Marks, 'The Myths of Reparations' (1978) 11 Central European History 231, at 236.

119 The A Bonds covered 12 billion gold marks concerning the unpaid part of a 20 billion gold marks provided by the treaty of Versailles as interim payment for reparations, while the B Bonds amounted to 38 billion gold marks. Together, A Bonds and B Bonds had a face value of 50 billion gold marks or 12,5 billion US dollars at the time. The remainder of German war debt were allocated in C Bonds, that is, a total of 82 billion gold marks. Interestingly, Sally Marks noted that "C Bonds, which contained the bulk of the German obligation, were deliberately designed to be chimerical […] and their primary function was to mislead public opinion in the receiver countries into believing that the 132-billion-mark figure was being maintained)." See Marks, *op.cit.*, at 237.

downfall to the payment of reparations, there was an increasing suspicion among the allies that German authorities were actively depreciating the Deutsch mark to avoid the payment of its war debt.[120]

Naturally, the occupation of the Ruhr led to an international crisis and to a debate on its legality.[121] On 30 November 1923, the Reparations Commission created two Committee of Experts with the respective tasks of "considering the means of balancing the Budget and the measures to be taken to stabilize [German] currency" and "estimating the amount of exported capital and of bringing it back into Germany."[122] The work of this expert group is credited with ending the occupation of the Ruhr and the plan passed into history as the Dawes plan due to the chairmanship of Charles G. Dawes.[123]

Dawes was an American General, banker and future vice-president of the United States. Even still, it would be another member sitting in the Dawes committee who would take the lead on the debates regarding reparations. This leadership role was assumed by Owen D. Young, who is often attributed with the intellectual fatherhood of the Dawes plan.[124] As a result of his influence on the matter, Young was appointed by the Reparations Commission as the first Agent General for Reparation Payments, that is, the official in charge of administering the implementation of the plan.[125]

Once the committee chaired by Dawes issued its report presenting a way out to the stalemate on reparation payments, the matter was passed on to the hands of diplomats and numerous government officials. From 16 July to 16 August 1924, delegations from Belgium, France, Italy, Germany, Great Britain, and the United States met in London to discuss the implementation of the plan. France was particularly weary of a possible German default, but other delegations tried to persuade the French officials to abandon the use of force as mechanism of compliance.[126]

---

120 See Marks, *op.cit.*, at 238.

121 See Ernest Schuster, 'The Question as to the Legality of the Ruhr Occupation' (1924) 18 American Journal of International Law 407.

122 See Rufus Cutler Dawes, *The Dawes Plan in the Making* (The Bobbs-Merrill Company 1925), at 285–286.

123 See Nicholas Roosevelt, 'The Ruhr Occupation' (1925) 4 Foreign Affairs 112.

124 Viz Marks, *op.cit.*, at 246.

125 George A Finch, 'The London Conference on the Application of the Dawes Plan' (1924) 18 American Journal of International Law 707, at 707.

126 See Peter Jackson, *Beyond the Balance of Power: France and the Politics of National Security in the Era of the First World War* (Cambridge University Press 2013), at 454.

Among the French delegates present in London was former ICC president Étienne Clémentel, who was now the minister of Finance in the Herriot government. During the negotiations, Clémentel suggested that the evacuation of the Ruhr should be conditioned to the adoption of a commercial treaty with Germany.[127] Furthermore, such instrument was to be equipped with an arbitral mechanism vested with coercive sanctions for the declaration of an eventual German default.[128]

The commercial treaty was not adopted, but arbitration was ultimately embedded in the governance of reparation payments. The Dawes plan gave rise to a series of agreements,[129] and in all these documents an arbitration clause was inserted. For instance, the agreement signed in London on 9 August 1924 between the German government and the Reparations Commission contained an arbitration clause that read as follows:

> Any dispute which may arise between the Reparation Commission and the German Government with regard to the interpretation either of the present agreement and its schedules or of the experts' plan or of the German legislation enacted in execution of that plan, shall be submitted to arbitration in accordance with the methods to be fixed and subject to the conditions to be determined by the London conference for questions of the interpretation of the experts' plan.[130]

127 See Jackson, *op.cit.*, at 454.

128 Jackson states the following: "French negotiators had called for arbitration agreements as part of the architecture of the new security system they had proposed at Chequers the previous June. In subsequent negotiations in Paris, Herriot had admitted the possibility of a role for arbitration in the process of declaring a German default. All of this was in keeping with the importance attributed to arbitration, and the rule of law more generally, in Radical Party international doctrine. It was entirely consistent with Cartel policy prescriptions, therefore, when French negotiators 'expressed keen interest' in the idea of using arbitration to resolve future disputes on the reparations commission. Henri Fromageot, the chief jurisconsulte at the Quai d'Orsay, indicated to his British colleagues that his political superiors favoured such a solution." See Jackson, *op.cit.*, at 456.

129 There were four agreements stemming from the Dawes plan. The first one was adopted on 9 August 1924 by the Reparations Commission on behalf of the Allied and Associated Powers. A second agreement was adopted on 30 August 1924 between the States present in London to discuss the agreement of 9 August 1924. A third agreement was entered by Germany and Allied and Associated Powers the same 30 August 1924 concerning the expert plan for the payment of German reparations. Finally, a fourth agreement was also adopted on 30 August 1924 amending the Treaty of Versailles in its Annex II, Part VII. See Finch, *op.cit.*

130 See Reparation Commission and Germany, 'Agreement between the Reparation Commission and the German Government, Signed at London, August 9, 1924' (1925) 19 American Journal of International Law, Supplement Ibid., at 25, Article III, letter b.

A more detailed arbitration clause was laid out in an agreement entered by the Allied Powers and Germany, which was signed in London on 30 August 1924. Pursuant to that clause, the arbitral tribunal charged with the task of interpreting the Dawes plan was to function as follows:

> The procedure for the settlement of disputes contemplated in Article III (b) of the said agreement of August 9, 1924, shall be as follows:
>
> Subject to the powers of interpretation conferred upon the Reparation Commission by paragraph 12 of annex II to Part VIII of the Treaty of Versailles and subject to the provisions as to arbitration existing elsewhere, and in particular in the Experts' Plan or in the German legislation enacted in execution of that plan, all disputes which may arise between the Reparation Commission and Germany with regard to the interpretation either of the agreement concluded between them, the Experts' Plan, or the German legislation enacted in execution of that plan, shall be submitted for decision to three arbitrators appointed for five years; one by the Reparation Commission, one by the German Government, and the third, who shall act as president, by agreement between the Reparation Commission and the German Government, or failing such agreement, by the president for the time being of the Permanent Court of International Justice.
>
> Before giving a final decision and without prejudice to the questions at issue, the president, on the request of the first party applying therefor, may order any appropriate provisional measures in order to avoid an interruption in the regular working of the plan and to safeguard the respective rights of the parties.
>
> Subject to any decision of the arbitrators to the contrary the procedure shall be governed by the provisions of the Convention of The Hague of October 18, 1907, on the pacific settlement of international disputes.[131]

The clause in question laid out a somewhat detailed procedural framework to govern arbitral proceedings arising in connection to reparation payments. One must immediately note that the jurisdiction of the arbitral tribunal was directly derived from the Reparation Commission's prerogative to interpret the Treaty of Versailles. Indeed, the Reparation Commission had been vested with "wide latitude as to its control and handling of the whole reparation problem

131 See Allied Governments and Germany, 'Agreement between the Allied Governments and the German Government Concerning the Agreement of August 9, 1924, between the German Government and the Reparation Commission' (1925) 19 American Journal of International Law, Supplement 36.

as dealt with in this part of the present treaty and shall have the authority to interpret its provisions,"[132] which was now passed on to the arbitral body in charge of overseeing the implementation of the Dawes plan. In sum, an arbitral body received delegated authority from the Reparation Commission to oversee the implementation of the plan put in place to govern the systemic aspects of war debt.

The constitution of the arbitral tribunal would suffer modifications even before the body had begun its works. Instead of three members, provided by the clause quoted above, it came to be agreed that the arbitral tribunal should be composed of five members – and two of its members were supposed to be nationals of neutral countries during the war. In addition, it was decided that the president of the tribunal was to be an American citizen. These changes were introduced in order to allow that "the members of the tribunal appointed by common agreement of the parties or impartial authority, outnumber those nominated by one party alone in the proportion of 3 to 2, and to take some of the weight off the shoulders of the chairman."[133] The appointment of arbitrators, then, was to be done as follows: the German government and the Reparation Commission would appoint one arbitrator each, and the three remaining members of the tribunal would be appointed either by common agreement or, failing such agreement, by the president of the PCIJ.

Concretely, the Reparation Commission and Germany appointed respectively Charles Rist, a lawyer and economist of French nationality, and A. Mendelssohn-Bartholdy, a lawyer and economist of German nationality. Then, through party agreement, Marc Wallenberg, a Swedish banker, and A.G Kröller, a Dutch industrialist, were appointed as co-arbitrators. Finally, also through party-agreement, Walter P. Cooke, an American lawyer, was selected to sit as president of the tribunal. Cooke would preside over the first case heard by the tribunal but would later be replaced following his re-assignment as the American delegate to the Reparation Commission. His replacement was Thomas Nelson Perkins, also an American lawyer, who would preside over the second and third cases heard by the tribunal.

There were only three occasions in which the tribunal was called to interpret the Dawes plan, answering several questions on the matter of reparation payments. It was clear that the economic impact of the decisions taken by the tribunal were of an unprecedented nature, as the awards rendered were bound

132 See Allied Powers, Associated Powers and Germany, *op.cit.*, Part VIII, Annex II, paragraph 12.

133 See John Fischer Williams, 'The Tribunal for the Interpretation of the Dawes Plan' (1928) 22 American Journal of International Law 797, at 798.

to deeply affect the German economy and global economic flows.[134] One finds in these proceedings an early example of the transnational authority of arbitration for the governance of an ever more globalized economy.

All questions submitted for interpretation were filed by Germany and essentially sought to reduce the burden of its reparation payments. In this regard, the decisions rendered by the Dawes arbitral tribunal tried to guarantee the maximum payment of war debt while maintaining the stability of German finances.

In the first award rendered, dated 24 March 1926, the tribunal was called to evaluate the scope of the annuities provided for by the Dawes plan – annuities that were envisioned as a yearly sum to be paid by Germany and representing a fraction of German obligations arising from the peace treaties. The background issue was to ascertain whether the payments made under the Dawes plan covered all Germany's war liabilities, which would have the practical effect of discharging it from any extra payments in excess to the Dawes annuities. In particular, the tribunal was called to answer whether certain payments made in relation to insurance funds of Alsace-Lorraine and Upper Silesia[135] and payments of civil and military pensions earned in Alsace-Lorraine on 11 November 1918 were comprised in the Dawes annuities.[136] In addition, the tribunal had also to decide whether restitutions in species provided for by Article 238 of the Treaty of Versailles and payments made by Germany to Great Britain for the supply of coal to the steamship Jerusalem were covered by the annuities.

The first three questions were answered in the affirmative, while the other two were answered in the negative. This meant that sums paid in connection to the insurance funds of Alsace-Lorraine and Upper Silesia were to be discounted from the annuities, as well as the sums paid in relation to civil and military pensions in Alsace-Lorraine. Conversely, restitution under Article 238 of the Treaty of Versailles was to be considered as a separate obligation.[137] In

134 See, for instance, the following account: "These two latter decisions of 1927 and 1928 dealt with very large figures. In particular the decision of 1927 would, had it been given in favor of Germany, have reduced the amount of the Dawes Annuities by something like 9,000,000,000 gold marks – say, $1,800,000,000 or £450,000,000 – a much larger sum, so far as the writer knows, than has ever been at issue in any lawsuit, national or international." See Williams, *op.cit.*, at 801–802.

135 These payments were ordered by the Council of the League respectively on 21 June 1921 and 9 December 1924.

136 See Walter P Cook and others, 'Award Delivered on March 24, 1926', *Reports of International Arbitral Awards/Recueil des Sentences Arbitrales* (United Nations 2006), at 876–877.

137 In this regard, the tribunal followed the Reparation Commission argument that "property taken away from Allied territory during the war was not to be regarded as properly

relation to the sums due for the supply of coal to the steamship Jerusalem, the tribunal considered that the "transactions which took place were of a private character" and that "the British Government did not act as Government but saw fit to supply coal to those responsible for the s.s. Jerusalem against a consideration."[138]

A second award was rendered on 29 January 1927, after the tribunal was again called to analyse the scope of the Dawes annuities. This time, the concrete question submitted to the arbitrators was whether compensation paid or to be paid by the German government to their nationals resulting from the retention, liquidation or transfer of German national's property, rights, or interests under the provisions of the treaty were to be discounted from the annuities. The tribunal held that such compensation was not covered by the Dawes annuities, for these payments were to be "looked upon as destined to the exclusive economic benefit of the Allied and Associated Powers."[139]

A third arbitral award was issued on 29 May 1928. As it had happened in the previous two cases submitted by Germany, the arbitrators had once again to determine the scope of the Dawes annuities. Germany now presented three separate questions, that were nevertheless analysed by the tribunal jointly as one fundamental issue. In essence, the tribunal had to decide whether Germany was to be given a credit against the annuities for the value of enemy private property, rights and interests taken in Allied or Associated States pursuant to Articles 297 or 243 of the Treaty of Versailles.[140] The conclusion of the tribunal was that the proceeds of the liquidation of German private property, rights, and interests by the Allies and Associated countries could not be considered a contribution to the annuities, for the Dawes plan expressly provided for the sources of the payments and these proceeds were not one of such sources.[141]

German; not being properly German, its restoration could not give rise to pecuniary credit in favour of Germany." See Cook and others, *op.cit.,* at 882.

138 See Cook and others, *op.cit.*, at 882.

139 Thomas Nelson Perkins and others, 'Award No. II, Delivered on January 29, 1927', *Reports of International Arbitral Awards/Recueil des Sentences Arbitrales* (United Nations 2006), at 890.

140 Thomas Nelson Perkins and others, 'Award No. III, Delivered on May 29, 1928', *Reports of International Arbitral Awards/Recueil des Sentences Arbitrales* (United Nations 1928), at 894–895.

141 The tribunal held the following: "In the opinion of the Tribunal the proceeds of the property in question cannot be held to be a contribution to the annuities. The Experts begin in Section IX of Part I of the Plan by providing that Germany shall make payment from three sources: (A) from her ordinary budget; (B) from Railway Bonds and Transport Tax; and (C) from Industrial Debentures. They then analyse these sources and the amount which in their opinion can be derived in the several years from each, and in Section X they

Beyond the great variety of economic issues governed by this arbitral tribunal, as seen from the cases cited, one must also highlight the procedural convergence of these arbitrations with the proceedings conducted under the PCA framework. There existed a considerable intertextuality between the arbitration agreements under the Dawes plan and the 1907 Hague Convention. Most notably, the last paragraph in the arbitration clause inserted in the agreement entered by the Allied Governments and Germany provided that, subject to the discretion of arbitrators, "the procedure shall be governed by the provisions of the Convention of The Hague of October 18, 1907, on the pacific settlement of international disputes."[142]

This intertextuality created a bridge between the arbitral tribunal interpreting the Dawes plan and the codified procedural practice of the PCA. Furthermore, the Dawes arbitral tribunal was seated in the Hague, which made the circulation of informal knowledge between the two bodies a likely event. In formal terms, all three decisions discussed above were similar to those rendered in PCA proceedings.[143] At this point in time, it was still common to find PCA decisions at the crossroads of French and Anglo-American judicial traditions. Accordingly, these awards would be relatively short and contain at least two sections. In the first part, the tribunal would state the issue at stake, the procedural background and decision rendered, being structured pursuant to the French judicial style of "*phrase unique*" (Whereas ... Whereas ... Therefore). Then, in the second part, the tribunal would state the reasons for the of the decision in a more Anglo-American discursive manner.

Even still, the arbitral tribunal created by the Dawes plan had been vested with great procedural discretion and could deviate from that procedural framework in case it considered appropriate. Consequently, the Dawes arbitral tribunal introduced some innovations in the conduct of international arbitral proceedings.[144] In particular, the arbitral tribunal embraced the practice

summarise their conclusions. Thereafter in Section XII they provide that all these payments shall be made in gold marks or their equivalent in German currency into the Bank of Issue to the credit of the 'Agent for Reparation Payments.' The proceeds of the liquidation are not one of the sources named by them. They are not realised in German currency, and they are not paid into the Bank of Issue to the credit of the Agent for Reparation Payments." See Perkins and others, *op.cit.*, at 897.

142 See Allied Governments and Germany, 'Agreement between the Allied Governments and the German Government Concerning the Agreement of August 9, 1924, between the German Government and the Reparation Commission.'

143 In this regard, see Permanent Court of Arbitration, *Island of Palmas* (*United States/The Netherlands*). Available at: <https://pca-cpa.org/en/cases/94/>. Accessed on 7 April 2022. Still, the French judicial style was diminishing in influence.

144 For an overview, see Williams, *op.cit.*, at 799.

of laying out terms of reference to guide the administration of proceedings, a practice that is now a standard feature in arbitral proceedings and which was not quite so common at the time. These terms of reference the tribunal labelled "Terms of Submission," being used to organize the proceedings both in relation to its scope and duration. Thus, the "Terms of Submission" would provide an exact delimitation of questions submitted to the tribunal, as well as the schedule of submissions and hearings.[145]

Another procedural innovation introduced was the practice of having successive submissions instead of concomitant ones. It was noted by commentators at the time that "this procedure is obviously more convenient than what used to be in an international matter the regular procedure by which the two disputing governments fired both at the same time when each was therefore perforce in ignorance of the opponent's contentions."[146] These continuities and discontinuities in procedural practice under the Dawes arbitral tribunal provide evidence of a gradual and cumulative development of arbitral technique, which would then inform and feed supervening codification initiatives.

2.1.2 The Authority of Arbitral Procedure in the Administration of Enemy Debt under the Treaty of Versailles

Economic war was a central part of the war efforts. Beyond the seizure of enemy property in the adversary's territory, prohibitions on trading with the enemy were imposed throughout the duration of the war.[147] With the closure of hostilities and the widespread desire to re-establish the normality of trade, these measures would haunt peace negotiators.

The Treaty of Versailles offered the possibility of vindicating a broad array of private rights,[148] including what was then called "enemy debt," that is, pecuniary obligations between private parties of belligerent countries.[149] Indeed, it became clear that a considerable number of pending payments for private

145 The submissions were four in total, and were composed of the "case," "counter-case," reply and rejoinder. See Williams, *op.cit.*, at 799.

146 See Williams, *op.cit.*, at 799.

147 See Blühdorn, *op.cit.*, at 142.

148 For an overview of Mixed Arbitral Tribunals' jurisdiction, see JP Niboyet, 'Les Tribunaux Arbitraux Mixtes organisés en éxecution des traités de paix' (1922) 7 Bulletin de l'Institut Intermediaire International 215, 222–234. See also Karl Strupp, 'The Competence of the Mixed Arbitral Courts of the Treaty of Versailles' (1923) 17 The American Journal of International Law 661; Paul De Auer, 'The Competency of Mixed Arbitral Tribunals' (1927) 13 Transactions of the Grotius Society XVII.

149 See Articles 296 and 297, in Allied Powers, Associated Powers and Germany, *op.cit.*, at 175–185.

contractual relations between the nationals of belligerent parties had to be settled. The mechanism created to govern these private relations brought together amicable and contentious forms of dispute management into one single transnational procedural framework. The settlement of enemy debt is of particular importance to understand how the authority of arbitration was gradually placed at the intersection of public and private international law,[150] becoming a preferential locus for the governance of transnational economic relations.

Indeed, the mechanism introduced to administer enemy debt highlights the fluid boundaries between public and private international law jurisdictions, and the constitutive role of hybridity in the expansion of arbitral authority. The singularity of such a novel jurisdiction did not go unnoticed at the time. Niboyet, for example, argued then that the "*juridiction organisée en exécution des derniers traités de paix est donc quelque chose de tout nouveau et d'intermédiaire entre la juridiction interne et l'arbitrage international.*"[151]

In order to operationalize this transnational jurisdiction, the Treaty of Versailles provided for the contracting parties to "prohibit within their territory all legal process relating to payment of enemy debts, except in accordance with the provision of this Annex."[152] Then, a multi-tiered process was established comprising a network of Clearing Offices and Mixed Arbitral Tribunals to conduct the micro-governance of enemy debt.

The first level of the mechanism consisted of local Clearing Offices, which were bodies charged with the task of processing, verifying, collecting, accounting, and distributing any relevant payments.[153] Interestingly, the procedural regime laid out in the peace treaties made the contracting States the ultimate guarantors of enemy debt,[154] and this created a situation in which States would

150 This was clearly stated by some tribunals, which considered that "[*l*]*e droit conféré aux particuliers par le Traité est un droit direct et indépendant qui doit être considéré pour lui-même si les conditions auxquelles l'art. 297 le subordonne sont … réalisées; on n'est pas fondé à le contester en invoquant des dispositions du Traité relatives aux rapports entre États.*" See JC Witenberg, 'Les jugements des Tribunaux Arbitraux Mixtes et le plan Dawes' (1927) 54 Journal du Droit International 307, 310.

151 See Niboyet, *Tribunaux*, at 216.

152 See Article 296, Annex, para. 3, in Allied Powers, Associated Powers and Germany, *op.cit.*, at 178.

153 See Article 296, Annex, para. 1–15, in Allied Powers, Associated Powers and Germany, *op.cit.*, at 177–180.

154 The Treaty of Versailles, for instance, reads as follows: "Each of the High Contracting Parties shall be respectively responsible for the payment of such debts due by its nationals, except in the cases where before the war the debtor was in a state of bankruptcy or failure, or had given formal indication of insolvency or where the debt was due by a company

have to advance the corresponding amount for all payments certified by the Clearing Offices mechanism. Pursuant to this system, each State would then be responsible for recovering any sums advanced on behalf of their nationals,[155] making it clear that enemy debt was as much of a public concern as it was a private one.

Concretely, procedure before Clearing Offices functioned as follows. First, a private creditor would notify one's local Clearing Office (the "Creditor Clearing Office") of a claim to enemy debt – and the notice was to be accompanied by all the relevant documents to substantiate the claim. Then, the Creditor Clearing Office would notify the claim to the corresponding local Clearing Office of the debtor (the "Debtor Clearing Office"). Finally, the Debtor Clearing Office would notify the debtor, who could admit or contest the claim.

Two outcomes were possible. If the debt was admitted, the amount at stake would be credited by the Debtor Clearing Office to the Creditor Clearing Office, which would ultimately pay the amount due. If the debt was contested, then reasons had to be provided for such non-admission of debt. This would lead the two Clearing Offices to analyse the matter together in view of bringing the parties to an agreed settlement. However, if the Debtor and Creditor Clearing Offices could not agree on whether the debt was due, or in case a dispute existed between creditor and debtor, then it would be possible to submit the dispute to either an *ad hoc* arbitral tribunal, to the competent Mixed Arbitral Tribunal, or, under very restricted circumstances, to the courts of the debtor's place of domicile.[156]

Mixed Arbitral Tribunals was the preferred second-tier jurisdiction overseeing the settlement of enemy debt. These bodies enjoyed semi-permanent status, being bilaterally created by the former belligerent countries in the terms of

whose business has been liquidated under emergency legislation during the war. Nevertheless, debts due by the inhabitants of territory invaded or occupied by the enemy before the Armistice will not be guaranteed by the States of which those territories form part." See Allied Powers, Associated Powers and Germany, *op.cit.*, Article 296, letter b.

155 See Allied Powers, Associated Powers and Germany, *op.cit*, Article 296, Annex, para. 14.

156 This was laid out in the following terms: "Where the two Clearing Offices are unable to agree whether a debt claimed is due, or in case of a difference between an enemy debtor and an enemy creditor or between the Clearing Offices, the dispute shall either be referred to arbitration if the parties so agree under conditions fixed by agreement between them, or referred to the Mixed Arbitral Tribunal provided for in Section VI hereafter. At the request of the Creditor Clearing Office the dispute may, however, be submitted to the jurisdiction of the Courts of the place of domicile of the debtor." See Article 296, Annex, para. 16, in Allied Powers, Associated Powers and Germany, *op.cit.*, at 180.

the peace treaties. In the case of the Treaty of Versailles, Mixed Arbitral Tribunals were established between each of the Allied and Associated Powers with Germany.

At the time, some ink was spilled on the nature of Mixed Arbitral Tribunals, for "international" was an adjective then reserved to state-to-state relations. There were few that saw these bodies as essentially international.[157] Among those, some would consider them as *"véritables tribunaux internationaux, ayant pouvoir d'établir eux-mêmes leur procedure."*[158] Others accorded partial internationality to Mixed Arbitral Tribunal, arguing that they performed limited international jurisdictional acts stemming from the specific international attributions vested on them.[159] Many, however, did not hesitate to see these bodies as a special type of domestic jurisdiction. It was then argued that the only particularity of Mixed Arbitral Tribunals in relation to domestic jurisdictions relied on the fact that their decisions were enforceable abroad without the need of exequatur.[160] That said, now one may safely state that Mixed Arbitral Tribunals were an early example of a transnational arbitral jurisdiction, placed at the intersection of the national/international and public/private axis.

The concrete organization of procedure varied from one Mixed Arbitral Tribunal to the next, for each of them was vested with discretion to dispose of their own procedural framework. Recent scholarship has grouped into three models the diverse procedural experiences of these many Mixed Arbitral Tribunals.[161] The first model was the one developed by the Franco-German Mixed Arbitral

157 Addressing the American experience, which was much more international to the extent that it fully embedded diplomatic protection within the MAT, see Arthur Burchard, 'The Mixed Claims Commission and German Property in the United States of America' (1927) American Journal of International Law 472, 476.

158 See Witenberg, *op.cit.*, at 308.

159 Blühdorn considers the following: *"En général, on entend par 'tribunal international' tout tribunal qui doit décider un litige entre deux États. Selon l'article 304-b, al.2, les T.A.M. étaient aussi compétents pour décider des différends nés entre particuliers ; ils n'étaient certainement pas, dans cette fonction, des tribunaux internationaux. Par contre, quand les T.A.M. avaient à décider si une dette ou créance tombait ou nous sous le coup des dispositions de l'article 296, ils devaient bien être considérés comme tribunaux internationaux. Car il s'agissait alors de la question de savoir si l'État de l'office débiteur devait ou non porter sous sa garantie une certaine somme au crédit de l'État adverse."* See Blühdorn, *op.cit.*, at 144.

160 For an overview of the discussion of the nature of Mixed Arbitral Tribunals, see Requejo Isidro and Hess, *op.cit.*, at 264–265.

161 On the three models, see Requejo Isidro and Hess, *op.cit.*, at 254.

Tribunal, which would considerably influence the work of the Italian-German tribunal. The second model was the one adopted by the Anglo-German Mixed Arbitral Tribunal. This model was strongly inspired by the English procedural tradition and was adopted as a template by the Japanese-German Mixed Arbitral Tribunal. The third model was the framework put forth by the Belgium-German Mixed Arbitral Tribunal, which served as inspiration for the bodies constituted by Yugoslavia, Czechoslovakia, and Poland.

However, the three models were not completely at odds. A certain procedural pattern was usually followed by most of these bodies, regardless of the way procedure came to be codified.[162] Accordingly, time-limits would be established for the submission of claims, the statement of claim had to lay out a description of facts, the law applicable and the evidence to be produced. The conduction of proceedings was structured around one single hearing, which was a practice adopted to avoid imposing unnecessary burdens on parties domiciled abroad. In this regard, one must bear in mind that these bodies were usually seated at the capital city of Allied and Associated powers. For example, the Franco-German and the English-German Mixed-Arbitral Tribunals were respectively seated in Paris and London, not in Berlin.

Most Mixed Arbitral Tribunals did not require representation by lawyers. Even still, State agents played a considerable role in the proceedings. State agents could act as counsel for a respondent State or for their nationals whenever these were not represented by a lawyer. In particular, State agents would come to mediate the relation of individual claimants and Mixed Arbitral Tribunals, which "eventually amounted to a kind of filtering of claims."[163] Even when parties were represented by lawyers, State agents had the right to plead and even settle claims. Thus, the prerogatives of State agents somewhat limited the margin of action of individuals before Mixed Arbitral Tribunals, as they could go as far as contradict the legal and factual claims of their nationals.[164]

Decisions of these bodies were final,[165] but the "nature" of such judgments was unclear. Were they founded on law or on equity? This was not expressly provided in the peace treaties, but it was widely understood that arbitrators sitting in Mixed Arbitral Tribunals were to act as judges and not as *amiable compositeurs*. This approach, it was then noted, was in line with "*les tendances de l'arbitrage international, qui penche de plus en plus – et ce avec raison – à*

162 See Requejo Isidro and Hess, *op.cit.*, at 255–256.

163 See Requejo Isidro and Hess, *op.cit.*, at 251.

164 See Requejo Isidro and Hess, *op.cit*, at 251–252.

165 See Treaty of Versailles, Articles 304-g. Interestingly, the MATs involving Hungary were amended to include an appeal mechanism to the PCIJ on 28 April 1930.

obliger les tribunaux arbitraux à rendre leurs décisions, non pas selon une conception plus ou moins vague d'équité, mais selon les règles de droit."[166] However, insofar as the treaties provided for, arbitrators were given the prerogative to rule certain issues on the basis of equity. For instance, the administration of procedure, including the administration of evidence, as well as the quantification of compensation were matters left to arbitrator's equitable decision.[167]

In general, the law applicable was primarily the provisions in the peace treaties, which meant that public international law was superimposed over domestic law to govern private relations between nationals of former belligerent countries. Domestic law would apply in a supplementary fashion only, and it was expected that Mixed Arbitral Tribunals should be able to advance the uniformization of private international law through the development of rules capable of being widely adopted by national courts.[168]

The example of accounts held in German and French banks by their respective "enemy" nationals is illustrative of the ramifications connected to the administration of enemy debt by Mixed Arbitral Tribunals. It is noteworthy that the relation between banks and "enemy" clients were put on hold during the war, but the accounts themselves were often operational despite the ongoing hostilities.[169] With the end of the war, the amounts held in these accounts had to be settled in the terms of Article 296 of the Treaty of Versailles, discussed earlier.

Great difficulty was faced by French nationals to recover sums held in German banks through the mechanism of clearing offices. Such difficulty had been partly attributed to the "passive resistance" of the German Clearing Office, which became quite uncooperative due to the French occupation of the Ruhr.[170] As a consequence, the Franco-German Mixed Arbitral Tribunal produced relevant case law pertaining to the recovery of sums held by French nations in German banks.

---

166 See Blühdorn, *op.cit.*, at 190.

167 See Ch Yotis, 'De l'influence de la notion de justice et d'équité sur l'application des traités de paix par les Tribunaux Arbitraux Mixtes' (1923) 50 Journal du Droit International 249, at 250–252.

168 See Blühdorn, *op.cit.*, at 227.

169 Archambault describes the situation as follows: "*Pendant tout le cours des hostilités, les relations entre les banques et leurs clients furent interrompues: cependant, les banques continuèrent la plupart du temps à exécuter les conventions intervenues avant la guerre : encaissement de coupons, créditement d'intérêts, etc ..., de sorte que les comptes ne cessèrent pas de fonctionner.*" In M Archambault, 'La jurisprudence des Tribunaux Arbitraux Mixtes sur les comptes courants' (1924) 19 Revue de Droit International Privé, 507.

170 See Archambault, *op.cit.*, at 508.

The leading ruling which would guide arbitrators in their decisions was laid in the case *Puymaigre v. Diskonto Gesellschaft.*[171] Applying Article 299, a, of the Treaty of Versailles,[172] the Franco-German Mixed Arbitral tribunal established that all current accounts held in a belligerent country were to be considered foreclosed as of the date marking the beginning of the war. Accordingly, it would be the balance at that date that would have to be paid to the titular of the account. In this regard, beyond ordering payment, arbitrators were often called to decide on the exchange rate applicable to these pecuniary obligations, for they were denominated in a foreign currency – *i.e.* German marks.

The mechanism introduced by the peace treaties laid the burden of currency devaluation on the debtors, guaranteeing to creditors that amounts due as enemy debt would be paid pursuant to the exchange rate applicable during the month preceding the outbreak of the war. The Treaty of Versailles regulated the applicable exchange rate applicable to enemy debt as follows:

> Debts shall be paid or credited in the currency of such one of the Allied and Associated Powers, their colonies or protectorates, or the British Dominions or India, as may be concerned. If the debts are payable in some other currency they shall be paid or credited in the currency of the country concerned, whether an Allied or Associated Power, Colony, Protectorate, British Dominion or India, at the pre-war rate of exchange.
>
> For the purpose of this provision the pre-war rate of exchange shall be defined as the average cable transfer rate prevailing in the Allied or Associated country concerned during the month immediately preceding the outbreak of war between the said country concerned and Germany.
>
> If a contract provides for a fixed rate of exchange governing the conversion of the currency in which the debt is stated into the currency of the Allied or Associated country concerned, then the above provisions concerning the rate of exchange shall not apply.
>
> In the case of new States the currency in which and the rate of exchange at which debts shall be paid or credited shall be determined by the Reparation Commission provided for in Part VIII (Reparation).[173]

171 See Archambault, *op.cit.*, at 512–517.

172 The provision in question read as follows: "Any contract concluded between enemies shall be regarded as having been dissolved as from the time when any two of the parties became enemies, except in respect of any debt or other pecuniary obligation arising out of any act done or money paid thereunder, and subject to the exceptions and special rules with regard to particular contracts or classes of contracts contained herein or in the Annex hereto." See Article 299, a, in Allied Powers, Associated Powers and Germany, *op.cit.*, at 190.

173 See Article 294, d, in Allied Powers, Associated Powers and Germany, *op.cit.*, at 176–177.

Concretely, by investing Mixed Arbitral Tribunals with oversight regarding the problem of currency devaluation, arbitrators were given the last say over the redistribution of wealth in micro-economic relations emerging out of enemy debt – which would be deeply impacted depending on the exchange rate applied to these pecuniary obligations. This is just one instance among many in which such a central role was played by Mixed Arbitral Tribunals in the micro-governance of war related economic relations, but it suffices to show how arbitration authority was progressively acquiring a larger and larger share in the transnational administration of economic justice.

2.2 *The Stillborn Procedure of Compulsory Arbitration*

Compulsory arbitration was an item in the pacifist's wish-list since the first Hague Peace Conference of 1899, when it was referred to as "obligatory arbitration." That year, the Russian delegation, headed by Feodor Martens, had suggested a limited mechanism of compulsory arbitration in relation to pecuniary disputes, but even this timid proposal was strongly opposed by the German government.[174] It was understood that PCA arbitration could only be established on a voluntary basis and the dream of compulsory arbitration subsisted unachieved.

The Covenant of the League reproduced the time-tested formula of voluntary arbitration under its Article 13, pursuant to which "[m]embers of the League agree that whenever any dispute shall arise between them which they recognise to be suitable for submission to arbitration or judicial settlement and which cannot be satisfactorily settled by diplomacy, they will submit the whole subject-matter to arbitration or judicial settlement."[175] Some stakeholder's of the League, however, advocated for the primacy of arbitration in a system of collective security and disarmament.

Disarmament and collective security were issues hotly debated in the early years of the League of Nations. Many felt, especially in France, that the "Anglo-Saxon" influence over the League was the main obstacle to implement a mechanism of collective security.[176] Georges Scelle, for instance, would have said that the League's lack of enforcement mechanism was attributable to a "mystical pacifism practised by old women and Anglo-Saxons."[177]

---

174 See Brown Scott, *The Conference of 1899*, at 597.

175 See Article 13 of the Covenant in League of Nations, 'The Covenant of the League of Nations' (1920) 1 League of Nations Official Journal 3, at 6.

176 This was translated in a French civil society campaign to reform the League, so as to mitigate its Anglo-Saxon features and its lack of a mechanism of collective security. See Jackson, *op.cit.*

177 See Jackson, *op.cit.*, at 446.

Despite these views, the influential American pacifist movement greatly favoured the idea of creating a system of collective security built upon a mechanism of compulsory arbitration. In reality, the encounter of American pacifist activists with French left-wing politicians would take the idea off the ground. When the Cartel des Gauches gained power in France, led by Edouard Herriot, it placed compulsory arbitration at the centre of international policy. The general contours of the policy were based on an unofficial project prepared by James Shotwell and Tasker Bliss.[178]

The brand-new French policy on collective security and arbitration would be labelled "Arbitration, Security and Disarmament," and it was unveiled to the world by Herriot himself during the Fifth Assembly of the League on 5 September 1924.[179] In the occasion, Herriot evoked the legacy of Léon Bourgeois and the traditional adherence of France to arbitration. In a way, Herriot's government attempted to revive Bourgeois vision of a more "muscular" League of Nations,[180] which had been rejected by the United States and the United Kingdom during the peace conference.[181]

On the other side of the channel, Britain was also governed by a left-wing government. Nevertheless, the labour cabinet headed by Ramsey Douglas merely reproduced the longstanding British approach to peacekeeping. Douglas recognized that arbitration could play a role in the definition of aggression,[182]

---

178 See James Thomson Shotwell, 'The "American Plan" and the Protocol' (1924) 10 International Conciliation 527. For a more in-depth analysis, see Carl Bouchard, 'Le « plan américain » Shotwell-Bliss de 1924 : une initiative méconnue pour le renforcement de la paix' (2001) Guerres mondiales et conflits contemporains 203.

179 See Jackson, *op.cit.*, at 460.

180 See Léon Bourgeois, *Pour la Société des Nations* (Bibliothèque-Charpentier 1910).

181 See Jackson, *op.cit.*, at 462.

182 Politis, presenting the Protocol at the Twenty-Fifth Plenary Meeting of the Fifth Assembly of the League, noted the following: "At the root of all the rules contained in the Protocol there is the general principle that, henceforward, wars of aggression are condemned. Henceforward, no war of aggression will be tolerated; only acts of legitimate defence or acts undertaken on behalf of or with the authorisation of the community of the signatory States will be allowed, and every private war, every war of aggression, will not only be condemned and regarded as an international crime, but will be attended by sanctions and accompanied by the necessary penalties to prevent it, and, in case of need, to suppress it. [...] Only one more stone was wanting to complete the structure which we had attempted to build. The Protocol condemns wars of aggression and offers all parties in all cases a pacific procedure involving a final and binding decision which is enforced by sanctions. With a view to the immediate and infallible application of these sanctions, we had to decide which was the State originally responsible for a war of aggression – in other terms, to define and determine the aggressor in each case. This definition is an easy matter and we found it without difficulty. It is sufficient to say that any State is the aggressor which resorts to war in violation of the engagement contracted by it either under the Covenant or under the Protocol. It is, however, extremely difficult to apply this definition in

but it was his view that enforcement mechanisms were not necessary. For the British, a toothless rule of law would be sufficient to secure peace.[183]

The Herriot's government, for its part, was adamant on producing a system of collective security based on compulsory arbitration. France mobilized its diplomatic troops to advance this vision,[184] marshalling the support of its central and eastern European allies such as Poland and Czechoslovakia. In an orchestrated move at the Fifth Assembly, the League came to adopt a resolution introducing the formula "Arbitration, Security and Disarmament" in its agenda.[185] In due course, this work program would directly give birth to the Protocol for the Pacific Settlement of International Disputes (2.2.1) and the General Act for the Pacific Settlement of International Disputes (2.2.2).

2.2.1 The Protocol for the Pacific Settlement of International Disputes of 1924

One knows that the covenant of the League did not go as far as declaring the illegality of war. Member states had an obligation to submit their disputes to arbitration, judicial settlement, or enquiry by the Council, but war was kept as a lawful settlement mechanism of international disputes. Pursuant to the

---

each particular case. [...] The Committee accordingly attempted to devise an automatic procedure which would obviate any discussion whatever and would make it possible to determine forthwith, by a combination of various external criteria, which was the State originally responsible for a war of aggression. We believe that we have found a solution by means of a system of 'presumption.' Our proposal is that you should say that there is a presumption, which shall hold good until the contrary has been established by a unanimous decision of the Council and which arises in a series of hypotheses, the importance of which I commend to your most particular attention. These hypotheses are three. The first is that of a State which resorts to war after refusing arbitration or refusing to submit to the decision by which the dispute was finally settled. The next hypothesis is that of a State which resorts to war in violation of the provisional measures enjoined by the Council during proceedings for a pacific settlement. The third and last hypothesis is that of a State resorting to war in disregard of a decision recognising that the question in dispute is exclusively within the domestic jurisdiction of the other party, or by failure to employ the last chance of conciliation offered in Article 11 of the Covenant." See League of Nations, 'Records of the Fifth Assembly – Text of the Debates – Twenty-Fifth to Twenty-Eight Plenary Meetings, October 1st and 2nd, 1924 – Arbitration, Security and Reduction of Armaments: Protocol for the Pacific Settlement of International Disputes: Reports of the First and Third Committees' (1924) 23 League of Nations Official Journal 192, 194–195.

183 See Jackson, *op.cit.*, at 462.

184 The implementation of the policy at the League was entrusted to Aristide Briand, Paul-Boncour, de Jouvenel, René Cassin and Louis Loucheur. See Jackson, *op.cit.*, at 461.

185 See Jackson, *op.cit.*, at 462.

Covenant of the League, war could always be waged 3 months after an arbitral or judicial decision settling a given dispute was rendered.[186]

The Protocol for the Pacific Settlement of International Disputes, commonly known as Geneva Protocol, constituted an attempt to move away from the unilateral use of force. Relying on the creation of a system of compulsory arbitration, it was hoped that its adoption would make the world a step closer to the prohibition of war. Notably, the instrument reduced the lawful use of force to cases of self-defence and to the enforcement of jurisdictional decisions. Within this framework, it was expected that contracting parties would then be able to pursue disarmament polices.[187]

One must note that collective security and the peaceful settlement of disputes were perceived as separate but interdependent matters, leading to the joint and concerted efforts of various organs of the Assembly in the furtherance of the agenda "Arbitration, Security and Disarmament."[188] Notably, the

---

186 The Covenant, in its Article 12, provided as follows: "The Members of the League agree that, if there should arise between them any dispute likely to lead to a rupture, they will submit the matter either to arbitration or judicial settlement or to enquiry by the Council, and they agree in no case to resort to war until three months after the award by the arbitrators or the judicial decision, or the report by the Council. In any case under this Article the award of the arbitrators or the judicial decision shall be made within a reasonable time, and the report of the Council shall be made within six months after the submission of the dispute." See League of Nations, *The Covenant*, at 6.

187 See Nikolaos Politis and Edvard Beneš, 'Records of the Fifth Assembly – Text of the Debates – Annex 30, A.135(I).1924.IX – Arbitration, Security and Reduction of Armaments – General Report Submitted to the Assembly on Behalf of the First and Third Committees' (1924) 223 League of Nations Official Journal, Special Supplement 479, at 288.

188 The resolution read as follows: "The Assembly, Noting the declarations of the Governments represented, observes with satisfaction that they contain the basis of an understanding tending to establish a secure peace: Decides as follows: With a view to reconciling in the new proposals the divergences between certain points of view which have been expressed and, when agreement has been reached, to enable an international conference upon armaments to be summoned by the League of Nations at the earliest possible moment: (i) The Third Committee is requested to consider the material dealing with security and the reduction of armaments, particularly the observations of the Governments on the draft Treaty of Mutual Assistance, prepared in pursuance of Resolution XIV of the Third Assembly and other plans prepared and presented to the Secretary-General since the publication of the draft Treaty, and to examine the obligations contained in the Covenant of the League in relation to the guarantees of security which a resort to arbitration and a reduction of armaments may require; (2) The First Committee is requested: (a) To consider, in view of possible amendments, the articles in the Covenant relating to that settlement of disputes; (b) To examine within what limits the terms of Article 36, paragraph 2, of the Statute establishing the Permanent Court of International Justice might be rendered more precise and thereby facilitate the more general acceptance of

Assembly's first committee was entrusted with the study of potential reforms regarding the peaceful settlement of disputes, while its third committee was charged with the matter of security and disarmament proper.[189] The rapporteurs of each committee would be respectively Nikolaos Politis (former Greek foreign minister and law professor) and Edvard Beneš (Czech foreign minister).

A central element for the operation of compulsory arbitration was the concept of justiciability.[190] Justiciable disputes, that is those disputes having a legal character, would have to be settled by the PCIJ. Conversely, non-justiciable ones, say disputes having a political character, were to be settled through compulsory arbitration.[191] The exception to the system of compulsory arbitration were issues pertaining to the domestic jurisdiction of a given state. It is clear from the above that great faith was placed on arbitral procedure, as this form of dispute resolution was given jurisdiction over the most sensitive disputes between States.

It is interesting to note that the framers of the Geneva Protocol thought to be creating a new type of settlement procedure, one that would be simultaneously more flexible and structured than arbitration as it existed at the time. Placed as the centre piece of a system of collective security, arbitral authority was not to be structured over party-appointment.[192] Furthermore, as noted at the time, it was felt that "an 'arbitration' under Article 4 of the Protocol may be expected not to be a purely legal procedure."[193]

This project, in fact, pushed forward a vision of arbitration as a type of equitable authority rather than a jurisdictional one, for arbitrators were not to be bound by law in their decisions. This was particularly true in relation to perceived legal gaps, in light of which arbitrators would be expressly allowed to rule on equity. Even still, arbitral awards issued within this framework were

---

the clause and thus strengthen the solidarity and the security of the nations of the world by settling by pacific means all disputes which may arise between States." See Politis and Beneš, *op.cit.*, at 479.

189 For an overview of the drafting process, see Politis and Beneš, *op.cit.*, at 479–480.

190 See Hersch Lauterpacht, 'La Théorie des Différends Non Justiciables en Droit International', *Collected Courses of the Hague Academy of International Law*, vol 34 (Martinus Nijhoff Publishers 1930). For Lauterpacht's extedend analysis of the issue, see Hersch Lauterpacht, *The Function of Law in the International Community* (Oxford University Press 2011).

191 See Article 4 of the Protocol for the Pacific Settlement of International Disputes in League of Nations, 'Protocol for the Pacific Settlement of International Disputes' (1924) 21 League of Nations Official Journal, Special Supplement 21, at 22.

192 See Politis and Beneš, *op.cit.*, at 482.

193 See John F Williams, 'The Geneva Protocol of 1924 for the Pacific Settlement of International Disputes' (1924) 3 International Affairs 288, at 303.

vested with coercive means of enforcement, for enforceability was seen as an essential element for the development of an effective arbitral procedure. Under the Geneva Protocol, awards would no longer rest on "loyalty and good faith of the parties."[194] Rather, compulsory arbitration would be both an equitable and a coercive type of authority.

The Council of the League would be at the driver's seat of the mechanism of compulsory arbitration. The procedural framework laid out in the Protocol consisted of a multi-tiered dispute resolution mechanism. Indeed, the first step in the process was a similar mechanism to good offices, which would be performed by the Council. Persisting the dispute, the Council had the obligation to persuade the parties to submit their dispute either to judicial or arbitral settlement. Failing such submission, compulsory arbitration could be initiated upon the request of one of the parties.

If arbitration was initiated, the Council would then act in a supervisory capacity in relation to the proceedings. This included the prerogative to take the necessary steps to constitute the tribunal or to set the terms of reference for the arbitrators (delimiting their powers and the procedure) if the parties failed to do so by themselves. Still, one important dimension of the procedure was not under the direct determination of the Council, which was the delimitation of the contentious issues. These would either be defined unilaterally by one of the parties or, failing such determination, by the arbitrators themselves – which would have to determine them on the basis of the parties' submissions.[195]

A fall-back device was established in case compulsory arbitration was not initiated. In such a scenario, the Protocol remanded the full dispute to the Council. The mechanism was premised on the fictitious, or at least, tacit agreement of the parties. In other terms, it was considered that "[r]efusal to arbitration implies the consent of both parties to final settlement of the dispute by the Council."[196]

The decision to be taken by the Council, however, would have to be reached by the unanimous agreement of all Council members – excluded from the tally the representatives of the parties themselves. Such decision would carry the same weight of an arbitral award and lead to the same consequences at the enforcement stage. Interestingly, if the Council could not reach a unanimous decision, then the dispute would be compulsorily submitted to arbitration. In

194 See Politis and Beneš, *op.cit.*, at 482.
195 See Politis and Beneš, *op.cit.*, at 486.
196 See Politis and Beneš, *op.cit.*, at 486.

this scenario, there would be no margin left to party autonomy with proceedings being entirely controlled by the Council.[197]

A final step in the mechanism concerned enforcement proceedings. Again, the Council was the central body charged with the administration of coercion and several steps were to be taken by it to assure compliance. First, the Council should "exert all its influence to secure compliance."[198] If non-compliance persisted, then the Council could propose enforcement measures in accordance with Article 13 of the Covenant. This meant that coercive measures would have to have an economic or financial character only, as it "has not appeared possible to go further and to employ force against a State which is not itself resorting to force."[199] That said, there existed the possibility of the Council authorising the successful party in the arbitration to deploy force against a non-compliant counterpart. Here, any type of armed resistance by the non-compliant party could trigger the use of force under Article 16 of the Covenant.

A curious feature was embedded in this mechanism of compulsory arbitration, which was the possibility of, upon request from the parties, obtaining an advisory opinion from the PCIJ on any point of law in the dispute. The provision resulted from the concern that arbitrators could eventually not have legal training, and this was then a way of bypassing such potential problem.[200] These advisory opinions, however, would not bind the arbitrators. There was one situation in which the relation between compulsory arbitration and the advisory jurisdiction of the PCIJ would slightly change. If it was raised by one of the parties that the issue at stake fell solely within its domestic jurisdiction,

---

197 See Politis and Beneš, *op.cit.*, at 487.

198 Article 4(6) of the Protocol for the Pacific Settlement of International Disputes reads as follows: "The signatory States undertake that they will carry out in full good faith any judicial sentence or arbitral award that may be rendered and that they will comply, as provided in paragraph 3 above, with the solutions recommended by the Council. *In the event of a State failing to carry out the above undertakings, the Council shall exert all its influence to secure compliance therewith.* If it fails therein, it shall propose what steps should be taken to give effect thereto, in accordance with the provision contained at the end of Article 13 of the Covenant. Should a State in disregard of the above undertakings resort to war, the sanctions provided for by Article 16 of the Covenant, interpreted in the manner indicated in the present Protocol, shall immediately become applicable to it" (emphasis added). See *League of Nations, Protocol for the Pacific Settlement of International Disputes*, at 23.

199 See Politis and Beneš, *op.cit.*, at 487.

200 See Politis and Beneš, *op.cit.*, at 486.

arbitrators would be in a position of requesting *ex officio* the opinion of the PCIJ, and the opinion on this issue would bind the arbitrators.[201]

In addition, as the PCIJ was granted a supervisory function over the life of the Protocol, there subsisted the question of whether an arbitral award under the Protocol could be revised on the grounds that the arbitrators misinterpreted the treaty. The question was raised in the following terms by an observer at the time:

> Does this mean that if a Committee of Arbitrators gives an award which upon the true construction of the Protocol it was not open to them to make, the question might be brought before the Permanent Court by means of an application to have the award declared invalid? This question may have importance in connection with the point whether it is open to arbitrators to give an award which involves a revision of treaty arrangements.[202]

This question, despite its intellectual interest, rapidly became irrelevant, for the Geneva Protocol would come to be dead letter.[203] Certainly, there were notable contributions introduced by this instrument. From the perspective of the law on the use of force, it introduced the prohibition of wars of aggression, which was an attempt to further reduce the scope of the use of force in international law.[204] In particular, it adopted a formal presumption of aggression, based on the simple idea that the use of force in violation of the Covenant of the League, of the Geneva Protocol itself or of the authority of the Council amounted to aggression.[205] Furthermore, the shadows of the instrument would extend over other interstate arbitration treaties, such as the arbitration agreements in the Pact of Locarno.[206]

---

201 See Article 5 of the Protocol for the Pacific Settlement of International Disputes in League of Nations, *Protocol for the Pacific Settlement of International Disputes*, 23.

202 See Williams, *op.cit.*, at 302.

203 See Maurice Vaïsse, 'La Société des Nations et le Désarmement' in United Nations Library (ed), *The League of Nations in Retrospect: Proceedings of the Symposium* (Walter de Gruyter 1983), at 482.

204 See Politis and Beneš, *op.cit.*, at 482.

205 See Article 10 of the Protocol for the Pacific Settlement of International Disputes in League of Nations, *Protocol for the Pacific Settlement of International Disputes*, at 24–25.

206 The Security Pact signed at Locarno provided in its Article 3 for the peaceful settlement of "all questions of every kind." A set of arbitration treaties was then adopted, providing for the submission of all disputes covered by Article 13 of the Covenant to arbitration or judicial settlement. For the text of these instruments, see Appendix Two in George Glasgow, *From Dawes to Locarno* (Harper & Brothers Publishers 1926), 168 et seq.

Even still, on the core issue of compulsory arbitration, the Protocol for the Pacific Settlement of International Disputes gave birth to a stillborn offspring. This is most clear when one contemplates the completely different path taken by the General Act for the Pacific Settlement of International Disputes of 1928.

2.2.2 The General Act for the Pacific Settlement of International Disputes of 1928

The Assembly of the League established in 1927 a committee on Arbitration and Security,[207] which was then entrusted by an Assembly resolution dated 26 September 1927 with the task of taking action "with a view to promoting, generalising and co-ordinating special or collective agreements on arbitration and security."[208] The outcome of this mandate was the production of the General Act for the Pacific Settlement of International Disputes, opened to signature on 26 September 1928.

This instrument was a proper codification initiative, trying to coordinate, and give some uniformity to the numerous jurisdictional arrangements governing the pacific settlement of international disputes. Nikolaos Politis, who was once again assigned as rapporteur on the pacific settlement of disputes, presented the General Act as a compilation into a single instrument of three model treaties.[209] These instruments, at minimum, could be used as a template for States to structure their bilateral jurisdictional commitments.[210] The three model treaties were the following ones: a Bilateral Convention for the Settlement of All International Disputes; a Bilateral Convention for Judicial Settlement, Arbitration, and Conciliation; and a Bilateral Conciliation Convention.[211] From this

207 See Quincy Wright, 'The General Act for the Pacific Settlement of International Disputes' (1930) 24 American Journal of International Law 582, 583.

208 See Nikolaos Politis, 'Records of the Ninth Ordinary Session of the Assembly – Meetings of the Committees – Minutes (Reduction of Armaments) – A. 86(1).1928.IX. – Annex 7. Pacific Settlement of International Disputes, Non-Aggression and Mutual Assistance – Report Submitted to the Assembly by M.N. Politis' (1928) 67 League of Nations Official Journal, Special Supplement 117, 117.

209 See Politis, *op.cit.*, 117.

210 The draft resolution advanced by the Committee of Arbitration and Security, in its paragraph 8, read as follows: "Invites all States whether Members of the League or not, and in so far as their existing agreements do not already achieve this end, to accept obligations in pursuance of the above purpose either by becoming parties to the annexed General Act or by concluding particular conventions with individual States in accordance with the model bilateral conventions annexed hereto or in such terms as may be deemed appropriate". See Politis, *op.cit.*, 118.

211 See League of Nations, 'Annex 2. Three Model Bilateral Conventions in Regard to Conciliation, Arbitration and Judicial Settlement' (1928) 63 League of Nations Official Journal, Special Supplement 26.

perfunctory overview, one quickly realizes that the General Act was not structured as a multilateral framework *stricto sensu*.

Being a compilation of model treaties, the instrument could operate as a mere bilateral arrangement. This is the underlying reason why its entry into force was conditioned to the accession of only two States – even if accessions would remain open to any number of interested States. Similarly, procedural arrangements laid out in other treaties would take precedence over the framework established by the General Act itself, in which cases the General Act would perform a complementary function.[212]

For its modular architecture, the General Act gave States great margin of discretion in relation to modes of accessions. These could vary from the adoption of the instrument in its entirety to a partial accession to some combination of its chapters.[213] The instrument additionally allowed for a large array of reservations to be made.[214] This "à la carte" approach, however, has been singled out as one of the central deficiencies of the General Act.[215]

Interestingly, the duration of the instrument was not indeterminate, a feature that can be understood as meant to reassure Contracting States that they could always revisit their consent to the instrument. Accordingly, the General Act would be in effect for a period of 5 years, which would then be tacitly renewed for periods of 5 years whenever a contracting party failed to manifest its intention to denounce the instrument at least 6 months prior to the expiration of the 5-year term.[216]

In terms of the codification of procedural technique, arbitration under the General Act would be conducted by a five-member arbitral tribunal – with two appointed by each party and the remaining three being jointly chosen.[217] These three arbitrators would have to be nationals of a third state, each of a different nationality, and none of them could be residents in the territory of any of the parties to the dispute. In case the joint appointment failed, an interesting method would be triggered to fill the missing spots at the arbitral tribunal. The appointment would be delegated to a third State jointly chosen by the parties, to two States chosen by each party, or to the President of the PCIJ (failing all

212 See Article 29 in League of Nations, 'Annex 1. General Act' (1928) 63 League of Nations Official Journal, Special Supplement 20, 23.

213 See Article 38 in League of Nations, *Annex 1. General Act*, 25.

214 See Article 39 in League of Nations, *Annex 1. General Act*, 25.

215 See Lucius Caflisch, 'Cent ans de règlement pacifique des différends interétatiques' in Wojciech W Kowalski, *Collected Courses of the Hague Academy*, vol 288 (Martinus Nijhoff Publishers 2001) 318.

216 See Article 45 in League of Nations, *Annex 1. General Act*, 26.

217 See Article 22 in League of Nations, *Annex 1. General Act*, 23.

of the preceding methods).[218] This whole mechanism was envisioned "for the purpose of ensuring still more completely the impartiality of the Tribunals."[219]

This method for constitution of the arbitral tribunal testifies to the codifiers' suspicions in relation to the independence and impartiality of party-appointed arbitrators. In fact, the trend towards reducing the space for party appointment was seemingly on the rise in public international law, as similar concerns had also influenced the method of constitution of the arbitral tribunals hearing claims related to the implementation of the Dawes plan.

The General Act also tried to codify rules governing relevant procedural incidents. For instance, it contained a provision on *lis pendens*, vesting the body first seized with the prerogative to rule on its own competence.[220] Similarly, it introduced provisions on multi-party proceedings and third-party interventions.[221] Furthermore, the instrument granted all dispute resolution bodies the prerogative of issuing provisional measures.[222] However, there were no provisions on the enforcement of settlement agreements, judicial decisions or arbitral awards, as the instrument established only a vague obligation laid upon the parties of abstaining "from all measures likely to react prejudicially upon the execution."[223]

Overall, parties to arbitration proceedings under the General Act would be granted great discretion on procedural and substantive rules to be applied by the tribunal. This ought to be regulated through a special arbitration agreement (*compromis*) and, in the absence of such stipulations, the PCA framework would govern the procedure while the article 38 of the PCIJ statute would determine the law applicable.[224] By default, proceedings would be confidential.[225]

More important for the scope of this study is the deviation of the General Act from the approach taken by the Protocol for the Pacific Settlement of International Disputes. The former privileged conciliation and the jurisdiction of the PCIJ to the detriment of arbitration. In particular, conciliation proceedings,

---

218 See Article 23 in League of Nations, *Annex 1. General Act*, 23.

219 See Politis, *op.cit.*, at 118.

220 See Article 30 in League of Nations, *Annex 1. General Act*, 24.

221 See Articles 34 in League of Nations, *Annex 1. General Act*, 24.

222 See Article 33 in League of Nations, *Annex 1. General Act*, 24.

223 Article 33(3) of the General Act reads as follows: "The parties undertake to abstain from all measures likely to react prejudicially upon the execution of the judicial or arbitral decision or upon the arrangements proposed by the Conciliation Commission and, in general, to abstain from any sort of action whatsoever which may aggravate or extend the dispute." See League of Nations, *Annex 1. General Act*, 24.

224 See Articles 18 and 26 to 28 in League of Nations, *Annex 1. General Act*, 22–23.

225 See Article 10 in League of Nations, *Annex 1. General Act*, 21.

which should last by default no longer than 6 months, had as its central task the production of an agreed solution to the dispute. Furthermore, conciliators would be central in laying down the terms of such settlement agreement as well as establishing facts in the manner of commissions of inquiry.[226]

Arbitration, under the General Act, was introduced as a subsidiary mechanism to both conciliation and judicial settlement. It would only be opened to Parties in case the conciliation process had failed, and the dispute could not be referred to the PCIJ.[227] Hence, whenever "parties are in conflict as to their respective rights," arbitration would not be available unless the parties expressly provided otherwise.[228]

In reality, the General Act seemingly marks a changing attitude towards arbitral authority in the realm of interstate disputes. The hopes that were once deposited on arbitration for the maintenance of peace were now being transferred to the PCIJ.[229] Interestingly, one observes contrasting trends in relation to procedural activity before the PCA and the PCIJ during the interwar years. Comparing the PCA docket between 1899 and 1921, one finds the submission of a total of 18 cases, while between 1921 and 1939 only 5 cases were submitted to the PCA.[230] Conversely, one observes a remarkable activity before the PCIJ. In the period spanning from 1922 to 1940, the world court registered 29 contentious cases and 27 advisory proceedings.

The phenomenon is explained not just by geopolitical contingencies, but also by a growing push towards the judicialization of international dispute-settlement in public international law. The advent of a permanent international judicial instance immediately overshadowed arbitration. Indeed, the creation of the PCIJ led Argentina to propose to the Assembly of the League the dissolution of the PCA.[231] Certainly, the proposition was not successful, but it represents a certain zeitgeist. Even among those that promoted the peaceful settlement of State-to-State disputes, arbitration was looking like an old-fashioned outfit, or a second-best option opened when judicial settlement was unavailable.

226 See Articles 11 and 15 in League of Nations, *Annex 1. General Act*, 21–22.

227 See Article 21 in League of Nations, *Annex 1. General Act*, 22.

228 See Article 18 in League of Nations, *Annex 1. General Act*, 22.

229 On the creation of the PCIJ and its practice, see Ole Spiermann, 'Who Attempts Too Much Does Nothing Well: The 1920 Advisory Committee of Jurists and the Statute of the Permanent Court of International Justice' (2002) 73 British Yearbook of International Law 187; Ole Spiermann, *International Legal Argument in the Permanent Court of International Justice: The Rise of the International Judiciary* (1st edn, Cambridge University Press 2004).

230 See Permanent Court of Arbitration, *Annual Report 2006* (PCA 2006), 42–43.

231 See Caflisch, *Cent ans*, 316.

3 Not All Roads Lead to Rome

The interplay between pacificism, legalism and commercial interests has always been central to the advancement of uniformization through codification projects of the most diverse colours. Indeed, many have believed that the uniformization of law was one way to "build and maintain peace by fostering an orderly and universally beneficial commercial exchange."[232]

Even still, the question on how to implement these codification projects was, as still is, very much open to debate. This section explores competing strategies for the codification of arbitration at both intergovernmental and non-governmental fora. On the one hand, UNIDROIT would be a leading force advocating for the adoption of a uniform arbitral legislation to be enacted by an international convention (3.1). On the other hand, the interwar years would be marked by an effervescent non-state regulatory activity, giving rise to often competing, but also converging, private arbitration codes (3.2).

3.1 *The Failure of the UNIDROIT Project of Uniform Arbitration Law*

UNIDROIT is an institution pertaining to the uniform law ecosystem, whose official name is the International Institute for the Unification of Private Law. It is currently a self-standing international organization, but its creation can be traced back to the early days of the League of Nations. Indeed, UNIDROIT was originally the organ within the League charged with the task of working towards the unification of private law. Created in 1926 by the Council of the League, the institute opened its doors in Rome on 30 May 1928 with the sponsorship of the Italian fascist government and with an opening speech delivered by Benito Mussolini.[233] This is not an attempt to imply that legal unification was fundamentally a fascist project, but rather to stress that even governments strongly opposed to multilateralism, like Mussolini's, would lend their support for the advancement of legal unification.

The Italian interest over the matter was not accidental. Since the times of Mancini and the Italian unification, Italian legal scholars felt that the task of codification was not to be bound to national borders.[234] UNIDROIT itself was the creation of Vittorio Scialoja, an Italian Senator, professor of Roman law and Deputy Secretary-General of the League.[235] Scialoja was a prominent member of the Italian movement for the unification of private law, being behind not

232 See Kronke, *op.cit.*, 183.

233 See Kronke, *op.cit.*, 185.

234 See Halpérin, *Nationalisme*, 77 et seq.

235 See Mario Matteucci, 'The History of UNIDROIT and the Methods of Unification' (1973) 66 Law Library Journal, 286.

just the creation of UNIDROIT but also the 1927 project for a Franco-Italian code of obligations. It has been noted that Scialoja "was convinced that after a century of nationalization of private law time was ripe for returning to a common law of 'civilized' nations.'"[236]

The creation of UNIDROIT in 1928 introduced one more centre for the pursuit of a codified arbitration law. In addition to the Hague, Geneva and Paris, Rome had the ambition of playing a major part in the codification of private law in general and of arbitration law in particular. Some five years after its creation, in 1933, the institution would already put together a working group with the mission of producing a draft uniform law for arbitration.[237] Only three years later, a preliminary draft was published.

A central figure in this endeavour was René David. The great comparatist was not just a strong supporter of the unification of arbitration law,[238] but the leading advocate regarding the adoption of a uniform arbitration law. In 1930, then a 24-year-old law professor, David took over the role of UNIDROIT's deputy secretary-general.[239] Two years later, he would produce a comprehensive report for UNIDROIT titled "*L'arbitrage conventional en droit privé.*"[240]

As a result of his expertise on the matter, David came to act as the main drafter of the UNIDROIT project of a uniform arbitration law.[241] In this regard,

236 See Kronke, *op.cit.*, 184.

237 The working group was chaired by Mariano d'Amelio (President of UNIDROIT at the time and former president of the Italian Court of Cassation). In addition to d'Amelio, the group was composed of the following members: René David (then deputy secretary-general of UNIDROIT), Simon Rudstein (counsel to the Polish Ministry of Foreign Affairs), Emil Sandström (justice at the Swedish Supreme Court), B.A. Wortley (law professor at Manchester University), and Giuseppe Righetti (then UNIDROIT's secretary-general). See René David, 'Un projet de loi uniforme sur l'arbitrage' in *Introduction à l'étude du droit comparé: Recueil d'Études en l'honneur d'Edouard Lambert* (LGDJ 1938), 885.

238 David advocated for the cause in the following terms: "*La diversité actuelle des législations en matière d'arbitrage est pour les milieux intéressés, et spécialement dans les rapports internationaux, une cause de troubles sérieux. Telle ou telle solution, consacrée par un droit donné, constitue parfois un obstacle au développement normal de l'arbitrage ; plus souvent la difficulté provient de ce qu'est mal défini le droit applicable en l'espèce. La validité de la convention arbitrale risque constamment d'être mise en doute, les effets produits par cette convention sont précaires et incertains; si une sentence a été rendue, son exécution peut être entravée ou rendue plus onéreuse du fait que cette sentence est qualifiée d'étrangère dans le pays de l'exécution. L'unification des lois sur l'arbitrage présenterait donc pour le commerce une utilité considérable.*" See David, *Un projet de loi uniforme sur l'arbitrage*, 884.

239 Kronke, *op.cit.*, 186.

240 See René David, *Rapport sur l'Arbitrage Conventionnel en Droit Privé: Étude de Droit Comparé* (L'Universale – Tipografia Poliglotta 1932).

241 See UNIDROIT, 'Comité d'étude Pour l'arbitrage. Chambre de Commerce Internationale : Discussion Du Comité d'Etudes de l'Arbitrage Commercial International Sur l'avant-Projet

a preliminary draft law was published by UNIDROIT already in 1936. This document is an interesting piece in the puzzle to understand the evolution of arbitration law and the ways arbitral authority came to be codified in the years to come. On the one hand, the draft announces ideas that were not yet dominant but that would become mainstream in the future. The case in point is the reliance on party autonomy as a means to promote the transnationalisation of arbitration practice. In the interwar years, this was not such a popular approach. On the other hand, the draft deviated from features that would become widespread in the practice of arbitration. Notably, the fundamental divergence concerned the function of arbitration itself and one may wonder whether the adoption of the draft could have taken the practice of arbitration to a different developmental path.

It is desirable to look at these two assertions with more attention. In relation to the role of party autonomy in the 1936 draft, it is appropriate to highlight the residual role played by party autonomy in the operation of the 1923 Protocol on Arbitration Clauses. Indeed, the 1923 instrument relied more on the notions of *pacta sunt servanda* and good faith than on that of party autonomy. As noted previously in this work, the binding character of arbitral authority stemmed from the "sanctity of the contract."[242] In addition, even if Article 2 of the 1923 Protocol subjected arbitral procedure to party autonomy, it vested the law of the seat with oversight over the will of the parties.[243]

The 1936 UNIDROIT draft, however, took the step of promoting the transnationalisation of arbitration authority by expanding the importance of party autonomy. In its article 1, the 1936 draft expressly allowed parties to choose the uniform instrument as the applicable law to an arbitration agreement regardless of their residency or nationality. This marks a very early attempt to de-nationalize arbitration legislation, favouring a uniform instrument transnationally valid to the detriment of municipal jurisdictions and its legislation.[244]

---

d'une Loi Internationale Sur l'arbitrage En Droit Privé (Doc. 13) : I. – Extrait Du Procès-Verbal de La 12ème Session, 19 Décembre 1935; II. – Procès-Verbal de La 13ème Session, 9 et 10 Janvier 1936' (1936) U.D.P 1936 – Etude III – Arbitrage – Doc. 17 12.

242 See MacKinnon and others, *op.cit.*, 1413.

243 Article 2 of the 1923 Protocol reads as follows: "The arbitral procedure, including the constitution of the arbitral tribunal, shall be governed by the will of the parties and by the law of the country in whose territory the arbitration takes place." See Secretary-General, *Protocol on Arbitration Clauses, Note by the Secretary-General.*

244 Article 1 of the 1936 draft reads as follows: "The present law shall apply when, at the time an arbitration agreement is concluded, the parties thereto have their respective habitual residences in different countries where the present law is in force. This law shall apply in such a case even when at the time a dispute arises the parties have their habitual residences in the same country. If one of the parties is a corporation or a partnership firm its

The intertextuality of arbitration agreements, arbitration rules and arbitration laws were also turned into a major tool for the transnational advancement of the codification project. Accordingly, the coordination between party autonomy and institutional arbitration rules was perceived as a gateway to enlarge the province of the UNIDROIT instrument.[245] This approach was not taken without controversy even among the members of the working group and some tried to brush aside criticisms by highlighting that the uniform instrument would ultimately be part of the national legal system of contracting parties.[246]

Turning to the second assertion, that is, the ways in which the 1936 draft contrasted with actual developments in the codification of arbitral authority, it must be noted that the UNIDROIT project construed the mandate of arbitrators in a quite discrete manner. Article 30 of the draft introduced a rule allowing the award to be set aside in case of errors in the application of law whenever parties so agreed,[247] otherwise no recourse would be available. Albeit this might be seen as a manifestation of the finality of arbitral awards, at the time the provision was implemented to stress that arbitrators' mandate was fundamentally that of an *amiable compositeur*. Indeed, Article 30 was considered

---

habitual residence shall be deemed to be the place of the situation of the establishment that has made the arbitration agreement, even if such establishment is only a branch. The nationality of the parties shall not be taken into consideration. The present law shall also apply whenever the parties have so provided." See UNIDROIT, 'Preliminary Draft of an International Law on Arbitration' (UNIDROIT 1936) S.D.N.-U.D.P. 1935–Études: III, Arbitrage Doc. 20 4.

245 David comments read as follows: "*Étant donné que le projet ne distingue pas entre convention expresse et soumission à un règlement d'arbitrage, il suffira, pour que la loi uniforme soit applicable, que les parties se soient référées à un reglement d'arbitrage prévoyant l'applicattion de la loi uniforme. Les groupements et institutions qui publient des règlements d'arbitrage pourront par conséquent élargir le domaine d'application de la loi uniforme, si celle-ci donne satisfaction à la pratique, et ils auront ainsi la possibilité de préparer l'abolition, en matière d'arbitrage, d'un dualisme de législations qui n'est pas sans inconvénients mais que le Comité n'a pas cru pour l'instant possible d'éviter.*" See David, *Un projet de loi uniforme sur l'arbitrage*, 885.

246 René David expressed this view as follows: "*Les critiques que soulève la théorie de l'autonomie de la volonté perdent du reste ici de leur valeur, car il est difficile de concevoir comment l'ordre public d'un pays pourrait être troublé du fait que des parties, résidant habituellement dans ce pays, auront éliminé sa loi interne particulière sur l'arbitrage pour appliquer dans leurs relations la loi uniforme, qui est une autre loi interne du même pays.*" See David, *Un projet de loi uniforme sur l'arbitrage*, 886.

247 Article 30 of the draft read as follows: "The award shall also be set aside if, contrary to the express stipulation of the parties, the arbitrators have not respected the rules of law." See UNIDROIT, *Preliminary Draft*, 10.

to grant arbitral tribunals, by default, the prerogative to rule on equity.[248] In a world where the 1936 draft came to dominate the practice of arbitration, arbitrators ruling on law would have been the exception, while tribunals ruling on equity would have been the norm.

In addition, it was felt that uncooperative parties to arbitration agreements were to be discouraged from settling their disputes through arbitration,[249] and Article 5 of the draft introduced a rule providing for the tacit renunciation of arbitration agreements. This provision read as follows:

> A party may no longer rely on an arbitration agreement in so far it relates to a particular difference, where he has shown his intention not to rely thereon or not to be bound thereby.
>
> The fact of claiming interim measures of protection shall not prevent an arbitration agreement from being relied on.[250]

The terms of said article may cause surprise to contemporary observers, but one must bear in mind that at the time arbitration was still widely perceived as a type of alternative dispute resolution mechanism – and one being construed as fundamentally voluntary and consensual. In a way, Article 5 takes party autonomy to its last consequences, preferring to refer parties to municipal courts than to turn arbitration into a coercive and judicialized procedure. Within this framework, the introduction of a claim before municipal courts despite the existence of an arbitration agreement, the failure to appoint an arbitrator, or any other type of uncooperative behaviour could

---

248 This is made clear in the following extract: "*L'article 30, en exigeant dans ces cas pour l'annulation une stipulation des parties, renverse absolument ce qui était la règle dans les pays latins et notamment en France: il fait de l'amiable composition la règle et de l'arbitrage proprement dit l'exception. Dans le système du projet, les arbitres sont en principe des amiables compositeurs, c'est-à-dire qu'ils doivent bien statuer conformément à la loi, mais que leur sentence ne peut être annulée si, en fait, elle n'est pas conforme à la loi. Les arbitres ne cessent d'être des amiables compositeur, dans le système du projet que s'il existe entre les parties une stipulation expresse leur retirant ces pouvoirs et les obligeant à statuer en droit.*" See David, *Un projet de loi uniforme sur l'arbitrage*, 888.

249 This view is expressed by David in the following terms: "*Il est certain toutefois que l'arbitrage ne rend pas les mêmes services et que le recours à des arbitres doit, dans la plupart des cas, être découragé, lorsque, dès l'origine, l'une des parties manifeste sa mauvaise volonté, en refusant de participer à la constitution de la juridiction arbitrale ou de collaborer aux opérations de l'arbitrage.*" See David, *Un projet de loi uniforme sur l'arbitrage*, 889.

250 See Article 5 of the 1936 draft in UNIDROIT, *Preliminary Draft*, 5.

give rise to an inference regarding the tacit renunciation of the arbitration agreement.

As a type of ADR, the impartiality of all members of the tribunal was not yet a mandatory feature in the 1936 draft. Notably, party-appointed arbitrators could not be disqualified on the grounds of lack of independence and impartiality. This was a duty that had to be fulfilled only by the president or arbitrators appointed by a court or a third party, all of whom could be disqualified for a lack of independence and impartiality.[251]

Furthermore, this early version of the UNIDROIT instrument attempted to end the system of double exequatur fostered by the 1927 Geneva Convention. Hence, it introduced an alternative system based on reciprocity, which entrusted the place of enforcement with oversight regarding arbitral awards' afterlife. As one knows, this approach would never take hold, but the mechanism imagined is quite an interesting one to analyse. The draft introduced a series of rules attempting to merge enforcement and annulment into the same proceedings. Under Article 28 of the draft, once exequatur had been granted in a jurisdiction where the uniform law was in force, that award would be enforceable in all other jurisdictions adopting the uniform instrument.[252] By the same token, if enforcement was refused or the award was annulled, it would be immediately unenforceable in all countries under the uniform regime. These solutions would be made operative by Article 26,[253] which vested the place where enforcement was first sought with privileged control over the life of the award.

251 See Article 12 of the 1936 draft in UNIDROIT, *Preliminary Draft*, 6.

252 Article 28 of the draft read as follows: "When leave has been given to issue execution of an award by a judicial authority of one of the countries in which the present law is in force, the award may be the subject of proceedings for enforcement in any one of such countries. Enforcement shall nevertheless be refused if the award is contrary to public policy in the country where execution is claimed or if it has been made in respect of some matter which the law of such country does not permit to be submitted to arbitration." See UNIDROIT, *Preliminary Draft*, 9.

253 See David, *Un projet de loi uniforme sur l'arbitrage*, 890–891. Article 26 of the 1936 draft had the following text: "A judicial authority shall, of its own accord, refuse leave to issue execution, if the award is contrary to public policy or if the arbitrators have decided some question that was not capable of being submitted to arbitration according to the law of the place where leave to issue execution has been claimed. A judicial authority shall also refuse leave to issue execution if, in a country where the present law is in force, leave has already been given to issue execution to the award, or if the authority concerned in one of such countries has adjourned its decisions in accordance with article 27 hereof." See UNIDROIT, *Preliminary Draft*, 9.

Overall, the criteria for refusing enforcement were reduced to violations of public policy and inarbitrability as provided by the place of enforcement.[254] Yet, a party against whom enforcement was sought was given the right, within the same enforcement proceedings and upon broader grounds, to apply for the annulment of the award. In other terms, annulment was envisioned as a procedural incident in enforcement proceedings. All of this was part of the concerted effort to merge enforcement and annulment into the same procedure – an innovation considered by the drafters as a major improvement in the normative regime governing arbitral awards.[255]

As an incident in enforcement proceedings, an application for annulment was capable of adjourning the analysis of enforcement if the applicant was able to show a *prima facie* a case for setting the award aside.[256] The grounds for annulment were not particularly innovative, and the award could be set aside if the arbitration agreement was not valid, if the tribunal was not regularly constituted, if the tribunal exceeded its powers, if there were violations of due process, and/or in cases of violation of certain formalities.[257]

---

254 See Article 28, second paragraph of the 1936 draft in UNIDROIT, *Preliminary Draft*, 9.

255 David notes the following: "*Un autre point essentiel du projet, qui selon ses auteurs constitue une amélioration très sensible de la situation de droit actuellement existante, est la liaison qui a été établie entre, d'une part, la procédure d'exequatur, dont nous venons de voir les effets, et, d'autre part, l'instance possible en annulation de la sentence. [/] Il paraît extrêmement désirable que, soit en première instance, soit comme instance d'appel, juge de l'exequatur et tribunal de l'annulation soient la même autorité, étant donné la connexité qui, de manière évidente, lie les deux problèmes. Les auteurs du projet se sont efforcés de parvenir à cette solution. Toutefois il n'était pas possible d'y parvenir d'une manière complète, l'autorité compétente dans les deux cas ne pouvant pas être désignée avec précision dans une loi internationale, qui doit tenir compte de la diversité des organisations judiciaires des États. On a donc dû se borner à faciliter la solution du problème dans le sens jugé désirable, d'une part abandonnant aux lois particulières des différent pays la détermination des recours que comporte la décision donnée à la demande d'exequatur, d'autre part en établissant que l'annulation de la sentence doit être demandée dans le pays où l'exequatur de la sentence a été demandé.*" See David, Un projet de loi uniforme sur l'arbitrage, 887.

256 Article 27 of the 1936 draft read as follows: "A judicial authority may adjourn the consideration of an application for leave to issue execution if a party cited to appear shows that he has a *prima facie* case for setting aside the award. If, when a reason for setting aside an award has been invoked, a judicial authority nevertheless gives leave to issue execution, it may require the party claiming execution to give security, pending proceedings for setting aside the award." See UNIDROIT, *Preliminary Draft*, 9.

257 See Article 29 of the 1936 draft, which provided the following: "The award shall be set aside in any of the following cases: (1) if there is no valid arbitration agreement; (2) If the award has been made by an irregularly constituted arbitral tribunal, or a challenge to an arbitrator has been wrongly disallowed; (3) If the arbitral tribunal has exceeded its

Moving away from the two assertions made above, in many respects, the 1936 draft merely echoed and codified ongoing trends in the uniformization of arbitral practice. For instance, the draft made a clear attempt to put a definitive end to the dying practice of having tribunals composed of even number of arbitrators. The document did not go as far as prohibiting even-number arbitral tribunals, but it set as a default rule that tribunals should be composed of an odd number of arbitrators.[258] Similarly, the instrument gave a formal contour to the title of president, which is another interesting example of the draft's alignment with ongoing trends in arbitration at the time. Despite the fact that some arbitral legislations would contain references to a third arbitrator, an umpire or a *surarbitre*, the title of president was favoured by the 1936 draft in order to make it clear that there was no hierarchy among the arbitrators when it came to their jurisdictional function as the role of the president was an administrative one.[259]

This 1936 preliminary draft would become the object of strong criticism and would ultimately be replaced by a revised version published in 1940. The new version incorporated comments from a number of stakeholders, including those of the ICC. The participation of the ICC in the production of the 1940 version of the UNIDROIT draft is quite interesting. René David himself was invited to a session of the ICC arbitration committee,[260] held in Paris on 26 February 1937, to discuss the document produced in 1936. In this occasion, considerable

jurisdiction or its powers, in such a case, however, the setting aside may be merely partial; (4) If the proceedings have not been conducted with impartiality; (5) if the award has been made after the expiration of the period fixed by the parties to the arbitration agreement, or by article 21 hereof; (6) If the award has not been signed in accordance with the terms of art.22; (7) If one of the parties has been prejudiced by reasons of the award being only a partial one; (8) If no reasons have been given for the award when the parties to the arbitration agreement have agreed that the award should contain such reasons." In UNIDROIT, *Preliminary Draft*, 9–10.

258 Article 7 of the 1936 draft read as follows: "The arbitrator or arbitrators may be appointed either by the arbitration agreement itself or after it has been entered into. If the agreement does not state the number and manner of appointment of the arbitrators each party shall appoint an arbitrator. Unless otherwise agreed when there is an even number of arbitrators, they shall, before entering on the reference, appoint another arbitrator who shall as of right be president of the arbitral tribunal; when an odd number of arbitrators has been appointed they shall appoint one of themselves to act as president of the arbitral tribunal. In case the arbitrators cannot agree thereon, such appointment shall be made by the court at the request of one of the parties." See UNIDROIT, *Preliminary Draft*, 5.

259 The administration of the proceedings and the direction of the debates were the preserve of the president. See Article 16 of the 1936 draft in UNIDROIT, Preliminary Draft, 7.

260 This was the research branch of the ICC arbitration network at the time. The original title of the committee was "*Comité d'Étude de l'Arbitrage de la Chambre de Commerce Internationale.*"

objections to the project were raised, even if some members of the ICC Court, such as Charles Neff, André Boissier and René Arnaud, expressed "*le regret de voir ces objections se manifester contre une innovation dont la Chambre devrait admettre tout au moins le principe.*"[261] David, for his part, would defend the project, while trying to accommodate the concerns voiced.[262] Even if a compromise solution was ultimately found, the debates at the ICC showed how difficult and controversial would be to move forward with codification projects such as this.

An important point of discord concerned the attempted unification of exequatur and annulments proceedings. A certain J. W. Wynaendts, seating as delegate of the Dutch ICC National Committee, raised concerns as to the appropriateness of foreclosing the possibility to seek annulment at the seat of arbitration. Notably, the Geneva enforcement framework was seen as a preferable regime than the one sketched at UNIDROIT.[263]

Even more controversial in the discussions at the ICC was the approach to arbitrator's mandate espoused by UNIDROIT in its Article 30. Thor Carlander, the delegate of the Swedish ICC National Committee and Vice-President of the ICC Court, noted that the Swedish legal system expected arbitrators to always

261 See UNIDROIT, 'Amendements Proposés Par La Chambre de Commerce Internationale Sur l'Avant-Projet d'une Loi Internationale Sur l'arbitrage En Droit Privé' (1937) S.d.N. – U.D.P 1937 – Etude III – Arbitrage – Doc. 26 32.

262 See UNIDROIT, *Amendements CCI*.

263 He expressed the following views: "*Après avoir fixé le principe de l'effet international de l'exequatur à l'art 28, le projet stipule à l'art. 37 que l'exequatur peut être demandé, notamment, au lieu où la sentence a été prononcée. Et plus loin, il stipule que l'annulation de la sentence doit être demandée au lieu où l'exequatur a été demandé. Il s'ensuit que le ressortissant d'un pays A pourrait être condamné dans un pays étranger B aux termes d'une sentence revêtue de l'exequatur dans ce pays ; qu'il pourrait voir son action en annulation refusée toujours dans le pays B et qu'ainsi la sentence serait finalement exécutée dans le pays A sans qu'il ait pu avoir aucun recours dans son propre pays. Pour peu que dans un pays quelconque se trouvent des personnes de moralité douteuse qui acceptent la fonction d'arbitre et qu'un juge de ce pays soit disposé à déclarer exécutoire cette 'sentence', celle-ci pourrait être exécutée dans n'importe quel État qui aurait accepté la loi uniforme. Cette conséquence des articles 28 et 37 paraît tout à fait inacceptable du point de vue des pays où, comme aux Pays-Bas, tant la procédure arbitrale que la procédure judiciaire sont entourées de plusieurs garanties qui font défaut ailleurs. Les dangers que comporte à cet égard le système du projet risqueraient de décourager le recours à l'arbitrage plutôt que le développer. Aussi, le Comité National néerlandais préférait-il que l'on s'en tient au système de la Convention de Genève et 1927 où la partie condamnée a toujours la possibilité de contester la validité de la sentence devant le juge de son propre pays. Autrement, les États refuseront d'aliéner une part si importante de leur souveraineté et la loi uniforme ne sera pas adoptée.*" See UNIDROIT, *Amendements CCI*, 30–31.

rule on law, proposing the elimination of Article 30 altogether.[264] Similar concerns were voiced by the Swiss and Dutch ICC National Committees.[265]

In reality, the objections were not related to the eventual possibility of an arbitrator to act as an *amiable compositeurs*. Rather the objection lied on the fact that the David's project had the ambition to turn the *amiable composition* into the default approach to arbitrators' mandate. Despite David's attempts to convince his interlocuters otherwise, most members of the ICC arbitration committee insisted on the need to consider the concerns raised.[266] With that in mind, some advocated a complete reversal of Article's 30 logic,[267] highlighting the following:

> *Tout en maintenant la possibilité d'un arbitrage par amiable composition, – procédure qui rallie tous les suffrages du Comité – cette nouvelle rédaction pose nettement le principe que le respect des règles de droit par l'arbitre doit être la règle et non, comme l'implique le libellé actuel, l'exception.*[268]

The discussion had at the ICC arbitration committee was reported to the ICC Congress held in Berlin on 30 June 1937. René David was again invited by the ICC to act as an ambassador of the UNIDROIT project.[269] Discussions at the Congress were not limited to the observations made by the ICC arbitration committee, and at the very opening of the session the delegations of Australia and the United Kingdom manifested their opposition to the project of a uniform law on arbitration.[270]

As discussions advanced, in an article-by-article analysis of the project, the larger ICC constituency discussed again whether arbitrators ought to be vested with the prerogative of ruling on equity by default. Most of the present were in favour of the suppression of Article 30, overturning the default prerogative allowing arbitrators to rule *ex aequo et bono*. Interestingly, the observations made in favour of the provision by the delegate of Czechoslovakia, a certain

264 See UNIDROIT, *Amendements CCI*, 35.

265 See UNIDROIT, *Amendements CCI*, 35–36.

266 See UNIDROIT, *Amendements CCI*, 36.

267 The new text proposed read as follows: "*La sentence est en outre annulé, si les arbitres n'ont pas respecté les règles du droit, sauf si les parties ont expressément stipulé que la juridiction arbitrale serait dispensée d'appliquer ces règles.*" See UNIDROIT, *Amendements CCI*, 60.

268 See UNIDROIT, *Amendements CCI*, 61.

269 See UNIDROIT, *Amendements CCI*, 67.

270 See UNIDROIT, *Amendements CCI*, 68–69.

Peter Sachs, provides a good illustration of the views espoused by those who wanted to advance the authority of arbitration as an equitable one:

> *Le Dr. Peter* SACHS (*Tchécoslovaquie*) *estime que l'arbitrage doit se distinguer de la procédure judiciaire, d'une part, par un formalisme moins rigoureux, et de l'autre, par la possibilité laissé aux arbitres de juger ex aequo et bono. Après avoir rappelé les services que rends l'arbitrage de la C.C.I., l'orateur conclut en émettant le vœu que les sentences rendues en droit par les arbitres soient l'exception et l'équité la règle.*[271]

In the end of the congress, and with many caveats, the ICC adopted a resolution in support of the UNIDROIT uniform instrument.[272] Still, even with the reservations made, the American, Australian and British National Committees refused to support the terms of the resolution.[273]

That same year of 1937, all the considerations raised by the ICC were carefully analysed within the UNDROIT working group charged with the drafting of the uniform arbitration law,[274] and some modifications were introduced

271 See UNIDROIT, *Amendements CCI*, 74.

272 The resolution adopted read as follows: "*La Chambre de Commerce Internationale, qui n'a cessé de préconiser le règlement par arbitrage des litiges entre industriels ou commerçants de pays différents, et qui, par ses commissions de conciliation et sa Cour d'Arbitrage commercial international, a assuré la solution sans recours aux tribunaux de nombreux différends internationaux réitère son vœu de voir les États qui ne l'ont pas encore fait, ratifier dès que possible le Protocole de Genève de 1923 relatif aux clauses d'arbitrage et la Convention de 1927 pour l'exécution des sentences arbitrales étrangères. Elle invite également ses Comités Nationaux à recommander à leurs Gouvernements respectifs de prendre les mesures nécessaires pour supprimer les difficultés auxquelles donnent encore lieu l'exécution des sentences arbitrales étrangères et la diversité des conditions régissant la convention arbitrale. D'autre part, la Chambre de Commerce Internationale se félicite qu'un projet de loi uniforme sur l'arbitrage en droit privé ait été élaboré par l'Institut International de Rome pour l'unification du droit privé. Lorsque ce projet aura été adopté par les principaux États, il facilitera le recours à l'arbitrage pour les contrats conclus avec l'étranger, notamment en reconnaissant un effet universel à l'exequatur prononcé dans un pays où la loi uniforme sera en vigueur. La Chambre de Commerce Internationale donne donc en principe son approbation au projet de loi uniforme, sous réserve des amendements ci-après qui tendent essentiellement à donner priorité, sur certains points, à la convention des parties, notamment lorsque celles-ci se seront référées à un règlement particulier tel que le Règlement de la Cour d'Arbitrage de la Chambre de Commerce Internationale.*" See UNIDROIT, *Amendements CCI*, 75–76.

273 See footnote (oo) of the resolution in UNIDROIT, *Amendements CCI*, 75.

274 See UNIDROIT, 'Procès-Verbaux, Sixième Session, Stockholm, 30 Septembre – 1er Octobre 1937' (1938) S.d.N. – U.D.P 1938 – Etude III – Arbitrage – Doc. 28.

to accommodate the observations emanating from the ICC. Albeit Article 30 was kept in the draft, its text completely changed the approach to arbitrators' mandate, aligning it with the comments made by the ICC arbitration committee and the ICC Berlin Congress. Accordingly, the new text made it clear that, unless otherwise agreed by the parties, arbitrators were required to rule *in iure stricto* and not *ex aequo et bono*.[275]

All these changes materialized in the draft published in December 1940, which conveyed the modifications above and an explanatory report on each of its provisions.[276] Even still, the UNIDROIT project of uniform arbitration law would never be adopted, and the reasons for its failure seem to be threefold.

First, the project was received with great scepticism by Anglo-American lawyers. Both in relation to form and substance, it was felt that the UNIDROIT project was fundamentally based on the "continental tradition."[277] Worse, Anglophone lawyers felt that the transposition of the draft from French to English resulted in unintelligible provisions.[278]

Second, the uniformization of arbitration law was not perceived as an autonomous project. Rather, it was construed as one element in the broader march for the unification of commercial law. In this regard, many felt that there were bigger fish to fry in the pond of uniform commercial law. Moreover, it was also felt within the uniformization movement that the UNIDROIT project was overall unambitious and did not actually promote the uniformization of arbitration law. It was then argued that, at best, the "draft of the Rome Institute may be an international law of commercial arbitration – to be called 'uniform law' it has, strictly speaking, no claim."[279]

Finally, one must realize that politics matter. As the League of Nations crumbled, the fascist government in Italy, which had withdrawn from the League in 1937, turned UNIDROIT into an independent organization. A new statute was drafted in 1939 and by 1942 all member countries working with UNIDROIT under the League of Nations accepted to join the new autonomous body.[280] However, with the winds of war blowing over the world, the appetite for State-led multilateral governance faded.

---

275 See UNIDROIT, *Procès-Verbaux, Sixième Session*, 7.

276 See UNIDROIT, 'Avant-Projet d'une Loi Uniforme Sur l'arbitrage Dans Les Rapports Internationaux En Droit Privé et Rapport Explicatif' (Institut International pour l'Unification du Droit Privé 1940) UDP 1940 – Projet III (1).

277 See Ernst J Cohn, 'The Unification of the Law of Commercial Arbitration' (1938) 24 Transactions of the Grotius Society 1, 3.

278 See Cohn, *op.cit*, 4.

279 See Cohn, *op.cit.*, 7.

280 See Kronke, *op.cit.*, 187.

3.2 *The Expansion of Non-State Codification of Arbitral Authority*

One knows by now that international arbitration was born as the preserve of States. However, a practice and a scholarship on "private aspects of international arbitration" gradually surfaced in the interwar years, dealing with this *sui generis* type of international dispute opposing a state and private party.[281] In parallel, the interwar years saw the advent of a mostly private type of international arbitration, i.e., international commercial arbitration.

It has been shown in this monograph that the birth of what was then called private international arbitration is very much tied to efforts to promote the uniformization and codification of commercial law. Certainly, there were several State-led normative initiatives to reckon with this emerging private form of international arbitration, and these have already been analysed at length in this chapter. However, alongside these positive law projects, considerable non-state normative activity co-existed and often competed with State-led ones. Notably, the 1920s and 1930s witnessed private bodies spearheading the codification of arbitral authority at the global stage in an unprecedented way.

Despite the relative failure of many of these normative projects,[282] the energy put towards the codification of arbitration in relation to cross-border commercial disputes was certainly not lost. Beyond laying the groundwork for

281 See, for instance, Simon Rudstein, 'L'arbitrage International en Matière Privée', *Collected Courses of the Hague*, vol 23 (Brill NV 1926).

282 Nussbaum describes the ICC and AAA arbitration experiments in the following terms: "Noteworthy are the discouraging experiences of the Court of Arbitration and Conciliation, founded in 1921 by the International Chamber of Commerce in Paris. This court enjoyed the prestige and powerful support of the Chamber of Commerce and under its regulations offered all guarantees of fairness, relative inexpensiveness, and facile proceedings. The nonsuccess of the court is all the more significant. Until 1939 (a period of eighteen years) only 77 cases were settled in the court by award, and 120 cases by 'conciliation' before either the 'Conciliation Commission' or the arbitrators. Moreover, the few figures available indicate that a deduction must be made from the figures given in order to ascertain the number of disputes between parties of different nationalities. Almost a third of the parties were French, which indicates that the court was employed in inner French litigation to a considerable extent. In this country the American Arbitration Association established a New York and London Arbitration Service in 1932 and, cooperating with the Pan-American Union, the Inter-American Commercial Arbitration Commission in 1934. Both enterprises were conspicuous failures." See Nussbaum, *Treaties*, 238. In a similar vein, Bagge noted that "[i]t is, therefore, astonishing that the Arbitration Tribunal of the International Chamber of Commerce, being at present the only existing real international arbitration tribunal in commercial cases, is not used any more than it is." See Algot Bagge, 'International Chamber of Commerce and the Development of International Arbitration' (1939) 10 Nordisk Tidsskrift for International Ret 3, 4.

future codification initiatives, these early non-State arbitration codes stand as records of the evolution of arbitral technique. In particular, these documents manifest points of convergence and tension in the way various stakeholders of the private forms of international arbitration envisioned its fundamental elements.

Recent literature on the history of international arbitration has tended to flatten these normative developments in a story of flux and reflux of State sovereignty in relation to international commercial arbitration, as if the transnational expansion of arbitral authority was dictated only by resistance or disinterest from sovereign states.[283] However, a closer look at the codification of international commercial arbitration shows a symbiotic relation between the elaboration of these numerous private arbitration codes and the task of economic reconstruction following WWI. In this regard, many revolving doors between the world of "private" and "public" stakeholders are already quite visible.

This study will now trace the development of three distinctive non-state normative projects fostering the codification and uniformization of international commercial arbitration, all of which reflect the constituent forces competing and cooperating for the control over the destiny of arbitral authority. In the next few pages, this study will survey the creation of the ICC Court of Arbitration in 1923 (3.2.1), the establishment by the American Arbitration Association of its so-called American Arbitration Tribunal in 1931 (3.2.2), and the International Law Association's work on a model arbitration clause and a set of arbitration rules to govern *ad hoc* international commercial arbitration proceedings (3.2.3).

283 This, for instance, is an argument put forward by Lemercier and Sgard: "*En particulier, c'est un principe très affirmé de la souveraineté des juridictions nationales qui est opposé fortement au projet de l'arbitrage. Accepter d'exécuter une sentence étrangère c'est en effet entériner, dans son ordre judiciaire, des règles de droit et des garanties de procédure d'un État étranger. C'est donc un principe de reconnaissance mutuelle qui est posé et que les souverains ne sont pas encore prêts, dans les années 1920, à entériner. Ainsi, les longs débats qui aboutissent à la Convention si décevante de 1927 sont structurés par cette rencontre problématique entre la souveraineté des différents États-membres, beaucoup plus que par la question d'une « justice privée ». A contrario, à l'ONU en 1958, l'enjeu de souveraineté est sinon absent, du moins largement désinvesti des enjeux symboliques encore si puissants dans les années 1920. À ce point, nous voyons donc converger, dans l'arène multilatérale, ces deux tendances de fond qui sous-tendent l'ensemble de notre histoire : la construction d'une institution et d'une pratique privées qui acquièrent efficacité et reconnaissance; et le retrait face à elles des souverains.*" See Lemercier and Sgard, *op.cit.*, at 98.

3.2.1 The Rise of ICC Arbitration

The ICC is the quintessential case in point, being usually portrayed as the leading force in the creation of international commercial arbitration itself.[284] The "merchants of peace," the preferred epithet of the ICC forefathers, were no strangers to international politics and participated actively in it.[285] Indeed, one must note that the first set of ICC Rules was drafted by a group of men gravitating around governments, international organizations, and professional associations.

This brand new institutional and normative framework was produced by a committee set up in 1920 under the chairmanship of Charles Lyon-Caen. Besides Lyon-Caen,[286] the group was composed of delegates from ICC National Committees – namely Edward Huysmans (Belgium), Oliver Bodington (Great Britain), Von Hermert (The Netherlands), S.G. Archibald (United States), Ugo Capitani and Roberto Pozzi (Italy).[287] Few other members would join the committee at a later stage, notably Thor Carlander (Sweden), Owen D. Young (in his capacity as chairman of the US Chamber of Commerce) and Raymond Streat (in his capacity as secretary of the Manchester Chamber of Commerce).[288]

The work of the Lyon-Caen's committee led to the adoption of a resolution in the London Congress of the ICC IN 1921, calling for the legalization of arbitration clauses, the liberalization of the nationality criteria for arbitrators, the adoption of uniform domestic rules on the enforcement of arbitral awards, and the adoption of uniform national rules governing commercial arbitration's

284 See, for instance, Lemercier and Sgard, *Arbitrage privé international et globalisation(s)*; Romero, Jolivet and Grisel, *Aux Origines de l'Arbitrage Commercial Contemporain*; and Schinazi, *The Three Ages of International Commercial Arbitration.*

285 For an institutional history of the early days of the ICC, see Ridgeway, *op.cit.* See also John H Fahey, 'The International Chamber of Commerce' (1926) 94 The Annals of the American Academy of Political and Social Science 126. For an overview of the ICC 's engagement with international politics during the interwar years, see Shane R Tomashot, 'Selling Peace: The History of the International Chamber of Commerce, 1919–1925' (Georgia State University 2015).

286 One must note that Charles Lyon-Caen was a member of that select group of *Belle Époque* international lawyers who were part of the *Institut de Droit International.* He had been a French delegate in a number of international conferences on commercial law and was also a rapporteur working on the unification of the law of bills of exchanges under the League of nations. For Lyon-Caen's profile, see André Lalande, 'Ch. Lyon-Caen' (1935) 89 Revue internationale de l'enseignement 235. See also See Charles Lyon-Caen and others, *Unification de La Législation Sur La Lettre de Change et Le Billet à Ordre – Rapport Général et Rapports Individuels* (Société des Nations 1923).

287 See Ridgeway, *op.cit.*, 319.

288 See Ridgeway, *op.cit.*, 321.

procedure.[289] Importantly, the work of the committee chaired by Lyon-Caen substantiated the creation of the ICC Court, the institutional body introduced to administer ICC arbitration and conciliation.

The ICC in general, and the Court in particular, seemingly emulated the structure of the League of Nations. The institutional framework of the ICC counted with a network of "National Committees" so as to provide some territorial hold to the organization, a General Congress and a permanent Council.[290] While the ICC Court had been entrusted with "all questions connected with arbitration,"[291] its functioning was supervised by the ICC Council.

That said, it is beyond question that the ICC Court was given great control over the life of arbitration proceedings since its inception in 1923. Such purview included the prerogative to decide the seat of the arbitration and the task of centralizing communications in the proceedings.[292] It would also be the ICC Court the one charged with the task of writing the *compromis*, a feature implemented to serve as a guarantee against the longstanding hesitancy on the validity of arbitration clauses.[293] This early practice would later give rise to a formalized document laying down detailed procedural rules for each proceeding, currently known as Terms of Reference.[294] Moreover, the control over the length of arbitral proceedings, including the time arbitrators had available to render their awards, had also been vested in the ICC Court early on.[295]

That said, the institutional control over proceedings was somewhat shared between the ICC Court and the National Committees, for the latter were given a say over arbitrator's appointment.[296] Similarly, the two bodies shared tasks in relation to the control of communications within the proceedings.[297]

---

289 See Ridgeway, *op.cit.*, 319–320.

290 See INTERNATIONAL CHAMBER OF COMMERCE, BROCHURE NO. 20: THE ORGANIZATION OF THE INTERNATIONAL CHAMBER OF COMMERCE (INTERNATIONAL HEADQUARTERS 1922).

291 See Article V/XXV and VI/XXVI of the 1922 ICC Rules in ICC, 'Former Rules of the Court of Arbitration of the International Chamber of Commerce (1922)' in Arthur Nussbaum (ed), *International Yearbook on Civil and Commercial Arbitration* (Oxford University Press 1928), 266–267.

292 See Articles IX/XXIX and XI/XXXI in ICC, *Former Rules of the Court of Arbitration of the International Chamber of Commerce (1922)*, 267.

293 See Romero, Jolivet and Grisel, *op.cit.*, 419.

294 See Romero, Jolivet and Grisel, *op.cit.*, 417.

295 See Article XV/XXXVI of the 1922 Rules in ICC, *Former Rules of the Court of Arbitration of the International Chamber of Commerce (1922)*, 269.

296 Article VI/XXVI, letter a, of the 1922 reads as follows: "The Court of Arbitration shall request the National Committees to furnish it with the names of technically qualified arbitrators, as and when required, for appointment as arbitrators in the cases submitted to it, and from amongst them the Committee shall proceed to appointment." See ICC, *Former Rules of the Court of Arbitration of the International Chamber of Commerce (1922)*, 267.

297 See Article IX/XXIX of the 1922 ICC Rules in ICC, *Former Rules of the Court of Arbitration of the International Chamber of Commerce (1922)*, 267.

Interestingly, the ICC procedural framework favoured the appointment of sole-arbitrators – and it would be up to the ICC Court to designate the adjudicator.[298] This favour towards the sole-arbitrator formally persists to this day,[299] but practice expressed in most arbitration agreements has made three arbitrators the dominant tribunal composition in international commercial arbitration nowadays.

Evidently, the ICC Court was not the only body with purview over arbitral proceedings, for arbitral tribunal themselves would share such prerogative. Notably, the ICC Rules have always entrusted arbitrators with considerable discretion regarding the rules governing the procedure.[300] Also, in the division of labour between the ICC Court and arbitrators, the arbitral tribunal was the one vested with authority over the construction of legal facts and norms.[301] Still, such authority was nuanced by the early development of a practice of award scrutiny, allocating to the institution a certain supervisory role in relation to the adoption of the award.

When the ICC Rules were first enacted, award scrutiny had not been contemplated. The practice, however, would soon emerge and lead to an amendment formalizing it.[302] This took place in 1927, when a provision on award scrutiny was introduced to the ICC Rules. At this point, review was limited to formal aspects of the award.[303] A few years later, in 1934, another amendment to the rules would enlarge the scope of award scrutiny, allowing the ICC Court to call attention to interesting points concerning the merits of the

298 See XII/XXXII of the 1922 ICC Rules in ICC, *Former Rules of the Court of Arbitration of the International Chamber of Commerce* (1922), 267.

299 See, in particular, Article 12(2) of the 2021 ICC Rules, which reads as follows: "Where the parties have not agreed upon the number of arbitrators, the Court shall appoint a sole arbitrator, save where it appears to the Court that the dispute is such as to warrant the appointment of three arbitrators. In such case, the claimant shall nominate an arbitrator within 15 days from receipt of the notification of the decision of the Court, and the respondent shall nominate an arbitrator within 15 days from receipt of the notification of the nomination made by the claimant. If a party fails to nominate an arbitrator, the appointment shall be made by the Court." In ICC, *Arbitration Rules in Force as from 1 January 2021* (ICC 2021), 23.

300 See Article XIII and XXXII of the 1922 ICC Rules in ICC, *Former Rules of the Court of Arbitration of the International Chamber of Commerce* (1922), 268.

301 See Article XIX of the 1922 ICC Rules in ICC, *Former Rules of the Court of Arbitration of the International Chamber of Commerce* (1922), 269.

302 See Romero, Jolivet and Grisel, *op.cit*, 417.

303 Article 21 of the 1927 ICC Rules reads as follows: "Before completing the award the arbitrators or arbitrator shell submit the same to the Court of Arbitration for examination as to its form. No award shall under any circumstances be issued until approved as to its form by the Court of Arbitration." In ICC, *Rules of Conciliation and Arbitration of the International Chamber of Commerce* (1928), 263.

dispute.[304] Currently, the ICC Court is allowed to "lay down modifications as to the form of the award and, without affecting the arbitral tribunal's liberty of decision, may also draw its attention to points of substance."[305] In short, it is the ICC's prerogative to resist the issuance of the award by denying its approval to the decision submitted by arbitrators.[306]

The birth of ICC arbitration is also a significant chapter in the struggle between those that wanted to advance arbitration as a purely contractual type of equitable authority divested of legal enforcement, and those who wanted to construe arbitration as a quasi-judicial mechanism for which legal enforcement ought to be central.

This clash had already taken place in the early days of the International Congresses of Chambers of Commerce, but it became more visible after the creation of the ICC. If back in the era of congresses the camp promoting arbitration as a quasi-judicial authority carried the day, the 1922 ICC Rules would stand as a partial victory for the partisans of equitable arbitration. The spoils of the battle can be found in the article on the enforcement of awards of the 1922 ICC Rules. Indeed, the relevant provision relied primarily on the parties' honour and good faith as guarantees to the enforcement of arbitral awards. In addition, a mechanism of naming and shaming would serve as a reassurance to protect ICC arbitration against dishonourable parties.[307]

This first ICC procedural framework was considerably influenced by a notable member of the Lyon-Caen committee, i.e., Owen D. Young. He believed that the ICC should offer three different types of services – in Young's words, "conciliation," "arbitration outside the law" and "arbitration within the law."[308] In this regard, it has been said that "[t]he rules of conciliation and arbitration as finally promulgated by the Council on July 10, 1922, show no important variation from the Young plan of international commercial arbitration."[309] Conversely, Roberto Pozzi, who had been entrusted by the Lyon-Caen committee with the task of producing a preliminary draft of the ICC arbitration rules, and who had been a long-time advocate of tying together arbitral authority

304 See Romero, Jolivet and Grisel, *op.cit.*, 425–426.

305 See Article 34 of the 2021 ICC Rules in ICC, *Arbitration Rules in Force as from 1 January 2021*, 39.

306 See the final part of Article 34 of the 2021 ICC Rules in ICC, *Arbitration Rules in Force as from 1 January 2021*, 39.

307 See Articles XX and XLI, letters a, b and c in ICC, *Former Rules of the Court of Arbitration of the International Chamber of Commerce (1922)*, 270.

308 See Ridgeway, *op.cit.*, 322.

309 See Ridgeway, *op.cit.*, 324.

and legal enforcement, would see his draft amended to accommodate Young's vision of arbitration.[310]

It is for this reason that there are three sections in the first ICC Rules, with one devoted to conciliation, another to arbitration in countries where arbitral awards were not enforceable, and a third section governing arbitration in countries where awards were legally enforceable – or to use Young's words once again, "conciliation," "arbitration outside the law" and "arbitration within the law."

Within this framework, conciliation proceedings were fundamentally based on the dispute resolution mechanism established between the New York Chamber of Commerce and the Bolsa de Comercio de Buenos Aires.[311] Arbitration, for its part, was construed as an equitable authority and the office of the arbitrator was established as an honorific one.[312] For instance, arbitrators were not to expect payment for their services.[313]

More importantly, a study of awards rendered under the ICC framework shows that in the interwar years only 9 of 70 awards referred to a law applicable.[314] Some have argued that this reliance on equity would be an attempt of the ICC to distinguish itself from "technical arbitrations."[315] Others have connected such an approach to the ICC's ambition to differentiate itself from State courts, as well as to an institutional desire to release ICC awards from judicial purview.[316] It is not unlikely that these considerations crossed the minds of those involved in the early codification of ICC arbitration, but it is also important to highlight the relevance of epistemic struggles for the soul of arbitral authority at the time.

In public and private international law circles, two camps had been opposing each other to control what arbitral authority was supposed to be. On one side, there were those engaging with arbitration as a part of the broader administration of justice, that is, a legal authority proper. On the other side, however,

310 See Ridgeway, *op.cit.*, 324–325.

311 See Ridgeway, *op.cit.*, 320.

312 See Romero, Jolivet and Grisel, *op.cit.*, 411.

313 Article XIX/XL, letter e, of the 1922 ICC Rules read as follows: "The arbitrators shall be entitled to reimbursement of all expenses, but shall render their services gratuitously; except that, in so far as it is recognized that in such countries and industries fees are customarily provided for arbitrators, the Court of Arbitration may, in its discretion, allow arbitrators' fees to be included in the costs of arbitration at rates customary to such countries or industries." In ICC, *Former Rules of the Court of Arbitration of the International Chamber of Commerce* (1922), 269–270.

314 See Romero, Jolivet and Grisel, *op.cit.*, 412.

315 See Lemercier and Sgard, *op.cit.*, 31.

316 See Romero, Jolivet and Grisel, *op.cit.*, 413.

there were those who wanted to promote arbitration as an equitable authority, one detached from law and its manipulation of coercive sanctions. In the interwar years, this controversy was far from being settled. If the correlation of forces favoured equitable arbitration in 1922, the ICC could not ignore the partisans of legal arbitration. In due course, the tables would be turned, and equitable arbitration would become nothing more than a point of curiosity.

A final element to be discussed regarding the birth of ICC arbitration has to do with the population bringing it to life. The ICC Court, one of the main custodians of the private forms of international arbitration, had as its second President Nikolaos Politis.[317] Politis, one should not forget, was an eminent public international lawyer, who had been the leading voice at the League of Nations in relation to the agenda "Arbitration, Security and Disarmament." Étienne Clémentel, a key negotiator of the London Agreements, was the first president of the ICC, while Owen D. Young, the intellectual father of the Dawes and Young settlement plans, also had a claim to the paternity of the ICC Rules. Looking at this group of people, one cannot but realize the fluid boundaries between the constituencies of public and private international arbitration in the interwar years.

3.2.2 The AAA's Code of Arbitration

Turning away from the ICC, an interesting counterpoint is that related to the codification efforts sponsored by the American Arbitration Association. The ICC and the AAA certainly shared common goals, which would lead them to enter into a cooperation agreement by the end of the 1930s.[318] Even still, the early arbitration frameworks created by the ICC and the AAA can be contrasted in several ways.

Perhaps the most fundamental difference between the two institutions was their constituency. While the ICC had internationalism in its DNA, the AAA was fundamentally an American organization. As a consequence, the foundation of the "American Arbitration Tribunal," as it was called back in the 1930s, aimed first and foremost at the promotion and uniformization of American arbitration.[319] Nevertheless, it was evident that an institution presiding over

317 See Romero, Jolivet and Grisel, *op.cit.*, 415.

318 See Sandra K Partridge, 'Frances Kellor and the American Arbitration Association' (2012) 67 Dispute Resolution Journal 16, 20.

319 This is made clear in a handbook published in 1931 by Frances Kellor under the auspices of the AAA: "The American Arbitration Association is composed of members, associates and organizations affiliated together for the purpose of advancing the practice of arbitration in the United States, and it maintains for this purpose the American Arbitration Tribunal.

American-related commercial disputes was bound to become relevant at the world stage. As American influence over the global economy kept increasing, American arbitration practice would continuously expand its purview over cross-border economic flows.

Certainly, this emerging American outlook to arbitration was not disconnected from the geopolitical context of its time. According to Frances Kellor, a "new Era in American arbitration began in 1920," and "its incentive came from World War I and the resolve to avoid future wars insofar as the settlement or control of disputes through arbitration could accomplish that end."[320] One must note that Kellor, a leader of American arbitration, never distinguished between domestic or international arbitration. Her approach to arbitral technique was all-encompassing.

The AAA was born out of the merger between the Arbitration Society of America and the Arbitration Foundation of the New York Chamber of Commerce. The Society was the oldest of the two organizations, being created in 1922 after the adoption of the New York Arbitration Act. It has been said that the Society was responsible for extending the reach of arbitration in the United States beyond trade associations, for "[i]t freed arbitration from commodity and geographical limitations to serve all of the people all of the time."[321]

The Foundation, for its part, had been created in 1925, under the auspices of the New York Chamber of Commerce – then considered in the United States as "the keeper of arbitration since 1768."[322] The initiative was led by Charles Bernheimer, the same one who had been actively involved in the arbitration

As an essential part of its plan for organized arbitration, the Association maintains a national panel of arbitrators and such special panels as individual trades may require. [...] The Association prepares and keeps up to date the arbitration rules and practice in connection therewith which offer a standard and uniform procedure that may be used in any type of controversy and that is readily adaptable to any jurisdiction in the United States. These rules and practice implement the arbitration law of the jurisdiction where the arbitration is to be held and they supply a procedure when the prevailing law fails to do so. By reason of the diversity in arbitration laws, the rules are general in character so as to admit of greater adaptability in the forty-eight state jurisdictions and the practice contains the necessary administrative directions for putting the rules into effect." See Frances Kellor, *Code of Arbitration: Practice and Procedure of the American Arbitration Tribunal* (Commerce Clearing House Inc 1931), 1.

320 See Frances Kellor, *American Arbitration: Its History, Functions and Achievements* (Harper & Brothers Publishers 1948), 9.

321 Kellor, *American Arbitration*, 11.

322 Kellor, *American Arbitration*, 15.

debates at the International Congresses of Chambers of Commerce. The two institutions harboured conflicting views with regards to the practice of arbitration, which ultimately manifested a political divide between progressives and conservatives. In this regard, Kellor described the struggle as follows:

> So deep-rooted were the differences between the champions of the new and preservers of the old order, that arbitration, the reconciler of differences, was likely to be split into factions. In the one group, lawyers, professional men, small traders, and the average citizen combined to support the new order; in the other group, substantial business interests combined to continue commercial arbitration very much as it had come down through the ages.[323]

Curiously, the creation of the AAA ensued from a conciliation process of sorts. The Society and Foundation agreed to appoint a six-member committee to settle their diverging views on the future of arbitration, with each party appointing half of the committee members. This committee spent a year "reconciling the differences, co-ordinating the various projects, and formulating a combined program."[324] In the end, the ultimate recommendation of the panel of conciliators was to merge the two organizations, which then led to the creation of the AAA in 1926.

Evoking the continental European legal tradition, the first set of AAA rules was labelled "Code of Arbitration." The institutional infrastructure in charge of administering the rules was equipped with a Permanent Advisory Council charged with the administration of cases and the appointment of arbitration tribunals under AAA Rules.[325] Then, an Arbitration Law Committee was created as an advisory body established "for the purpose of considering, from time to time, the intricate questions of law that arise from matters heard and determined in the American Arbitration Tribunal."[326] Finally, at the apex of this system, there was the AAA Board of Directors. The Board's chair was Frances Kellor, who had been the only female founder of the AAA, and already a well-known lawyer, social scientist, and activist.[327]

---

323 Kellor, *American Arbitration*, 16.

324 Kellor, *American Arbitration*, 17.

325 In 1931, the Permanent Advisory Council was composed of Frank H. Sommer (chairman), Hermann Irion (vice-chairman); William Fellowes Morgan Jr. (secretary); and Lee J. Eastman, Nathan Isaacs, Frances Kellor, S. Whitney Landon, Floyd B. Odlum, Franklin E. Parker Jr, and Thomas B. Paton (members). See Kellor, *Code of Arbitration*, 2.

326 See Kellor, *Code of Arbitration*, 2.

327 See Partridge, *Frances Kellor and the American Arbitration Association*, 18.

Under the AAA Rules, arbitration was presented as a "quasi-judicial proceeding" and the office of the arbitrator was similarly construed as a "quasi-judicial" one.[328] As a consequence, arbitrators were expected to act as judges – albeit private ones. Accordingly, the AAA Rules did not provide for the possibility of arbitrators ruling on equity and foreclosed the possibility to entrust them with the task of promoting an "amicable composition."[329]

In its "Suggestions for the Guidance of Arbitrators," an early guideline instrument with soft norms on the many facets of the office of the arbitrator, the AAA defined the scope of the arbitrator's authority as follows:

> The Arbitrator has authority to decide all matters, submitted to him by the parties, including, under most of the arbitration statutes, questions of law as well as of fact. He is not bound by technical rules of evidence but he should not reject material evidence and may admit all evidence. He should permit all parties to be present or to be represented and should receive the testimony of all witnesses presented and all exhibits offered.[330]

Even still, the prevailing view at AAA in this moment portrayed arbitral authority fundamentally as a cognitive authority instead of a normative one. The primary role of arbitrators was to construe legal facts and not norms per se. Accordingly, being a lawyer was not seen as a necessary qualification to act as an arbitrator under the AAA framework,[331] but in the years to come the practice of arbitration would end up colonized by lawyers.

Great idealism still existed on both sides of the Atlantic in relation to the office of the arbitrator, and most failed to portray the role of the arbitrator as a professional career or service subject to a market exchange. In fact, arbitrators were expected to act "[in] the interests of the public good and commercial

328 See Kellor, *Code of Arbitration*, 60 and 75.

329 See Kellor, *Code of Arbitration*, 61.

330 See Suggestion for the Guidance of Arbitrators, Annex II in Kellor, *Code of Arbitration*, 198.

331 In this regard, Frances Kellor highlights the following: "Arbitrators need have no knowledge of the law unless the parties indicate that attorneys or jurists shall be named as arbitrators. Only a small percentage of the matters adjudicated under the Arbitration Rules involve questions of law; but if it appears, from the submission or clause that such a question is likely to arise, the parties may indicate that they wish to have an attorney or jurist named as the arbitrator or as one of the arbitrators." See Kellor, *Code of Arbitration*, 84.

peace."[332] In short, similar to the approach taken at the early days of ICC arbitration, the AAA also framed the office of the arbitrator as an honorary one. Consequently, under the AAA rules the arbitrator should not expect to receive payment for the services rendered.

Another important feature of this early set of AAA Rules concerned the finality of arbitral awards, for the decision on the merits of the dispute was final and binding, foreclosing any possibility of review by State courts.[333]

AAA arbitration also encompassed considerable institutional oversight. Any references to the AAA Rules contained in an arbitration agreement would suffice to ground the authority of the American institution.[334] Certainly, AAA Rules did not provide for the scrutiny of awards, but it provided for the maintenance of a list of arbitrators institutionally vetted. Parties were not obliged to choose arbitrators from this list, but being listed added a layer of credibility to prospective arbitrators and created a strong incentive for parties to select from the rooster. With the implementation of a list of arbitrators, the AAA would perform the role of a professional gatekeeper, governing the concrete distribution of arbitral authority to chosen individuals.[335] This feature entrusted the institution with a considerable hold over the development of arbitrators' careers, and an indirect control regarding the performance of their duties.

---

332 See Kellor, *Code of Arbitration*, 76; and Rule XII of the AAA Rules, Annex 1, in Kellor, *Code of Arbitration*, 194.

333 See Kellor, *Code of Arbitration*, 163.

334 Rule XVI provides as follows: "The parties shall be deemed to have made these Rules a part of the arbitration agreement whenever, in the submission or clause or other written agreement, they provide for arbitration thereunder; and they shall be bound only by the precise terms of these Rules as contained herein." See AAA Rules, Annex 1, in Kellor, *Code of Arbitration*, 195.

335 Frances Kellor notes the following: "To overcome this delay and difficulty, the American Arbitration Association maintains permanent panels of qualified and impartial persons from which the parties are entitled to make their nominations in the manner hereinafter prescribed. The members of these panels are invited to serve by the Arbitration Committee and they accept only on its invitation and not on the direct request of a party. [...] These panels are composed of persons, distinguished in public service or skilled in the various branches of the trades or professions, who, in their acceptance, agree to serve without compensation and when called upon by the Arbitration Committee after they have been nominated by the parties. While it is not obligatory on the parties to make their selections from these panels they offer a way out of the deadlock in which parties, suspicious of each other's nominees, frequently find themselves; and they assure highly qualified judges who have no personal interest in either party or in the controversy. The members of these panels have a certificate of appointment as members thereof and receive instructions concerning the duties of their office." See Kellor, *Code of Arbitration*, 78–79.

In addition, the AAA also disposed of a further instrument to control the office of the arbitrator, which was the administration of an oath of office.[336] This somewhat anachronistic obligation, which would not gain course in the practice of transnational arbitration, was put in place to comply with the arbitration legislation of various American states.[337] As a consequence, the oath served simultaneously as an instrument of institutional and State control over the life of the arbitration, for it had to be sworn "by an officer authorized by law to administer an oath to the effect that he will faithfully and fairly hear and examine the matter in controversy and that he will make a just award according to the best of his understanding."[338]

The uniformization project led by the AAA was not limited to the codification of procedural rules. It also produced several standard forms to be readily used throughout the proceedings, including a model arbitral award. This template was divided in three parts. The first one would indicate the terms of the arbitrator's mandate and the administration of the oath of office. Then, a second part would contain the reasoning and decisions arrived at by the tribunal. Finally, a third section would be devoted to the signature of the arbitrators.[339]

Like the ICC, the expansion of AAA's purview relied on standard arbitration clauses. In this regard, the AAA arbitration framework in force in the 1930s conveyed two different model clauses, one to be adopted in "domestic trade contracts" and another one for "foreign trade contracts." The first clause was much more concise and did not provide for the seat, the number of arbitrators or their method of appointment. Conversely, the clause governing international contracts established by default New York as the seat of the arbitration, provided for a three-member tribunal and introduced a method of appointment in which each party would appoint one arbitrator, and the two party-appointed arbitrators would then select the third one.[340]

---

336 See Form of Oath, Annex VIII, in Kellor, *Code of Arbitration*, 274.

337 Section 5, letter e, of the Suggestions reads as follows: "The Arbitrator is in sole charge of hearings and has the following obligations: [...] (e) To take an oath when the hearing opens (if so required by the prevailing law. If the oath has been signed before the hearing, it should be exhibited to the parties at the opening of the proceedings." See Suggestions for the Guidance of Arbitrators, Annex II, in Kellor, *Code of Arbitration*, 199.

338 See Kellor, *Code of Arbitration*, 109.

339 For the model award, see Annex VIII, in Kellor, *Code of Arbitration*, 284.

340 Compare the two standard clauses. The "Standard Clause for Domestic Trade Disputes" read as follows: "Any controversy or claim arising out of or relating to this contract or the breach thereof, shall be settled by arbitration, in accordance with the Rules, then obtaining, of the American Arbitration Association, and judgment upon the award rendered

3.2.3 The ILA Efforts for the Codification of Arbitral Procedure

In addition to these developments in institutional arbitration, it is also important to draw attention to another non-State actor that was increasingly involved in the codification of private forms of international arbitration, *i.e.*, the International Law Association – commonly known as ILA. Created in Brussels in 1873 under the name of "Association for the Reform and Codification of the Law of Nations," the ILA became known as such in 1895.[341] The early days of its existence were animated by the familiar faces of that elite community of *Belle Époque* international lawyers, among which it is worth to note the following: Carlos Calvo, Gustave Rolin-Jaequemyns, Jean Gaspar Bluntschli, Augusto Pierantoni, and David Dudley Field.[342]

The core mandate of the ILA was to work towards the codification of both public and private international law. Evidently many of its initiatives overlapped with that of its sister organization, the IDI. Still, while the IDI hoped to become a "senate of jurists,"[343] the ILA catered to a broader constituency. Accordingly, the stakeholders of the ILA would "consist of Jurists, Economists, Legislators, Politicians and others taking an interest in the question of the reform and Codification of Public and Private International Law, the Settlement of Disputes by Arbitration, and the assimilation of the laws, practice and procedure of the Nations in reference to such laws."[344]

---

may be entered in the highest court of the forum, state or federal, having jurisdiction." In contrast, the "Standard Clause for Foreign Trade Contracts" read as follows: "Any controversy or claim arising out of or relating to this contract or the breach thereof, shall be settled by arbitration, in accordance with the Rules, then obtaining, of the American Arbitration Association. This agreement shall be enforceable and judgment upon any award rendered by all or a majority of the arbitrators may be entered in any court having jurisdiction. The arbitration shall be held in New York City or wherever jurisdiction may be obtained over the parties. Three arbitrators shall be selected. Unless the parties have mutually agreed upon qualified persons, one arbitrator shall be appointed by each party and the two so chosen shall designate the third. If either party fails or neglects within a period of fourteen days after written notice by the other to select an arbitrator upon its part, or if the two selected by the parties cannot agree upon a third arbitrator within seven days after they have been chosen, the Arbitration Committee of the American Arbitration Association, upon the request of either party, shall appoint such arbitrator or arbitrators from its National Panel within a period of fourteen days thereafter." See Annex III in Kellor, *Code of Arbitration*, 205.

341 See Ruth Frendo, 'The Archives of the International Law Association' (2017) 17 Legal Information Management 97, at 97.

342 See International Law Association, *Reports of the First Conference Held at Brussels, 1873 and of the Second Conference Held at Geneva, 1874* (West, Newman & Co 1903), 6.

343 Rolin-Jaequemyns, *Communications Relatives à l'Institut de Droit International*, 667.

344 See Frendo, *op.cit.*, 97.

If State-to-State arbitration was a central element of the ILA's original codification program, some fifty years after its creation the organization would develop a steady work stream on the codification of commercial arbitration. In 1922, the ILA Conference had the opportunity to discuss the creation of the ICC Court on the basis of a paper presented by Robert Fraser. Acting as the delegate of the London Chamber of Commerce, Fraser praised the creation of a permanent institution to replace *ad hoc* arbitral tribunals,[345] and proposed a resolution promoting the unification of arbitral procedure.[346] The association did adopt Fraser's proposal, and the paper led to the appointment of a committee to further work on the issues he raised.[347]

With the creation of the commercial arbitration committee, two reports were then presented at the 1924 ILA conference on the unification of arbitral procedure. One document was submitted by English rapporteurs and another by French rapporteurs. The two reports covered different issues. The English report focused on the enforcement of foreign arbitral awards, giving special attention to English legislation, while the French report focused on the institutionalization of international commercial arbitration.[348] The committee decided to issue a resolution calling states to unify their regimes on the enforcement of foreign arbitral awards through the adoption of international treaties, drawing attention to the advantages of conducting arbitration before the ICC Court.[349]

At the following congress of the ILA, held in 1926, the ICC would be invited to join the debates in the commercial arbitration committee. In that occasion,

---

345 Fraser argued the following: "Arbitral tribunals appointed *ad hoc* are open to the objection of the absence of any guarantee that a uniform interpretation of obscure passages in contracts would be observed or definite principles applied. The International Chamber therefore favours the institution of permanent arbitral Courts of a high standard, to which commercial men could appeal for the adjustment of differences, if and when they arise, without unnecessary friction, cost, or delay, and whose awards would be enforceable in the country where execution is claimed." See International Law Association, *Report of the Thirty-First Conference Held at the Palace of Justice, Buenos Aires, 24th August – 30th August, 1922* (Sweet & Maxwell 1923), 187–188.

346 Fraser proposed a resolution that read as follows: "That this Association approves the proposal of the International Chamber of Commerce for the establishment of standardised Commercial Courts of Arbitration; and appeals to the Governments of all Commercial States to engage in the studies requisite to the unification of Commercial Law and arbitral procedure and for the prompt execution of Awards." See International Law Association, *Report of the Thirty-First Conference*, 189.

347 See International Law Association, *Report of the Thirty-Third Conference Held at the Riddarhuset and the Riksdaghuset, Stockholm, September 8th to 13th, 1924* (Sweet & Maxwell 1925), 362.

348 See International Law Association, *Report of the Thirty-Third Conference*, 356–362.

349 See International Law Association, *Report of the Thirty-Third Conference*, 362.

René Arnaud addressed the attendants and explained the operations of the ICC Court.[350] The members of the committee had also to opportunity to discuss whether arbitral tribunals ought to be composed by a sole-arbitrator or whether it should be a collegiate body. Interestingly, there was a strong view that "[t]he system by which each party appoints an arbitrator, who themselves choose an umpire, has proved in practice to be wasteful and extravagant," as a result of the fact that "two arbitrators usually degenerate into mere advocates for the party appointing them, and the parties have to pay the fees of three arbitrators instead of one."[351]

In the Warsaw congress of the ILA, held in 1928, the commercial arbitration committee devoted considerable attention to the 1927 Geneva Convention on the Execution of Foreign Arbitral Awards. A report presented to the committee, drafted by T. Willes Chitty and Victor Aronson, did not fully endorse the instrument. In fact, it was considered that "the enforcement of such awards should be discretionary and not obligatory" and that "[i]f however the system is to be adopted of making enforcement compulsory, subject to certain exceptions, the exceptions ought to be more precisely and accurately defined than is at present case."[352] Furthermore, the report claimed that under the Geneva regime of enforcement, foreign arbitral awards were given a higher status than those obtained in a purely domestic context, which was perceived as undesirable.[353] A lively exchanged ensued. René Arnaud, once again present, took the floor to defend the convention at various occasions.[354] Similarly, Kuhn and Hofmannsthal also defended the convention, considering that the terms of the report would jeopardize the enforceability of foreign arbitral awards.[355]

In light of the controversy, the report in question was remanded to the appreciation of the ILA Executive Council, which decided to send it back to the committee for further consideration. When the 1930 ILA conference opened in New York, Wyndham A. Bewes, the new designated rapporteur on commercial arbitration, stood the ground of his predecessors. For him, there was no reason to modify the 1928 report, "the more so since their views have been

350 See International Law Association, *Report of the Thirty-Fourth Conference Held at the Imperial Palace and the Chamber of Commerce, Vienna, August 5th to August 11th, 1926* (Sweet & Maxwell 1927), at 637 et seq.

351 See International Law Association, *Report of the Thirty-Fourth* Conference, 624.

352 See International Law Association, *Report of the Thirty-Fifth Conference Held at Warsaw, August 9th to 16th, 1928* (Sweet & Maxwell 1929), 172–173.

353 See International Law Association, *Report of the Thirty-Fifth Conference*, 173.

354 See International Law Association, *Report of the Thirty-Fifth Conference*, at 178, 182 and 187.

355 See International Law Association, *Report of the Thirty-Fifth Conference*, 181.

substantially adopted by the British Government Department in drafting the Bill to put the Convention in force."[356]

The contention seems to reflect a certain English attitude towards the 1927 Geneva Convention, which was likely grounded on a fear that the British imperial system of commercial arbitration might be in jeopardy. The Bewes report went further in its exhortation against the convention, praising "the astute" English Arbitration Act of 1930 for deviating from the regime of enforcement established in Geneva.[357] Robert Fraser would take the floor in support of this view, arguing that "the Convention of 1927 […] was a premature proceeding."[358] The members of the committee, upon the proposition of Charles Bernheimer, one of the founding members of the AAA, thought it would be more productive to shift gears from multilateralism to bilateralism and to focus on the uniformization of institutional arbitral procedure.[359] This was indeed the course of action taken by the ILA, reflected in the resolution adopted that year in relation to commercial arbitration.[360]

---

356 See International Law Association, *Report of the Thirty-Sixth Conference Held at New York in the Hourse of the Association of the Bar, September 2nd to 9th, 1930* (Sweet & Maxwell 1931), 238.

357 See International Law Association, *Report of the Thirty-Sixth* Conference, 240.

358 See International Law Association, *Report of the Thirty-Sixth* Conference, 243.

359 Charles Bernheimer expressed the following view: "It is futile to endeavour to do too much along general international lines, but rather we should foster the endeavour between two nations of like characteristics. […] The award is what we are looking for, namely, that the Courts should both enforce the acts of a foreign country as regards the compelling of arbitration to proceed under the contract of submission, submission in that case relating to existing disputes under a contract – the "clause compromissoire" – in the first place, and that the Courts of the respective countries should honour by comity, by friendliness between nations, what the Courts in another country have pronounced to be sound in relation to arbitration. The other point which has been greatly discussed between ourselves is the addition 'provided these arbitrations have been conducted under institutions of high standing and which possess necessary facilities.' […] Now, that experience has shown us that if arbitrations are conducted without institutional background they are apt to run wild." See International Law Association, *Report of the Thirty-Sixth* Conference, 244–245.

360 The resolution read as follows: "Be it resolved, that in order to safeguard the security of transactions in international commerce it is necessary that agreements between Governments be entered into to regulate the essentials of arbitration practice and procedure between nationals of their respective countries, and to provide for the reciprocal enforcement of commercial arbitration agreements and awards made pursuant thereto. Provided these arbitrations are conducted under institutions of high standing which possess necessary facilities." See International Law Association, *Report of the Thirty-Sixth* Conference, 243.

At its Oxford conference, held in 1932, the ILA dealt only tangentially with commercial arbitration.[361] Indeed, in a discussion on the uniformization of trade terms (notably a so-called "Warsaw rules" giving uniformity to C.I.F. contracts), it was decided that ICC arbitration was not to be the default settlement mechanism of C.I.F. contracts.[362]

Two years later, in 1934, the Budapest congress had the opportunity to discuss the draft of a model arbitration clause, which was, essentially, a succinct code of commercial arbitration procedure.[363] Made of seventeen articles, many of which were composed of multiple paragraphs, this model clause governed the constitution of the tribunal, the conduct of proceedings, cost allocation and enforcement of the awards. This was a quite interesting normative instrument, as it had unique features in comparison to an ever more uniform procedure in international commercial arbitration.

For instance, if the use of a model clause was the preferred strategy to structure arbitral authority, the emerging practice related to the design of these clauses – that would become the dominant one – was not to regulate every detail of procedure in the clause itself but rather refer to a separate set of detailed procedural rules. Also, the default rule under the ILA model clause provided for an arbitral tribunal composed of two arbitrators and priority was given to consular and judicial authorities in its composition,[364] an odd approach in complete disconnect with the rules of the ICC or the AAA surveyed above.

These unusual features were not well received by the members of the commercial arbitration committee. There were many that considered the instrument undesirable, with a certain Arne Rygh expressing the view that "our international Chamber of Commerce does the work better than anyone else could do it."[365] Similarly, a certain A.C.W. Beerman considered that "this question should be decided by the International Chamber of Commerce, whose

361 See International Law Association, *Report of the Thirty-Seventh Conference Held at Oxford in the Hall of the Union Society, August 8th to 12th, 1932* (Eastern Press 1933); International Law Association, *Report of the Thirty-Eighth Conference Held at Budapest in the Hungarian Academy of Science, September 6th to 10th, 1934* (Eastern Press 1935).

362 See International Law Association, *Report of the Thirty-Seventh Conference*, 282.

363 See International Law Association, *Report of the Thirty-Eighth Conference*, 113–115.

364 Article 4 of the model clause read as follows: "*Les deux parties contractantes désignent pour leurs arbitres respectifs, leur Consul et à défaut le Président du Tribunal jugeant au premier degré les affaires commerciales dans le ressort duquel se trouve le lieu où il sera procédé à l'arbitrage.*" See International Law Association, *Report of the Thirty-Eighth Conference*, 114.

365 See International Law Association, *Report of the Thirty-Eighth Conference*, 118.

arbitration is very satisfactory in practice, and I think it is only a question of fairness that the International Law Association should not encroach in the same territory."[366] Along the same lines, René Arnaud, speaking on behalf of the ICC, was of the view that such a model clause would be counterproductive in light of the work of the ICC, and proposed to accommodate some of the concerns and observations of the ILA in the ICC rules.[367]

There were also those who proposed amendments to the model clause, especially in relation to the role of consular and judicial authorities in arbitration.[368] Still, several members of the ILA commercial arbitration committee also resisted the growing predominance of the ICC. This was the case of Wyndham A. Bewes, an influential member of the committee, who noted that "our friends in the International Chamber of Commerce do not want to go so far as to wish for a monopoly of arbitration."[369] Finally, the draft model clause was not adopted, instead the ILA decided to "continue its work, and should take into consideration the experience already acquired on this subject by the various expert bodies."[370]

And so it was done. The Congress held in Paris in 1936 would continue its labour on the uniformization of arbitral procedure, dealing more directly with the fragmentation of arbitration rules. The report penned by R.S. Fraser and C. John Colombo is an excellent example of the position of arbitration as part of a broader movement for the unification of private law. In particular, one finds an early reference to the *lex mercatoria* as a force pushing forward the

366 See International Law Association, *Report of the Thirty-Eighth Conference*, 118.

367 Arnaud expressed the following: "*Il serait sans doute regrettable de proposer aux industriels et commerçants qui font des affaires avec l'étranger une nouvelle clause d'arbitrage qui risquerait de faire double emploi avec la clause d'arbitrage de la Chambre de Commerce Internationale. D'ailleurs si la Chambre de Commerce Internationale est essentiellement un groupement d'hommes d'affaires et si l'arbitrage est par nature une procédure qui intéresse spécialement les hommes d'affaires, il n'en est pas moins vrai que dans l'élaboration et le perfectionnement de son règlement d'arbitrage la Chambre de Commerce Internationale a toujours tenu à s'entourer de l'avis des juristes. Elle a reconnu, en effet, que la procédure arbitrale doit, pour être valable, se conformer aux règles impératives des lois des divers pays. C'est précisément surtout pour tenir compte des observations des juristes en même temps que des leçons de l'expérience que la Chambre de Commerce Internationale a été amenée à amender à plusieurs reprises son règlement d'arbitrage ; elle sera toujours prête à prendre connaissance avec le plus grand intérêt à des observations que pourraient faire, sur son règlement, les juristes si compétents en matière de droit international que groupe l'International Law Association.*" See International Law Association, *Report of the Thirty-Eighth Conference*, 124.

368 See International Law Association, *Report of the Thirty-Eighth Conference*, 119–121.

369 See International Law Association, *Report of the Thirty-Eighth Conference*, 122.

370 See International Law Association, *Report of the Thirty-Eighth Conference*, 125–126.

uniformization of commercial arbitration.[371] The report, however, would serve as a preliminary basis for a broader comparative study to substantiate a further initiative on the unification of commercial arbitration.[372]

The outcome of this comparative study was presented in the 1938 congress, held at the end of August in Amsterdam. Despite the imminence of a full-scale world war, expressed in the German bombing of Guernica in April 1937, the Japanese invasion of China in July 1937, and the German annexation of Austria in March of that 1938, the ILA carried on with business as usual. Notably, the commercial arbitration committee produced a report on the uniformization of arbitration procedure, which conveyed both a model clause and a set of arbitration rules.[373]

The conclusions of this report highlighted some convergence in the normative framework governing commercial arbitration across the countries studied, except for the varying attitudes towards the mechanism of *amiable composition* and the possibility of submitting an appeal against the arbitral award.[374] With regard to the former, the following was noted:

---

371 This is expressed in the following terms: "As members of the International Law Association, we all recognise the importance of the unification of Private International Law, of which the immutable principles of commercial arbitration enshrined in the *lex mercatoria* form an integral part. Those who seek peace need to pursue it, and this is done when insistence is placed on the due observance of *lex mercatoria* – and, in particular, the right for contracting parties to prescribe in their contracts the conditions upon which they are prepared to contract, including the sufficiency of the arbitration clause to afford them a square deal in ease of difference". See International Law Association, *Report of the Thirty-Ninth Conference Held at Paris in the Cour de Cassation, September 10th to 15th, 1936* (Richard Clay & Sons 1937), 98, para 11.

372 The terms of the decision were the following ones: "In conclusion, your Committee consider that co-operation between existing organisations should be secured, with the object of reaching the unification of the rules observed in arbitration, and to effect the uniform and reciprocal enforcement of arbitral awards in all countries. Towards the attainment of this object, your Committee consider that the various branches of the I.L.A. should be invited to contribute Reports of the practice obtaining in their respective countries in commercial arbitration. It will then be the task of your Committee to advise, in the light of such Reports, to what extent unification may be practicable in the near future." See International Law Association, *Report of the Thirty-Ninth Conference*, 98, para 12.

373 See International Law Association, *Report of the Fortieth Conference Held at Amsterdam in the Royal Colonial Institute, August 29 to September 2, 1938* (Richard Clay & Sons 1939), 209 et seq.

374 In this regard, the report read as follows: "An examination of these reports and memoranda shows that, apart from the very material departure from legal and arbitral procedure obtaining in some Continental countries with reference to '*amiables compositeurs,*' or the application of the principle of equity as differently understood and applied according to the country in which it is employed, there is really no fundamental difference in

> The system of "*amiables compositeurs*," on the other hand, has always been viewed with considerable apprehension by Anglo-American countries, as it exempts arbitrators to which it applies (*i.e. de facto* arbitrators as distinguished from *de jure* arbitrators) from adhering to the forms and procedure prescribed by ordinary courts of justice, and further empowers them to decide a dispute in their discretion, irrespective of the law applicable to the case.[375]

The view espoused by the report was that "it is obviously desirable that greater international uniformity should be established in the practice of commercial arbitration."[376] In this regard, the report acknowledged the draft uniform instrument produced by UNIDROIT, but cautioned that "the draft law prepared by the Rome Institute does not appear to your Committee likely [...] to gain the approval of commercial countries such as Great Britain, or the British Dominions, or the United States of America."[377] It was argued that the UNIDROIT project of uniform law "proceeds too much upon the conception of arbitration as it exists in some codes of law on the Continent of Europe."[378]

For the ILA constituency, the ideal uniform legislation would enforce only "independent and impartial arbitration on the basis of judicial procedure and prohibit the substitution for such arbitration when agreed on of '*amiables compositeurs*.'"[379] In addition, such ideal piece of uniform legislation would provide for an exception to the enforcement of arbitration agreements when

the main principles of substantive rules governing commercial arbitration in the leading States. Such main differences as exist relate principally to the rules of evidence and procedure, and to such as affect the qualification of the terms of contract by custom and usage, which vary considerably in the countries concerned. Thus, most Continental States refuse to allow parties to a dispute to be witnesses at all, and the award is principally decided on documentary evidence. Another point which presents serious difficulties is the right of appeal to courts of law, which in some countries appears to be too freely available. Even when the parties have waived their right of appeal in advance, there still exists, in some Continental States, the remedy of 'annulment,' and also a 'claim for revision' which is capable of delaying unduly the enforcement of an award. There is no doubt that such proceedings may result in extreme hardship and are opposed to the general desire of international commerce to obtain a speedy, final and inexpensive determination of disputes by arbitration." See International Law Association, *Report of the Fortieth Conference*, 209–210, para 3.

375 See International Law Association, *Report of the Fortieth Conference*, 210, para 4.

376 See International Law Association, *Report of the Fortieth Conference*, 210, para 5.

377 See International Law Association, *Report of the Fortieth* Conference, 212, para 10.

378 See International Law Association, *Report of the Fortieth Conference*, 212, para 10.

379 See International Law Association, *Report of the Fortieth Conference*, 213.

"it would be considered as offending against the common conscience of civilised nations," as well as limit the role of courts in arbitral proceedings and the right to appeal from arbitral awards.[380] This idealized version of uniform legislation was never drafted, for the ILA preferred to engage in a process of codification of *ad hoc* arbitration relying on party autonomy for its enactment.

Indeed, the ILA produced a new model arbitration clause and a set of arbitration rules, both of which were much more in line with the common practices in the emerging field of international commercial arbitration. This time, the model clause was quite succinct. Instead of codifying procedure, the clause referred to a separate ILA Rules for International Commercial Arbitration (also called "Amsterdam Rules 1938"). Additionally, the model clause contained optional standard provisions governing the number of arbitrators and their mode of appointment.[381]

The so-called Amsterdam Rules 1938 was fundamentally a procedural code for *ad hoc* arbitration. Differently from the AAA and ICC Rules, no institutional machinery was entrusted with authority over the arbitration proceedings. It is true that the chairperson of the commercial arbitration committee of the ILA would act as appointing authority whenever needed and would review challenges on the impartiality of arbitrators,[382] but this would be the maximum extent of institutional control over the proceedings. The decisions of arbitrators would be final and binding, unless the parties expressly agreed on the right to appeal.[383]

Evidently, considering the hostility of a majority of ILA members, the Amsterdam Rules attributed no role to *amiable composition*. Much to the contrary, arbitrators were expected to "conduct their proceedings in a judicial manner."[384] In addition, it was provided that "[t]he award of the arbitrators or an umpire shall be made in accordance with the law of the country which it has been agreed to regulate the construction, validity and performance of the contract."[385] Hence, one cannot but note that the provision in question did not yet espouse the doctrine of separability, a technical feature that would become central for the operation of arbitral procedure in the years to come.

---

380 See International Law Association, *Report of the Fortieth Conference,* 213.

381 See International Law Association, *Report of the Fortieth Conference,* 216.

382 See Article 9 and 12 of the Amsterdam Rules 1938 in International Law Association, *Report of the Fortieth Conference,* 218.

383 See Article 29 of the Amsterdam Rules 1938 in International Law Association, *Report of the Fortieth Conference,* 223.

384 See Article 21 of the Amsterdam Rules 1938 in International Law Association, *Report of the Fortieth Conference,* 221.

385 See Article 23 of the Amsterdam Rules 1938 in International Law Association, *Report of the Fortieth Conference,* 222.

In any event, similarly to what happened in 1934 when the first draft of the ILA model arbitration clause was analysed, controversy ensued. Notably, there were considerable questions as to the strategy of uniformization pursued by the ILA.[386] André de Boissier, Secretary-General of the ICC Court, opposed the project arguing, *inter alia*, that "arbitration can only succeed if a central and permanent body is responsible for the administration of the rules referred to by the parties in their contract."[387] Interestingly, René David, also present at the Amsterdam congress, intervened to express his "desire and that of many members of the Conference that this Association should work for unification of arbitration law."[388]

Against the continued controversy, and the gap between "Anglo-Saxon" and "Continental" positions on arbitration, the matter was remanded to the Executive Council of the ILA for further consideration.[389] Still, comparably to what happened to other initiatives, the war would also suddenly halt this ongoing process of uniformization.

Despite the sudden interruption, the work done in the interwar years by the ICC, the AAA and ILA serve as evidence of the many non-state *fora* in which the codification of arbitration was also being pursued. In this increasingly polycentric and transnational governance regime, certain people would circulate from Paris to London to Geneva and beyond. These legal globe-trotters – like René David, F.D. MacKinnon, Charles Bernheimer, René Arnaud and Owen D. Young, to name a few – would labour for the promotion and codification of arbitral authority at venues that were both private (the ILA, the ICC, the AAA) and public (the League of Nations or in national governments).

Similarly to their *Belle époque predecessors*, this generation of individuals circulated easily in different social and political spaces, creating a permanent conversation on arbitration technique. Consequently, these many *loci* in which the codification of arbitration was being pursued already looked like a tight-nit network enabling a continuous and transnational process of production, formalization and reproduction of arbitral knowledge and authority.

386 A certain M.M. Morelli noted that "*au point de vue du droit d'un État donné, les parties ne peuvent déterminer, par leur volonté, la loi qui devra régler un rapport quelconque que si cette possibilité est admise par les règles de droit international privé du même État,*" an issue that would create great obstacles for the uniformization of arbitration via the strategy undertaken by the ILA in his view. See International Law Association, *Report of the Fortieth Conference*, 226.

387 See International Law Association, *Report of the Fortieth Conference*, 228.

388 See International Law Association, *Report of the Fortieth Conference*, 232.

389 See International Law Association, *Report of the Fortieth Conference*, 238.

CHAPTER 5

The Illusion of Fragmentation

The proliferation of arbitral rites and fora, materialized in numerous sets of procedural rules and distinctive institutional frameworks, produces an illusion of fragmentation. This mirage of diversity, best encapsulated in the seemingly divergent development paths taken by the World Bank and UN systems of arbitration, disguise an ever-increasing process of homogenization. As counterintuitive as this may seem, the multiplication of procedural and institutional regimes rather than manifesting a cacophonous evolution of arbitral authority materializes a piece-meal process of transnational codification. Certainly, all of this reflects a decentralized, or rather polycentric, form of global governance. This polycentric governance is founded upon a common grammar structuring arbitral authority, based upon a gradual, progressive and intentional convergence of public and private forms of arbitration in the realm of transnational economic disputes.

This chapter aims at uncovering the many layers of technical, political and professional struggles in the pile of failed and successful codification of projects that made possible such developments. In particular, it will be shown that, instead of creating a fork in the road that would forever bifurcate investment from commercial arbitral authority, the adoption of the Convention on the Settlement of Investment Disputes and the United Nations Convention on the Recognition and Enforcement of Foreign Arbitral Awards are foundational elements of an interdependent and intertextual (if not uniform) form of transnational arbitral authority.

Concretely, the chapter will be divided in two parts. First, it will address the birth of ICSID, which cannot be understood in disconnect from several parallel normative projects addressing the problem of arbitration between private parties and governments (1). Then, in a second moment, the chapter will discuss how the United Nations generated a tiered arbitral normative regime, inaugurated by the adoption of the New York Convention, in which some UN organs were vested with legislative oversight in relation to the codification and expansion of arbitral authority (2).

1 New Forum Old Practices

It is no secret that "[t]he history of the development of the international law on the responsibility of states for injuries to aliens is [...] an aspect of

 | DOI:10.1163/9789004728998_006

the history of 'imperialism.'"[1] Interestingly, at the dawn of the age of empire, important voices in international law held the view "that people who go into other countries shall realize that they are not entitled to have the laws and police regulations and methods of judicial procedure and customs of business made over to suit them."[2]

In a world divided in empires, punctuated by some few independent countries, the Calvo doctrine was not particularly outrageous to investors. Hence, foreigners were to expect nothing more than treatment equal to that accorded to nationals of a given country. As imperial legislation was often the law applicable to foreign investments at capital importing regions of the world, capital exporting States felt a lot more comfortable with affording domestic treatment to foreigners.

Yet, as empires crumbled in the aftermath of the world wars, a great many things that were once merely municipal relations under imperial law were now exposed to the perceived vagaries of international legality. Things were not made easier when decolonization led to the emergence at Bandung of a third world simultaneously zealous of its national sovereignty and eager to host foreign investments.[3]

In parallel, as the UNGA resolution 1710 (XVI) declared the 1960s the development decade,[4] one would observe the emergence of several different initiatives addressing dispute settlement between governments and private parties.

1 See Philip C Jessup, 'Responsibility of States for Injuries to Individuals' [1946] Columbia Law Review 903, 906.

2 See Elihu Root, 'The Basis of Protection to Citizens Residing Abroad' (1910) 4 American Journal of International Law 517, 527.

3 This tension is expressed in the final communiqué issued at Bandung: "The Asian-African Conference recognised the urgency of promoting economic development in the Asian-African region. There was general desire for economic co-operation among the participating countries on the basis of mutual interest and respect for national sovereignty. The proposals with regard to economic co-operation within the participating countries do not preclude either the desirability or the need for co-operation with countries outside the region, including the investment of foreign capital. It was further recognised that the assistance being received by certain participating countries from outside the region, through international or under bilateral arrangements, had made a valuable contribution to the implementation of their development programmes." See 'Final Communiqué of the Asian-African Conference of Bandung (24 April 1955)' 1, para 1. Available at: <http://www.cvce.eu/obj/final_communique_of_the_asian_african_conference_of_ba ndung_24_april_1955-en-676237bd-72f7-471f-949a-88b6ae513585.html>. See also Balakrishnan Rajagopal, *International Law from below: Development, Social Movements, and Third World Resistance* (Cambridge University Press 2003), 74 et seq.

4 See UNGA, 'United Nations Development Decade. A Programme for International Economic Co-Operation (I)' (United Nations Publications 1962) A/RES/1710(XVI).

Some of these initiatives would be concerned primarily with the conduct of States regarding foreign investors, as was the case of the Abs-Shawcross project – which would later be taken over by the newly born OECD and led to a dead end.[5] Nevertheless, there was a renewed quest for a codified arbitral procedure specifically focused on disputes involving States and private parties (1.1). Ultimately, the conjunction of these many efforts for the promotion of foreign investments would lead to the creation of a brand-new specialized institution and a corresponding procedural regime (1.2).

1.1 *A Renewed Quest for a Codified Procedure*

The triumph of the allies in 1945 was also the triumph of Kelsen over Schmitt in legal theory.[6] Indeed, codified positive law would emerge as a central pillar of the world order birthed at the dawn of WWII, for written-down State sanctioned rules would serve as the safe harbour for the legal mind in the postwar years. The renewed quest for the codification of arbitration is very much connected to these theoretical developments, in which the establishment of a clear-cut threshold for the validity of legal norms was the Eldorado to be conquered.

Although arbitration was no longer the *belle époque* panacea that it once was, its role in the transnational administration of justice was secured and had to be formalized. On the one hand, arbitral authority had a residual function to perform in the oversight of inter-state disputes, which would lead the ILC to devote considerable resources for its codification (1.1.1). On the other hand, there was an emerging role to be played by arbitral authority in the settlement of disputes between governments and private parties, a matter which was given great attention by UNIDROIT (1.1.2).

1.1.1 The ILC Work on Arbitral Procedure

In 1949, at the end of the ILC's first session, the codification of arbitral procedure was identified as a priority for the upcoming work of that novel UN body.[7] As one knows, the ILC was established by UNGA resolution 174(II) dated 21 November 1947.[8] The body was to be composed of "persons of recognized

---

5 See Antonio Parra, *The History of ICSID* (2nd edn, Oxford University Press 2017), 12–15.

6 See Hans Kelsen, 'Théorie du droit international public', in *Collected Courses of the Hague Academy of International Law*, vol. 84 (Martinus Nijhoff Publishers 1953).

7 See United Nations, *Yearbook of the International Law Commission, 1949, Summary of Record and Documents of the First Session Including the Report of the Commission to the General Assembly* (United Nations Publications 1956), 281, para 19.

8 For an analysis of the ILC, see Laurence Boisson de Chazournes, 'The International Law Commission in a Mirror – Forms, Impact and Authority' in United Nations (ed), *Seventy Years of the International Law Commission: Drawing a Balance for the Future* (Brill NV); Alain Pellet,

competence in international law,"[9] and was vested with the mandate to promote "the progressive development of international law and its codification."[10] The ILC's powers were derived from Article 13(1) of the Charter, pursuant to which the UNGA "shall initiate studies and make recommendations for the purpose of [...] promoting international co-operation in the political field and encouraging the progressive development of international law and its codification."[11]

The ILC's involvement with arbitration aimed at producing a "general law of arbitration."[12] Albeit focused on interstate arbitration, it became clear over time that some of its work could also serve as guidance for disputes between governments and private parties.[13] The French professor George Scelles was the member of the ILC appointed to act as special rapporteur on the topic,[14] and he would consequently become the leading figure in a decade of work on the codification of arbitral procedure at the UN. In particular, the ILC would have the opportunity to analyse at length various reports and preliminary drafts on the topic in its second, fourth, fifth, ninth and tenth sessions.

During those many years, what was first conceived as a draft hard-law instrument, a convention on arbitral procedure, was later replaced by a soft law approach – a document codifying a set of model rules on arbitral procedure. For this reason, the ILC work on the topic can be divided into two periods,

'Between Codification and Progressive Development of the Law: Some Reflections from the ILC' (2004) 6 International Law FORUM du droit international 15; Herbert W Briggs, 'Reflections on the Codification of International Law by the International Law Commission and by Other Agencies', in *Collected Courses of the Hague Academy of International Law*, vol. 126 (Brill NV 1969).

9 See Article 2(1) of UNGA Resolution 174(II) in United Nations, 'Official Records of the Second Session of the General Assembly, Resolutions, 16 September-November 1947' (United Nations 1948) A/519, 105.

10 See Article 1(1) of UNGA Resolution 174(II) in United Nations, *Official Records of the Second Session of the General Assembly, Resolutions, 16 September-November 1947*, 105.

11 See Article 13(1) of the UN Charter in United Nations, 'Charter of the United Nations'. Available at: <https://www.un.org/en/about-us/un-charter/full-text>.

12 See Kenneth S Carlston, 'Draft Convention on Arbitral Procedure of the International Law Commission' (1954) 48 American Journal of International Law 296, 296.

13 This is expressed by the ILC in the following terms: [...] now that the draft is no longer presented in the form of a potential general treaty of arbitration, it may be useful to draw attention to the fact that, if the parties so desired, its provisions would, with the necessary adaptations, also be capable of utilization for the purposes of arbitrations between States and international organizations or between international organizations. In the case of arbitrations between States and foreign private corporations or other juridical entities, different legal considerations arise. However, some of the articles of the draft, if adapted, might be capable of use for this purpose also." See United Nations, *Yearbook of the International Law Commission*, 1958, vol. II, document A/3859, footnote 16.

14 See United Nations, *Yearbook of the International Law Commission 1949*, at 281, para 21.

one ranging from 1950 to 1955, when the prevailing goal was to produce a treaty to govern arbitral procedure, and another spanning from 1955 to 1958 when the idea of a set of model rules took hold of the ILC's workstream.[15]

During the first phase of the ILC's work on arbitral procedure, a draft convention was in fact completed and submitted to governments already in 1952.[16] In light of the commentary received, a new version of the document was produced in 1953 and then submitted to the UNGA that same year.[17] By 1955, the UNGA had collected commentaries from member States and invited the ILC to take them into consideration.[18] Concretely, the mood of Member States was "decidedly unfavourable to adoption of a convention,"[19] leading the ILC to change gears and start working on a soft instrument instead of a hard one.[20] The draft convention was converted into a set of model rules, which were adopted by UNGA's Resolution 1262(XIII) dated 14 November 1958.[21]

---

15 As noted above, Scelle acted as special rapporteur on the topic for all the duration of the ILC's involvement with the codification of arbitral procedure. However, the remaining members of the ILC would change over time. In addition to Scelle (France), the following members also took part, to different degrees, in the works on the codification of arbitral procedure: Roberto Ago (Italy), Gilberto Amado (Brazil), Ricardo J. Alfaro (Panama), Milan Bartos (Yugoslavia), James L. Brierly (United Kingdom), Roberto Córdova (Mexico), Douglas L. Edmonds (United States), Abdullah El-Erian (Egypt), Faris Bey el-Khouri (Syria), Gerald Fitzmaurice (United Kingdom), J.P.A. François (The Netherlands), Shuhsi Hsu (China), Manley O. Hudson (United States), Vladimir K. Koretsky (USSR), F.I. Kozhevnikov (USSR), Thanat Khoman (Thailand), S.B. Krylov (USSR), Ahmed Matine-Daftary (Iran), Luis Padilla Nervo (Mexico), A. E. F. Sandström (Sweden), Jean Spiropoulos (Greece), Jesús Maria Yepes (Colombia), Francisco V. García-Amador (Cuba), Hersch Lauterpacht (United Kingdom), Radhabinod Pal (India), Carlos Salamanca Figueroa (Bolivia), Alfred Verdross (Austria), Kisaburo Yokota (Japan), Jaroslav Zourek (Czechoslovakia).

16 See Kenneth S Carlston, 'Codification of International Arbitral Procedure' (1953) 47 American Journal of International Law 203, 204.

17 See UNGA Resolution 797 (VIII) in United Nations, 'Resolutions Adopted by the General Assembly at Its Eight Session during the Period from 15 September to 9 December 1953' (United Nations 1954) A/2640 51.

18 See UNGA Resolution 989 (X) in United Nations, 'Resolutions Adopted by the General Assembly during Its Tenth Session from 20 September to 20 December 1955' (United Nations 1956) A/3116 47.

19 See United Nations, *Yearbook of the International Law Commission, 1958, Volume II, Documents of the Tenth Session Including the Report of the Commission to the General Assembly*, vol II (United Nations Publications 1958), 2.

20 For the debate on the matter, see records of the ILC 419th Meeting in United Nations, *Yearbook of the International Law Commission, 1957, Volume I, Summary Records of the Ninth Session, 23 April – 28 June 1957* (United Nations Publications 1957), 181–185.

21 The resolution reads as follows: "Recalling its resolutions 797 (VIII) of 7 December 1953 and 989 (X) of 14 December 1955, Considering that arbitration is one of the means for the pacific settlement of disputes referred to in the Charter of the United Nations, Having

As another instance of cross-fertilization, one must note that the ILC work on the codification of arbitral procedure took the Hague Conventions for the Pacific Settlement of International Disputes of 1899 and 1907 as starting points, qualifying those instruments as a "*véritable codification officielle*."[22] The roadmap was complemented by references to the Locarno Pact, the General Act of 1928 (in its updated form implemented by the UNGA Resolution of 28 April 1949), and the Pact of Bogota of 1948.[23]

A perceived problem with the original draft produced by the ILC was that it did not confine itself to a mere restatement of arbitral practice in a codified form. Rather, the instrument introduced features framed as desirable developments to further the authority of arbitration.[24] An example of these

considered chapter II, on arbitral procedure, of the report of the International Law Commission covering the work of its tenth session, Taking note of the comments in that report to the effect, in particular, that the draft articles on arbitral procedure contained therein would have no binding effect on States unless accepted by them and save to the extent that each one is accepted by them in treaties of arbitration or in a *compromis*, Taking into consideration the observations of Governments and the statements made in the Sixth Committee at the thirteenth session of the General Assembly, (1) Takes note of chapter II of the report of the International Law Commission covering the work of its tenth session; (2) Expresses its appreciation to the International Law Commission and the Secretariat for their work on arbitral procedure; (3) Brings the draft articles on arbitral procedure contained in the report of the International Law Commission to the attention of Member States for their consideration and use, in such cases and to such extent as they consider appropriate, in drawing up treaties of arbitration or *compromis*; (4) Invites Governments to send to the Secretary General any comments they may wish to make on the draft, and in particular on their experience in the drawing up of arbitral agreements and the conduct of arbitral procedure, with a view to facilitating a review of the matter by the United Nations at an appropriate time." In United Nations, 'Resolutions Adopted by the General Assembly during Its Thirteenth Session, Volume II, 20 February – 13 March 1959' (United Nations) A/4090/Add.1, 53.

22 See Georges Scelle, 'Procédure arbitrale: rapport de Georges Scelle, rapporteur spécial, A/CN.4/18', *Yearbook of the International Law Commission*, vol II (United Nations Publications 1950), 117.

23 See Scelle, *Procédure arbitrale*, 117.

24 Scelle expresses this ambition as follows: "*C'est une œuvre de législation internationale dont l'effet est novatoire. Toute codification, qu'elle soit d'ordre interne ou d'ordre international, a essentiellement pour objet de substituer de nouvelles normes juridiques à des normes préexistantes qu'elle abroge ipso facto, même lorsqu'elle les incorpore de manière formelle : ce n'est plus la règle coutumière, ou la règle conventionnelle ancienne qui sont en vigueur entre les signataires de l'instrument codificateur. C'est la règle exprimée par l'instrument conventionnel de codification. C'est en cela que la codification se distingue du restatement ou de ce qu'on appelait en France, sous la monarchie, la « Rédaction des coutumes », ou en Espagne les Recopilaciones.* [...] *Ajoutons que notre liberté est grande puisque, d'une part, nous n'avons pas d'instructions et que, d'autre part, l'article premier de notre statut nous*

innovations was that of entrusting the ICJ with oversight in relation to arbitral procedure, which was coupled with a move towards the judicialization of arbitration – something evocative of the old ambition of implementing compulsory arbitration. States, however, vocally opposed this approach.[25] The majoritarian view at the UNGA resisted the notion of "jurisdictional" arbitration, and this was recorded in the following terms:

> The majority considered that the draft would distort the traditional institution of arbitration; that it would turn that institution into a jurisdictional procedure, whereas according to custom it was diplomatic in character, and would link it with the institutional jurisdiction of the International Court of Justice by making it, as it were, a court of first instance; that the draft would face Governments with unacceptable demands for the surrender of sovereignty; and lastly, that it would cause the Commission to abandon its primary task – the codification of the law on the subject – and thus, on the pretext of developing the institution of arbitral procedure, damage it by considerably reducing its field of application.[26]

The tension between "diplomatic" *versus* "jurisdictional" arbitration can be read as an iteration of the longstanding clash between the equitable and legal approaches to the authority of arbitration. On one side of the camp, one finds those that construed the authority of arbitration as extending beyond the realm of positive law through the operation of party autonomy/consent. On the other side, there were those who wanted to affirm the frontiers of arbitration as overlapping with the province of positive law.

In this regard, Scelle's first report to the ILC is quite interesting. The special rapporteur greatly resisted including the notion of "*amiable composition*"

---

incite à promouvoir le progrès du droit, ce qui implique éventuellement sa révision. Toute révision comporte par définition un effort de lege ferenda. En l'espèce, c'est au progrès et à l'efficacité de l'institution arbitrale qu'on nous invite à travailler. En ce faisant, nous ne portons aucune atteinte au principe dit de la souveraineté des Etats puisqu'il s'agit, en dernière analyse, d'une œuvre purement consultative en vue d'un résultat purement conventionnel." See Scelle, *Procédure arbitrale*, 118.

25 Georges Scelle, a supporter of the approach, noted that "[…] it was clear that the general tendency was to reject the draft and that states, naturally enough, continued to regard arbitration as a diplomatic and not a judicial procedure." See the records of ILC 417th Meeting in United Nations, *Yearbook of the International Law Commission, 1957, Volume I, Summary Records of the Ninth Session, 23 April–28 June 1957*, 173.

26 See United Nations, *Yearbook of the International Law Commission, 1958, Volume II, Documents of the Tenth Session Including the Report of the Commission to the General Assembly*, 2.

in that of arbitration. This conclusion rested on a three-pronged reasoning. First, he considered equity as different from *amiable composition*, presenting the ruling *ex aequo bono* as a type of analogical reasoning performing a gap filing function. Second, Scelle noted that an equitable ruling could be *praeter legem*, but never *contra legem* – while an "*amiable compositeur*" could go as far as ruling *contra legem*. Finally, Scelle affirmed that "*l'arbitre est un juge et le juge est tenu au respect du droit*."[27] Within this framework, an *amiable composition* would rather be a form of mediation than arbitration.[28]

The legalization of equity as proposed by Scelle was seemingly an attempt to include in the mandate of arbitrators the ability to reason by analogy, but to exclude the possibility of reasoning against positive law. This seems to be based on the dogma that there can be no proper administration of justice outside State sanctioned norms. Even if Scelle's argued that he was not attempting to vest arbitration with a "real" form of jurisdiction (which he defined as a permanent and compulsory institutional judicial organisation), his report does put forth a jurisdictional view of arbitration. Under the regime he proposed, the authority of arbitration is drawn first and foremost from positive law itself and not from consent, with the main task of the arbitrator being that of echoing the voice of the legislator.[29]

In this regard, the ILC took steps to make the "offer to arbitrate" a legal one, that is, binding and inviolable. The preamble of the ILC Model Rules highlights that the undertaking to arbitrate is a "legal obligation which must be carried out in good faith."[30] Interestingly, the arguments laid out for such an approach hint at the notion of separability – a doctrine that was not yet fully developed.[31] Overall, the approach in question alludes to the debate on the

27 See Scelle, *Procédure arbitrale*, 116.

28 See Scelle, *Procédure arbitrale*, 116.

29 Scelle argues the following: "*Ce qui, du point de vue de la technique juridique caractérise essentiellement l'arbitrage, c'est que la sentence arbitrale est rendue « en droit » et à notre avis son caractère obligatoire lui vient d'abord de ce qu'elle est l'expression de la règle de droit et ensuite seulement de l'engagement pris de s'y conformer. Cet engagement est secondaire et pourrait être implicite, car il découle nécessairement du fait que l'arbitre statue en droit; il est en effet inconcevable qu'un sujet de droit, lorsqu'il est en présence de l'expression concrète de la règle de droit, dans un cas déterminé, puisse songer à se dérober à son application. La sentence arbitrale est obligatoire par elle-même automatiquement.*" See Scelle, *Procédure arbitrale*, 116.

30 See the Preamble of the Model Rules in International Law Commission, 'Model Rules on Arbitral Procedure with a General Commentary, 1958', *Yearbook of the International Law Commission*, vol II (United Nations Publications 1958), 83.

31 In his report on behalf of the ILC, Georges Scelles affirms the following: "First and most vital among these essential principles of arbitration is, in our view, the inviolability of the

validity of arbitral clauses that had taken place in the realm of private international law in the 1920s, addressing similar problems under a different light. For instance, Scelle noted that "[g]overnments accustomed to the diplomatic technique of arbitration frequently incline to the view that, until a *compromis* relating specifically to a particular dispute has been reached or made final, no legal obligation exists."[32]

An important contribution of the ILC was to elevate some elements of arbitral procedure to the status of "principles of general international law" in the preamble of the ILC Model Rules.[33] These general principles of arbitration would encompass, beyond the autonomous legal obligation to arbitrate, the possibility of arbitrating both future and existing disputes, the requirement of the written form for arbitration agreements, the voluntary nature of arbitration, and the equality of parties in arbitral proceedings.[34] By doing this, the ILC Model Rules took interstate arbitration a step closer to the codified practice

---

promise given to have recourse to it, or of the undertaking to arbitrate, regarded as an obligation in itself, or, if it is desired to emphasize this, a partial surrender of sovereignty. The same applies to any international treaty or agreements, provided only that it has an individuality which can be identified and proved. The 'undertaking to arbitrate' may, of course, be embodied in the compromis itself, as its first provision, especially in the case of an ad hoc compromis or a concrete case of arbitration. The idea cannot, however, be entertained that if there is no compromis, or if the compromis has not yet been drawn up, a "bare undertaking" to arbitrate is not binding because it is only an abstract promise relating to hypothetical or future disputes. That would be tantamount to declaring null and void arbitration treaties or arbitration clauses such as our Commission has itself included, on several occasions, in the various bodies of rules it has drafted." See United Nations, *Yearbook of the International Law Commission, 1958, Volume II, Documents of the Tenth Session Including the Report of the Commission to the General Assembly*, 3.

32 See United Nations, *Yearbook of the International Law Commission, 1958, Volume II, Documents of the Tenth Session Including the Report of the Commission to the General Assembly*, 3.

33 See comments on the model rules in International Law Commission, *Model Rules on Arbitral Procedure*, 86.

34 The Preamble of the Model Rules reads as follows: "The undertaking to arbitrate is based on the following fundamental rules: (1) Any undertaking to have recourse to arbitration in order to settle a dispute between States constitutes a legal obligation which must be carried out in good faith. (2) Such an undertaking results from agreement between the parties and may relate to existing disputes or to disputes arising subsequently. (3) The undertaking must be embodied in a written instrument, whatever the form of the instrument may be. (4) The procedures suggested to States parties to a dispute by these model rules shall not be compulsory unless the States concerned have agreed, either in the compromis or in some other undertaking, to have recourse thereto. (5) The parties shall be equal in all proceedings before the arbitral tribunal." See International Law Commission, *Model Rules on Arbitral Procedure*, 83.

in the realm of international commercial arbitration, further closing the gap between public and private forms of arbitration.

Albeit not considered a general principle of arbitration, the instrument produced by the ILC made it clear that the arbitral tribunal was the master of procedure. The document vested arbitrators with great discretion with regards to the conduct of proceedings, which included the prerogative to decide on its language and to "formulate or complete the rules of procedure" in case parties could not agree upon such framework.[35] This approach was in line with the jurisdictional undertones given to the mandate of arbitrators, who were likely expected to perform their duties having as a guiding principle the good administration of justice.

The ILC's approach to the question of arbitrability is also worthy of consideration. In the preliminary stages of debate, rather than referring the issue to the arbitral tribunal itself, the solution initially favoured was to place such matters under the purview of the ICJ unless otherwise agreed by the parties.[36] Yet, this approach would evolve over time and lead to a dual-fold mechanism. If the tribunal had already been constituted, it would be the tribunal itself the body entrusted to rule on the arbitrability of the dispute. However, if the tribunal was not constituted, then it would be the ICJ the one with oversight on the matter.[37]

In fact, the ICJ was called to perform several supervisory roles in relation to the institutional control of proceedings. For instance, inspired by the General Act of 1928, the ICJ would be the fall-back appointing authority in charge of nominating arbitrators if parties could not do so.[38] Similarly, it would be the ICJ the body in charge of ruling on the challenges against the president of the tribunal or a sole arbitrator.[39]

Furthermore, it is relevant to note the cross-fertilization between national and international arbitration law operating at the level of the ILC. Despite his mandate being focused on interstate arbitration, the Special Rapporteur

35 See Articles 12(1) and 13 in International Law Commission, *Model Rules on Arbitral Procedure*, 9.

36 See Scelle, *Procédure arbitrale*, 120–121.

37 See Article 1 of the ILC Model in Rules International Law Commission (n 717) 83. See also George Scelle's Report to the Tenth Session of the UN General Assembly in United Nations, *Yearbook of the International Law Commission, 1958, Volume II, Documents of the Tenth Session Including the Report of the Commission to the General Assembly*, 4–5.

38 See Article 3 in International Law Commission, *Model Rules on Arbitral Procedure*, 83–84. See also Scelle, *Procédure arbitrale*, 122.

39 See Article 6(2) in International Law Commission, *Model Rules on Arbitral Procedure*, 84.

would not shy away from transposing domestic solutions to the international plane. This was the case of the mechanism first envisioned for the challenge arbitrators, which was borrowed from French arbitration law.[40] Although the suggestion was not retained in the final instrument adopted by the ILC, it evidences the permanent fluidity between municipal and international arbitral knowledge.

Another element that deserves attention is the principle of competence-competence, which was enshrined in the final instrument and that entrusted the tribunal with the prerogative of having the first say on its jurisdiction.[41] Georges Scelle expressly sought inspiration for its enunciation in Article 14 of the 1875 IDI Rules and in Article 73 of the 1907 Hague Convention.[42] Here, one is able to observe in vivid colours the different archaeological layers grounding a procedural tool of fundamental importance for the operation of transnational arbitral authority – *i.e.* competence-competence. Commenting on what would become Article 9, Scelle made the following observations:

> This is axiomatic. Every judicial organ is the judge of its own competence, gives rulings on any objections raised to it, and may adapt its procedure to the substance. This applies whether its competence is based on law or on a *compromis*. For a court to refuse a ruling on the ground that its competence was challenged would be a denial of justice on its part. As early as 1875, article 14 of the draft rules on international arbitral procedure prepared by the Institute of International Law provided that: 'If the doubt concerning the jurisdiction depends on the interpretation of a clause in the *compromis*, the parties are presumed to have given the arbitrators power to settle the question, unless otherwise stipulated.' [...] Reference may also be made to article 73 of the Convention of 1907, Article 36, paragraph 6, of the Statute of the International Court of Justice, etc. Since the International Law Commission took a definite stand on this matter in compiling its 1953 draft on the basis of Judge Lauterpacht's report, it appears unnecessary to dwell on it here.

An important deviation taken by the ILC Model Rules in relation to the commonly codified practice of arbitration concerned the finality of arbitral awards.

40 See Scelle, *Procédure arbitrale*, 127.

41 See Article 9 in International Law Commission, *Model Rules on Arbitral Procedure*, 9.

42 See United Nations, *Yearbook of the International Law Commission, 1958, Volume II, Documents of the Tenth Session Including the Report of the Commission to the General Assembly*, 8.

Indeed, one finds in the preparatory works of the instrument that "[n]either the Special Rapporteur nor the Commission itself has accepted the categorical theory that an arbitral award should be treated as final even if found to be morally unacceptable or practically unenforceable."[43] As a consequence, the ILC instrument contained three different means through which an award could be controlled.

The first one was the possibility of applying for an interpretation of the award whenever there was uncertainty concerning its meaning and scope. The application would be submitted to the tribunal itself, but the ICJ was listed as a fall-back option in case the tribunal could not rule on the application and the parties failed to agree on an alternative solution.[44]

Then the instrument provided for a mechanism of annulment. Among the ILC members, including the special rapporteur himself, there were those who wanted to entrust the ICJ with jurisdiction regarding annulment, expecting it to act as a proper court of cassation.[45] Still, many criticized this solution as "making for the establishment of a hierarchy among international tribunals, and as tending to limit their independence."[46] Thus, an intermediate solution was found, in which parties would be granted three months to agree upon another tribunal to rule on the annulment, failing which agreement jurisdiction would be devolved to the ICJ.[47] Evidently such a short time-frame for agreement was established with the expectation that the ICJ would be the *de facto* body overseeing annulment proceedings,[48] an expectation that is made even clearer in Article 37 of the instrument.[49] When it came to the grounds of

43 See United Nations, *Yearbook of the International Law Commission, 1958, Volume II, Documents of the Tenth Session Including the Report of the Commission to the General Assembly*, 11.

44 See Article 33 in International Law Commission, *Model Rules on Arbitral Procedure*, 86.

45 See United Nations, *Yearbook of the International Law Commission, 1958, Volume II, Documents of the Tenth Session Including the Report of the Commission to the General Assembly*, 11.

46 See United Nations, *Yearbook of the International Law Commission, 1958, Volume II, Documents of the Tenth Session Including the Report of the Commission to the General Assembly*, 11.

47 See Article 36 in International Law Commission, *Model Rules on Arbitral Procedure*, 86.

48 The three-month time-limit had been suggested by Kisaburo Yokota to prevent a losing party from evading the "execution of the award by challenging its validity and spinning out the discussions with the other party regarding the court which was to decide the question of nullity." See ILC's 450th meeting in United Nations, *Yearbook of the International Law Commission, 1958, Volume I, Summary Records of the Tenth Session, 28 April-4 July 1958*, vol I (United Nations Publications 1958), at 99, para 46.

49 Article 37 of the ILC Model Rules read as follows: "If the award is declared invalid by the International Court of Justice, the dispute shall be submitted to a new tribunal constituted

annulment, they were not particularly innovative. Four grounds were enunciated, i.e., excess of powers, corruption, violation of due process and the invalidity of the arbitration agreement.[50]

Finally, the ILC Model Rules contained a provision on the "revision of the award," which was a feature drawn expressly from the 1899 and 1907 Hague Conventions and from the Pact of Bogotá.[51] The mechanism was to be operated by the tribunal itself, but the ICJ was once again the body of choice in case the tribunal could not discharge its task and the parties could not agree otherwise. Revision was not meant as a regular appeal, but as a means of addressing the discovery of new facts that could impact the decision of the tribunal.[52]

1.1.2 The UNIDROIT Work on Arbitration between Governments and Individuals

One knows that the 20th century is marked by a growing interest regarding arbitration as a mechanism to administer disputes between governments and private parties. The irreversible participation of the State in market exchanges tended to generate much confusion in legal theory, with the dichotomy between public and private law becoming ever more blurred as the State claimed the reigns of the economy.

Worse. The more exchanges between "private" and "public" entities took place, the more disputes followed. Already in its Budapest Conference, held in 1934, the ILA inquired on the creation of a permanent court of international private law.[53] The discussion was furthered in 1936, with a report on the creation of mixed arbitral tribunals of private law.[54] Evidently, the war would bring these concerns to a state of latency.

When the world awoke from its horrific nightmare at the end of World War II, the economic order drawn by the victorious nations would be one where the State would play a vital role. It was not just the Soviet Union and its centrally planned economy who relied on the State, for the capitalist economies of the

---

by agreement between the parties, or, failing such agreement, in the manner provided by article 3." This provision is silent on the next steps following an annulment decision rendered by a body that was not the ICJ and there are no other articles dealing with this issue. See International Law Commission, *Model Rules on Arbitral Procedure*, 86.

50 See Article 35 in International Law Commission, *Model Rules on Arbitral Procedure*, 86.

51 See United Nations, *Yearbook of the International Law Commission, 1958, Volume II, Documents of the Tenth Session Including the Report of the Commission to the General Assembly*, 12.

52 See Article 36 in International Law Commission, *Model Rules on Arbitral Procedure*, 86.

53 See International Law Association, *Report of the Thirty-Eighth Conference*, 245.

54 See International Law Association, *Report of the Thirty-Ninth* Conference, 111.

West were operated by a Keynesian macro-economic model attributing a central role to State initiative.

Within this framework, it is not surprising to find out that in 1948 UNIDROIT was very much interested in arbitration between governments and individuals. That year, Mario Matteucci, then UNIDROIT's Secretary-General, penned a report highlighting the increasing importance of disputes between governments and private parties,[55] acknowledging the fact that "the State has greatly expanded its sphere of activity into the field of economics."[56] The report further considered the many obstacles faced by private parties when vindicating their contractual rights against foreign states, as well as its relation to the issue of State immunity. Although sovereign immunity was not yet established as a legal rule, it was already considered a rule of "international politeness."[57]

Reading the document, one has a feeling that the creation of an international court with jurisdiction over such disputes might have been the preferred course of action. Still, the solution was perceived as a difficult one due to "doctrinal reluctance to recognize individuals as subjects of international law."[58] Conversely, arbitration was presented as a viable alternative to the stalemate, and the reasons underlining this proposition would be threefold: as arbitration was based on consent, proceedings would not be affected by considerations over sovereign immunity; the ability to choose arbitrators would make arbitral decisions more acceptable to States; given that arbitrators would not necessarily be bound to apply municipal law, this would generate a sense of impartiality and potentially make States more at ease with proceedings.[59]

55 See UNIDROIT, 'Première session du Comité de travail pour l'Étude de l'Arbitrage entre Gouvernements et Particuliers, Procès-Verbal, Rome, le 11 mai 1948' (UNIDROIT 1948) U.D.P. 1948–Études: XXV, Doc. 2, 1.

56 See UNIDROIT, 'Arbitration between Governments and Individuals, Draft Report (Revised Edition)' (UNIDROIT 1948) U.P.L. 1948–Papers: XXV-Arbitration between Governments and Individuals-Doc. 1(1), 1.

57 See UNIDROIT, *Arbitration between Governments and Individuals, Draft Report* (*Revised Edition*), 4.

58 See UNIDROIT, *Arbitration between Governments and Individuals, Draft Report* (*Revised Edition*), 5.

59 These reasons were laid out in the report under the following terms: "Since the arbitration was consented to in advance, States who submit to it do not impair the principle of immunity from the process of another jurisdiction. Since the contending parties each usually have the right to select an arbitrator, each State can choose one of its own citizens; this seems better than accepting the decision of a body composed entirely of foreign judges. Since arbitrators in an international arbitration are not bound as a rule to apply a particular national law, this serves as guarantee of impartiality, and States, parties to arbitration proceedings, cannot help finding this more acceptable." See UNIDROIT, *Arbitration between Governments and Individuals, Draft Report* (*Revised Edition*), 6.

In reality, without referring directly to party autonomy and transnationalism, Matteucci's report anticipates these ideas as a way forward for the settlement of disputes between States and private parties. First, the principle of State immunity could be bypassed by the notion of consent, which is nothing other than the sovereign disguise of party autonomy. Second, the appointment of arbitrators by parties themselves, another manifestation of party autonomy, could foster the trust deposited upon adjudicators. Third, in a contractual dispute born out of a treaty,[60] arbitrators ought to have the jurisdiction to rule on matters related to the treaty itself.[61] Finally, the detachment of arbitral authority from any given national law could ensure the "impartiality" of proceedings. Voilà transnational arbitral authority sketched in 1948.

This approach was expressly based on the assumption that "States would be more disposed to submit to arbitration in international litigation, than to accept the judgment of judges of another State or a genuine international court."[62] Nevertheless, the question remained of whether an arbitration clause governing disputes between States and private parties would be valid, a matter that was not at all uniformly dealt with by municipal or international law. Indeed, it was widely understood that the 1923 Protocol on the Validity of Arbitration Clauses governed only "disputes between persons," leaving States out of its purview.[63] As a consequence, given the interdependence between the 1923 Protocol and the 1927 Convention, it was understood that the enforcement

60 Very early in the drafting process, the question emerged of whether an adjudicator ruling on a contract born out of a treaty would have jurisdiction over the treaty itself. Charles Carabiber, who was not a member of the UNIDROIT working group and attended the meeting held in Paris in March 1949 as a "special guest", raised the issue of "*au cas où le contrat dont découle le litige, est conclu sur la base d'un traité de commerce entre des États, si le juge pourra connaître de l'interprétation non seulement du contrat lui-même, mais aussi de la convention internationale qui est à la base du contrat.*" See UNIDROIT, 'Comité d'Études Pour l'Arbitrage Entre Gouvernements et Particuliers, Procès-Verbal, Deuxième Session, Paris, Les 10 et 11 Mars 1949' (UNIDROIT 1949) U.D.P. 1949–Études: XXV-Arbitrage entre Gouvernements et Particuliers-Doc. 5, 12.

61 J.G. Allanby, the LCA delegate, argued that "*la sentence d'arbitrage doit statuer sur toutes les circonstances qui, même si dans la compétence de la Cour internationale de la Haye, concernent le contrat, y compris l'interprétation du traité, même si cette interprétation peut tomber.*" See UNIDROIT, *Comité d'Études Pour l'Arbitrage Entre Gouvernements et Particuliers, Procès-Verbal, Deuxième Session, Paris, Les 10 et 11 Mars 1949*, 13.

62 See UNIDROIT, *Arbitration between Governments and Individuals, Draft Report* (*Revised Edition*), 6.

63 See UNIDROIT, *Arbitration between Governments and Individuals, Draft Report* (*Revised Edition*), 7.

mechanism introduced by the Geneva Convention of 1927 would only govern arbitration between private parties.[64]

As one can see, there was great uncertainty regarding arbitration between States and private parties. Despite the successful experience of Mixed Arbitral Tribunals implemented for the settlement of WWI disputes, these bodies were seen as a *sui generis* adjudicative arrangement – something at the crossroads of arbitral and judicial dispute settlement.[65] In addition, various countries prohibited or greatly limited the avenues for arbitration between states and private parties. At the time, this was the case of France, Belgium, Spain, Argentina and Chile.[66]

Within this framework, it must be highlighted that Matteucci's report may be the source of a seminal idea for the future of what is now called investor-state arbitration. Notably, the document contains a very early written trace of the idea to elevate arbitration clauses governing investor-state disputes to the level of treaties governing economic relations between States themselves. The suggestion was made in the following terms:

> The arbitration clause in a contract does not entirely solve the problem for, as we have seen, many countries do not recognize its validity where the State is a party to the contract and other countries, although recognize its validity, hedge it about with so many formalities and restrictions as to make it valueless. Hence it is suggested that reference should be made to such arbitration clauses in trade agreements between States

64 This is made clear by UNIDROIT: "Even the States which signed the Geneva Convention of 1927 on the enforcement of foreign awards, are not bound to apply such agreement to awards other than those rendered under an arbitration clause as provided for in the above mentioned Protocol of 1923, namely awards in arbitration proceedings between individuals. When a Government is part to an arbitration there is still no international convention requiring the enforcement of foreign awards." See UNIDROIT, *Arbitration between Governments and Individuals, Draft Report (Revised Edition)*, 11–12.

65 This view is expressed at UNIDROIT in the following terms: "Although these mixed tribunals were called 'arbitral' they enjoyed some of the characteristics of a real international tribunal because they were not founded on the basis of a '*compromis*' or of an arbitration clause agreed upon between individuals and States, nor were they the sole creatures of the contending parties. [...] Mixed arbitral tribunals are thus rightly defined as 'mixed jurisdiction' having at one and the same time both arbitral and judicial functions: They do undoubtedly partake of the nature of an international tribunal." See UNIDROIT, *Arbitration between Governments and Individuals, Draft Report (Revised Edition)*, 13–14.

66 See UNIDROIT, *Arbitration between Governments and Individuals, Draft Report (Revised Edition)*, 10–11.

> so that differences arising under contracts between such Governments and individuals would have to be arbitrated, since such a clause would not only be applied to differences between the two contracting States or between subjects of said States, but also between one or more subjects of a State on one side, and the other States on the other.

The same document called for the adoption of a multilateral convention governing the validity of arbitration clauses and enforcement of arbitral awards in disputes involving states and private parties.[67] Matteucci envisioned a strategy to achieve maximum adherence to such instrument by placing these arbitral proceedings under the purview of "a body enjoying special international authority" – and the PCA was contemplated as a possible candidate for this job.[68]

The Matteucci Report would serve as the basis for UNIDROIT to pursue the project of a multilateral convention governing the settlement of contractual disputes between States and foreign nationals. The draft instrument would be elaborated by Algot Bagge, who was the former President of the Anglo-German Mixed Arbitral Tribunal,[69] and who was appointed as chairperson of the committee created by UNIDROIT to work on the matter.[70] Even still, Matteucci would continue to exert great influence over the drafting process.[71]

At least four meetings were held by UNIDROIT from 1948 to 1950 to discuss this draft convention, bringing a broad array of arbitration stakeholders into the process. Indeed, UNIDROIT would receive inputs on its work from the ILA, the ICC, the AAA, the LCA and even the USSR Chamber of Commerce. The ICC was particularly active in these discussions, to the point of hosting one of the

---

67 See UNIDROIT, *Arbitration between Governments and Individuals, Draft Report (Revised Edition)*, 16.

68 See UNIDROIT, *Arbitration between Governments and Individuals, Draft Report (Revised Edition)*, 17.

69 See UNIDROIT, *Comité d'Études Pour l'Arbitrage Entre Gouvernements et Particuliers, Procès-Verbal, Deuxième Session, Paris, Les 10 et 11 Mars 1949*, 5.

70 See UNIDROIT, *Première session du Comité de travail pour l'Étude de l'Arbitrage entre Gouvernements et Particuliers, Procès-Verbal, Rome, le 11 mai 1948*; UNIDROIT, *Comité d'Études Pour l'Arbitrage Entre Gouvernements et Particuliers, Procès-Verbal, Deuxième Session, Paris, Les 10 et 11 Mars 1949*.

71 See UNIDROIT, *Première session du Comité de travail pour l'Étude de l'Arbitrage entre Gouvernements et Particuliers, Procès-Verbal, Rome, le 11 mai 1948*, 3–5. See also UNIDROIT, 'Avant Projet d'une Convention Internationale Permettant de Recourir à La Cour Permanent d'arbitrage de La Haye, Pour Le Règlement Des Différends Nés Des Contracts Commerciaux Conclus Entre États et Particuliers' (UNIDROIT 1949) U.D.P. 1949–Études: XXV-Arbitrage entre Gouvernements et Particuliers-Doc.3.

meetings of the UNIDROIT working group.[72] Algot Bagge, who also acted as ICC delegate in the same working group he chaired, would not shy away from relying on the ICC to feed him information. Notably, he commissioned a study to the ICC on the instances in which States appeared before the ICC Court.[73]

The ICC, for its part, lobbied to make its Court the default forum for arbitration involving states and private parties, advocating that the PCA should be a fall-back option only.[74] This proposition made its way to one of the many versions of the draft convention due to Algot Bagge's influence over the text,[75] and as a result of the resistance that some stakeholders had in relation to the PCA. For instance, the representatives of the USSR Chamber of Commerce were opposed to the adoption of the PCA as an institutional framework to govern disputes between States and private parties.[76] Nevertheless, the prevailing view portrayed the PCA as the most suitable institution to administer these proceedings.[77] Even the AAA viewed the PCA favourably, but it cautioned that a study was needed to figure out "how this proposal would fit into the powers of the United Nations, the International Court of Justice, [and] the proposed International Trade Organization."[78]

Besides these obstacles to the adoption of the PCA as a forum for the settlement of investor-State disputes, there were also material issues that would make it difficult to administer future cases of this nature at the Hague. On the one hand, it was felt that PCA member states would have to hold a diplomatic conference allowing such a mandate expansion.[79] On the other hand, the PCA was severely understaffed. At that moment in time, its Secretariat comprised

72 See UNIDROIT, *Comité d'Études Pour l'Arbitrage Entre Gouvernements et Particuliers, Procès-Verbal, Deuxième Session, Paris, Les 10 et 11 Mars 1949*.

73 See UNIDROIT, *Comité d'Études Pour l'Arbitrage Entre Gouvernements et Particuliers, Procès-Verbal, Deuxième Session, Paris, Les 10 et 11 Mars 1949*, 4.

74 See UNIDROIT, *Comité d'Études Pour l'Arbitrage Entre Gouvernements et Particuliers, Procès-Verbal, Deuxième Session, Paris, Les 10 et 11 Mars 1949*, 6.

75 See UNIDROIT, 'Comité d'Études Pour l'Arbitrage Entre Gouvernements et Particuliers, Procès-Verbal, Troisième Session, Rome, Les 8 et 9 Juin 1949' (UNIDROIT 1949) U.D.P. 1949–Études: XXV-Arbitrage entre Gouvernements et Particuliers-Doc. 6 3.

76 See UNIDROIT, *Comité d'Études Pour l'Arbitrage Entre Gouvernements et Particuliers, Procès-Verbal, Deuxième Session, Paris, Les 10 et 11 Mars 1949*, 7; UNIDROIT, *Comité d'Études Pour l'Arbitrage Entre Gouvernements et Particuliers, Procès-Verbal, Troisième Session, Rome, Les 8 et 9 Juin 1949*, 4.

77 See UNIDROIT, *Comité d'Études Pour l'Arbitrage Entre Gouvernements et Particuliers, Procès-Verbal, Deuxième Session, Paris, Les 10 et 11 Mars 1949*, 4.

78 See UNIDROIT, *Comité d'Études Pour l'Arbitrage Entre Gouvernements et Particuliers, Procès-Verbal, Deuxième Session, Paris, Les 10 et 11 Mars 1949*, 9.

79 See UNIDROIT, *Comité d'Études Pour l'Arbitrage Entre Gouvernements et Particuliers, Procès-Verbal, Troisième Session, Rome, Les 8 et 9 Juin 1949*, 6.

only the Secretary-General, a M. Snouck, and another person – so the PCA Secretariat would have to take onboard more people in order to accommodate an eventual new mandate.[80]

Beyond the ICC Court and the PCA,[81] the model of Mixed Arbitral Tribunals also emerged as a potential solution to the administration of disputes between governments and private parties. However, Bagge himself noted that, despite their success, Mixed Arbitral Tribunals "*ont été institués pour remplir une mission assez particulière selon les limites tracées par les traités de paix.*"[82]

In terms of legislative technique, the UNIDROIT working group preferred the adoption of a very concise text, composed only of five articles stating some of its core features. The most advanced version of the project was produced by Matteucci and discussed within UNIDROIT on March 1950.[83] Algot Bagge chaired the meeting, but once again sat as the representative of the ICC as he would often do. Also present was Robert Sandiford, representing the ILA, and Gunnar de Sydow, acting as the working group's secretary.[84]

The instrument's Article 1 delimited its scope, providing that it applied to disputes arising out of commercial contracts containing an arbitration agreement between a contracting state and a private party residing in the territory of another contracting state.[85] Notably, the reference to commercial contracts

---

80 See UNIDROIT, *Comité d'Études Pour l'Arbitrage Entre Gouvernements et Particuliers, Procès-Verbal, Troisième Session, Rome, Les 8 et 9 Juin 1949*, 6.

81 Bagge noted that one of the central tasks of the UNIDROIT working group on arbitration between government and private parties was to "*[d]éterminer les avantages qu'il y a confier cette tâche à l'une des deux Cours Internationales déjà existantes, à savoir la Cour d'Arbitrage de la C.C.I. et la Cour Permanente de la Haye, ou à toutes les deux, soit séparément, soit en liaison et dégager les mesures qu'il convient prendre dans ces différents cas.*" See UNIDROIT, *Comité d'Études Pour l'Arbitrage Entre Gouvernements et Particuliers, Procès-Verbal, Deuxième Session, Paris, Les 10 et 11 Mars 1949*, 5.

82 See UNIDROIT, *Comité d'Études Pour l'Arbitrage Entre Gouvernements et Particuliers, Procès-Verbal, Deuxième Session, Paris, Les 10 et 11 Mars 1949*, 5.

83 See UNIDROIT, 'Comité d'Études Pour l'Arbitrage Entre Gouvernements et Particuliers, Procès-Verbal, Quatrième Session, Rome, Les 3, 4 et 10 Mars 1950' (UNIDROIT 1951) U.D.P. 1951–Études: XXV-Arbitrage entre Gouvernements et Particuliers-Doc. 8 4–5.

84 See UNIDROIT, *Comité d'Études Pour l'Arbitrage Entre Gouvernements et Particuliers, Procès-Verbal, Quatrième Session, Rome, Les 3, 4 et 10 Mars 1950*, 1.

85 The text of the provision read as follows: "*La présente Convention est applicable aux différends découlant d'un contrat commercial conclu entre l'une des Hautes Parties contractantes et un particulier ayan sa résidence habituelle dans le territoire d'une autre Haute Partie contractante, pourvu que les parties au contrat aient stipulé que tels différends seront tranchés par arbitrage conformément aux règles de la Convention. Les Hautes Parties contractantes se déclarent intéressées à introduire une clause d'arbitrage, dans toute l'étendue*

was introduced by Matteucci in order to harmonize the text of the draft with the language of the Geneva Convention of 1927.[86] This is yet another example of the cross-fertilization between different codification projects, one that shows very clearly an intentional convergence between public and private forms of international arbitration.

In reality, a central concern of UNIDROIT related to the transposition of the Geneva regime to govern disputes between States and private parties. It was felt that the new instrument could be used to formally fill that perceived gap of the Geneva regime, that is, the one related to the recognition and enforcement of arbitral awards rendered in cases involving States. Accordingly, Article 2 of the draft introduced the obligation of contracting parties to recognize and enforce awards rendered under the instrument itself.[87]

The next three articles dealt with the choice of forum. Article 3 provided that the PCA, or any other arbitral institution with "*un caractère international,*" could be chosen to administer proceedings under the proposed convention,[88] while Article 4 and 5 referred to the applicable procedural rules in case the PCA or the ICC were chosen.[89] In this regard, the working group appended a concise and novel set of procedural rules governing arbitration between private parties and governments under the PCA institutional framework. The deviation from the standard PCA procedural rules is curious, but likely resulted from the feeling that a set of rules designed to deal with disputes between sovereign states was not entirely adequate to govern hybrid situations as the ones involving States and private parties.

The eventual proceedings before the PCA would be structured around two phases, consisting of written submissions ("*instructions écrites préparatoires*") and oral hearings ("*débats devant le tribunal*") and the two phases were

possible, dans leurs contrats ci-dessus visés." In UNIDROIT, 'Avant-Projet d'une Convention Internationale Sur l'arbitrage Entre Gouvernements et Particuliers' (UNIDROIT 1950) U.D.P. 1950–Études: XXV-Arbitrage entre Gouvermenement et Particuliers-Doc. 7.

86 See UNIDROIT, *Comité d'Études Pour l'Arbitrage Entre Gouvernements et Particuliers, Procès-Verbal, Quatrième Session, Rome, Les 3, 4 et 10 Mars 1950*, 5.

87 See UNIDROIT, *Avant-Projet d'une Convention Internationale Sur l'arbitrage Entre Gouvernements et Particuliers*, 1; UNIDROIT, *Comité d'Études Pour l'Arbitrage Entre Gouvernements et Particuliers, Procès-Verbal, Quatrième Session, Rome, Les 3, 4 et 10 Mars 1950*, 6.

88 See UNIDROIT, *Comité d'Études Pour l'Arbitrage Entre Gouvernements et Particuliers, Procès-Verbal, Quatrième Session, Rome, Les 3, 4 et 10 Mars 1950*, 6–7.

89 See Annex 1 and Annex 2 in UNIDROIT, *Avant-Projet d'une Convention Internationale Sur l'arbitrage Entre Gouvernements et Particuliers.*

regulated respectively in the annex's Articles 7 and 8.[90] Article 9 provided for the secrecy of tribunal deliberations and the finality of the award. The award, which had to be reasoned, was to be the product of a majority decision, failing which the president would provide the deciding vote.[91] The same provision entrusted the tribunal with the prerogative to allocate costs, which were to include the fees of the tribunal itself. In addition, the annex's Article 10 governed the case in which the arbitration proceedings would be entirely based on the written submissions. This would take place only upon party agreement and the tribunal could always decide to hold a hearing if it felt this was necessary.[92]

Interestingly, the draft rules for PCA arbitration between governments and private parties can be seen as another piece in the gradual colonization of transnational arbitration by legal professionals. Indeed, arbitrators were to be chosen from a roster set up by the PCA itself, an element of institutional control already favouring legal professionals. Such favour was compounded by the fact that this list of 20 names had to be composed of at least 10 "*jurisconsultes*."[93] Furthermore, in a three-member tribunal, the person appointed to act as president had to be chosen from the pool of legal professionals contained in the roster.[94]

---

90 On the one hand, Article 7 governed the written submissions, providing that the procedural calendar was determined by the PCA Secretariat in consultation with the president of the tribunal. In fact, it was the prerogative of the PCA Secretariat, always in consultation with the president of the Tribunal, to "*contrôler que l'Instruction soit complète et, au besoin, demander aux parties de faire les compléments d'instruction nécessaires*". On the other hand, Article 8 was entitled "*Les débats devant le tribunal*", but beyond governing the oral hearings, it contained the most important rules governing the procedure. For instance, failing agreement otherwise, Article 8 provided for The Hague as the default seat of arbitration. The same provision established the tribunal's competence-competence, stating that "[*l*]*e tribunal statue définitivement sur sa competence*". Also, the President of the Tribunal was entrusted with the task of drafting the terms of reference, which would include *inter alia* the object of the dispute, the contentious points, the law applicable and the language of the proceedings. Parties were expected to contribute to the drafting of this document, yet, failing agreement on any element, the tribunal was given the last word on the matter. See Annex 1, Article 7, in UNIDROIT, *Avant-Projet d'une Convention Internationale Sur l'arbitrage Entre Gouvernements et Particuliers*, 6–7.

91 See Annex 1, Article 9, in UNIDROIT, *Avant-Projet d'une Convention Internationale Sur l'arbitrage Entre Gouvernements et Particuliers*, 9.

92 See Annex 1, Article 10 UNIDROIT, *Avant-Projet d'une Convention Internationale Sur l'arbitrage Entre Gouvernements et Particuliers*, 10.

93 See Annex 1, Article 4, in UNIDROIT, *Avant-Projet d'une Convention Internationale Sur l'arbitrage Entre Gouvernements et Particuliers*, 4.

94 See Annex 1, Article 5, in UNIDROIT, *Avant-Projet d'une Convention Internationale Sur l'arbitrage Entre Gouvernements et Particuliers*, 5; UNIDROIT, *Comité d'Études Pour l'Arbitrage*

The second annex to the draft convention referred to the section B, articles 5 to 28 of the ICC arbitration rules in force in January 1934. A third and final annex conveyed the following three model clauses:

> *Première clause* – Tous différends découlant du présent contrat seront tranchés définitivement suivant la Convention sur l'arbitrage entre gouvernements et particuliers, signée à … le …
>
> *Deuxième clause* – Tous différends découlant du présent contrat seront tranchés définitivement par la Cour permanent d'arbitrage suivant le Règlement d'arbitrage annexé à la Convention sur l'arbitrage entre Gouvernements et particuliers, signée à … le …
>
> *Troisième clause* – Tous différends découlant du présent contrat seront tranchés définitivement suivant le Règlement de conciliation et arbitrage de la Chambre de Commerce Internationale par un ou plusieurs arbitres nommés conformément à ce Règlement.[95]

During the session held on March 1951, great care was again given to the intertextuality of the UNIDROIT project in relation to both the 1923 Protocol and 1927 Convention.[96] Furthermore, the PCA procedural rules discussed above were turned into a working document of a standalone draft convention providing for the jurisdiction of the PCA over commercial disputes between governments and private parties.[97] Finally, in that same meeting, Gunnar de Sydow presented an alternative draft focusing on the international validity of arbitration clauses entered between States and private parties, as well as addressing the enforcement of the corresponding arbitral awards emerging out of these arbitration clauses.[98]

Entre Gouvernements et Particuliers, Procès-Verbal, Quatrième Session, Rome, Les 3, 4 et 10 Mars 1950, 21.

95 See Annex 3 in UNIDROIT, *Avant Projet d'une Convention Internationale Permettant de Recourir à La Cour Permanent d'arbitrage de La Haye, Pour Le Règlement Des Différends Nés Des Contracts Commerciaux Conclus Entre États et Particuliers*, 13.

96 See UNIDROIT, *Comité d'Études Pour l'Arbitrage Entre Gouvernements et Particuliers, Procès-Verbal, Quatrième Session, Rome, Les 3, 4 et 10 Mars 1950*, 10–20.

97 See UNIDROIT, *Comité d'Études Pour l'Arbitrage Entre Gouvernements et Particuliers, Procès-Verbal, Quatrième Session, Rome, Les 3, 4 et 10 Mars 1950*, 20.

98 De Sydow, who passed into oblivion, would be a central player in the 1958 United Nations Conference on International Commercial Arbitration. Indeed, it would be upon his proposition that the New York Convention would come to include a provision on the validity of arbitration agreements, as it will be seen in due course in this study. See UNIDROIT,

Even still, for unclear reasons, all this work would suddenly stop at UNIDROIT. Few years later, in 1962, the PCA itself would produce a set of rules to govern arbitrations involving States and private parties. Information on its drafting process is not readily available. Yet, one knows that the "PCA Rules of Arbitration and Conciliation for Settlement of International Disputes Between Two Parties of which only one is a State" were produced by the PCA's Secretariat as a model set of procedural rules, which greatly relied on party autonomy for their enactment.[99]

The text of the document itself contained "a certain number of general stipulations which are customary in practice,"[100] and paid considerable attention to its interplay with the Hague Conventions of 1899 and 1907. In particular, the PCA Model Rules laid out provisions on the principle of competence-competence,[101] party-appointment of a three-member tribunal,[102] and two fall-back appointment methods under the purview respectively of the Bureau (i.e., the PCA's Secretariat) and the Secretary General of the PCA.[103]

The instrument also contained a section with a novel set of procedural rules governing disputes between governments and private parties.[104] In particular, these procedural rules made express reference to some interesting technical features, namely the possibility of filing counterclaims,[105] the prerogative to issue procedural orders and provisional measures,[106] and the procedural discretion

---

Comité d'Études Pour l'Arbitrage Entre Gouvernements et Particuliers, Procès-Verbal, Quatrième Session, Rome, Les 3, 4 et 10 Mars 1950, 9–10.

99 An explanatory note to the model rules, explained the following: "The Set of Rules has the character of a model. The parties are at liberty, if they deem this desirable, to fix other rules of procedure." See PCA, 'Rules of Arbitration and Conciliation for Settlement of International Disputes Between Two Parties of Which Only One Is a State. The Hague, February, 1962' (1963) 57 American Journal of International Law 500, 57.

100 See PCA, *Rules of Arbitration and Conciliation for Settlement of International Disputes Between Two Parties of Which Only One Is a State*, 57.

101 See Article 4 in PCA, *Rules of Arbitration and Conciliation for Settlement of International Disputes Between Two Parties of Which Only One Is a State*, 501.

102 See Article 5 in PCA, *Rules of Arbitration and Conciliation for Settlement of International Disputes Between Two Parties of Which Only One Is a State*, 501.

103 See Articles 5 and 6 in PCA, *Rules of Arbitration and Conciliation for Settlement of International Disputes Between Two Parties of Which Only One Is a State*, 501–502.

104 See Section B, Articles 10 to 34 in PCA, *Rules of Arbitration and Conciliation for Settlement of International Disputes Between Two Parties of Which Only One Is a State*, 502–505.

105 See Article 11 in PCA, *Rules of Arbitration and Conciliation for Settlement of International Disputes Between Two Parties of Which Only One Is a State*, 502.

106 See Article 12 and 24 in PCA, *Rules of Arbitration and Conciliation for Settlement of International Disputes Between Two Parties of Which Only One Is a State*, at 502, 504.

of the tribunal in the conduct of proceedings.[107] Furthermore, the PCA Model Rules codified the obligation of tribunals to provide reasons for its awards and to rule on the basis of law, unless parties agreed otherwise.[108] The award would be binding on the parties, but no reference to was expressly made – and its enforcement relied first and foremost on parties' good faith.[109]

As one knows, the codification projects discussed in this section failed. A convention governing disputes between states and private parties was not adopted under the auspices of UNIDROIT, and both the ILC and PCA Model Rules did not become popular instruments in the transnational administration of justice. Yet, as some of the other "unsuccessful" codification projects already analysed in this study, the efforts devoted by the ILC, UNIDROIT and the PCA would serve to foster the production, formalization and circulation of arbitration knowledge. Furthermore, the engagement with institutional and normative frameworks like the PCA, the ICC, the Geneva regime and the Hague Conventions of 1899 and 1907 demonstrate the continuous process of convergence and uniformization of transnational arbitral authority. Rather than fragmentation or isolation, one observes considerable deference to coherence and coordination, which so often has been manifested in cross-references, cross-fertilization, and intertextuality between the many documents produced.

1.2 *A Star is Born: the Creation of ICSID*

The creation of ICSID is inscribed in the effervescent geopolitical landscape of the 1960s. As the "development decade" unfolded,[110] numerous initiatives had been launched to foster capital flows across the globe. This agenda did not concern the Eastern bloc, but it did mobilize great energies in the so-called third world. Since the 1950s, the United States had relaunched its treaty program of Friendship, Commerce and Navigation, adopting some 17 of these precursors' instruments to investment treaties.[111] The first BIT proper would come to life in

107 See Articles 15, 19, 21 and 22 in PCA, *Rules of Arbitration and Conciliation for Settlement of International Disputes Between Two Parties of Which Only One Is a State*, 503–504.

108 See Articles 29–30 in PCA, *Rules of Arbitration and Conciliation for Settlement of International Disputes Between Two Parties of Which Only One Is a State*, 505.

109 See Article 31 in PCA, *Rules of Arbitration and Conciliation for Settlement of International Disputes Between Two Parties of Which Only One Is a State*, 505.

110 See UNGA, *United Nations Development Decade. A Programme for International Economic Co-Operation (I)*.

111 See Parra, *The History of ICSID*, 19.

1959, between Germany and Pakistan, a landmark in a long and complex history of investment protection.[112]

Embedding arbitral authority in the protection of foreign investments was not itself innovative. It has been seen in this book that the adoption of the Drago-Porter Convention in 1907 was meant to curb gunboat diplomacy through the use of arbitration. This constituted an early manifestation of the transnationalisation of arbitral authority, drawing contractual disputes to the orbit of what was perceived as an interstate dispute settlement mechanism (*i.e.* international arbitration). Already then, by referring contractual debt to the purview of arbitrators, the field was immediately broadened up.

All of this, however, does not quite explain how the World Bank came to create one of the leading arbitration institutions in the world – and certainly the most important one when it comes to investment disputes. Emerging out of the United Nations Monetary and Financial Conference held at Bretton Woods in 1944,[113] the International Bank for Reconstruction and Development, then informally labelled "World Bank," had been entrusted with the task of financing the reconstruction of war-torn countries following WWII. Gradually, it began shifting its focus to the funding of development projects in developing countries.[114]

If it is not surprising that the World Bank would be following attentively the many initiatives emerging under the UN development decade, its concrete involvement with arbitration may seem somewhat accidental. At the time, there were three potential avenues for the World Bank's normative contribution for the promotion of foreign investments. The first was the adoption of a code of conduct, a project that had been taken over by the OECD following the Abs-Shawcross initiative. Then, there was the creation of a multilateral insurance scheme – a path that would be kept in abeyance until the 1980s, ultimately leading to the creation of MIGA. Finally, there was the creation of an institutional platform for the settlement of investment disputes, which is the object of this section.

The creation of ICSID was an initiative spearheaded by the World Bank's bureaucracy, counting with the omnipresent influence of Aron Broches. In the pages that follow, this study will first address the preliminary debates for the elaboration of the ICSID framework at the level of the bank's Executive

112 See Kate Miles, *The Origins of International Investment Law* (Cambridge University Press 2013), 19 et seq.

113 See Aron Broches, 'International Legal Aspects of the Operations of the World Bank' in Collected Courses of the Hague Academy of International Law, vol. 98 (Brill NV 1959), 301.

114 See Parra, *The History of ICSID*, 2.

Directors (1.2.1), and then it will dive into a detailed analysis of the broader legislative process, especially the regional consultations, underlying the adoption of the Washington Convention (1.2.2).

1.2.1 *A Bureaucrat Turned Lawgiver at the Committee of the Whole*

If the World Bank was to do something to promote foreign investments, certainly it was felt that dispute settlement was a low hanging fruit.[115] The zeitgeist pointed towards the creation of a specialized framework to govern disputes between governments and private parties. The World Bank, especially its President Eugene Robert Black, was gradually getting involved in arbitral proceedings. In most instances, Black would be called to act as an appointing authority in arbitration cases, but the institution would also be implicated in the settlement of investment disputes all throughout the 1950s through good offices, conciliation and mediation.[116]

Within this context, it was not too far-fetched for the World Bank to engage with the institutionalization of arbitration and conciliation. Preliminary discussions on the topic began in August 1961 and extended until June 1962 at the level of the bank's Executive Directors.[117] The governance of the World Bank is tripartite, made of a Board of Governors, Executive Directors and a President.[118] Originally, the Board of Directors (also called Committee of the Whole) was composed of 12 Executive Directors, but this number has now expanded to 25.[119] The bank's five largest shareholders (USA, Japan, China, Germany, and France and the UK tied in the fifth place) each appoint one Executive Director, and the remaining members are appointed by the Board of Governors.[120]

115 Aron Broches, in an interview to Robert E. Asher for the World Bank's Oral History Program, stated the following: "Well, since we were under general pressure to do something in the field of encouragement of foreign investment, I thought dispute settlement was the least controversial approach, and also something that wouldn't require a large organization. It wouldn't require money, and I thought it was something that the Bank ought to take up." See Robert E Asher, 'The World Bank/IFC Archives, Oral History Program, Transcript of Interview with Aron Broches, 23 May 1984' 35. Available at: <https://oralhistory.worldbank.org/transcripts/transcript-oral-history-interview-aron-broches-held-april-18-and-may-23-1984-second>.

116 See Aron Broches, 'SecM 62–17 (January 19, 1962) Note by the General Counsel Transmitted to the Executive Directors', *History of ICSID the Convention*, vol 2 (ICSID Publication 2009), 7, para 5.

117 See Parra, *The History of ICSID*, 23–24.

118 See Article V in World Bank, 'IBRD Articles of Agreement'. Available at: <https://www.worldbank.org/en/about/articles-of-agreement/ibrd-articles-of-agreement>.

119 See World Bank, 'Board of Directors'. Available at: <https://www.worldbank.org/en/about/leadership/directors>.

120 See Parra, *The History of ICSID*, 3.

Decision-making at the Board of Directors mirrors shareholding rights.[121] Accordingly, it has been noted that "Executive Directors have a dual character, as officials of the Bank and as representatives of the member or members that appointed or elected them."[122]

It was Aron Broches, then General Counsel of the World Bank, who introduced the potential creation of an arbitration institution in the bank's agenda.[123] Importantly, Broches was not just aware of the ongoing debates on arbitration involving States and private parties taking place elsewhere, but he also drew ideas from these discussions.[124] When the matter was presented to the Executive Directors of the World Bank for the first time, Broches framed it as a four dimensional issue: first, there was the problem of applying municipal laws to investment disputes; second, there were the shortcomings of diplomatic espousal as a means of investment protection; third, there was the question of the validity of arbitration agreements involving States and private parties; and finally, there was a lack of a specialized institution to administer foreign investment disputes, given that the ICC was often unacceptable to governments and the PCA was not open to private parties.[125]

The solution envisioned by Broches to overcoming these obstacles was grounded on State consent (voluntary arbitration instead of a compulsory model), direct access offered to private parties in relation to arbitral jurisdiction, recognition that an arbitration agreement between a private party and a government is a "binding international undertaking," the creation of a new institutional and procedural framework for the conduct of these cases, and the establishment of conciliation as an alternative to arbitration.[126] In any event, none of this was to interfere, unless provided otherwise by States themselves, "with the customary principle of international law pursuant to which

121 See World Bank, *Board of Directors*.

122 See Parra, *The History of ICSID*, 3–4.

123 See Aron Broches, 'SecM 61–192 (August 28, 1961): Note by A. Broches, General Counsel; Transmitted to the Executive Directors: "Settlement of Disputes between Governments and Private Parties,"' *History of ICSID the Convention*, vol 2 (ICSID Publication 2009).

124 Broches noted the following: "The many studies which have been undertaken in recent years concerning ways and means to promote private foreign investment have almost invariably discussed the problem of the settlement of disputes between foreign private investors or entrepreneurs and the Government of the country where the investment is made. In many cases these studies have recommended the establishment of international arbitration and/or conciliation machinery." See Broches, 'Note, 29 August 1961' (n 806) 1.

125 See Broches, *Note, 29 August 1961*, 2.

126 See Broches, *Note, 29 August 1961*, 2.

claims cannot be brought before an international tribunal until local remedies (whether administrative or judicial) have been exhausted."[127]

In the preliminary discussions of the project, one will quickly realize that the debates were not informed by a deep understanding of how arbitration worked. In fact, some of the questions raised by the Executive Directors demonstrate little to no knowledge about such dispute settlement mechanism. In this regard, Aron Broches performed a pedagogical role, explaining the basics of arbitration and conciliation. For instance, one finds in the records an Executive Director who asked "what the position would be in the case of an agreement to arbitrate, if one of the parties refused to cooperate on the ground that the claim made by the other party was not within the terms of the undertaking to arbitrate."[128] In his propaedeutics of arbitration, Broches presented the principle of competence-competence by affirming that it was a "well-established rule of international law that, unless the parties otherwise provide, the arbitral tribunal is the judge of its own jurisdiction."[129]

Albeit well documented,[130] it is never superfluous to emphasize Broches' central role in the creation of the ICSID framework. Born in Amsterdam at the outset of WWI, Broches had extensive legal training in both the Netherlands and the United States.[131] By 1939 he already held a Master and a PhD in Law from the University of Amsterdam. Moving to the United States during WWII, he completed a Bachelor of Laws at Fordham University Law School in 1942. Then, seemingly serving the Dutch government-in-exile, he became legal adviser to the Dutch Embassy in New York and then served as a Secretary in the Dutch delegation at the Bretton Woods Conference. He would become a staffer at the World Bank as early as 1946, reaching the grade of General Counsel in 1959.[132]

Aron Broches' involvement in the drafting of the Washington Convention is the quintessential example of the legislative power of bureaucracy, providing a great illustration of a bureaucrat turned lawgiver. On the one hand, the Bank's Articles of Agreement did not entrust the institution with the prerogative of

127 See Broches, *Note, 29 August 1961*, 2.

128 See Broches, *Note, 19 January 1962*, at 10, para 22.

129 See Broches, *Note, 19 January 1962*, at 10, para 25.

130 For instance, see Parra, *The History of ICSID*, at 25 et seq.; Andreas Llowenfeld, 'The ICSID Convention: Origins and Transformations' (2009) 38 Georgia Journal of International and Comparative Law 37, 50 et seq.

131 For an overview of his profile, see biographical note in Broches, *International Legal Aspects of the Operations of the World Bank.*

132 See H Oliver, 'The World BankI/IFC Archives, Oral History Program, Transcript of Interview with Aron Broches, July 11, 1961' 1. Available at: <https://oralhistory.worldbank.org/transcripts/transcript-oral-history-interview-aron-broches-held-july-11-1961-summary>.

drafting a treaty like the ICSID Convention. Rather, it was upon Broches advice that the World Bank would consider within its "implied powers to undertake any other actions to further its objectives."[133] On the other hand, it was not Broches' expertise in arbitration or the weight of his scholarship that made him a legitimate codifier of ICSID arbitration. Instead, it would be his professional credentials as a senior officer at the World Bank that would vest him with the legitimacy to lead this institutional project. If Broches would come to be one of the so-called "grand old man" of arbitration,[134] at that point he was something of an outsider to the field in a similar manner to what had been the case for some of the founding fathers of the ICC Court and Secretariat.[135]

That said, one must highlight that the conversations at the Board of Directors would be amplified within governmental bureaucracies, for these officials also acted as delegates for one or more countries. Accordingly, despite their lack of concrete knowledge concerning arbitration, Executive Directors would consult their constituencies and receive instructions on how to act in relation to the project.

As a result of these consultations, Executive Director John M. Garland expressed that his constituency was not fully convinced that the PCA was an unworkable option to the settlement of disputes between governments and private parties.[136] Jacques Waitzenegger, an Alternate Executive Director representing France, expressed the view that "the relationship of the proposed Centre with the Permanent Court of Arbitration and other similar bodies was not clear," for which reason the French government would reserve its position until further clarifications were made.[137] Helmut Koinzer, an Alternate Executive Director appointed by Germany, noted that the institutional framework eventually created should be very lean, pointing to the ICC and the PCA as a template for guidance, while stressing that matters of "jurisdiction, procedure and applicable law might be dealt with in bilateral agreements between interested countries (or in the absence of such bilateral agreements it could be

133 See Parra, *The History of ICSID*, 26.

134 See Dezalay and Garth, *Dealing in Virtue*.

135 See Lemercier and Sgard, *op.cit.*, 143 et seq.

136 See World Bank, 'Memorandum of Meeting of Executive Directors on the Subject of "Settlement of Investment Disputes", Tuesday, March 13, 1962', vol II–1 (ICSID Publication 2009), at 17, para 21.

137 See World Bank, *Memorandum, 13 March 1962*, at 16, para 18.

decided ad hoc)."[138] In essence, most felt that a more detailed proposal was needed, and the General Counsel was asked to work in that direction.[139]

Such a proposal came in June 1962 under the title of "Working Paper in the form of a Draft Convention prepared by the General Counsel and transmitted to the Executive Directors."[140] The document was much more elaborate, containing a total of 7 fully developed provisions and 4 placeholders.[141] Some comments were also appended whenever it was felt that a provision needed further explanation. Yet, this was merely a preliminary draft, a document presented "in order to facilitate further discussion of the question."[142]

The whole mechanism envisioned by Broches relied essentially on the principle of *pacta sunt servanda*, not party autonomy.[143] Similar to what had been the case in the 1923 Protocol on the Validity of Arbitration Clauses, *pacta sunt servanda* and good faith would be structuring ideas underlying the World Bank's procedural framework. Hence, it would be the sanctity of the contract the reason to uphold the legality of a written undertaking to arbitrate and to enforce a corresponding arbitral award.[144] Furthermore, Broches' project provided for the creation of a new arbitral institution – a centre – to hear claims both by and against States.[145] This final part was meant to make it clear that private parties were to be given direct access to the novel institutional framework.

138 Koinzer further noted that "Germany had concluded a number of so-called investment promotion treaties with different countries, and hoped to conclude more, making the bank's proposal 'a valuable supplement.'" See World Bank, *Memorandum, 13 March 1962*, at 14, para 6.

139 See World Bank, *Memorandum, 13 March 1962*, at 19, para 34.

140 See ICSID, *History of the ICSID Convention*, vols 2–I (ICSID Publication 2009), 19.

141 See Aron Broches, 'R 62–1 (SD) (June 5, 1962) Working Paper in the Form of a Draft Convention Prepared by the General Counsel and Transmitted to the Executive Directors', in ICSID, *History of the ICSID Convention*, vol 2 (ICSID 2009). One of these placeholders was Article VIII, which was supposed to govern the recognition of arbitral awards. Under that heading, a provision would be inserted "to the effect that Contracting States will give to awards rendered pursuant to the Convention the most favourable treatment they give to foreign arbitral awards whether under their internal law or pursuant to the Geneva Convention of 1927 on the execution of foreign arbitral awards or the United Nations Convention of 1958 on the recognition and enforcement of foreign arbitral awards." See Article VIII in Broches, *Working Paper, 5 June 1962*, 46.

142 See Broches, *Working Paper, 5 June 1962*, 20.

143 See Aron Broches, 'SID/63-2 (February 18, 1963) Paper Prepared by the General Counsel and Transmitted to the Members of the Committee of the Whole', in ICSID, *History of the ICSID Convention*, vol 2 (ICSID Publication 2009), 79–80.

144 See Article II in Broches, *Working Paper, 5 June 1962*, 22–23.

145 See Article I in Broches, *Working Paper, 5 June 1962*, 21.

One must highlight that, at this point of the drafting process, the project was silent on how to proceed with the enforcement of arbitral agreements and awards. As noted, Broches relied on good faith to assure compliance, presenting his approach as "an adaptation of a generally accepted principle of international arbitration to the effect that 'recourse to arbitration implies an engagement to submit in good faith to the award' (Article 37 of the Hague Convention of 1907)."[146]

The creation of a so-called "International Conciliation and Arbitration Centre" was the object of the draft's Article 3, establishing an international legal organization with "full juridical personality."[147] Overseeing all the operations of the new body, there would be an Administrative Council composed of representatives of member States, all of which with equal voting powers.[148] Still, the institution was to keep a connection with the World Bank,[149] but it would be equipped with its own Secretariat.[150] In addition, an idea was floated that the new institution should also maintain close ties with the PCA. Notably, it was suggested that the two bodies could share staff, and the premises of the PCA could be eventually used to conduct proceedings under the new centre's framework.[151]

More importantly, the future centre was to be vested with oversight in relation to arbitrators' appointments through the establishment of a panel of "qualified" individuals willing to act as arbitrators and conciliators.[152] It was argued that these panels would have "limited significance," for parties would be allowed to appoint arbitrators and conciliator from outside the list kept by the institution. Still, this feature represents an important instance of professional control over the career of arbitrators, for being included in one such panel would serve as a credential of technical expertise. Furthermore, the maintenance of a roster of arbitrators consists of another example of the interplay between the PCA and ICSID frameworks, for Broches argued that "[t]he

146 See Broches, *Working Paper, 5 June 1962*, 23.

147 See Broches, *Working Paper, 5 June 1962*, 25.

148 See Broches, *Working Paper, 5 June 1962*, 26–28.

149 See Broches, *Working Paper, 5 June 1962*, 25–26.

150 See Article III(10) and III(11) in Broches, *Working Paper, 5 June 1962*, 28.

151 See Articles III(2) and VII(4) in Broches, *Working Paper, 5 June 1962*, 25 and 44. Regarding the institution's staff, the draft's Article III(11)(2) provided the following: "The office of Secretary-General or Deputy Secretary General shall be incompatible with the exercise of any political function, and with any employment or occupation other than employment by the Bank or by the Permanent Court of Arbitration, except as the Administrative Council, with the concurrence of the President, may otherwise decide." See Broches, *Working Paper, 5 June 1962*, 29.

152 See Article III(13) in Broches, *Working Paper, 5 June 1962*, 30.

method adopted in the draft largely follows the system of the Hague Conventions of 1899 and 1907."[153]

The remaining articles of the document dealt with the jurisdiction of the centre and laid out rules to govern conciliation and arbitration proceedings. Jurisdiction was based on consent and restricted to disputes involving member States and nationals of other member States.[154] The principle of competence-competence was enshrined in the document regarding both conciliation and arbitration proceedings,[155] but it also vested the Centre's Secretary General with a prima facie purview over the jurisdiction of the Centre.[156]

There was great parallelism between the procedural framework laid out to govern arbitration and conciliation.[157] Still, as had been the case in other codification endeavours, the bipartition of the two mechanisms evoked that longstanding divide between contractual and jurisdictional approaches to transnational dispute settlement. Therefore, the two proceedings would diverge precisely in relation to their output – *i.e.*, a quasi-judicial decision in the case of arbitration proceedings, and a recommendation for a settlement agreement in the case of conciliation proceedings.

In the specific case of arbitration, the draft vested the tribunal with discretion to determine the law applicable whenever parties failed to agree otherwise, precluding the possibility of a *non liquet*.[158] Also, as a jurisdictional mechanism, the tribunal was given the prerogative to render provisional measures.[159] Albeit providing for the final and binding character of the award,[160] as well as its enforceability,[161] this early draft already contemplated a mechanism for the interpretation and revision of the award. On the one hand, interpretation would be available whenever there was a dispute as to the meaning and the scope of the award. On the other hand, revision would be allowed in cases where facts unknown were discovered and could have a decisive bearing in the outcome of the arbitration.[162]

153 See Broches, *Working Paper, 5 June 1962*, 30.
154 See Article IV in Broches, *Working Paper, 5 June 1962*, 33.
155 See Article IV(5) in Broches, *International Legal Aspects of the Operations of the World Bank*, 37.
156 See Article IV(4) in Broches, *Working Paper, 5 June 1962*, 35.
157 Compare Articles 5 and 6 of the draft in Broches, *Working Paper, 5 June 1962*, 37–43.
158 See Article VI(5) in Broches, *Working Paper, 5 June 1962*, 41.
159 See Article VI(6) in Broches, *Working Paper, 5 June 1962*, 41–42.
160 See Article VI(10) in Broches, *Working Paper, 5 June 1962*, 42.
161 See Article VI(11) in Broches, *Working Paper, 5 June 1962*, 42–43.
162 See Article VI(12) in Broches, *Working Paper, 5 June 1962*, 43.

Two meetings of the so-called Committee of the Whole were held on 18 and 27 December 1962 to discuss Broches' working paper.[163] In these meetings, a central issue of debate was the relationship between the World Bank and the future centre, with views being expressed that this should be a looser one.[164] In fact, it was then held that, if institutional close ties were to exist, these should be maintained with the PCA. This proposition was extensively defended by a Mr. Lieftinck – the Executive Director representing the Netherlands.[165] The same Mr. Lieftinck, who commented at length on Broches' paper, expressed concerns over the role of State consent regarding the operation of the arbitration agreement. For him, the legally binding nature of the promise to arbitrate should be further stressed, for "[c]ontracting states should not be enabled to free themselves of this obligation by their own stipulation."[166] Albeit desirable, Broches was unsure as to how to proceed "without obscuring or casting doubt on the fact that the obligation was intended to be equally binding on the private party."[167]

Also in these preliminary discussions, some Executive Directors raised concerns over the scope of jurisdiction of the future body. The Executive Director for India, C.S. Krishna Moorti, highlighted that "arbitration and conciliation could be had only under certain exceptional circumstances with reference to closely defined jurisdiction; the aim should be to provide for the minimum of action for the Centre, and this should be the maximum expected of any state."[168] In this regard, Broches affirmed that "the proposed new machinery should not be a substitute for local courts and local law," covering only what he called "the abnormal case."[169] A similar concern was raised by Fernando Ilanes,

163 See World Bank, 'SID 62–1 (December 28, 1962) Memorandum of the Meeting of the Committee of the Whole; December 18, 1962', in ICSID, *History of the ICSID Convention*, vol II–1 (ICSID Publication 2009); World Bank, 'SID/62-2 (January 7, 1963) Memorandum of the Meeting of the Committee of the Whole, December 27, 1962', in ICSID, *History of the ICSID Convention*, vol II–1 (ICSID Publication 2009).

164 See World Bank, *Memorandum, 28 December 1962*, at 55, para 12.

165 See World Bank, *Memorandum, 28 December 1962*, at 55–56.

166 See World Bank, *Memorandum, 28 December 1962*, at 55, para 9.

167 See World Bank, *Memorandum, 28 December 1962*, at 57, para 22.

168 See World Bank, *Memorandum, 28 December 1962*, at 57–58, para 28.

169 See World Bank, *Memorandum, 28 December 1962*, at 58, para 32. In another study prepared by Broches argued the following: "Although adherence to the Convention does not impose any legal obligation on any party thereto to agree to conciliation or arbitration under the auspices of the Centre, would such adherence not expose governments to pressures by investors to agree to such conciliation or arbitration on a wide scale? To the extent that the Convention would ensure the effectiveness of conciliation and arbitration procedures, investors might well show an increased interest in having recourse thereto. But such international methods of settlement of disputes should be reserved for special

who represented several South American States, echoing Latin America's longstanding commitment to the Calvo doctrine.[170] Despite these considerations, Broches intentionally advocated for leaving such scope vague.[171]

In addition, concerns were raised as to the interplay between the new institution and other normative initiatives underway. Notably, Otto Donner, the German Executive Director, noted that his government was sympathetic to the creation of the Centre, but expressed the view that further consideration should be given to the consistency between the draft proposed by Broches and the BITs adopted by Germany.[172] In particular, he noted that "his government would wish it to be made clear that the convention would not preclude a state from submitting to arbitration questions concerning the interpretation of an investment treaty, where the treaty itself made provision for arbitration of such questions."[173] In hindsight, the fears of the German official may seem unwarranted, but it demonstrates the uniformization concerns at play in the creation of ICSID.

Finally, there were voices at the Committee of the Whole who considered that "legal experts" should be brought to bear upon the project. This, for

---

situations as indicated earlier in this paper. Adherence to the Convention would constitute a recognition that there may be circumstances in which recourse to international methods for the settlement of disputes between governments and foreign investors may be appropriate. Experience indicates that governments decide on the basis of an evaluation of their enlightened self-interest how far they wish to go in offering incentives to foreign investors. This applies to such matters as tax exemptions and transfer guarantees as well as to special arrangements for the settlement of disputes." See Broches, *Paper, 18 February 1963*, 82.

170 See World Bank, *Memorandum, 7 January 1963*, at 61, para 6.

171 In a paper prepared to further clarify his proposals, he observed the following: "Should there be a definition of the type of dispute for which the facilities of the Centre would be available? There is a general understanding, which could be recorded in a Preamble to the Convention, that the machinery created by the Convention and the rules laid down in the Convention are designed to deal primarily with investment disputes. It is also generally understood that the scope of the Convention should be limited to legal disputes as distinguished from political or commercial disputes, and this could also be suitably expressed in a Preamble. Once this intention is expressed, there seems to be no need to go further and give a precise definition of the disputes for which the services of the Centre would be available. To give a precise definition of investment dispute would be extremely difficult. More seriously, it might lead to undesirable jurisdictional controversies in cases where parties have agreed to submit a dispute to conciliation or arbitration under the auspices of the Centre, and one of the parties later refuses to carry out the agreement claiming that the dispute is of a kind outside the defined scope of the Convention." See Broches, *Paper, 18 February 1963*, 83.

172 See World Bank, *Memorandum, 7 January 1963*, at 62, para 8.

173 See World Bank, *Memorandum, 7 January 1963*, 63, para 13.

instance, was the view of Ms. Brun, who represented the Nordic countries.[174] Yet, Broches considered that it was too soon to enlarge the conversation, for the Executive Directors should first discuss the "general principles" underlying the draft.[175]

Just as the work towards the creation of ICSID got off the ground, the term of Eugene Black as President of the World Bank came to an end in December 1963. Black, a veteran of WWI and former American investment banker,[176] had been a strong supporter of arbitration and conciliation within the World Bank. He was even personally involved in the conclusion of an arbitration agreement in a dispute involving French bondholders and the City of Tokyo.[177] Black was replaced by George Woods in January 1963, but he made sure to tell the incoming President that the creation of ICSID was a "good idea."[178] Yet, Woods preferred to acquaint himself with the many aspects of his new job, which led to some delays in the discussion of the ICSID project.[179]

As soon as Woods understood the project, he became "one of its most ardent proponents."[180] He then called a series of meetings in June 1963 to resume its

174 See World Bank, *Memorandum, 7 January 1963*, at 64, para 20.

175 See World Bank, *Memorandum, 7 January 1963*, 63, para 15.

176 For Black's profile, see World Bank, 'Eugene R. Black: 3rd President of the World Bank Group, July 1, 1949–December 31, 1962'. Available at: <worldbank.org/en/archive/history/past-presidents/eugene-robert-black>.

177 See Parra, *The History of ICSID*, 22.

178 See Robert W Oliver, 'A Conversation with Aron Broches, Washington D.C., November 7, 1985' 4. Available at: <https://oralhistory.worldbank.org/transcripts/transcript-oral-history-interview-aron-broches-held-november-7-1985-main-transcript>.

179 Broches, in an interview to Robert Oliver, noted the following: "There is something else with which I was connected where Woods, I thought, acted very well. I am referring to the International Centre for the Settlement of Investment Disputes. I started working on that in '62. Black liked it, but he left before discussions really got going. Black told Woods, 'George this is a good idea'. In his first weeks, Woods said, 'I understand that you are working on that. I like the idea, but there are so many things to find out in my new job, I'd like to put that on the back burner until I have time to study it. Then I'll talk to you, but I don't want to deal with a matter I don't understand'. Then about June, he said, "O.K. Counsel, talk, examine me', and I had to examine him. I had to ask him questions. I said, 'You're doing pretty well'. He said, 'Now we're going to talk to Directors. We'll talk first to Directors whose importance is somewhat peripheral. I will do the talking. Unless I say something completely idiotic, you stay out of it; but then in discussions you take over'. Afterwards he said, 'How did I do?' I said, 'fine'. He said, 'Yeh, but I didn't know what I was saying'. Second round, 'Did I do better now?' I said exactly the same thing, and he said, 'I think I know what I was saying'. The third time was lunch with the heavies, U. S., U. K. et cetera and he said, 'Now I feel comfortable'." See Oliver, *Conversation, November 7*, 4.

180 See Parra, *The History of ICSID*, 25.

discussion.[181] The debates reflected the evolving views concerning whether the new institution should be established at all, how to organize such an institution and the links it should keep with the World Bank. Based on these many exchanges, Broches produced a new document entitled "First Preliminary Draft of a Convention on the Settlement of Investment Disputes between States and Nationals of other States."[182] This was a fully elaborated draft convention made of a preamble, 11 articles and their corresponding comments. Evidently, the new document retained the core of the Working Paper, while incorporating the modifications suggested by the Executive Directors and further elaborating on elements originally left missing.

This First Preliminary Draft was analysed by the Committee of the Whole on 10 September 1963.[183] At this meeting, George Woods announced that, following the conclusion of the debates at the level of Executive Directors, the document would be amended whenever appropriate, transmitted to the World Bank's Member States for comments, and serve as working document for the regional consultations with legal experts organized with the assistance of the Regional Commissions of the United Nations.[184] Concretely, no major change was made to the First Preliminary Draft, with most of the discussions revolving around the question as to how wide should be the circulation of the draft.[185]

With the final touches given to the document, a new version of the Preliminary Draft was finalized on 15 October 1963,[186] and circulated ahead of the

181 See World Bank, 'SID/63-8 (June 5, 1963) Memorandum of the Meeting of the Committee of the Whole, May 28, 1963.', *History of the ICSID Convention*, vol II–1 (ICSID Publication 2009); World Bank, 'SID/63-10 (June 13, 1963) Memorandum of the Meeting of the Committee of the Whole, June 4, 1963', *History of the ICSID Convention*, vol II–1 (ICSID Publication 2009); World Bank, 'SID/63-11 (June 19, 1963) Memorandum of the Meeting of the Committee of the Whole, June 6, 1963', in ICSID, *History of ICSID Convention*, vol II–1 (ICSID Publication 2009); World Bank, 'SID/63-12 (June 21, 1963) Memorandum of the Meeting of the Committee of the Whole, June 11, 1963', in ICSID, *History of the ICSID Convention*, vol II–1 (ICSID Publication 2009).

182 See Aron Broches, 'SID/63-15 (August 9, 1963) First Preliminary Draft of a Convention on the Settlement of Investment Disputes between States and Nationals of Other States', in ICSID, *History of the ICSID Convention*, vol 2 (ICSID Publication 2009).

183 See World Bank, 'SID/63-16 (September 20, 1963) Memorandum of the Discussion by the Executive Directors, September 10, 1963', in ICSID, *History of the ICSID Convention*, vol II–1 (ICSID Publication 2009).

184 See World Bank, *Memorandum, 20 September 1963*, 174–175.

185 See World Bank, *Memorandum, 20 September 1963*, 177–179.

186 See World Bank, 'Preliminary Draft of a Convention on the Settlement of Investment Disputes between States and Nationals of Other States. Working Paper for Consultative Meetings with Legal Experts Designated by Governments', in ICSID, *History of the ICSID Convention*, vol II–1 (ICSID Publication 2009).

regional consultations. The preamble, which would be later enshrined in the Washington Convention with some minor changes, conveyed the general purposes and objectives of the future treaty. These foundational notions were the promotion of economic development, the protection of the legitimate exercise of national sovereignty, the alternative character of the dispute resolution mechanisms set forth in the instrument, and the obligational character of a promise to arbitrate.[187]

The institutional architecture of the new centre was laid out in Article I, throughout some 20 sections. The basic structure did not deviate from what had been delineated in the Working Paper, which was heavily inspired in the PCA institutional framework.[188] Similarly to its Hague ancestor, the new institution would have an Administrative Council, a Secretariat and a list of arbitrators (labelled panel in the phraseology adopted). Considering the comments received from the Executive Directors, the links between the World Bank and the Centre were made looser. Notably, the President of the Bank would no longer preside over the day-to-day activities of the new institution. Even if the President of the Bank was to act as the chairperson of the Administrative Council of the new institution, it would be the Centre's Secretary-General the one to assume the role of its principal officer.[189]

The PCA was another source of inspiration in terms of jurisdiction, and the mention of the term "jurisdiction" itself was grounded upon "the precedent of the Hague Convention of 1907 which speaks of the 'jurisdiction of the Permanent Court' [...] even though that Court, like the proposed Centre does not itself exercise judicial or quasi-judicial functions."[190] The text of this provision also reflected the restrictive scope of the Centre's jurisdiction as suggested by the Executive Directors, even if this was done more or less vaguely, as advocated by Broches.[191] Accordingly, the Preliminary Draft provided that "[t]he jurisdiction of the Centre shall be limited to proceedings for conciliation and arbitration with respect to any existing or future investment disputes of a legal character between a Contracting State and a national of another Contracting State".[192] This provision would be further elaborated throughout the following phases of the drafting process, until it reached the final formulation as enshrined in the Washington Convention. At this point, the reference to legal

187 See Broches, *First Preliminary Draft, 9 August 1963*, 135–136.
188 See Parra, *The History of ICSID*, 46.
189 See Article I(10)(1) in World Bank, *Preliminary Draft, 15 October 1963*, 194.
190 See World Bank, *Preliminary Draft, 15 October 1963*, 203.
191 See Broches, *Paper, 18 February 1963*, 83.
192 See Article II(1) in World Bank, *Preliminary Draft, 15 October 1963*, 202.

investment disputes was included to set the boundaries between legal investment disputes and "political, economic or purely commercial disputes," as the latter would fall outside the purview of the new body.[193]

The provisions on conciliation did not change substantially from the Working Paper to the First Preliminary Draft and finally to the Preliminary Draft. Notably, the Preliminary Draft clarified that the powers and functions of conciliation as enshrined in the document reflected "generally accepted concepts of the conciliation function."[194] In particular, the commentary to the relevant provisions referred to Article 15(1) of the 1928 General Act for the Pacific Settlement of International Disputes and to Article XXII of the 1948 American Treaty on Pacific Settlement (the Pact of Bogotá).[195] This testifies once again to the cross-fertilization between codification projects, all of which gradually created and reinforced uniform boundaries between potentially overlapping dispute settlement mechanisms.[196]

The arbitration provisions in the draft circulated ahead of the regional consultations was also analogous to what had been laid out in Broches' Working Paper, with some slight textual variation. That said, one must highlight few other instances of cross-fertilization between codification projects. Notably, the provisions on the legal undertaking to arbitrate, on competence-competence, as well as the ones on the constitution, power and functions of the tribunal were considerably inspired on the ILC Model Rules on Arbitral Procedure.[197]

One must also note that the Preliminary Draft innovated in relation to the Working Paper by dealing with the disqualification of arbitrators, and by introducing some rules on the recognition and enforcement of arbitral awards. However, the Preliminary Draft was still quite vague in its approach of these issues. On the one hand, the rule on disqualification merely stated that a Party could apply for the disqualification of an arbitrator on the basis of "any fact."[198] On the other hand, the rules on recognition and enforcement succinctly provided that the award was final and binding, and that Contracting States would recognize and enforce these awards within its territory.[199] These elements

193 See comment in Broches, *First Preliminary Draft, 9 August 1963*, 149.

194 See comment in Broches, *First Preliminary Draft, 9 August 1963*, 154; World Bank, *Preliminary Draft, 15 October 1963*, 210.

195 See comment in Broches, *First Preliminary Draft, 9 August 1963*, 154; and World Bank, *Preliminary Draft, 15 October 1963*, 210.

196 See Article IV(13) in Broches, *First Preliminary Draft, 9 August 1963*, 159.

197 See Parra, *The History of ICSID*, 46–47.

198 See Article V(2) in World Bank, *Preliminary Draft, 15 October 1963*, 223.

199 These provisions read as follows: "Section 14. The award shall be final and binding on the parties. Each party shall abide by and comply with the award immediately, unless

introduced by the Preliminary Draft would be considerably developed in the next drafting phases.

A most important innovation brought by the Preliminary Draft was the introduction of a third type of post-award remedy. Originally, Broches contemplated in his Working Paper only interpretation and revision as mechanisms of review, but in the Preliminary Draft he added annulment alongside the original two. Interpretation and revision were remedies existing under the 1907 Hague Convention for the Pacific Settlement of International Disputes, and the text proposed by Broches seemingly builds on that framework.[200] Conversely, it is not entirely clear how and why the provision on annulment came to be developed.

No great explanation is given for this addition, nor any extensive comment is offered in relation to the provision. Certainly, annulment was a common feature in commercial arbitration treaties. Here, one could imagine that Broches would have borrowed from these instruments, but then one cannot but remark that the grounds for annulment were slightly different and the procedural mechanism completely distinct. The former, particularly, was centred on an *ad hoc* Committee, which would be vested with jurisdiction over annulment.[201] This had no resemblance with the approach adopted by the 1927 Geneva Convention or the 1958 New York Convention, both of which vested municipal courts with jurisdiction over annulment proceedings.[202]

Then, one could draw attention to the 1958 ILC Model Rules on Arbitral Procedure. Indeed, the grounds for annulment conveyed in the World Bank's Preliminary Draft were almost an identical copy of Article 35 of the ILC Model Rules.[203] However, procedure was once again very different, for the ILC vested the ICJ with jurisdiction over annulment proceedings.[204] Broches himself

---

the Tribunal shall have allowed a time limit for the carrying out of the award or any part thereof, or the enforcement of the award shall have been stayed pursuant to Sections 11, 12 or 13 of this Article. Section 15. Each Contracting State shall recognize an award of the Tribunal as binding and enforce it within its territories as if it were a final judgment of the courts of that State." See Articles IV(14) and IV(15) in World Bank, *Preliminary Draft, 15 October 1963*, 218.

200 Compare sections 11 and 12 of Article IV in the World Banks Preliminary Draft with Articles 82 and 83 in the 1907 Hague Convention. See Brown Scott, *The Conference of 1907, Plenary Meetings of the Conference*, 569.

201 See Article IV(13)(2) in Broches, *First Preliminary Draft, 9 August 1963*, 159.

202 See Article V of the New York Convention and Articles 1 to 3 of the 1927 Geneva Convention.

203 See Article 35 of the ILC Rules in International Law Commission, *Model Rules on Arbitral Procedure*, 86.

204 See Article 36 of the ILC Rules in International Law Commission, *Model Rules on Arbitral Procedure*, 86.

would later remark that the reason why "the International Law Commission's model rules in regard to annulment had not been followed was that the parties could not present their case to the International Court of Justice unless the State of the investor's nationality were willing to espouse his cause."[205]

In this case, was the ICSID annulment proceedings a product of Broches creativity? It may be so, but it is not unreasonable to think otherwise. Indeed, in the preparatory works of the IDI Rules, one finds a proposition strikingly similar to what would become the ICSID annulment proceedings. As discussed previously in this study, the rapporteur of the project, Levin Goldschmidt, had envisioned the possibility of entrusting *ad hoc* arbitration tribunals with the jurisdiction to deal with the annulment of arbitral awards.[206] Interestingly, this somewhat forgotten project resurfaced during the ILC work on the codification of arbitral procedure.[207] In this context, one may wonder whether Broches, or anyone in his team, sought inspiration there for this new development.

1.2.2 *Expanding the Debates: Legal Experts and Regional Consultations*

The Preliminary Draft was discussed at length in four regional meetings held between December 1963 and May 1964. These regional consultations took place in Addis Ababa (Ethiopia),[208] Bangkok (Thailand),[209] Geneva (Switzerland)[210] and Santiago (Chile),[211] with the attendance of more than 80 legal experts from Africa, the Americas, Asia and Western Europe – and were always chaired by

205 See World Bank, 'Settlement of Investment Disputes. Consultative Meeting of Legal Experts. Geneva, February 17–22, 1964. Summary Record of Proceedings', *in* ICSID, *History of the ICSID Convention*, vol II-1 (ICSID Publication 2009), 129–130.

206 See Goldschmidt, *op.cit.*, 451.

207 See United Nations, *Yearbook of the International Law Commission, 1958, Volume II, Documents of the Tenth Session Including the Report of the Commission to the General Assembly*, n 8.

208 For the records of the Addis Ababa consultation, see World Bank, 'Settlement of Investment Disputes. Consultative Meeting of Legal Experts. Addis Ababa, December 16–20, 1963. Summary Record of Proceedings', *in* ICSID, *History of the ICSID Convention*, vol II–1 (ICSID Publication 2009).

209 For the records of the Bangkok consultation, see World Bank, 'Settlement of Investment Disputes. Consultative Meeting of Legal Experts. Bangkok, Thailand, April 27–May 1, 1964. Summary Record of Proceedings', *in* ICSID, *History of the ICSID Convention*, vol II–1 (ICSID Publication 2009).

210 For the records of the Geneva regional meeting, see World Bank, *Consultative Meeting of Legal Experts. Geneva, February 17–22, 1964.*

211 For the records of the Santiago consultation, see World Bank, 'Settlement of Investment Disputes. Consultative Meeting of Legal Experts. Santiago, Chile, February 3–7, 1964. Summary Record of Proceedings', in ICSID, *History of the ICSID Convention*, vol II–1 (ICSID Publication 2009).

Broches himself.[212] Nevertheless, at a time where decolonization was still underway, various delegates of African and Asian States were governmental officials from European countries. The issue is well illustrated by the example of François Giscard d'Estaing, a French officer and cousin of future French president Valéry Giscard d'Estaing,[213] who attended the consultations as part of the delegation of the Tchad and the Central African Republic.

Still, times were a-changin' and the order was rapidly fading, sang Bob Dylan that same year of 1964. If the decolonization of Africa was yet to be completed, post-colonial concerns were voiced by several delegations in the meetings at Bangkok and Santiago. Interestingly, some of the comments foresaw many of the topics now hotly debated in the context of ISDS reform, such as its catch-all jurisdictional provisions or its perceived democratic deficit.

For instance, Robert Ghanem, a Lebanese official from the Ministry of Justice, considered that "it would not be fair to apply it [the draft convention] to old investments, particularly those made when the host State was not master of its own destiny."[214] Broches, however, argued that "it would be going too far to say that treatment of old investments was irrelevant to the investment climate for future investments" and that "investors considering an investment in a country would be guided, at least in part, by the experiences of old investors."[215]

Also cautious was the Indian representative, Bhaskar Namdeo Adarkar, who felt that the World Bank's project "placed the foreign investor and the State on a par regardless of any law, national or international, or the terms of any contract or other arrangements between the State and the foreign investor."[216] Contrary to Broches' views, he considered that the vague definition of the new Centre's jurisdiction would generate more disputes rather than minimize their likelihood, exposing States to a pressure to arbitrate inarbitrable disputes in order to avoid reputational damage.[217] Broches counter-argued that, rather

---

212 See Parra, *The History of ICSID*, 48.

213 For background information on François Giscard d'Estaing, see Pol Bruno, 'La Saga Des Giscard' [1980] *Le Nouvel Observateur* 94, 122.

214 See World Bank, *Consultative Meeting of Legal Experts. Bangkok, Thailand, April 27–May 1, 1964*.

215 See World Bank, *Consultative Meeting of Legal Experts. Bangkok, Thailand, April 27–May 1, 1964*, 536.

216 See World Bank, *Consultative Meeting of Legal Experts. Bangkok, Thailand, April 27–May 1, 1964*, 470.

217 This was expressed as follows: "Section 2(3) of Article II on jurisdiction allowed a party to submit a dispute to the Centre even before the State's consent had been obtained, and then to try to use the good offices of the Secretary General to secure the consent of the State. As a precise definition of disputes within the jurisdiction of the Centre was

than a code of conduct, the draft was merely procedural, and that "it gave the investor no right whatever but only a procedural capacity in cases where States had consented to proceedings under the Convention."[218]

In Santiago, Francisco da Cunha Ribeiro, a Brazilian lawyer and member of the Brazilian monetary authority, evoking the traditional public international law view under which international arbitration was "a legal institution designed for the peaceful solution of disputes between nations," punctuated that "foreign investors would be granted a legally privileged position, in violation of the principle of full equality before the law."[219] Similarly, Julio Barboza, an Argentinean diplomat, considered that "unjust discrimination would exist if some persons could be excepted from the principle of equality of all before the law" and that "there were no firmly established precedents for the use of arbitration between an individual and a State."[220] In general, it was felt that the draft would be an affront to fundamental principles democratically enshrined in national constitutions and ultimately a violation of national sovereignty. Broches once again defended his project, stressing that "when a State agreed

lacking, it would be difficult for the Secretary-General to decide whether he should take the matter up with the State concerned or try to discourage the investor from pursuing his request. The Convention in fact conferred an additional right on the foreign investor without placing additional obligations on him, and thus the basic principle of reciprocity, fundamental in all international agreements, was not present. Refusal of consent could cause considerable damage to the reputation of the State for fair dealing if that refusal were to be misinterpreted as being due to an unwillingness on the part of the State to submit to international jurisdiction. Such a refusal might very well be entirely bona fide as where, for instance, the matter concerned national policy, or again if the matter did not involve discrimination between foreign and national investors or conflict with any contractual obligation of the State. In such cases no purpose would be served by submitting it to an international tribunal because an award involving a change in the national law would be unenforceable. If a distinction were not drawn between cases where the dispute itself was not arbitrable according to the principles laid down in the Convention or otherwise internationally agreed upon, and those others where the State was unwilling or unable to submit itself to international jurisdiction, the Convention would either compel every State to agree to conciliation or arbitration in every case for fear of an adverse inference or, alternatively, it would create an unnecessary and unwarranted impediment to the flow of foreign investment instead of promoting it, which was the object of the Convention." See World Bank, *Consultative Meeting of Legal Experts. Bangkok, Thailand, April 27–May 1, 1964*, 470–471.

218 See World Bank, *Consultative Meeting of Legal Experts. Bangkok, Thailand, April 27–May 1, 1964*, 472.

219 See World Bank, *Consultative Meeting of Legal Experts. Santiago, Chile, February 3–7, 1964*, 306.

220 See World Bank, *Consultative Meeting of Legal Experts. Santiago, Chile, February 3–7, 1964*, 308.

to submit a dispute to arbitration or conciliation, it was exercising a sovereign right, namely that of limiting its own sovereignty."[221]

In addition to this broader debate underpinned by Latin America's deference to the Calvo doctrine, the regional consultations produced minute commentary on the technical operation of investment dispute settlement. Topics like the nationality of investors,[222] as well as the disqualification of conciliators and arbitrators,[223] generated comments taken onboard by Broches for further elaboration. In addition, there were considerable debates concerning the applicable law to investment disputes and the means of annulling an award.

The topic of choice of law emerged in the analysis of the powers and functions of the tribunal. Delegates raised concerns as to the scope of party autonomy in relation to the choice of applicable law, as well as to tribunal's discretion in determining such law failing party agreement.[224] As an example, P.T. Mpanjo, a member of Cameroon's delegation, cautioned that the project entrusted the tribunal with the prerogative of defining the applicable law in the absence of express choice, asking whether "[i]f an act of nationalization were to be questioned before a tribunal, would the tribunal be competent to decide upon the legality of such a sovereign act, and if so, by reference to which system of law?"[225] In these instances, Broches would try to defuse criticisms to the project, highlighting that, failing agreement otherwise, "it [the tribunal] would look into all the legal aspects of any dispute brought before it from the standpoint not only of domestic, but also of international law, to see if the rights of either party had been infringed."[226] Without articulating it so clearly, or even realizing it, Broches constantly advocated for the transnationalisation of arbitrators' mandate, imagining investment adjudication beyond the divide

221 See World Bank, *Consultative Meeting of Legal Experts. Santiago, Chile, February 3–7, 1964*, 309.

222 See World Bank, *Consultative Meeting of Legal Experts. Addis Ababa, December 16–20, 1963*, at 260 and 285; World Bank, *Consultative Meeting of Legal Experts. Santiago, Chile, February 3–7, 1964*, at 325 and 361, 538–539; World Bank, *Consultative Meeting of Legal Experts. Geneva, February 17–22, 1964*, 448–450.

223 See World Bank, *Consultative Meeting of Legal Experts. Addis Ababa, December 16–20, 1963*, 276; World Bank, *Consultative Meeting of Legal Experts. Geneva, February 17–22, 1964*, 436; World Bank, *Consultative Meeting of Legal Experts. Bangkok, Thailand, April 27–May 1, 1964*, 529.

224 See World Bank, *Consultative Meeting of Legal Experts. Addis Ababa, December 16–20, 1963*, at 265–266; World Bank, *Consultative Meeting of Legal Experts. Geneva, February 17–22, 1964*, at 418–421; World Bank, *Consultative Meeting of Legal Experts. Bangkok, Thailand, April 27–May 1, 1964*, at 511 and 513.

225 See World Bank, *Consultative Meeting of Legal Experts. Addis Ababa, December 16–20, 1963*, at 267.

226 See World Bank, *Consultative Meeting of Legal Experts. Addis Ababa, December 16–20, 1963*, 267.

established between public and private international law. This vision, however, would find a strong resistance at the final stages of the drafting process.

A connected discussion had to do with the tribunal's prerogative to render rulings *ex aequo et bono*. Andreas F. Lowenfeld, then an Assistant Legal Adviser at the U.S. Department of State and yet to become a leading scholar in international economic law, suggested that arbitrators should be allowed *ex officio* to rule on equity.[227] The debate, however, was cut short, for the proposition was not supported by Broches or by any other delegations.

In Santiago, a long discussion ensued in relation to the provision on recognition and enforcement of arbitral awards. Several issues were raised, including the following ones: whether the draft could potentially impair the doctrine of sovereign immunity (and, if so, to what extent); whether enforcement within the territories of the States involved in the dispute should be distinguished from enforcement in third States; whether the provision on enforcement should be limited in scope only to enforcement of pecuniary obligations; whether there should be exceptions to enforcement, such as a public policy exception; and whether a distinction should be made between a binding award and an enforceable award.[228] Broches agreed that these matters deserved careful consideration, yet he highlighted that the provision on enforcement had been drafted with the intention "to protect the interests of the host States which while they were themselves internationally bound to comply with the award, might want an effective assurance that the private party would be compelled to do the same."[229]

Similarly, enforcement had also generated a clash of opinions between the delegations represented in Geneva. Some were of the view that enforcement and annulment should converge with the mechanisms provided for by the 1958 New York Convention, advocating in favour of court control at the place of enforcement and against setting the award at a par with municipal court decisions.[230] In light of these discussions, Broches formulated his vision of the hybridity and transnationality underlying the future ICSID Convention:

> The present draft was designed to establish a self-contained system as was found in judicial or arbitral proceedings between States under

---

227 See World Bank, *Consultative Meeting of Legal Experts. Santiago, Chile, February 3–7, 1964*, 330.

228 See World Bank, *Consultative Meeting of Legal Experts. Santiago, Chile, February 3–7, 1964*, at 342 et seq.

229 See World Bank, *Consultative Meeting of Legal Experts. Santiago, Chile, February 3–7, 1964*, at 346–347.

230 See World Bank, *Consultative Meeting of Legal Experts. Geneva, February 17–22, 1964*, at 424, 426 and 429.

> which there would be no recourse to an outside authority against decisions of tribunals or conciliation commissions; it was something midway between commercial and inter-State arbitration as the expert from the United Kingdom had pointed out. Since one of the purposes of the Convention was to give a greater sense of confidence not only to investors but also to capital-importing countries the latter would expect some assurance that compliance with an award made in their favour would be just as automatic as it would be if they lost the case.[231]

The comments received were collected by Broches and his team, feeding further drafting work. In the meanwhile, George Woods thought time had come to seek authorization from the Board of Governors in relation to a final instrument.[232] Rather than calling a diplomatic conference for that purpose, Woods considered that the future treaty should be finalized at the level of the Committee of the Whole with the assistance of a legal subcommittee to "which each Executive Director might appoint legal experts from as many of the countries represented by him as wished to be more directly associated with the preparatory work on the Convention."[233] Not without considerable resistance, specially from Latin American States,[234] the proposition came to be endorsed

231 See World Bank, *Consultative Meeting of Legal Experts. Geneva, February 17–22, 1964*, at 427.

232 See George Woods, 'SID/64-3 (June 10, 1964) Memorandum from the President to the Committee of the Whole', *in* ICSID, *History of the ICSID Convention*, vol II–1 (ICSID Publication 2009), 555.

233 See Woods, *Memorandum from the President (June 10, 1964)*, 556.

234 Felix Ruiz, a member of the Board of Governors appointed by Chile, issued the following statement, which provides a good summary of the position of Latin American States: "I should particularly like to stress the opinion of the countries whom I here represent with respect to the draft Agreement on Conciliation and Arbitration. We consider undesirable the resolution submitted to the Board of Governors; which recommends, and entrusts to the Board of Directors of the Bank, the drafting of an international agreement to create a center for conciliation and arbitration to which foreign private investors could have recourse for the settlement of their disputes with governments of the member countries, without necessarily having to exhaust the formalities and procedures of the national tribunals. It is believed that this would stimulate private investment in the underdeveloped countries. The legal and constitutional systems of all the Latin American countries that are members of the Bank offer the foreign investors at the present time the same rights and protection as their own nationals; they prohibit confiscation and discrimination and require that any expropriation on justifiable grounds of public interest shall be accompanied by fair compensation fixed, in the final resort, by the law courts. The new system that has been suggested would give the foreign investor, by virtue of the fact that he is a

by the World Bank's Board of Governors.[235] A vote had to be taken, gathering the support of 21 Member States against the opposition of all Latin American States and the Philippines – an event that became known as the "El No de Tokyo."[236]

Concretely, the legal subcommittee assisting the Committee of the Whole, labelled Legal Committee, did most of the heavy lifting in the final steps towards the adoption of the Washington Convention. This body was composed of representatives from 61 World Bank Member States, with the majority of Latin American countries sending delegates despite their opposition to the project.[237] Broches would once again take the lead of the discussions at the Legal Committee, as he chaired the body in his capacity of General Counsel of the World Bank.[238] Within the Legal Committee, a Drafting Subcommittee was also established to perform the concrete work of putting on paper the decisions taken.[239] Decision-making favoured consensus, and whenever such consensus was not reached in relation to any given provision, working groups would be appointed in order to formulate a generally acceptable provision.[240] Persisting controversy at the level of working groups, the issue would be referred to the Committee of the Whole at the discretion of the Legal Committee's

foreigner, the right to sue a sovereign state outside its national territory, dispensing with the courts of law. This provision is contrary to the accepted legal principles of our countries and, de facto, would confer a privilege on the foreign investor, placing the nationals of the country concerned in a position of inferiority. I must state, Mr. President, that the procedure suggested does not meet with the approval of our countries because it contravenes constitutional principles relating to this question that cannot be ignored." See ICSID, *History, vols. 2-I,* 606.

235 See Parra, *The History of ICSID*, 60–61.

236 See Llowenfeld, *The ICSID Convention*, 54.

237 See Parra, *The History of ICSID*, 67.

238 See World Bank, 'SID/LC/1 (November 17, 1964) Legal Committee on Settlement of Investment Disputes', *in* ICSID, *History of the ICSID Convention*, vols 2–II (ICSID Publication 2006), 647.

239 The Drafting Subcommittee was composed as follows: Messrs. Belin (USA), Burrows (UK), Kpognon (Dahomey), Lokur (India), Malaplate (France), Mantzoulinos (Greece), Melchor (Spain), Perez (Ecuador) and Pinto (Guatemala). See World Bank, 'SID/LC/SR/2 (December 17, 1964) Summary Proceedings of the Legal Committee Meeting, November 24, Morning', *in* ICSID, *History of the ICSID Convention*, vol II–2 (ICSID Publication 2006), 680.

240 See World Bank, *SID/LC/1 (November 17, 1964) Legal Committee on Settlement of Investment Disputes*, 648.

chairman[241] – a feature that provides another example of the hold Broches had over the elaboration of the ICSID Convention at all its drafting stages.

Meetings of the Legal Committee were held between 23 November and 11 December 1964.[242] The body worked on the basis of a document referred to as "First Draft," circulated on 11 September 1964,[243] which was essentially a revised version of the Preliminary Draft incorporating the comments received at regional consultations. From a formal standpoint, the First Draft was already very similar to the future Washington Convention. A preamble with seven paragraphs opened the document.[244] Then, what had been presented in the Preliminary Draft as articles were turned in the First Draft into chapters, with a total of ten chapters. Then, sections in the Preliminary Draft became in the First Draft articles numbered continuously, enshrining a total of 78 articles. Also, the First Draft introduced the name "International Center for the Settlement of Investment Disputes,"[245] for until then the body was referred to as "International Conciliation and Arbitration Center."[246]

After debates at the Legal Committee came to a close, Broches and his team elaborated a "Revised Draft," which would be finalized by January 1965.[247] That same January 1965, along with the Revised Draft, Broches transmitted to the Committee of the Whole a "Draft Report," which consisted of an explanatory note to accompany the future convention.[248] Some elements that were once featured as provisions in the early drafts were transposed to the report. This, for instance, had been the case of an express reference to the validity of consent to arbitration given in relation to existing and future disputes, which was transposed from the text of the instrument to its explanatory note.[249] The

---

241 See World Bank, *SID/LC/1 (November 17, 1964) Legal Committee on Settlement of Investment Disputes*, at 649.

242 See Parra, *The History of ICSID*, 67.

243 See World Bank, 'Z 12 (September 11, 1964) Draft Convention: Working Paper for the Legal Committee', *in* ICSID, *History of the ICSID Convention*, vol II–1 (ICSID Publication 2009).

244 The preamble in the draft corresponds almost exactly to the one adopted, except for the fact that its second paragraph no longer refers to sovereign equality. This specific provision read as follows in the draft: "BEARING IN MIND the possibility that from time to time disputes may arise in connection with such investment between Contracting States and nationals of other Contracting States and bearing in mind the desirability that such disputes be settled in a spirit of mutual confidence, and with due respect for the principle of equal rights of States in the exercise of their sovereignty". See World Bank, *First Draft*, at 611.

245 See Article 1(1) in World Bank, *First Draft*, 612.

246 See Article I, section 1 in World Bank, *Preliminary Draft, 15 October 1963*, 189.

247 See Parra, *The History of ICSID*, 80.

248 See Parra, *The History of ICSID*, 80.

249 See Parra, *The History of ICSID*, 81.

explanatory note also highlighted some choices made, such as that of leaving the definition of an investment an open-ended one.[250]

Indeed, the scope of the Centre's jurisdiction was an element that greatly evolved at these later stages of the drafting process. The debates at the Legal Committee were extensive and gave rise to a divide amongst its members, opposing those who favoured an open-ended approach to jurisdiction against those that preferred a closed definition of the types of investment disputes that could be heard under the new institutional framework.[251] As no consensus could be reached on the topic, a working group was created focusing on the various elements of the provision on jurisdiction – namely the issues of nationality, legal disputes, political subdivisions and the scope of the instrument.[252] Controversy on jurisdiction also ensued at the working group, so two draft provisions were produced, one styled as an open-ended approach and another as a closed one.[253] Several rounds of voting by shows of hand were performed, with the open-ended approach carrying the day.[254]

Similarly, the topics of recognition and enforcement were discussed with great attention. In the interest of time, as noted by Broches, he appointed a working group to address these issues even before the relevant provisions of the First Draft were analysed by the Legal Committee.[255] Originally, the First

250 See Aron Broches, 'R65-11 (January 19, 1965) Memorandum from the General Counsel and Draft Report of the Executive Directors to Accompany the Convention', in ICSID, *History of the ICSID Convention*, vols 2–II (ICSID Publication 2006) 957, para 26.

251 See Aron Broches, 'Report of the Chairman of the Legal Committee on Settlement of Investment Disputes', *in* ICSID, *History of the ICSID Convention*, vol II–2 (ICSID Publication 2006) 936.

252 See World Bank, 'SID/LC/SR/5 (December 21, 1964) Summary Proceedings of the Legal Committee Meeting, November 27, Morning', *in* ICSID, *History of the ICSID Convention*, vol II–2 (ICSID Publication 2006) 711.

253 See World Bank, 'SID/LC/SR/17 (December 30, 1964) Summary Proceedings of the Legal Committee Meeting, December 8, Afternoon', *in* ICSID, *History of the ICSID Convention*, vol II–2 (ICSID Publication 2006) 821; Mark Bomani, 'SID/LC/48 (December 7, 1964) WORKING GROUP IV Report on Scope of Jurisdiction of the Centre (Articles 26 and 29)', *in* ICSID, *History of the ICSID Convention*, vol II–2 (ICSID Publication 2006) 827–829.

254 The text as adopted was supported by experts appointed by the following countries: United Kingdom, Tanzania, Uganda, U.S.A., Netherlands, Sierra Leone, Denmark, Norway, Finland, Sweden, Nepal, Malaysia, New Zealand, Turkey, Nigeria, Yugoslavia, Korea, Japan, Liberia, Greece, Germany, Austria, Ivory Coast, Belgium, India, Costa Rica, Lebanon, Iran and Malagasy Republic. See Broches, *Report of the Chairman of the Legal Committee on Settlement of Investment Disputes*, 936.

255 See World Bank, 'SID/LC/SR/11 (December 29, 1964) Summary Proceedings of the Legal Committee Meeting, December 3, Morning', *in* ICSID, *History of the ICSID Convention*, vol II–2 (ICSID Publication 2006) 768. This working group was composed of delegates

Draft provisions governing the topic referred to the final character of awards,[256] imposing on future Contracting States the automatic duty to recognize and enforce binding awards rendered under the instrument.[257] In addition, they also evoked a "writ of execution" and "rules of civil procedure" applicable at the place of enforcement.[258] Confronted with such mechanism, the working group considered, *inter alia*, "the need for qualifying the automatic enforceability of awards," especially in relation to the requirement of "there being in existence a valid and authentic award, *i.e.* one which had not been annulled by an *ad hoc* Committee under Article 55, or one in respect of which execution had been refused by a competent authority after review pursuant to Article 57(3)."[259] The outcome of these discussions was a considerable revision of the provisions in question, giving rise to a much more detailed mechanism of recognition and enforcement.[260]

Another change conveyed in the Revised Draft concerned the relation of the Centre with the PCA. One must remember that all throughout the drafting process, there were provisions promoting collaboration between the new institution and the one at the Hague. The extent of such collaboration was at its peak in the first Working Paper presented by Broches in 1962,[261] but it would be gradually diminished overtime. A residual bridge between the two bodies existed in the First Draft, with an express reference to cooperation between ICSID and the PCA.[262] Upon suggestion of a member of the Indian delegation, Mr. Lokur, a vote was taken at the Legal Committee on whether reference to the PCA should be omitted from the instrument, but the decision was taken in favour of keeping it in the text.[263] That said, in a fairly unexplained manner,

from Germany, Greece, Sweden, Malgasy Republic, United States, El Salvador, Nigeria and Malaysia. See World Bank, 'SID/LC/SR/13 (December 30, 1964) Summary Proceedings of the Legal Committee Meeting, December 4, Afternoon', *in* ICSID, *History of the ICSID Convention*, vol II–2 (ICSID Publication 2006), 792.

256 See Article 56 in World Bank, *First Draft*, 636.

257 See Article 57 in World Bank, *First Draft*, 636–637.

258 See Article 57 in World Bank, *First Draft*, 636–637.

259 See Vidar Hellners, 'SID/LC/50 (December 8, 1964) WORKING GROUP VI Chairman: Mr. Vidar Hellners (Sweden) Report on Article 57', *in* ICSID, *History of the ICSID Convention*, vol II–2 (ICSID Publication 2006), 893.

260 See World Bank, 'SID/LC/SR/22 (January 11, 1965) – Summary Proceedings of the Legal Committee Meeting, December 11, Morning', *in* ICSID, *History of the ICSID Convention*, vol II–2 (ICSID Publication 2006), 899–904.

261 See Broches, *Working Paper, 5 June 1962*, 19–42.

262 See Article 2(2) in World Bank, *First Draft*, 613.

263 See World Bank, *SID/LC/SR/2 (December 17, 1964) Summary Proceedings of the Legal Committee Meeting, November 24, Morning*, at 680 and 684.

the whole paragraph in which the reference was contained did not make its way to the Revised Draft, and so all mentions of the PCA disappeared from the Washington Convention.

Some fine tuning was also performed by the Legal Committee. The provision on applicable law is a case in point. Although it has been said that this provision was adopted with "as little discussion as possible,"[264] the Legal Committee was responsible for giving it its current form. One ought to remember that the First Draft granted the tribunal the prerogative to apply rules of national and international law at its discretion failing agreement of the parties,[265] an approach evocative of a transnational vision of arbitrators' authority. In this regard, some raised concerns as to the default application of international law.[266] There were also those who took issue with the application of national laws other than those of the host State.[267] In light of the resistance found, Broches suggested reformulating the text. This would be done to highlight the primacy of party autonomy regarding the law applicable, with a default provision expressly referring to the law of the host State, and its conflict of laws regime. Within this framework, only a vague reference to the application of "principles of international law" would be kept in the text of the instrument.[268] This

264 See Llowenfeld, *The ICSID Convention*, 57.

265 Article 45(1) of the First Draft read as follows: "In the absence of agreement between the parties concerning the law to be applied, the Tribunal shall decide the dispute submitted to it in accordance with such rules of national and international law as it shall determine to be applicable. The term "international law" shall be understood in the sense given to it by Article 38 of the Statute of the International Court of Justice." See World Bank, *First Draft*, 630.

266 See intervention of Mr. Serb from Yugoslavia in World Bank, 'SID/LC/SR/14 (December 30, 1964) Summary Proceedings of the Legal Committee Meeting, December 7, Morning', *in* ICSID, *History of the ICSID Convention*, vol II–2 (ICSID Publication 2006), 801.

267 See comments of Mr Bilgen, from Turkey, and Mr. da Cunha, from Brazil, in World Bank, *SID/LC/SR/14 (December 30, 1964) Summary Proceedings of the Legal Committee Meeting, December 7, Morning*, 801.

268 Broches intervention was recorded as follows: "Mr. BROCHES (Chairman) thought that the misapprehension with respect to the power of foreign investors might have been justified in the past but he was doubtful whether it was justified under present conditions. He thought the parties should be free to tell the Tribunal which issues required its solution and which had already been solved by agreement between them. He thought the text might be improved so as to convey this idea and he would propose that the first part of the first sentence of paragraph (1) be replaced by the following sentence: 'The Tribunal shall decide disputes submitted to it in accordance with such rules of law as shall have been agreed upon between the parties. That would indicate that in the normal case one would expect the parties to choose the applicable law and would reflect the normal practice in the field of foreign investment agreements'. [...] Mr. BROCHES (Chairman) noting that the meeting appeared to be concerned with two problems, said the first one was which was

proposition was submitted to a vote and finally managed to form a majority,[269] standing as a victory of the camp advocating for a more traditional division of labour between public and private international jurisdictions.

The final discussions on the future Washington convention would be undertaken by the Committee of the Whole between February and March 1965. A fundamental contribution at this stage has to do with elements of the draft that had not been analysed by the Legal Committee, namely the instrument's preamble and its final provisions.[270] For instance, it was the Committee of the Whole that decided to exclude from the preamble any references to sovereign equality that were previously conveyed in this part of the document.[271] The justification of such decision was allegedly to make the document simpler and easier to read.[272]

Albeit keeping the stability of the text produced by Broches and the Legal Committee, the Committee of the Whole still introduced quite a few changes to the instrument ultimately adopted. This was the case of the provision on enforcement, which again generated considerable debate. The article on recognition and enforcement was slightly modified to appease some of the criticism made in relation to elevating arbitral awards to the status of national court rulings, a charge led by the German delegation that wanted to see included a public policy exception.[273] There were also attempts to return to debates that

---

the applicable 'national law' and the second, under what circumstances, if any, should international law be applicable. Taking these views into consideration, he would propose that the provisions following that dealing [sic] with an express choice of law agreement be redrafted to read as follows: 'Failing such agreement, the Tribunal shall apply the law of the State party to the dispute (including its rules on the conflict of laws) and such principles of international law as may be applicable.'" See World Bank, *SID/LC/SR/14 (December 30, 1964) Summary Proceedings of the Legal Committee Meeting, December 7, Morning*, 803–804.

269 See World Bank, *SID/LC/SR/14 (December 30, 1964) Summary Proceedings of the Legal Committee Meeting, December 7, Morning*, 804.

270 See World Bank, *SecM65-3 (January 4, 1965) Memorandum of the President to the Executive Directors, in* ICSID, *History of the ICSID Convention*, vol II–2 (ICSID Publication 2006), 942.

271 Compare paragraphs 2 of the Revised Draft with the final instrument adopted. See World Bank, 'Z-13 (December 11, 1964) Revised Draft of Convention on the Settlement of Investment Disputes between States and Nationals of Other States', *in* ICSID, *History of the ICSID Convention*, vol II–2 (ICSID Publication 2006), 912.

272 See World Bank, 'SID/65-11 (March 11,1965) Memorandum of the Meeting of the Committee of the Whole, March 4, 1965, Not an Approved Record. Continuation of the Discussion of Article 26(2), and Discussion of Article 54 and of the Preamble', *in* ICSID, *History of the ICSID Convention*, vol II–2 (ICSID Publication 2006), 1020.

273 See World Bank, 'SID/65-6 (February 25, 1965) Memorandum of the Meeting of the Committee of the Whole, February 23, 1965, Afternoon, Not an Approved Record. Continuation

took place at the Legal Committee. This was the case of the provision on the jurisdiction of the Centre. Indeed, some delegations tried to revisit the discussion on whether the jurisdiction of the institution should be open-ended or *numerus clausus*, without success.[274]

Finally, on 18 March 1965, the Committee of the Whole adopted the final document that would become known as the Washington Convention, giving birth to ICSID and its procedural framework.[275] In a tortuous way, the birth of ICSID was a momentous achievement for the expansion of a codified form of transnational arbitration. The document enshrined the procedural capacity of private parties before international jurisdictions, while creating a platform for the administration of contractual disputes between governments and private parties beyond the exclusive realms of public and private international law. Yet, its practical significance would only take-off in the 1990s, becoming in the following decade a central piece of global economic governance.

2 Hybrid Codification at the United Nations

The universal use of arbitration for the peaceful settlement of interstate disputes was a pipedream buried by two world wars and further dismissed by the judicialization of interstate dispute settlement. Even if one might find calls to implement a universal system of arbitration by the end of WWII,[276] any realistic observer would know that such project was doomed to failure at the interstate level. Still, a transnational legal grammar governing the authority

of the Discussion of Chapter IV, and Discussion of Chapters V, VI, VIII, IX and X', *in* ICSID, *History of the ICSID Convention*, vol II–2 (ICSID Publication 2006), 989–992.

274 See World Bank, 'SID/65 2 (February 17, 1965) Memorandum of the Meeting of the Committee of the Whole, February 16, 1965, Not an Approved Record. Discussion of Chapters I and II of the Draft Convention', *in* ICSID, *History of the ICSID Convention*, vol II–2 (ICSID Publication 2006), 972–973.

275 See Parra, *The History of ICSID*, 85.

276 Frances Kellor was of the view that, among others, the following measure should be adopted: "Either the same or another committee should carefully analyse the Conventions establishing the Permanent Court of Arbitration and the procedures and administration set up under these Conventions, with a view to making recommendations for its reorganization and adaptation to post-war requirements in the field of both public and private controversy and its possible reconstruction as a universal system of arbitration; or it should consider the drafting of a substitute system, should the adaptation of the Permanent Court not prove practicable." See Frances Kellor and Martin Domke, *Arbitration in International Controversy* (Commission to Study the Organization of Peace and American Arbitration Association 1944), 96–97.

of arbitration would emerge in the new world order structured around the United Nations, albeit one not centred on State-to-State disputes.

When the UN emerged as the main *locus* of global governance, it quickly turned its attention to the production of a multi-tiered arbitral code for the administration of transnational economic disputes. Obviously, the work was not done in a vacuum. The emergence of a codified legal grammar at the UN is partly explained by shifting interests in arbitration, which moved away from the administration of war and towards the governance of economic flows.

Importantly, so-called international commercial arbitration was in an ever-increasing expansion since the early 1920s – a phenomenon already discussed in this study. The adoption of the 1923 Geneva Protocol on the Validity of Arbitration Clauses and the 1927 Geneva Convention on the Execution of Foreign Arbitral Awards were both a reflection and a catalyst of such expansion. Yet, the many stakeholders labouring for the transnationalisation of arbitral authority perceived in the Geneva regime a number of flaws halting their efforts.

First, the Geneva regime was silent on disputes involving States and private parties – a gap that would be filled by the adoption of the Washington Convention. Second, it contained the problem of double exequatur, which was rather an unintended consequence of the 1927 Geneva Convention. Third, the Geneva regime attributed an extensive role to municipal rules of procedure and private international law, which increased the fragmentary nature of arbitral authority.

Hopes to curb these shortcomings were long deposited in a much-awaited uniform arbitration law in production at UNIDROIT since the 1930s.[277] By the early 1950s, however, it was clear that such project had hit a roadblock.[278] A

277 It has been noted that the ICC, in its Quebec Congress, emphasized that "[a]s long as the laws governing arbitration vary from one country to another, there will be uncertainty as to the validity of arbitration clauses and the possibility of enforcing arbitral awards in a foreign country". See Florian Grisel, 'Treaty-Making between Public Authority and Private Interests: The Genealogy of the Convention on the Recognition and Enforcement of Foreign Arbitral Awards' (2017) 28(1) European Journal of International Law 73, at 78.

278 The ICC progressively came to the conclusion that this uniform law would not be practical due to the difficulty of amending a great number of national laws. The change of course was highlighted in a resolution adopted at its 1951 Lisbon Congress: "The I.C.C. welcomes a continuation of studies for the unification of arbitration laws in all countries, on the basis of the draft proposed by the International Institute for the Unification of Private Law, but recognizes the complexities and difficulties of the subject. The I.C.C. considers that pending completion of these studies an immediate effort should be made (whether by amendment of the Geneva Convention of 1927 or by a new Convention) to remove the main defect which militates against the effectiveness of international arbitration and to permit the immediate enforcement of international arbitral awards. The I.C.C. calls

new approach was thus needed. In this regard, a hybrid and multi-tiered strategy for the codification of arbitration would be undertaken at the UN, one which relied simultaneously on hard positive law and soft normative instruments. On the one hand, the adoption of the United Nations Convention on the Recognition and Enforcement of Foreign Arbitral Awards, widely known as the New York Convention, would serve as the positive law element structuring a transnational normative regime governing arbitration (2.1). On the other hand, the creation of UNCITRAL would establish a focal point for the advancement of a codification agenda building upon the New York Convention (2.2).

2.1 *Piercing the Iron Curtain at New York*

It is nothing original to portray the New York Convention as a "universal constitutional charter for the international arbitral process."[279] Yet, few explore in detail the constituency present at this constitutional moment.[280] Many have praised the oracular dimension of that instrument as it would have "foreseen the evolution of arbitration law."[281] Still, little is said on the structuring effects of a codified normative grammar sponsored by the United Nations in 1958. Rather than oracular, the adoption of the New York Convention channeled the development of arbitration, foreclosing certain avenues while promoting other ones. None of this can be properly understood without diving deeper into the legislative process that led to the creation of this novel and influential normative framework.

One cannot but remark that the preparatory works conducing to the adoption of the New York Convention were quite different, and much broader, than the ones producing the instruments of the Geneva regime. Indeed, as discussed elsewhere in this study, the 1923 Protocol on the Validity of Arbitration Clauses and the 1927 Geneva Convention on the Execution of Foreign Arbitral Awards were drafted at the level of the Economic Committee of the League of Nations at the initiative of Member States. Furthermore, both Protocol and Convention were produced in a very short time span. Conversely, the New York Convention was the outcome of a full-fledged diplomatic conference, the United Nations Conference on International Commercial Arbitration

---

on all governments concerned to cooperate towards that end." See Grisel, *Treaty-Making between Public Authority and Private Interests*, 79.

279 See Gary B Born, *International Commercial Arbitration* (Kluwer law international 2021), 99.

280 See Grisel, *Treaty-Making between Public Authority and Private Interests*.

281 See Emmanuel Gaillard, 'The Urgency of Not Revising the New York Convention' in Albert Jan Van den Berg (ed), *50 Years of the New York Convention: ICCA international Arbitration Conference* (Kluwer law international 2009), 693.

held in 1958, which was preceded by five years of public debate. Furthermore, differently from the Geneva regime, the United Nations instrument was not produced at the initiative of governments themselves, but rather, triggered by an initiative of the ICC.

The New York Convention itself had been preceded by preparatory works undertaken at other *loci* engaged in the production of arbitral knowledge, both private and public ones to be sure. Evidently, the instrument is an inheritor of all the debates that had taken place at UNIDROIT and the ILA, respectively an intergovernmental organization and a professional association. More directly, however, it was the ICC the main vector through which non-State actors would impact the production of the future instrument. This fact has been vastly documented by recent scholarship on the history of international commercial arbitration.[282]

The story is well known: starting in 1950, the ICC created a working group to explore the issue of enforcement of arbitral awards, with the publication of a draft convention already in 1953.[283] Sitting in this working group one finds Jean Robert, acting as its chairman, René Arnaud, Pieter Sanders, Ernest Barda, Charles Carabiber, Robert Marx, James Mordan and Max Shoop.[284] The ICC proposal was animated by "its conviction that the system established under the 1927 Geneva Convention no longer corresponded to the requirements of international trade."[285] Its central aim was to cure something perceived as the system's main defect, i.e., "the enforcement of only those awards that are strictly in accordance with the rules of procedure laid down in the law of the country where the arbitration took place."[286] That same 1953, the ICC draft would be transmitted to the UN's ECOSOC.

Within this framework, the ICC tried to introduce a new regime abolishing double exequatur and postulating the notion of international arbitral awards detached from the purview of municipal law.[287] This latter feature is often highlighted, with reason, as a testament of ICC's commitment to party

282 See Schinazi, *Three Ages*, 127–132; Grisel, *Treaty-Making between Public Authority and Private Interests*; Lemercier and Sgard, *Arbitrage Privé*, 124–131.

283 See Lemercier and Sgard, *Arbitrage Privé*, 126.

284 See Grisel, *Treaty-Making between Public Authority and Private Interests*, at note 38.

285 See ICC, 'E/C.2/373 – Enforcement of International Arbitral Awards: Statement Submitted by the International Chamber of Commerce, a Non-Governmental Organization Having Consultative Status in Category A', at 7.

286 See ICC, *Statement Submitted by the International Chamber of Commerce*, 7.

287 See Articles II-IV of the ICC Draft in ICC, *Statement Submitted by the International Chamber of Commerce*, 12–13.

autonomy.[288] Yet, another ideological device was mobilized to justify the project, one drawing less attention from contemporary commentators, which was that of legal uniformization. Since the early days of the International Congresses of Chambers of Commerce, the ICC's predecessor, the unification of commercial law was pursued as a central item in the agenda of these "merchants of peace." True to its DNA, the ICC would have recourse to said ideological framework, presenting party autonomy as an instrument in the service of legal uniformity. In the report substantiating the ICC Draft transmitted to ECOSOC, the following was argued:

> In actual fact, the idea of an international award, *i.e.* an award completely independent of national laws, corresponds precisely to an economic requirement. It is certain that a commercial agreement between the parties, even for international transactions, will always be linked up with a given national system of law. Nevertheless, the fact that an award settling a dispute arising in connection with this agreement will produce its effects in different countries, makes it essential that it should be enforced in all these countries in the same way. The development of international trade depends on this.
>
> Only by giving full value to the autonomy of the will can this result be attained in the field of conflict of laws.[289]

The ICC proposal reached ECOSOC on 10 September 1953,[290] triggering a legislative process that would culminate in the 1958 United Nations Conference on International Commercial Arbitration and the adoption of the New York Convention. It has been argued that United Nation's involvement with the recasting of the Geneva regime provides evidence that "private interests de facto acted in a strategic, coordinated manner during the genesis of the New York Convention and achieved what had been rejected as provocative by national governments shortly before."[291]

Certainly, there is truth to this statement. The ICC was indeed one of the first non-governmental organizations to obtain consultative status at the UN ECOSOC,[292] and it managed to make its voice heard through the many delegates

288 See Schinazi, *Three Ages*, 128.
289 See ICC, *Statement Submitted by the International Chamber of Commerce*, 7–8.
290 See ICC, *Statement Submitted by the International Chamber of Commerce*.
291 See Grisel, *Treaty-Making between Public Authority and Private Interests*, 76.
292 See Grisel, *Treaty-Making between Public Authority and Private Interests*, 77.

who attended the United Nations Conference on International Commercial Arbitration with a dual allegiance to their home countries and to the ICC itself. This was the case of René Arnaud and Pieter Sanders – and the paternity of the instrument is often attributed to Sanders himself.

That said, one must guard against overblowing the role of the ICC network. Moreover, one must certainly not disregard other forces and struggles at play in New York. Much like the ICC, one also finds other important institutions, governmental and non-governmental alike, strongly engaged in this legislative process. This is the case of UNIDROIT, the ILA, the Hague Conference on Private International Law, all of which had "observers who actively participated in the deliberations of the Conference."[293]

Furthermore, the delegations gathered at New York from 20 May to 10 June 1958 brought together emissaries of 45 States, with a most considerable representation of the Eastern bloc countries.[294] Notably, it does not seem trivial that among the initial 23 signatories of the instrument, 6 were socialist countries – the Soviet Union included.[295]

Once the ICC document was received by ECOSOC, the body adopted resolution 520(VII) establishing an eight-member *Ad Hoc* Committee to "study the matter raised by the International Chamber of Commerce in light of all the relevant considerations and to report its conclusions to the Council."[296] The countries represented at this restricted group were Australia, Belgium, Ecuador, Egypt, Great Britain, India, Sweden, and the Soviet Union.[297]

It seems quite surprising that the USSR accepted to take part in this exercise, but the literature on the New York Convention is unphased by this fact. Conversely, it has been a cause of surprise that other countries associated with ICC arbitration, besides Sweden and Belgium, were not members of the committee. Some have explained it as a potential disinterest of the American, French, German, Italian and Swiss governments.[298] This would have been a rather curious situation, where France is disinterested by the project and the Soviet

293 See Martin Domke, 'The United Nations Conference on International Commercial Arbitration' (1959) 53 American Journal of International Law 414, 415.

294 The following seven socialist countries attended the conference: Albania, Bulgaria, Byelorussia, Czechoslovakia, Poland, Ukraine, the USSR, and the Yugoslavia. See UN, 'E/CONF.26/INF.1/Rev.2 – List of Representatives and Observers.'

295 See Domke, *The United Nations Conference on International Commercial Arbitration*, 415.

296 See ECOSOC, 'E/AC.42/4 – Report of the Committee on the Enforcement of International Arbitral Awards', at para 1.

297 See ECOSOC, *E/AC.42/4*, at para 2.

298 See Lemercier and Sgard, *Arbitrage Privé*, 127–128.

Union is actively engaged in the drafting process. Instead of disinterest, what seems to be at play is something of a different nature.

It may come as a surprise for the contemporary reader, but the Soviet Union made extensive use of arbitration within its frontiers for the administration of contracts in the context of its planned economy – a mechanism once known as "State Arbitration."[299] Even more important for this study is the pervasiveness of arbitration as a dispute resolution tool regarding trade relations entered by the socialist bloc. Evidently, when Stalin implemented socialism in one country to the detriment of the Trotskyist global revolution, this implied that USSR and its satellites would have to entertain economic relations with the capitalist world for the foreseeable future. Accordingly, when it came to international trade relations, the Iron Curtain was never as thick as it may be imagined.

Much more than porosities, longstanding economic exchanges took place. Given that international commercial relations were monopolized by the State and its entities,[300] international commercial arbitration in the socialist world was a matter of considerable interest in terms of economic cooperation. Tracing back its wide acceptance in the USSR to the early 1920s, a commentator highlighted that "[t]he experience of the socialist countries convincingly evidences a definitely positive outlook on the institution of international commercial arbitration."[301] Within this context, it should be evident that a reform of the enforcement regime of foreign arbitral awards was likely to attract attention beyond the Iron Curtain. And so it did, as will be seen further below.

---

299 See RS Baranov, 'Contract and Arbitration in Soviet State Economy' (1950) 1 Soviet Studies 383.

300 For a general analysis of the interplay between the State monopoly over international commercial relations and private international law, see Pavel Kalenský, 'Le droit international privé comparé des états socialistes dans leur coopération économique' *in Collected Courses of the Hague Academy of International Law*, vol. 208 (Martinus Nijhoff Publishers 1988), at 197–207.

301 See Sergei N Lebedev, 'International Commercial Arbitration in the Socialist Countries Members of the CMEA' *in Collected Courses of the Hague Academy of International Law*, vol 158 (Martinus Nijhoff Publishers 1978), 100–101. Another commentator noted that since the 1940s, "the Soviet Union can be said to have embarked on a systematic policy of concluding a large number of bilateral agreements containing provisions on commercial arbitration." See Peter Benjamin, 'Soviet Treaty Practice on Commercial Arbitration Since 1940' (1959) 53 American Journal of International Law 882, at 882.

Most of the delegates sitting at the ECOSOC *Ad Hoc* Committee were seemingly diplomats.[302] An exception can be clearly made in relation to the British delegate, Ben Atkinson Wortley, a Law Professor who worked at the intersection of private and public international law.[303] Thirteen public meetings were held from 1 to 15 March 1955 at the New York headquarters of the United Nations.[304] In addition to delegates of Member States, the IMF, UNIDROIT, the ICC and the ILA sent observers to the meetings.[305]

The *Ad Hoc* Committee did not plainly reject the ICC Draft, rather using it as a working document for its discussions. Nonetheless, and to no one's surprise, the body abandoned the expression "international arbitral awards." The change was very much connected to doctrinal views popular at the time, pursuant to which the epithet "international" ought to be reserved to interstate relations.[306] Overall, it is usually considered that the ECOSOC Draft marked a backlash against the ICC proposal – and this was also the perception shared by the ICC at the time.[307]

Indeed, the *Ad Hoc* Committee departed from core elements laid out by the ICC proposition. Besides the change in the title, the *Ad Hoc* Committee reverted back to the principle of reciprocity in relation to the implementation

302 The members of the *Ad Hoc* Committee were the following: A.H. Loomes (Australia), J. Nisot (Belgium), José Vicente Trujillo (Ecuador), M.B. Mehta (India), S. Dennemark (Sweden), Anatoly N. Nikolaev (USSR), and B.A. Wortley (UK). See ECOSOC, *E/AC.42/4*, at 2.

303 See BA Wortley, 'The Interaction of Public and Private International Law Today'; BA Wortley, 'The General Principles of Private International Law', *Collected Courses of the Hague Academy of International Law*, vol 194 (Martinus Nijhoff Publishers 1958); BA Wortley, 'Problèmes Soulevés En Droit International Privé Par La Législation Sur l'expropriation', *Collected Courses of the Hague Academy of International Law*, vol 67 (Martinus Nijhoff Publishers 1939).

304 See ECOSOC, *E/AC.42/4*, at para 4.

305 These institutions were represented by Gordon Williams (IMF), John N. Hazard (UNIDROIT), Morris S. Rosenthal and Roberta Lusardi (ICC), and Samuel Kopper (ILA). See ECOSOC, *E/AC.42/4*, at para 7.

306 In this regard, the following was noted: "The Committee considered that the expression 'International Arbitral Awards' used by the International Chamber of Commerce (E/C.2/373) normally referred to arbitration between States. Since this Draft Convention does not deal with arbitration between States, but deals with the recognition and enforcement in one country of arbitral awards made in another country, the Committee adopted the title 'Draft Convention on the Recognition and Enforcement of Foreign Arbitral Awards' which reflects more accurately the object of the Convention." See ECOSOC, *E/AC.42/4*, at para 17.

307 See Grisel, *Treaty-Making between Public Authority and Private Interests*, 80; Lemercier and Sgard, *Arbitrage Privé*, 128.

of the instrument,[308] nuancing the more liberal approach taken by the ICC.[309] Furthermore, the ECOSOC Draft re-introduced finality as a condition for the enforcement of arbitral awards, which in practice dismissed the ICC proposal to end with the mechanism of double exequatur.[310]

On 20 May 1955, ECOSOC submitted the Draft and Report produced by the *Ad Hoc* Committee to Member and non-Member States of the UN for analysis, to UNIDROIT for its information, as well as "to the International Chamber of Commerce and to twenty non-governmental organizations in consultative status considered to be interested in international commercial arbitration for their comments."[311] All observations received, a total of fifteen from governmental sources and four from non-governmental ones, were recorded in a Secretary-General's Report to ECOSOC dated 31 January 1956.[312] Interestingly, the

308 The *Ad Hoc* Committee reasoned as follows: "Thus, while the Geneva Convention is based upon the principle of reciprocity, the ICC Draft would provide for the enforcement in the territory of a Contracting State of arbitral awards made abroad, regardless of whether or not they were made in the territory of another Contracting State. Having regard to the object of the Draft Convention, the Committee thought it would not be desirable to establish a strict requirement of reciprocity. At the same time the Committee was aware that the adoption of the solution proposed by the ICC would make the Convention unacceptable to States willing to adhere to it only on condition of reciprocity. Accordingly, in Article I the Committee adopted a formulation which would permit any Contracting State to declare that it will apply the Convention only to arbitral awards rendered in the territory of another Contracting State (Article I, paragraph 2). On the other hand, a Contracting State not making such declaration would undertake to apply the Convention to arbitral awards rendered in any other country." See ECOSOC, *E/AC.42/4*, at para 20–21.

309 Article I in the ICC Draft read as follows: "The present Convention shall apply to the enforcement of arbitral awards arising out of commercial disputes between persons subject to the jurisdiction of different States or involving legal relationships arising on the territories of different States." See ICC, *Statement Submitted by the International Chamber of Commerce*, at 12.

310 The *Ad Hoc* Committee observed the following: "The ICC Draft had omitted from the conditions of enforcement that an arbitral award must be final. In order to properly safeguard the rights of the losing party, the Committee decided to reintroduce the requirement of finality which had been included in the Geneva Convention (Article 1(d)). This provision prescribes that in the country where the award was made, the award must be 'final and operative' and in particular, that its enforcement must not have been suspended. The expression 'final and operative was intended by the Committee to mean that an award must be a definitive adjudication of all matters at issue, and must have full legal force and effect." See ECOSOC, *E/AC.42/4*, at 9.

311 See UN Secretary-General, 'E/2822 – Report by the Secretary-General, Recognition and Enforcement of Foreign Arbitral Awards, 31 Jan 1956', at para 2.

312 The governments that submitted comments were the following: Austria, Belgium, Brazil, China, Denmark, France, Federal Republic of Germany, India, Japan, Republic of Korea,

ECOSOC Draft seemed to dissatisfy everyone, simultaneously displeasing those that wanted to liberalize and those that wanted to conserve the *status quo* on the enforcement of foreign arbitral awards.

Comments sent by Austria and Germany emphasized the need for the uniformization of arbitration law, highlighting how the draft fell short of such goal.[313] The Swiss government went further in the criticism of the Draft, arguing that a real improvement in relation to the 1927 Geneva Convention "is possible only to the extent that international arbitral awards are made more independent of the law of the country in which the arbitration takes place" and that "the will of the parties prevails over the law and that their will is the principal basis of the validity of the arbitral award, the exceptional cases in which enforcement of the award may be opposed being reduced to the strict minimum."[314]

Criticism was also levelled from governments that considered the ECOSOC Draft too liberal. In relation to the scope of the draft, the Chinese and Mexican governments advocated in favour of narrowing it down to strictly abide by the principle of reciprocity.[315] Brazil, moreover, wanted to reinforce double exequatur, proposing that the enforcement of foreign arbitral awards be subject to ratification at the seat.[316]

The non-governmental organizations were visibly unhappy with the approach taken by ECOSOC. In this regard, the Société de Législation Comparée (SLC) praised the notion of "international awards" as a "promise for the future."[317] The ILA, for its part, proposed the introduction of a few rules of

Lebanon, Mexico, Philippines, Switzerland, Union of Soviet Socialist Republics. The non-govermental organizations that submitted comments were the following: the ICC, the ILA, the Society of Comparative Law and the Société Belge d'Etudes et d'Expansion. See UN Secretary-General, *Report by the Secretary-General, 31 Jan 1956*, at 1–2.

313 See UN Secretary-General, *Report by the Secretary-General, 31 Jan 1956*, at 4–5.

314 See UN Secretary-General, *Report by the Secretary-General, 31 Jan 1956*, 8.

315 See UN Secretary-General, *Report by the Secretary-General, 31 Jan 1956*, 11–12.

316 See UN Secretary-General, *Report by the Secretary-General, 31 Jan 1956*, 17.

317 The SCL noted the following: "Lastly, the term 'international awards' contains a promise for the future; it suggests that international organizations may bend their efforts towards a larger and more relevant goal: namely, that arbitral awards may be made under the rules of procedure of international arbitration centres, the agreement of the parties stipulating that the arbitration proceedings shall be governed by those rules, the provisions of which would tend to remove arbitral awards from the sphere of national laws on procedure – usually far too rigid to meet the wishes of international commerce – and to place them rather, where their enforcement is concerned, under an international organ concerned with verifying their prima facie validity." See Annex II in UN Secretary-General, *Report by the Secretary-General, 31 Jan 1956*, 4–5.

conflict of laws,[318] and the incorporation of the 1923 Protocol on the Validity of Arbitration Clauses into the new enforcement treaty.[319] Evidently, the ICC defended its original proposal.[320]

Regardless of any comments, there was considerable support for calling a conference to conclude a new convention on the enforcement of arbitral awards.[321] Accordingly, on 3 May 1956, ECOSOC adopted Resolution 604 (XXI), calling a conference of plenipotentiaries to "conclude a convention on the recognition and enforcement of foreign arbitral awards" and "to consider, if time permits, other possible measures for increasing the effectiveness of arbitration."[322] In this regard, the ECOSOC draft, taking into account the comments received, was to be used as working document during the conference.[323]

Meanwhile, UN officials had brought to the ICC's attention that "if the ICC comes to the New York Conference to insist upon its original draft and to oppose the ECOSOC draft as a whole there would be a serious risk of the whole idea of a new convention running into heavy water."[324] Behind the scenes, the ICC was faced with a dilemma, either to insist on its draft as it was presented or engage with the proposal from ECOSOC. Some discussion took place within the ICC Commission on International Arbitration, with Pieter Sander defending a conciliatory position against Jean Robert who put forward a more combative approach.[325]

A certain convergence gradually emerged between the opposing views, and Sanders would provide the terms of the consensus: rather than struggling against the ECOSOC Draft, it was more strategic to focus on the provisions where more progress towards the ICC approach could be made.[326] Pursuant to the new strategy, the ICC decided to drop the discussion on international awards, centring its fire on double exequatur and governing law problems. With regards to double exequatur, the ICC would suggest that finality become

318 See Annex II in UN Secretary-General, *Report by the Secretary-General, 31 Jan 1956*, 14 and 20.

319 See Annex II in UN Secretary-General, *Report by the Secretary-General, 31 Jan 1956*, 8.

320 See Annex II in UN Secretary-General, *Report by the Secretary-General, 31 Jan 1956*.

321 See UN Secretary-General, *Report by the Secretary-General, 31 Jan 1956*, 2.

322 See ECOSOC, 'Resolution 604 (XXI). Recognition and Enforcement of Foreign Arbitral Awards', at 6. Available at: <https://treaties.un.org/doc/source/docs/E_RES_604_XXI-E.pdf>.

323 See ECOSOC, *Resolution 604 (XXI)*, 6.

324 See Grisel, *Treaty-Making between Public Authority and Private Interests*, 82.

325 See Grisel, *Treaty-Making between Public Authority and Private Interests*, 81–82.

326 See Lemercier and Sgard, *Arbitrage Privé*, 130.

an exception to resist enforcement, that is, a negative ground rather than a positive criterion for the enforcement of awards.[327]

It was a Tuesday afternoon, 20 May 1958, when the United Nations Conference on International Commercial Arbitration opened. Carl W.A. Schurmann, Dutch diplomat, was elected the conference's president by acclamation.[328] This does not seem like a casual or irrelevant event, especially as in two years' time Schurmann would be elected president of ECOSOC. These elements suggest that the Dutch plenipotentiary enjoyed a certain prestige among its peers, possessing political capital that could be used to advance some of the Dutch delegation's views on the way forward for the enforcement of foreign arbitral awards.

In relation to the remaining attendants of the conference, it should cause no great surprise that just a few of those belonged to a cohort of so-called arbitration specialists. To expect otherwise would be a sign of anachronism, for arbitration was not yet a full-fledged specialized legal field. Yet, among the specialists in attendance, one finds quite a few that were involved in other ventures for the codification of arbitration authority.[329] For instance, Gunnar de Sydow and Mario Matteucci, sent as plenipotentiaries for Sweden and Italy, had worked together in 1951 when UNIDROIT explored the possibility of adopting a convention to govern arbitration between governments and private parties, a project discussed elsewhere in this work. For their part, Pieter Sanders and René Arnaud were central actors in the ICC arbitration network and attended the conference as members of the Dutch and French delegations. In addition, among the observers, one also finds Martin Domke and René David, who respectively attended on behalf of the ILA and the SLC. David, one must remember, was the main force driving the UNIDROIT project of a uniform arbitration law in the 1930s, also discussed before in this work.

Despite this collection of familiar faces, in the hagiography of arbitration, it is Pieter Sanders and his so-called Dutch Proposal who is usually considered to have "saved the day by jettisoning the 'final and operative' requirement, and instead putting forward the two provisions which now figure as Articles III and V(1)(e) of the Convention as adopted."[330] Sanders himself recalled the drafting of the proposal in rather romanticized terms:

327 See Grisel, *Treaty-Making between Public Authority and Private Interests*, 83.

328 See UN, '1st Meeting [E/CONF.26/SR.1 – Opening of the Conference, Adoption of the Agenda, Adoption of the Rules of Procedure]', at 2.

329 For the complete list of representatives and observers, see UN, *List of Representatives and Observers*.

330 See Marike Paulsson, *1958 New York Convention in Action* (Kluwer Law International 2016), 12.

> It [the Dutch Proposal] was conceived during the first weekend of the Conference. I spent that weekend at the house of my father-in-law in a suburb of New York. I can still see myself sitting in the garden with my small portable typewriter on my knees. It was there, sitting in the sun, that the "Dutch proposal" was conceived. Upon return to New York on Monday, 26 May, this draft was presented to the Conference.[331]"

Recently, a more realistic account of the Dutch Proposal has emerged. It has been argued that "Sanders was not the solitary white knight often praised in the arbitration circles but, rather, the acting soldier of an invisible network of experts, with an exact understanding of how the debate had previously developed at the ICC."[332] Sanders certainly was not a solitary knight and was not the only one attending the conference who held double allegiances. The ICC team of lobbyists was considerable, and they could work both in the shadows and under the light of day.

Yet, this same literature seemingly portrays States as helpless bystanders. Notably, it is suggested that governments might have fallen prey to a lack of vision, for "after governments had rejected the 1953 ICC Preliminary Draft, they had no vision of the way ahead."[333] A closer look at the records of the conference points in another direction, as governments opposing the ICC project did not seem at a loss on how to move forward. The final text of the instrument is very far from both the ICC and *Ad Hoc* Committee's drafts, suggesting that a real drafting and negotiation process did take place at New York. A most notable example of this relates to the fact that the two preliminary drafts were silent regarding the recognition of the validity of arbitration agreements, while the New York Convention did end up covering this topic. Similarly, the inclusion of a reference to arbitral awards made by "permanent bodies" in Article 1, paragraph 2, was the outcome of an express request from socialist countries, which aimed at accommodating their particular experiences with arbitration.[334]

When the general debate at the conference began, the first to take the floor was Mario Matteucci, then Secretary-General of UNIDROIT and plenipotentiary for Italy. Matteucci was no stranger to the many difficulties facing the

331 See Peter Sanders, 'The Making of the Convention' *in Enforcing arbitration awards under the New York Convention: Experience and Prospect* (United Nations 1999), at 3.

332 See Grisel, *Treaty-Making between Public Authority and Private Interests*, 83.

333 See Grisel, *Treaty-Making between Public Authority and Private Interests*, 83.

334 See, for instance, the address of Mr. Pscolka for Czechoslovakia in UN, '4th Meeting [E/CONF.26/SR.4 – E/2704 and Corr.1, E/CONF.26/2, E/CONF.26/3 and Add.1, E/CONF.26/7]' 6. This amendment was the object of a long and heated debate regarding the necessity of it. See UN, '8th Meeting [E/CONF.26/SR.8 – E/2704 and Corr.1, E/CONF.26/L.10]'.

uniformization and codification of arbitration and was certainly not a mere pawn in the ICC chessboard. To the contrary, as a senior officer at the leading intergovernmental organization working on the unification of private law, his views would have been given great weight.

In his address, Matteucci expressed his agreement with the document produced by the *Ad Hoc* Committee, considering it a median solution that could please both the business community and States. Notably, he argued that an instrument founded solely on party autonomy was likely to raise great distrust from municipal courts. Interestingly, it was his view that "absolute liberalism was a thing of the past" as "[t]he sphere of private law was steadily and inevitably contracting as optional provisions gave ground to mandatory rules of law."[335] Still, he considered that the working document could be improved, namely by expanding the scope of awards that would fall under the future convention, by including a provision on the recognition of the validity of arbitral agreements, by simplifying the control at the place of enforcement in relation to the finality of the award, and by considering how to determine the *lex arbitri*.[336]

The cooperation between socialist and capitalist countries was another recurrent theme at these opening speeches. Polish delegate, Mr. Lychowski, would capture the zeitgeist, arguing that "the present division of the World into two great economic and social systems made it particularly important to conclude an international convention on arbitration," given that "[t]rade between countries belonging to those two systems had increased rapidly during the past few years and a concomitant increase was to be expected in the number of disputes."[337] Even more curious was the address of the plenipotentiary of the USSR, Mr. Bakhtov, for whom "[international] trade should be free of restriction, discrimination and artificial barriers."[338]

With Schurmann presiding the conference, it would be up to Sanders to speak on behalf of the Netherlands. His initial address is yet another testament to the fact that the end of double exequatur was not an invention of the ICC, but a feature that had been long in the making. He noted, in this regard,

335 See UN, '2nd Meeting [E/CONF.26/SR.2 – Adoption of the Rules of Procedure (Continued), Consideration of the Draft Convention on the Recognition and Enforcement of Foreign Arbitral Awards (E/2704 and Corr.1, E/2822 and Add. 1 to 6, E/CONF.26/2. 26/3 and Add.1, 26/4)]', at 7.

336 See UN, *2nd Meeting*, at 7–8.

337 See UN, *4th Meeting*, at 6.

338 See UN, '5th Meeting [E/CONF.26/SR.5 – E/2704 and Corr.1, E/2822 and Add.1 to 6, E/CONF.26/2, 26/3 and Add.1, 26/4, 26/7, E/CONF.26/L.6 and L.9]', at 4.

that "the Rome draft, and more recently the draft of the Council of Europe, had provided for only one exequatur."[339]

When the time had come for the debates on specific provisions, a long discussion ensued in relation to scope of application of the convention. This led to the creation of a working group, composed of delegates from Colombia, Czechoslovakia, France, India, Israel, Italy, Turkey, the USSR, the UK and West Germany.[340] Notably, there was a strong divide in relation to which type of foreign awards would be covered by the treaty, with a camp favouring a rule connected to the place of arbitration and an opposing one advocating for a rule based on the nationality of the award. The result of discussions led to a midway solution, accommodating both views.[341] Indeed, the proposition of the working group came to be enshrined in the final text adopted at the conference.

Another important contribution unrelated to the so-called Dutch Proposal pertains to what is now Article II of the New York Convention. As noted above, neither the draft produced by the ICC or the *Ad Hoc* Committee had a provision on the validity of arbitration clauses. This had been noted by several delegations present at New York and was the object of two amendment proposals, respectively presented by Poland and Sweden.[342] The conference, once again, devoted considerable attention to the issue.

Matteucci, while not opposing it, noted that the "Swedish proposal went a little beyond the provision in the Geneva Protocol which referred to international agreements whereas the text proposed by Sweden would cover all agreements."[343] The El Salvadorean delegate, Mr. Lima, raised many concerns, overall considering that a provision on arbitration agreements would be out of place in the instrument.[344] The French plenipotentiary, Mr. Holleaux, initially favoured the inclusion of such provision in the convention,[345] but then changed his mind after exchanging with the Belgian delegation – their view

339 See UN, *4th Meeting*, at 7.

340 See UN, '7th Meeting [E/CONF.26/SR.7 – E/2704 and Corr.1, E/2822 and Add.1 to 6, E/CONF.26/2, 26/3 and Add.1, 26/4, 26/7, E/CONF.26/L.6 to 13]', at 8.

341 See UN, 'E/CONF.26/L.42 – Report on Article 1, Paragraph 1 and Article 2 of the Draft Convention (E/2704 and Corr.1)', at 2.

342 See UN, 'E/CONF.26/7 – Poland: Amendments to the Title of the Convention and Articles 1, 3, 7, 8 10'; UN, 'E/CONF.26/C.3/L.1 – Sweden: Draft Additional Protocol on Arbitration Agreements: Submitted for Consideration by Working Party II'.

343 See UN, *7th Meeting*, at 9.

344 See UN, *7th Meeting*, 9–11.

345 See UN, *7th Meeting*, 10–11.

was that arbitration agreements escaped the mandate given to the plenipotentiaries present at the conference.[346]

The Dutch delegation got involved in the drafting of Article II at a very late stage of the conference and to a limited extent. This seems to have escaped Sanders' memory some years later,[347] but during the early discussions on the inclusion of a provision to govern arbitration agreements he only expressed that "[i]f the Conference wished to adopt a text similar to article I of the Protocol it must take a decision of principle in that connexion."[348] In light of the controversy, the President, Mr. Schurmann, called a vote on whether the conference was competent to address the validity of arbitration agreements, with a majority voting in favour of dealing with the matter.[349] Yet, a further vote was taken in relation to the position of the provision in the instrument, and the decision reached favoured an annexed Protocol.[350]

Working Party II, entrusted with the task of producing said Protocol,[351] was composed of Belgium, Poland, Sweden, Turkey, the USSR, the UK and West Germany. This group was chaired by Albert Herment, the Belgian plenipotentiary.[352] The draft protocol elaborated and presented to the conference was composed of three articles,[353] of which the first and third provisions would be merged and adapted into what is now Article II of the New York Convention. Deliberations at the plenary of the conference took place at its 21st

346 See UN, '9th Meeting [E/CONF.26/SR.9 – E/2704 and Corr. 1, E/2822 and Add.1 to 6, E/CONF.26/2, 26/3 and Add.1, 26/4, 26/7, E/CONF.26/L.7, L.8, L.12. L.14, L.16]'.

347 Recalling his experience at the New York Convention some 40 years after the conference, Sanders gives the impression that the provision governing arbitration agreements was fundamentally produced by the Dutch delegation. He expresses this thought as follows: "At the meeting of Tuesday, 27 May, this proposal was welcomed by many of the delegates. The meeting decided that the Dutch proposal would be the basis for further discussions. I will not go into details of these discussions and the amendments made. I will only mention that the Conference, initially, preferred not to deal in the Convention with the arbitration agreement, as the Dutch proposal did. Preference was first given to a separate Protocol, as we knew from the Geneva Protocol on Arbitration Clauses (Geneva, 1923) (the 1923 Geneva Protocol). Nevertheless, at a very late stage of the Conference, a provision on the arbitration agreement was inserted in the Convention, the present article II." See Sanders, *The Making of the Convention*, 3–4.

348 See UN, *9th Meeting*.

349 See UN, *9th Meeting*, at 12.

350 See UN, *9th Meeting*, at 12.

351 See UN, *9th Meeting*, 14.

352 See UN, 'E/CONF.26/8/Rev.1 – Final Act and Convention on the Recognition and Enforcement of Foreign Arbitral Awards', at 4.

353 See UN, 'E/CONF.26/L.52 – Text Additional Protocol on the Validity of Arbitral Agreements Submitted by the Working Party No. 2–5 June 1958'.

meeting, held in the afternoon of 5 June 1958. It is here where Sanders regains the stage, proposing to revisit the decision of having an annexed protocol,[354] and to replace it by a consolidated version of the three articles into a single provision.[355] The idea was resisted by the Belgian delegation, who considered that "[t]he advantage of having a convention with a separate protocol was that States could ratify one without ratifying the other."[356] Sanders' motion was put to a vote, carrying the day with a majority of 18 votes against 8 with 4 abstentions.[357]

The plenary would analyse each paragraph of Sanders' consolidated provision. Considerable redrafting would be performed, specially to highlight, as Matteucci noted,[358] that arbitration agreements could emerge from both contractual and non-contractual legal relationships – a technical observation that would make its way to the final text of the convention.

In relation to Article II(2) of the New York Convention, pursuant to Sanders' consolidated proposal, "[t]he expression 'agreement in writing' includes exchange of letters or telegrams between the parties and confirmation in writing by one of the parties without contestation by the other party." This seemed unacceptable to the Soviet delegate, K.K. Bakhtov, who proposed to revert to the Working Party's formulation of the provision. This position was shared by a majority of 19 votes to none with 5 abstentions.[359] Similarly, B.A. Wortley suggested that the third paragraph of the provision on arbitration agreements should reflect the text drafted by Working Party II instead of the reformulated version proposed by Sanders. Here again the plenary decided to reverse gears towards the solution envisioned at the Working Group by a large majority.[360]

If the Dutch influence over the rules governing the validity of arbitration agreements was limited, the same is not true in relation to the regime of enforcement and annulment of arbitral awards. In this regard, the so-called Dutch Proposal would serve as a backbone for the rules on that matter.[361] Consistent with the views espoused by the ICC Draft,[362] the proposal was put forward by

354 See UN, '21st Meeting [E/CONF.26/SR.21 – E/2704 and Corr.1, E/2822 and Add.1 to 6, E/CONF.26/2, 3 and Add.1, E/CONF.26/4, 7, E/CONF.26/L.16, L.28, L.49, L.52, L.55, L.56]', at 17.

355 See UN, 'E/CONF.26/L.54 – Netherlands: Amendment to Proposal Made by Working Party No. 2 (E/CONF.26/L.52)'.

356 See UN, *21st Meeting*, 17.

357 See UN, *21st Meeting*, 17.

358 See UN, *21st Meeting*, at 18, 20.

359 See UN, *21st Meeting*, 21.

360 See UN, *21st Meeting*, 22.

361 See UN, 'E/CONF.26/L.17 – Netherlands: Amendments to Articles 3, 4, 5'.

362 See Grisel, *Treaty-Making between Public Authority and Private Interests*, 86.

Sanders as a "single whole" with the main goal of eliminating double exequatur.[363] It would be upon Mario Matteucci's suggestion, seconded by Wortley and applauded by the ICC delegate, a Mr. Haight, that the Dutch Proposal became the working document for the provisions on annulment and enforcement.[364]

That said, one must not think that the conference was aloof and merely ratified Sanders views. Instead, the Dutch Proposal gave rise to considerable debates, occupying the attention of delegations during the 11th, 12th, 13th, 14th, 23rd and 24th meetings of the United Nations Conference on International Commercial Arbitration.[365] Several amendments were submitted,[366] including a new document presented by the Dutch delegation itself in association with the French and Western German delegations – then becoming the working document on the basis of which further discussions were undertaken.[367]

Amongst the many views exchanged in these debates, an interesting comment was made by Matteucci. For him, the Dutch Proposal, by concentrating the judicial control of awards at the place of enforcement, contained a "bold innovation" that "might prove unacceptable to jurists and to the competent administrative authorities."[368] In this regard, he raised concerns over contradictory decisions taken in concurrent enforcement and annulment proceedings, suggesting that "[t]he Netherlands delegation should try to find some means for removing that danger by stating clearly which jurisdiction was to be competent."[369]

---

363 See UN, '11th Meeting [E/CONF.26/SR.11 – E/2704/Rev.1, E/2822 and Add.1-6, E/CONF.26/2, 6/3 and Add.1, 26/4, 26/7, E/CONF.26/L.6-L.31]'.

364 See UN, 'ECOSOC, *11th Meeting*, at, 7–8 and 12.

365 See UN, *11th Meeting*; UN, '12th Meeting [E/CONF.26/SR.12 – E/2704 and Corr.1, E/CONF.26/7, E/CONF.26/L.8 and Corr.1, L.15/Rev.1, L.16, L.19, L.22, L.31 to L.34]'; UN, '13th Meeting [E/CONF.26/SR.13 – E/2704 and Corr. 1, E/2822 and Add.1 to 6, E/CONF.26/2, 26/3 and Add.1, 26/4, 26/7, E/CONF.26/L.8 and Corr.1, L.15/Rev.1, L.16, L.17, L.22 to L.25, L.30 to L.36]'; UN, '14th Meeting [E/CONF.26/SR.14 – E/2704 and Corr.1, E/2822, E/CONF.26/L.17, L.31, L.33/Rev.1, L.34. L.38 and L.40]'; UN, '23rd Meeting [E/CONF.26/SR.23 – E/CONF.26/L.60; Adoption and Signature of the Final Act and Convention (E/CONF.26/8, 9, E/CONF.26/L.28, L.49, L.58, L.61)]'; UN, '24th Meeting [E/CONF.26/SR.24 – Adoption and Signature of the Final Act and Convention (E/CONF.26/8 and 9, E/CONF.26/L.63), Report of the Credentials Committee (E/CONF.26/10)]'.

366 See UN, 'E/CONF.26/L.33 – Amendments Proposed by the Netherlands, Sweden, the Committee, France, Pakistan and Israel', at 33.

367 See UN, 'E/CONF.26/L.40 – France, Federal Republic of Germany and Netherlands: Amendment to Articles 3, 4 and 5'.

368 See UN, *13th Meeting*, 3–4.

369 See UN, *13th Meeting*, 3–4.

Ultimately, the matter of annulment and enforcement was referred to a working group upon the President's suggestion. This group was composed of delegates from Czechoslovakia, El Salvador, the Federal Republic of Germany, Guatemala, Italy, Japan, the Netherlands, Pakistan, Sweden, Switzerland, Tunisia, the USSR and the UK.[370] Under the chairmanship of Gunnar de Sydow, the records show that the text "adopted by the Working Party represented a compromise arrived at after exhaustive consideration of the views advanced at the Conference and of the requirements of the various legal systems governing arbitration proceedings in different countries."[371]

The output of this working group generated a text much closer to Articles IV, V and VI as adopted,[372] but the plenary meetings of the conference would make some further contributions to Articles V and VI in particular. Concretely, the working group had proposed a rule for the coordination of parallel enforcement and annulment proceedings, a provision that was absent in the Dutch Proposal. During its 17th meeting, the plenary of the conference decided to reformulate said provision.

As drafted by the working group, the provision contained two paragraphs, one on the enforcement of annulled or suspended awards, and another one on the enforcement of awards facing an application to set aside or suspend it.[373] The first paragraph of the rule designed by the working group was expanded and incorporated into Article V(1)(e), while the second paragraph, with some slight modifications, became Article VI of the New York Convention.[374]

At a very late stage of the conference, during its 23rd plenary meeting, the Soviet delegate, K.K. Bakhtov, raised the issue that Article V(1)(a) was too vague. As it stood, the provision established that recognition and enforcement of an

370 See UN, *14th Meeting*, 10.

371 See UN, '17th Meeting [E/CONF.26/SR.17 – E/2704 and Corr.1, E/CONF.26/L.31, L.37/Rev.1, L.43 and L.45]' 2.

372 See UN, 'E/CONF.26/L.43 – Text of Articles III, IV and V of the Draft Convention Proposed by Working Party III: 3 June 1958'.

373 The provision in question read as follows: "Article V – 1. If an award has been suspended in the country where it was given, the competent authority before which the award is sought to be relied, upon shall adjourn the decision on its enforcement. 2. If an application for the setting aside or suspension of the award had been made in the country where the award was given, the competent authority before which the award is sought to be relied upon may, if it considers it proper, adjourn the decision on the enforcement of the award and may also, on the application of the party claiming enforcement of the award, order the other party to give suitable security." See UN, *Text of Articles III, IV and V of the Draft Convention Proposed by Working Party III*, 3.

374 See UN, *17th Meeting*, 16.

FIGURE 2 K. K. Bakhtov, representative of the USSR, discussing a document with V. N. Savchenko, representative of the Ukrainian SSRS on 26 May 1958, United Nations, New York, UN7491448.

award could be refused if "the arbitration agreement or the arbitral clause is not valid under the law applicable to it."[375] Bakhtov proposed to replace that text with a formula conveying that refusal could stem from a situation where "the arbitration agreement or the arbitration clause is not valid under the national law to which the parties have subjected their agreement, or failing any indication thereon, under the law of the country where the award was made."[376] Certainly the proposition would be grammatically lapidated and further elaborated to include a reference to incapacity, but the core of Article V(1)(a) of the New York Convention is essentially rooted in Bakhtov's proposition, which was adopted by the plenary.[377] In yet another curious turn of events,

375 Such provision did not exist in the ICC or ECOSOC Drafts. It was formulated by the Working Party III. See UN, *Text of Articles III, IV and V of the Draft Convention Proposed by Working Party III*, at 1.

376 See UN, *23rd Meeting*, at 14.

377 The amendment was approved by 14 votes against 7 with 9 abstentions. See UN, *23rd Meeting*, 15.

it would be the Soviet delegate the one to introduce an express reference to party autonomy in relation to the applicable law to the arbitration agreement, reserving to the law of the seat only a fallback role.

The portrait just offered depicts a more nuanced picture than the ones usually addressing the adoption of the New York Convention. It is not the intention of this study to dismiss the role of the ICC and its professional network in the making of the convention, but rather to expand the analysis on the politics (and geopolitics) of legal technique at play in the legislative process conducive to the production of this foundational document.

On the one hand, there were considerable debates on the technical operation of arbitration at New York, with contrasting views very much connected to the ways in which different legal traditions engaged with arbitral authority. In these technical discussions, the voices of members of the ICC network, like Peter Sanders and René Arnaud, were not necessarily the most authoritative ones. In fact, the two were not even the plenipotentiaries for their delegations, acting as alternates. Instead, core contributions were given by other individuals, such as Gunnar de Sydow, B.A. Wortley and Mario Matteucci. The latter, due to his position at UNIDROIT, performed the role of custodian of expert knowledge on uniformization and codification, taking an active and preeminent role in all discussions.

On the other hand, one cannot but note the many instances in which socialist and capitalist countries worked together towards delineating the final contours of the United Nations arbitration regime. As economic cooperation seemed central at both sides of the Iron Curtain, it became possible to put the cold war momentarily to a halt. In addition to the tangible contributions of the Eastern bloc to the instrument adopted, the wide acceptance of the New York Convention beyond the ideological divide would serve to strengthen the legitimacy of the treaty. This, in turn, contributed to the consolidation of the United Nation, and its specialized bodies, as a privileged *locus* for the codification of arbitral authority.

2.2 *UNCITRAL as a Privileged Locus for the Codification of Arbitral Authority*

UNCITRAL was established by UNGA resolution 2205 (XXI) of 17 December 1966.[378] The process leading to the establishment of UNCITRAL took place a

378 See UNGA, 'Resolution 2005 (XXI): The Establishment of UNCITRAL, 17 December 1966', *in* UNCITRAL, *Yearbook of the United Nations Commission on International Trade Law*, vol I (United Nations Publications 1970), at 65. For accounts on the creation and functioning of UNCITRAL, see Endre Ustor, 'Le Développement Progressif Du Droit Commercial

few months after the Washington Convention was opened to signature on 18 March 1965. Yet, investment or the settlement of investment disputes did not appear on the radar of those involved in its creation. Rather, this body was envisioned as an organ in charge of promoting the "progressive development of the law of international trade," which was conceived essentially as commercial law for cross-border transactions.

A series of factors informed the decision to create UNCITRAL, such as the perceived modest results obtained up until that point by other institutions, the lack of coordination amongst the various formulating agencies and the limited representation and participation of developing countries in the processes of unification and harmonization of commercial law.[379] Furthermore, the creation of a new body to deal exclusively with the uniformization of the "law of international trade" was based upon the inexistence of an organ within the United Nations that was both technically competent on the matter and able to devote the resources necessary for the success of that endeavour.

UNCITRAL was set, therefore, as a central formulating agency for the legislative governance of cross-border trade. It was thought that this new body would be in the best position to coordinate the efforts of the diverse organs working on these matters, while commanding higher authority due to UN's broad constituency. In other terms, UNCITRAL was to act as "a kind of international clearing house for unification activities,"[380] i.e., a transnational legislative forum in which experts ought to play a central role. Indeed, the performance of a quasi-legislative function has been at the core of most of UNCITRAL's activities since

International. Un Nouveau Programme Juridique de l'ONU' (1967) 13 Annuaire Français de Droit International 289; René David, 'The Methods of Unification' (1968) 16 American Journal of Comparative Law 13; René David, 'La Commission Des Nations Unies Pour Le Droit Commercial International' (1970) 16 Annuaire Français de Droit International 435; John Honnold, 'The United Nations Commission on International Trade Law: Mission and Methods' (1979) 27 American Journal of Comparative Law 201.

379 See UN Secretary-General, 'Progressive Development of the Law of International Trade', *in* UNCITRAL, *Yearbook of the United Nations Commission on International Trade Law*, vol I (United Nations Publications 1970), at 41, para 210.

380 On this matter, the Secretary-General's report read as follows: "It would be essential to assure the most active and broadly-based support of Governments, and at the same time to provide for the participation of recognized authorities in this field of law. It would therefore appear advisable to provide that the membership of such a commission should be composed of an appropriate number of States, elected by the General Assembly, and to provide further, that the representatives of these States, appointed by them to serve on the commission, should be persons of eminence in the field." See UN Secretary-General, *Progressive Development of the Law of International Trade*, at 44, para 226.

its inception, and the body has developed a number of normative documents aiming at the unification of commercial law.

At the roots of UNCITRAL's creation lies a document entitled "Steps to be taken for the progressive development of private international law with a view of promoting international trade,"[381] which was submitted by the delegation of Hungary to the General Assembly.[382] It should not escape the reader's attention that this is another instance in which a socialist country, as it was the case of the Hungarian People's Republic at the time, was spearheading an initiative to promote trade through the codification of law. The proposal was an initiative of Endre Ustor, a Hungarian diplomat and jurist who is usually attributed the paternity of UNCITRAL. Ustor was a member of the International Law Commission and of the *Institut de Droit International*, two institutions labouring towards the codification of international law.

The document in point argued that it was time for the UN to adopt a new agenda concerning the progressive development of international law and that the legislative work within the UN system had been unduly focused on public international law. A narrow approach to international law, claimed the Hungarian delegation, would not find support in Article 13(1)(a) of the Charter, which referred to the progressive development of international law without the qualification of its public or private dimensions.[383] Therefore, the proposal ventured beyond the disciplinary divide, engaging with economic governance as a transversal issue of major interest to international law and with the law on international trade as a topic of central importance for economic

381 Background paper by the delegation of Hungary, see Delegation of Hungary, 'Steps to Be Taken for the Progressive Development of Private International Law with a View to Promoting International Trade,' *in* UNCITRAL, *Yearbook of the United Nations Commission on International Trade Law* (United Nations Publications 1970), at 5–12.

382 The Hungarian proposal was an initiative of Endre Ustor, a Hungarian diplomat and jurist who is usually attributed the paternity of UNCITRAL. Ustor was a member of the International Law Commission and of the *Institut de Droit International.*

383 Among other issues, the Hungarian submission discusses the previous work of the League of Nations for the development of international law, as well as explores the scope of the idea of progressive development of international law within the UN system. In particular, it notes that the expression "progressive development of international law" was crafted in the United Nations Conference on International Organizations, held in 1945 in San Francisco, as a way of striking a balance between stability and change in international law. The term came to be incorporated in Article 13 of the Charter, paragraph 1(a). In particular, the document asked "whether the United Nations General Assembly's activities aimed at the progressive development of international law under Article 13, paragraph 1 a, of the Charter can be extended beyond the traditional area of public international law." See Delegation of Hungary, *Steps To Be Taken*, at 8, para 32.

development.[384] The initiative was not oblivious to the obstacles that could be posed by the division of labour between public and private international lawyers. In this regard, it acknowledged that previous discussions at the Sixth Committee of the General Assembly regarding an expansion of the agenda of the International Law Commission to cover issues of private international law did not produce any concrete results precisely as consequence of this divide.[385]

The Hungarian initiative would gain momentum at the General Assembly and prompted further works, leading the UN Secretariat to produce a note entitled "Unification of the law of international trade."[386] This preliminary study, which was submitted to the Sixth Committee of the General Assembly, stated that "[t]he impetus for the unification of the law of international trade stems from difficulties typically faced by those who engage in international commercial transactions as a result of the multiplicity of, and divergencies in national laws."[387] In particular, the Secretary-General endorsed the idea advanced by the Hungarian delegation, pursuant to which it was necessary for the UN to be involved in the unification of municipal commercial law.

In light of this preliminary study, the General Assembly requested the UN Secretariat to submit a comprehensive report on the unification and harmonization of the law of international trade and included in the provisional agenda for its twenty-first session an item on the topic. The report in question, which was entitled "Progressive development of the law of international trade,"[388] laid the foundational contours for the creation of UNCITRAL. The document was based on a study commissioned to Professor Clive M. Schmitthoff, which was later revised by Professors Margarita Argúas, Dr. Taslim O. Elias, Professor Gyula Eörsi, Professor Willis L. Reese, and Professor Mustafa Kamil Yasseen.[389]

---

384 In relation to the centrality of the law on international trade for economic development, see Delegation of Hungary, *Steps To Be Taken*, at 11, para 56.

385 See Delegation of Hungary, *Steps To Be Taken*, 9–10.

386 See UN Secretary-General, 'Unification of the Law of International Trade: Note by the Secretariat', *in* UNCITRAL, *Yearbook of the United Nations Commission on International Trade Law*, vol I (United Nations Publications 1970), at 13–17.

387 See UN Secretary-General, *Unification of the Law of International Trade*, at 14, para 6.

388 See UN Secretary-General, *Progressive Development of the Law of International Trade*.

389 Professor Schmitthoff, an Anglo-German scholar specialized in the law of international trade and serving at the City of London College, was considered a leading authority in the field of international trade law. Professor Argúas was an Argentinean judge and scholar specialized in private international law. Dr. Taslim O. Elias was the Nigerian minister of justice at the time and would become a president of the International Court of Justice. Professor Eörsi was a Hungarian scholar specialized in comparative private law. Professor Reese was an American scholar specialized in private international law. Professor Yasseen was an Iraqi scholar specialized in public international law.

A central pillar of the Secretariat's report is the definition of international trade law as the "the body of rules governing commercial relationships of a private law nature involving different countries."[390] In this regard, the report produced a list of topics that would illustrate the scope of the law of international trade, which included the international sale of goods, negotiable instruments, the conduct of business activities, insurance, transportation, copyrights and industrial property, and, most notably for the purposes of this study, commercial arbitration.

When UNCITRAL held its first session, in 1968, commercial arbitration was included as a priority in its agenda.[391] By the following session, in 1969, the body would designate a Special Rapporteur to work on issues pertaining to the application and interpretation of conventions on international commercial arbitration.[392] The individual designated was yet another lawyer from a socialist country, the Romanian legal scholar Ion Nestor. Nestor was neither a novice to the field nor a completely unknown to his peers, having published a few years prior to his appointment a book entitled "Problems of Foreign Trade Arbitration in the Socialist Countries of Europe" that gained some attention in the West.[393]

Discharging his task as Special Rapporteur, Nestor presented his report in 1972 at UNCITRAL's fifth session.[394] The 58-page double-columned document would come to life as precious record of the evolution of arbitral codification, an in-depth diagnosis of the state of the art and a detailed roadmap for future work. Notably, Nestor argued in favour of adopting a model set of arbitration

---

390 See UN Secretary-General, *Progressive Development of the Law of International Trade*, at 20, para 10.

391 See UN, 'Report of the United Nations Commission on International Trade Law on the Work of Its First Session, 29 January – 26 February 1968', *in General Assembly, Official Records: Twenty-Third Session, Supplement No. 16 (A/7216)* (United Nations Publications 1968), at 13.

392 See UNCITRAL, 'Report of the Secretary-General: Summary of Comments by Members of the Commission on the Proposals of the Special Rapporteur on International Commercial Arbitration (A/CN.9/79)', *in* UNCITRAL, *Yearbook of the United Nations Commission on International Trade Law*, vol IV (United Nations Publications 1973) 129.

393 The book had been reviewed by Martin Domke in the American Journal of International Law. See Martin Domke, 'Reviewed Work: Problems of Foreign Trade Arbitration in Socialist Countries of Europe, by Ion Nestor' (1964) 58 American Journal of International Law 228.

394 See Ion Nestor, 'Problems Concerning the Application and Interpretation of Existing Multilateral Conventions on International Commercial Arbitration and Related Matters (A/CN.9/64)', *in* UNCITRAL, *Yearbook of the United Nations Commission on International Trade Law*, vol III (United Nations Publications 1972).

rules,[395] and suggested "to draw up a uniform law that could serve as a model, containing certain basic norms."[396] In due course, both of Nestor's recommendations would be taken up by UNCITRAL. The first of his proposals to see the light of day was the model set of arbitration rules, adopted as the 1976 UNCITRAL Arbitration Rules (2.2.1). A few years later, in 1985, it would be time for the long-awaited piece of uniform arbitral legislation to finally come to life, albeit in a *soft* instrument version – *i.e.* the 1985 UNCITRAL Model Law on International Commercial Arbitration (2.2.2).

2.2.1 The UNCITRAL Arbitration Rules

The sequence of events described above resulted from the conclusion that "the attempt to implement simultaneously all of the proposals of the Special Rapporteur would call for an amount of preparatory work [...] that could not be carried out in view of the other priority items on the Commission's agenda."[397] In essence, the decision to first work on a model set of arbitration rules for world-wide use in *ad hoc* arbitration was based on the idea that this was a more cost-effective task to accomplish. This perception was consubstantiated by the fact that other UN bodies, namely the ECE and ECAFE, had produced sets of uniform arbitration rules for regional application.[398] The European Arbitration Rules of the ECE, for instance, were chosen to govern contractual disputes

395 See Nestor, *Problems*, at 247.

396 See Nestor, *Problems*, at 247.

397 See UNCITRAL, *Summary of Comments on the Proposals of the Special Rapporteur on ICA*, at 134.

398 A concern for diversity also informed the decision to undertake the project of drawing up a model set of arbitration rules for *ad hoc* arbitration with global reach. In this regard, the following considerations were brought to UNCITRAL's attention: "The drawing up of a set of uniform rules for worldwide use, as suggested in paragraphs 65 and 66 above, may also contribute to the realization of the Special Rapporteur's further proposal that the Commission should promote the balanced use of arbitration facilities in both developed and developing countries and in trade involving countries having different economic systems (see proposal D in para. 28 above). Such a set of uniform rules, like the European and ECAFE Rules, presumably would include provisions (in the absence of agreement by the parties) on the venue of arbitration and the appointment of arbitrators by paying due attention to the use of existing appointing authorities and international arbitration centres concerned with disputes arising from international trade. It may be expected that recourse to such rules prepared for world-wide use would result in a more balanced use of arbitrators from the various regions of the world and may contribute to a more balanced use of existing arbitration facilities." See UNCITRAL, *Summary of Comments on the Proposals of the Special Rapporteur on ICA*, 135.

falling under the 1972 trade agreements entered by the United States and the Soviet Union.[399]

In 1973, at its sixth session, UNCITRAL members had the opportunity to analyse Ion Nestor's proposals. At that moment, there was great controversy on the feasibility of producing a uniform arbitration law. Some delegations felt that "the implementation of this proposal was virtually impossible," since "procedural law was much more difficult to unify than substantive law" as "the code of civil procedure was one of the branches in which national traditions were strongest."[400] Much less controversial was the discussion related to the production of model arbitration rules, a course of action supported by the majority of the UNCITRAL Member States.[401] The task was to be performed "[i]n consultation with regional economic commissions of the United Nations and centres of international commercial arbitration, giving due consideration to the Arbitration Rules of the United Nations Economic Commission for Europe and the ECAFE Rules for International Commercial Arbitration."[402]

The staff of the UN Secretary-General had been entrusted with the task of preparing a preliminary draft of the arbitration rules, which would be presented at UNCITRAL's eigth session, held in 1975. This preliminary draft was completed by 1974, having received the input from a Consultative Group created on the advice of the International Committee on Commercial Arbitration.[403] In addition, the draft was also influenced by Pieter Sanders, who had been commissioned by the Secretariat as a consultant on the issue.[404] As he

399 See UNCITRAL, *Summary of Comments on the Proposals of the Special Rapporteur on ICA*, 134.

400 See UNCITRAL, 'Report of the United Nations Commission on International Trade Law on the Work of Its Sixth Session, 2–13 April 1973', *in General Assembly Official Records: Twenty-Eight Session, Supplement No. 17 (A/9017)* (United Nations Publications 1973), at 21.

401 See UNCITRAL, *Report of UNCITRAL on Its Sixth Session*, at 21.

402 See UNCITRAL, *Report of UNCITRAL on Its Sixth Session*, at 23.

403 The International Committee on Commercial Arbitration was an institution bringing together officials of arbitral institutions and experts in the field The Consultative Group was composed of the following members: Carlos A. Dunshee de Abranches, Director-General of the Inter-American Commercial Arbitration Commission; Tokusuke Kitagawa, from Tokyo Metropolitan University; Donald B. Straus, President of the Research Institute of the American Arbitration Association; and Heinz Strohbach, from the Court of Arbitration of the Chamber of Commerce of the German Democratic Republic. See UN Secretary-General, 'Report of the Secretary-General: Preliminary Draft Set of Arbitration Rules for Optional Use in Ad Hoc Arbitration Relating to International Trade (UNCITRAL Arbitration Rules) (A/CN.9/97)', *in* UNCITRAL, *Yearbook of the United Nations Commission on International Trade Law*, vol IV (United Nations Publications 1975), at 163.

404 See UN Secretary-General, *Report of the Secretary-General: Preliminary Draft Set of Arbitration Rules*, 163.

would continue to take part in these codification projects, Sanders kept amassing symbolic capital, and began to serve as an informal custodian of arbitral knowledge. Unquestionably, Sanders was now one of the leading vectors for the circulation of arbitral knowledge and a most important moderator of the conversations on the codification of arbitral authority.

The document in question made an express effort to take into consideration the New York Convention, the European Convention on International Commercial Arbitration of 1961 (1961 Geneva Convention), and the Washington Convention.[405] The draft was also circulated amongst a large array of stakeholders, many of whom offered comments to the project.[406] The operation of the UNCITRAL rules was to be advanced through a model arbitration clause, as had been the practice for at least half a century by this time. The clause, which provided that "[a]ny dispute, controversy or claim arising out of or relating to this contract, or the breach, termination or invalidity thereof, shall be settled by arbitration in accordance with the UNCITRAL Arbitration Rules as at present in force,"[407] could be further enriched with "plugins" referring to an appointing authority, the number of arbitrators, and the language of proceedings.[408]

Although it focused on international commercial arbitration, having the goal to "facilitate arbitration in international trade,"[409] no efforts were made to limit the applicability of the future instrument to commercial disputes.[410] In

405 See UN Secretary-General, *Report of the Secretary-General: Preliminary Draft Set of Arbitration Rules*, 164.

406 The following stakeholders presented written comments to the preliminary draft: the ECE, the ICC, the Argentinian Chamber of Commerce, the Fifth International Arbitration Congress (held in Delhi between 7–10 January 1975), the Norwegian government, the Hungarian Chamber of Commerce, the Inter-American Commercial Arbitration Commission, the Inter-American Development Bank, and the Commission of European Communities. See UN Secretary-General, *Report of the Secretary-General: Preliminary Draft Set of Arbitration Rules*, 180–186.

407 See footnote (*) to the 1976 Arbitration Rules in UNCITRAL, 'Report of the United Nations Commission on International Trade Law on the Work of Its Ninth Session, 12 April – 7 May 1976', *in General Assembly Official Records: Thirty-First Session, Supplement No. 17 (A/31/17)* (United Nations Publications 1976), at 35.

408 See UN Secretary-General, *Report of the Secretary-General: Preliminary Draft Set of Arbitration Rules*, 164–166.

409 See UN Secretary-General, *Report of the Secretary-General: Preliminary Draft Set of Arbitration* Rules, 166.

410 In this regard, the following was noted: "An attempt to limit the applicability of the rules to 'international trade' by a binding provision in the rules would present difficult problems of definition and might open up new grounds for challenges to arbitration. It does not appear necessary to provide such a limiting provision, since the rules become applicable only when the parties have entered into a written agreement to this effect. The

particular, bridges were established between the UNCITRAL procedural regime and the PCA institutional framework. For instance, already at this early drafting stage, the PCA Secretary-General was expected to perform a residual supervisory role of the proceedings, enshrined in the prerogative to designate an appointing authority failing agreement of the parties in this regard.[411]

The prerogatives of the arbitral tribunal would include a first say on its jurisdiction (the so-called principle of competence-competence) and the purview over the administration of proceedings. Notably, the formulation of competence-competence in the preliminary draft was considerably inspired by Article 41 of the Washington Convention.[412] This fact expresses another instance of the cross-fertilization and intertextuality of codification projects.

Moreover, this preliminary draft also accommodated the possibility of arbitration in equity. One knows that the debate on *amiable composition* had long been a main trench in which the partisans of arbitration as an equitable (and contractual) authority opposed those that portrayed it as a jurisdictional one. Seemingly, the tension was not completely resolved in the 1970s. Deference to *amiable composition* was not so much a result of conviction over its importance, but rather a pragmatic gesture to certain parts of the world where it was still of currency.[413]

This document would be subject to a very general review at the eight session of UNCITRAL, leading to a request made to the Secretary-General to formulate a revised draft taking into account the discussions had and the commentary received. All of this was to be concluded by UNCITRAL's following session.[414]

---

problem of scope is consequently quite different from the one presented by a uniform law or convention which is applicable in the absence of specific agreement by the parties." See UN Secretary-General, *Report of the Secretary-General: Preliminary Draft Set of Arbitration* Rules, at 166.

411 See UNCITRAL, 'Report of the United Nations Commission on International Trade Law on the Work of Its Eight Session, 1–17 April 1975', *General Assembly Official Records: Thirtieth Session, Supplement No. 17 (A/10017)* (United Nations Publications 1975), 169.

412 See UN Secretary-General, *Report of the Secretary-General: Preliminary Draft Set of Arbitration Rules*, 174.

413 In the Secretary-General's report noted the following: "Paragraph 3 deals with arbitrators acting ex *aequo et bono* (as "*amiables compositeurs*"). In arbitration rules intended for world-wide use, this type of arbitration cannot be neglected. It is used in many countries of Western Europe, Africa, Asia and Latin America. The formula in paragraph 3 gives arbitrators acting as '*amiables compositeurs*' great freedom in arriving at their award, although it is generally accepted that such arbitrators are bound by rules of public order (*ordre public*), if not by 'jus cogens' in general." See UN Secretary-General, *Report of the Secretary-General: Preliminary Draft Set of Arbitration Rules*, 178.

414 See UNCITRAL, *Report of the United Nations Commission on International Trade Law on the Work of Its Eight Session, 1–17 April 1975*, 25.

And so it was done. In less than a year, the UN Secretariat produced not just a revised version of the rules,[415] but also a working paper presenting a set of alternative draft provisions that could be adopted,[416] and a note with a proposed schedule for arbitrators' fees.[417] Similarly to what had happened regarding the creation of ICSID, the development of the UNCITRAL Arbitration Rules was spearheaded by a body of bureaucrats serving, in this instance, at the UNCITRAL Secretariat under the purview of the UN Secretary-General.

Although the propositions made by the UNCITRAL Secretariat would be subject to the analysis of Member States, this somewhat faceless bureaucracy, with the assistance of the visible face of Pieter Sanders,[418] was vested with wide legislative latitude. In performing its task, the Secretariat further elaborated on the texts consulted for the preparation of the revised draft. Alongside the normative instruments already used in the preliminary document, the Secretariat sought inspiration from 1975 Rules of Conciliation and Arbitration of the ICC, the Rules of Procedure of the Inter-American Commercial Arbitration Commission, the Commercial Arbitration Rules of the AAA, and the Rules of Procedure of the Foreign Trade Arbitration Commission at the USSR Chamber of Commerce.[419]

The UNCITRAL Secretariat would establish normative links not just with other codification projects, but would also incorporate into codified format emerging rules taken from municipal case law. The most striking example of this relates to Article 21(2) of the 1976 UNCITRAL Arbitration Rules. In essence, this provision was put in place to reinforce the normative weight of the doctrine of separability. The text gained its final contours with the Secretariat's

415 See UN Secretary-General, 'A/CN.9/112 – Report of the Secretary-General: Revised Draft Set of Arbitration Rules for Optional Use in Ad Hoc Arbitration Relating to International Trade (UNCITRAL Arbitration Rules)', *in* UNCITRAL, *Yearbook of the United Nations Commission on International Trade Law*, vol VII (United Nations Publications 1976).

416 See UN Secretariat, 'A/CN.9/113 – Working Paper Prepared by the Secretariat; Revised Draft Set of Arbitration Rules for Optional Use in Ad Hoc Arbitration Relating to International Trade (UNCITRAL Arbitration Rules); Alternative Draft Provisions for the Draft UNCITRAL Arbitration Rules', *in* UNCITRAL, *Yearbook of the United Nations Commission on International Trade Law*, vol VII (United Nations Publications 1976).

417 See UN Secretariat, 'A/CN.9/114 – Note by the Secretariat: Draft UNCITRAL Arbitration Rules; Schedule of Fees of Arbitrators', *in* UNCITRAL, *Yearbook of the United Nations Commission on International Trade Law*, vol VII (United Nations Publications 1976).

418 See UN Secretary-General, *Revised Draft Set of Arbitration Rules*, 158.

419 See UN Secretary-General, *Revised Draft Set of Arbitration Rules*, 159.

revised draft,[420] but it had already been contemplated with a different wording in its preliminary version.[421] The commentary to this provision is quite insightful, highlighting the following:

> Paragraph 4 has been added in order to dispel any possible doubt as to the competence of the arbitrators to determine the existence or validity of a contract of which the arbitration clause forms a part. This paragraph gives effect to the view that the arbitration clause is 'separate' from the contract, as has been decided, inter alia, by the Supreme Court of the United States of America in 1967 in the case of Prima Paint Corporation v. Flood and Conklin Manufacturing Co. (388 U.S. 395). This view may also be considered to conform with the underlying intention of the parties when they entered into a written contract containing an arbitration clause. Consequently, a decision by the arbitrators that a contract is null and void will not affect the validity of the arbitration clause in that contract and will not undermine the competence of the arbitrators to make that decision.[422]

Having before it the documents prepared by the Secretariat,[423] the Member States present at the ninth session of UNCITRAL went on to thoroughly analyse the revised draft in a two-step process. First, the document would be reviewed by a working group, then it would be submitted to the final deliberation of the plenary of UNCITRAL's Member States. Among the members of the working group, many were state officials and diplomats,[424] some were specialists in international sales law,[425] but a few of them were private international lawyers with a good command of arbitral technique. This was the case of Sergei Lebedev, Howard Holtzmann, and Jerzy Jakubowski, all of whom had a publication

420 See Article 19(2) in UN Secretary-General, *Revised Draft Set of Arbitration Rules*, 164. See also Secretariat's commentary to this provision in UN Secretary-General, *Revised Draft Set of Arbitration Rules*, 174.

421 Indeed, the rule was enshrined in Article 18(4) of the Secretariat's preliminary draft. See UN Secretary-General, *Report of the Secretary-General: Preliminary Draft Set of Arbitration Rules*, 174.

422 See UNCITRAL, *Report of the United Nations Commission on International Trade Law on the Work of Its Eight Session, 1–17 April 1975*, 175.

423 See UN Secretary-General, *Revised Draft Set of Arbitration Rules*.

424 For instance, the chairperson of the working group was Roland Loewe. At this point, he was serving as a Director of the Austrian Ministry of Justice. See UNCITRAL, 'A/CN.9/(VIII)/Misc.1 – Provisional List of Participants', 2.

425 For example, Anthony Gordon Guest, delegate for the United Kingdom, was a specialist in commercial and contract law.

record on arbitration and who were very much interested in East-West dispute settlement.

Sergei Lebedev was a private international law professor, having served as President of the Maritime Arbitration Commission and a member of the Foreign Trade Arbitration Commission at the USSR Chamber of Commerce and Industry. He had also been involved in several municipal codification projects, including the elaboration of the Moscow Convention on Arbitration of 1972 and the CMEA Uniform set of Arbitration Rules of 1974.[426] Jakubowski was a law professor in Poland, who had also been actively involved in international commercial arbitration as a practitioner. He had served as the President of the Court of Arbitration at the Polish Chamber of Foreign Trade and acted as an arbitrator in *ad hoc* arbitrations seated in Egypt, France, West Germany, Italy, Spain and Sweden.[427] Holtzmann, for his part, would become a leading arbitration expert in the United States and would ultimately be appointed to sit at the Iran-US Claims Tribunal.[428] Of the three, Jakubowski would be elected by his peers as the rapporteur of the UNCITRAL working group in charge of the draft arbitration rules,[429] reaffirming the importance of jurists from the socialist bloc for the development and codification of transnational arbitral authority. In addition, Aron Broches, Pieter Sanders and Martin Domke also attended the meetings of the working group, in their capacity respectively as World Bank representative, UN consultant and ICC observer.

The working group met between 12 and 26 April 1976, holding a total of 17 meetings. Extensive debate took place in relation to all provisions of the revised draft prepared by UNCITRAL's Secretariat. In these discussions, two elements are worthy of a more paused consideration, which concern the requirement of the written form for the arbitration agreement and the tribunal's prerogatives to conduct proceedings within the UNCITRAL framework.

In relation to the first element, the debate had been raised by Anthony Guest, who represented the United Kingdom, and for whom "the applicability of the rules should not depend on the existence of an 'agreement in writing;' an oral agreement should suffice."[430] Holtzmann, Lebedev, and a majority of

426 For Lebedev's profile, see Lebedev, *op.cit.*, 93.

427 Jakubowski's professional background can be found in Jerzy Jakubowski, 'Some Legal Aspects of Industrial Co-Operation in East-West Relations', *in Collected Courses of the Hague Academy of International Law*, vol. 163 (Martinus Nijhoff Publishers 1979).

428 An overview of Holtzmann's career can be found in Arthur Rovine, 'In_Memoriam: Howard Holtzmann' (2014) 108 American Society of International Law Proceedings 506.

429 See UNGA, 'A/CN.9/9/C.2/SR.1 – UNCITRAL Ninth Session, Committee of the Whole II, Summary Records of the 1st Meeting', at 2.

430 See UNGA, *1st Meeting of the Committee of the Whole II*, at 4, para 25.

other delegates joined forces to defend the written form of the arbitral agreement, pointing to the fact that the New York Convention and most municipal arbitration legislation contained a similar requirement.[431] This provides an interesting example of the importance of uniformization concerns, for the ambition to keep the UNCITRAL Arbitration Rules aligned with the New York convention foreclosed further discussions on the desirability of recasting the written form requirement.

In relation to the second element, it is interesting to note that the Secretariat contemplated a broader role for discretion in the conduct of proceedings than would be ultimately adopted, an approach "following closely the wording of Article 14 in the ECE Arbitration Rules."[432] Equal treatment was then the only limitation imposed on the discretion of arbitrators in the administration of proceedings. Such discretion was gradually narrowed down in the drafting process, with the introduction in the revised draft of a further condition of fairness in addition to equal treatment.[433] Yet, fairness was perceived as a vague notion, leading to a more concrete elaboration of the scope of the tribunal's prerogative in the administration of proceedings. In the place of fairness, a concrete obligation placed on the tribunal to afford at any stage of the proceedings a full opportunity for each party to present its case was included alongside equal treatment.[434]

The final deliberations at the plenary session of UNCITRAL produced few but still relevant changes to the final text of UNCITRAL Arbitration Rules. The most notable of these changes concerns Article 1(2), which was amended to include an express reference to the priority of the applicable law over the will of the parties. Hence, the text that once read "[t]he Rules are subject to the law applicable to the arbitration" were changed to "[t]hese Rules shall govern the arbitration except that where any of these Rules is in conflict with a provision of the law applicable to the arbitration from which the parties cannot derogate, that provision shall prevail."[435] Such late amendments suggest that, even if the drafting process was led by bureaucrats and experts, State representatives kept a hold of the normative output produced at UNCITRAL. At the end of plenary deliberations, all UNCITRAL Members unanimously adopted the text of the

431 See UNGA, *1st Meeting of the Committee of the Whole II*, at 4, para 29 ss.

432 See UN Secretary-General, *Revised Draft Set of Arbitration Rules*, 172.

433 See Article 14 of the Revised Draft in UN Secretary-General, *Revised Draft Set of Arbitration Rules*, 163.

434 See UNCITRAL, *Report of the United Nations Commission on International Trade Law on the Work of Its Ninth Session, 12 April–7 May 1976*, at 176, para 76.

435 See UNCITRAL, *Report of the United Nations Commission on International Trade Law on the Work of Its Ninth Session, 12 April–7 May 1976*, at 33.

rules, enacting one of the most important instruments for the transnational uniformization of arbitral authority. Notably, it would be due to its arbitration rules that UNCITRAL came to be a legislative centre in the reform of investor-state dispute settlement.

Despite Endre Ustor's somewhat transnational vision, the creation of UNCITRAL was based on a well-established division of labour between public and private international lawyers. The mandate given to the body endorsed this divide by subscribing to the dichotomy of *acta jure imperii* and *acta jure gestionis*. In this regard, the scope of the law of international trade excluded "international commercial relations on the level of public law, such as those relating to the attitude and behaviour of States when regulating, in the exercise of their sovereign power, the conduct of trade affecting their territories," while including "international commercial relations on the level of private law entered into by governmental and other public bodies or, particularly in countries of centrally planned economy, by foreign trade corporations."[436]

In essence, UNCITRAL was not envisioned as a forum for the governance of the economic relations of States in their capacity as sovereigns, or even for the governance of international investments in their public law dimension. Under the idea of harmonization and unification of the law of international trade, UNCITRAL was meant to focus on the production of normative instruments to govern cross-border economic relations of a private nature. Nevertheless, the ever-increasing transnational character of arbitration would profoundly disrupt these assumptions, which would find its most notable expression with UNCITRAL's involvement in the legislative work concerning investment arbitration.

Notably, UNCITRAL's work on investment arbitration is the result of a double life undertaken by the UNCITRAL Arbitration Rules. Originally intended to govern commercial arbitration between private parties, these rules were adopted as an alternative to the ICSID system, especially in a series of cases against States that have denounced the Washington Convention (such as Bolivia, Ecuador and Venezuela). This somewhat accidental involvement with ISDS was consolidated with the adoption of the Rules on Transparency and the Mauritius Convention. Strangely, both of these instruments were themselves accidental, as they were side products of the revision process of the UNCITRAL Arbitration Rules undertaken between 2006 and 2010.

436 See UN Secretary-General, *Progressive Development of the Law of International Trade*, at 21, paras. 11–12.

Faced with an ever-growing backlash against the opacity of ISDS,[437] UNCITRAL had to decide to what extent its arbitration rules should contain detailed provisions on the matter. The resulting agreement at the time was that work on ISDS should not delay the revision process of the arbitration rules, but that "the topic of transparency in treaty-based investor-state arbitration was worthy of future consideration and should be dealt with as a matter of priority immediately after the completion of the current revision of the UNCITRAL Arbitration Rules."[438]

The success of the Mauritius Convention as a method of extending the application of the Rules on Transparency for treaties in force prior to the adoption of that set of rules raised UNCITRAL's status even higher as a centre for the production of procedural investment law. The body suddenly became an obvious choice of forum when talks on ISDS reform gained momentum.[439]

In 2017, UNCITRAL felt empowered to entrust its working group III with a broad mandate and a wide discretion to explore potential reforms for ISDS. In addition, the process was to be government-led, marking an express deviation from the traditional expert-led production process adopted at UNCITRAL. The mandate of working group III was laid out in the following terms:

> The Commission entrusted Working Group III with a broad mandate to work on the possible reform of investor-State dispute settlement. In line with the UNCITRAL process, Working Group III would, in discharging that mandate, ensure that the deliberations, while benefiting from the widest possible breadth of available expertise from all stakeholders,

437 There is a vast literature exploring the shortcomings of ISDS. See, for instance, Claire Cutler, 'Reclaiming Sovereignty: Resistance to Transnational Authority and the Investor-State Regime' in Peer Zumbansen (ed), *The Oxford Handbook of Transnational Law* (Oxford University Press 2021); Stephan W Schill, 'Reforming Investor – State Dispute Settlement: A (Comparative and International) Constitutional Law Framework' (2017) 20 Journal of International Economic Law 649; Michael Waibel and others, *The Backlash against Investment Arbitration* (Kluwer Law International 2010); Barnali Choudhury, 'Democratic Implications Arising from the Intersection of Investment Arbitration and Human Rights' 46 Alberta Law Review 983.

438 See UNCITRAL, 'Report of the United Nations Commission on International Trade Law on the Work of Its Forty-First Session (16 June-3 July 2008)', *in General Assembly Official Records, Sixty-third session, Supplement No. 17* (United Nations Publications 2008), at para 314.

439 See Gabrielle Kaufmann-Kohler and Michele Potestà, 'Can the Mauritius Convention Serve as a Model for the Reform of Investor-State Arbitration in Connection with the Introduction of a Permanent Investment Tribunal or an Appeal Mechanism?' [2016] SSRN Electronic Journal 27–31. Available at: <http://dx.doi.org/10.2139/ssrn.3455511>.

> would be Government-led, with high-level input from all Governments, consensus-based and fully transparent. The Working Group would proceed to: (a) first, identify and consider concerns regarding investor-State dispute settlement; (b) second, consider whether reform was desirable in the light of any identified concerns; and (c) third, if the Working Group were to conclude that reform was desirable, develop any relevant solutions to be recommended to the Commission. The Commission agreed that broad discretion should be left to the Working Group in discharging its mandate, and that any solutions devised would be designed taking into account the ongoing work of relevant international organizations and with a view to allowing each State the choice of whether and to what extent it wished to adopt the relevant solution(s).[440]

This new status as a centre for the governance of investment arbitration is seemingly the mirror-image of a change of paradigm concerning UNCITRAL's construction of its mandate. The concept of the "law of international trade,"[441] and the mission of promoting its progressive harmonization, is now construed in a more flexible way. Its direct engagement with matters that were traditionally framed as public law issues indicates that UNCITRAL no longer feels bound to exclusively promote the uniformization of municipal commercial law. Yet, the extent of this paradigm shift is unclear and the outcome of the process of ISDS reform can be decisive in shaping the future role UNCITRAL may play in the transnational governance of international investments. That said, these latest developments, regardless of their outcome, have shown that UNCITRAL is now a privileged and unsurmountable *locus* for the codification of transnational arbitral authority.

2.2.2 Codification beyond Legal Positivism: the UNCITRAL Model Law on International Commercial Arbitration

The UNCITRAL Model Law was a monumental achievement, for it was an item that had been present in the wish list of arbitration stakeholders for almost a century. Instead of producing a minute commentary of this instrument and its legislative history, a task that has already been accomplished by others,[442] the

440 See UNCITRAL, 'Report of the United Nations Commission on International Trade Law on the Work of Its Fiftieth Session (3–21 July 2017)', *in General Assembly Official Records, Seventy-second session, Supplement No. 17* (United Nations Publications 2017), at para 264.

441 See UNGA, *Resolution 2005 (XXI)*.

442 See Howard M Holtzmann and Joseph Neuhaus, *A Guide to the UNCITRAL Model Law on International Commercial Arbitration: Legislative History and Commentary* (Kluwer Law International 1989); Gerold Herrmann, 'UNCITRAL Adopts Model Law on International

following paragraphs will explore the underlying reasons for its success and its relevance for the codification of arbitral authority.

The model law is currently adopted or has inspired the arbitration legislation in 111 jurisdictions.[443] Two moves are fundamental for this achievement. On the one hand, it placed the emphasis of its codification efforts on arbitration administering disputes related to international commerce. On the other hand, and more importantly, UNCITRAL pursued a soft codification approach instead of a hard law one.[444] These two elements combined would defuse resistance within domestic procedural traditions, leading to a gradual acceptance of the solutions conveyed in the model law.

One knows by now that early references to the uniformization of arbitration legislation can be found already in the agenda of the 1906 edition of the International Congress of Chambers of Commerce.[445] It was also demonstrated by this monograph that UNIDROIT was committed for many years to the promotion of a uniform arbitration law, an endeavour put forward with the stewardship of René David. Similarly, when UNCITRAL was created, Ion Nestor was entrusted with the task of designing a work programme in relation to International Commercial Arbitration – and such a programme left the door open for the uniformization of arbitration law.

The obstacles were always evident, with Nestor himself stressing in the 1970s that "development in this direction is slow and in our view could not

---

Commercial Arbitration: (A Brief Account of the Final Text)' (1986) 2 Arbitration International 2; Gerold Herrmann, 'The UNCITRAL Model Law – Its Background, Salient Features and Purposes' (1985) 1 Arbitration International 6. See also Peter Binder, *International Commercial Arbitration and Mediation in UNCITRAL Model Law Jurisdictions* (Kluwer law international 2019).

443 See Binder, *op.cit.*, 20.

444 For an analysis of the use of soft-law instruments in arbitration in particular, see Felix Dasser, "Soft Law" in International Commercial Arbitration', *Collected Courses of the Hague Academy of International Law*, vol 44 (Brill | Nijhoff 2019); VV Veeder, 'Procedural Soft Law in International Arbitration', *Max Planck Encyclopedias of International Law* (Oxford University Press 2019); Gabrielle Kaufmann-Kohler, 'Soft Law in International Arbitration: Codification and Normativity' (2010) 1 Journal of International Dispute Settlement 283. For a general analysis of the use of soft instruments in the governance of transnational private relationships, see Diego P Fernández Arroyo, 'The Growing Significance of Sets of Principles to Govern Trans-Boundary Private Relationships' in UNIDROIT (ed), *Eppur si muove: The Agenda of Uniform Law – Essays in honour of Michael Joachim Bonell to celebrate his 70th birthday*, vol 1 (UNIDROIT 2016).

445 As noted before in this thesis, a resolution adopted in that occasion called the participants in the congress to work towards the promotion of a uniform arbitral legislation. See Canon-Legrand and Jottrand, *op.cit.*, 8.

be too extensive."[446] Notably, it was Nestor's suggestion that such uniformization was to be achieved on the basis of a model law instead of a treaty, a strategy that had been voiced for some time and that had been supported by the ICC since at least 1966.[447] Furthermore, it would also be Nestor's suggestion, drawing expressly from the teachings of René David, to focus UNCITRAL's uniformization efforts on arbitral proceedings related to international commercial disputes instead of those administering the settlement of exclusively municipal legal relations.[448]

The development of the UNCITRAL Model Law started not long after the completion of its Arbitration Rules. Already in 1978, in a consultative meeting held in Paris and attended, among others, by members of the UNCITRAL Secretariat, the African-Asian Legal Consultative Committee, the International Council for Commercial Arbitration and the ICC, it was considered that "the preparation of a Model Law on Arbitration would be a most appropriate way to achieve uniform standards in arbitration procedure, which is most desirable in international trade."[449]

---

446 See Nestor, *Problems*, at 247, para 181.

447 Pieter Sanders observes the following: "The idea of a Model Law on Arbitration is not new. Long ago, in the sixties, when the Council of Europe was preparing what was to become the Uniform Law of Strasbourg, 1966, the ICC had already suggested that it might be preferable not to draft a Uniform Law but a Model Law." See Pieter Sanders, 'Opening Address Professor Pieter Sanders', *UNCITRALs Project for a Model Law on International Commercial Arbitration* (Kluwer Law International 1984), at 24.

448 Nestor noted the following: "The Special Rapporteur feels that a practical and realistic solution would be to draw up a uniform law that could serve as a model, containing certain basic norms (for example, the form of the arbitration agreement and its effects, principles for the establishment of the arbitral tribunal, possibility of choosing a foreign arbitrator, definitive character of the arbitral award, possibility of choice between arbitration according to the rules of law and arbitration according to equity, means of recourse). This model law would relate directly only to disputes concerning international trade (excluding domestic commercial relationships and civil law relationships) and would be limited to procedures which determine the extent to which the State, through its judicial institutions, intends to retain what Professor Ren David calls 'a legitimate and necessary control over the conditions in which the arbitration foreseen by the parties is to be administered and the award of the arbitrators rendered'. René David is quite right when he states that insufficient account has been taken of 'the fact that arbitration in international commercial relationships, differed from arbitration in civil relationships or even in domestic commercial relationships and required a different approach'." See Nestor, *Problems*, 247, para 181.

449 See Iván Szász, 'Introduction to the Model Law of UNCITRAL on International Commercial Arbitration,' *in UNCITRALs Project for a Model Law on International Commercial Arbitration* (Kluwer law international 1984), at 35.

The idea would continue to brew until 1981, when the UNCITRAL's fourteenth session formally decided to vest its Working Group on International Contract Practices with the mandate to draft a model law on international commercial arbitration.[450] As usual, the drafting process would be launched on the basis of documents produced by the UN bureaucrats staffed at the UNCITRAL Secretariat.[451] The whole legislative activity within the working group would be rather quick, being completed in the time span of two years.[452]

A drafting body was constituted, composed of representatives from Austria, Czechoslovakia, France, Ghana, Guatemala, Hungary, India, Japan, Kenya, Philippines, Sierra Leone, Trinidad and Tobago, the USSR, the UK and the USA, but sessions were attended by State officers from other UNCITRAL members and from organizations like UNCTAD, the AALCC, the Commission of the European Communities, the Inter-American Juridical committee, the ICC and ICCA.[453] Ivan Szász, yet another jurist from the Eastern bloc, was elected the chairman of the working group.[454]

The case of Szász is very insightful on how the participation in a codification project may positively impact one's position in the professional hierarchy within the arbitral field. Szász was originally a law professor whose expertise centred on the international sales of goods, while his appointment as Hungarian delegate to UNCITRAL seems to be tied to the many positions he occupied

450 See UNCITRAL, 'Report of the United Nations Commission on International Trade Law', *General Assembly Official Records: Fortieth Session, Supplement No. 17 (A/40/17)* (United Nations Publications 1985), at 5.

451 The UNCITRAL Secretariat prepared a report entitled 'Possible features of a model law on international commercial arbitration' and a note entitled "Possible features of a model law on international commercial arbitration: questions for discussion by the Working Group'. See UNCITRAL, 'A/CN.9/216 – Report of the Working Group on International Contract Practices on the Work of Its Third Session (New York, 16–26 February 1982)', at 3.

452 See UNCITRAL, *Report of the Working Group on International Contract Practices on the Work of Its Third Session*; UNCITRAL, 'A/CN.9/232 – Report of the Working Group on International Contract Practices on the Work of Its Fourth Session (Vienna, 4–15 October 1982)'; UNCITRAL, 'A/CN.9/233 – Report of the Working Group on International Contract Practices on the Work of Its Fifth Session (New York, 22 February-4 March 1983)'; UNCITRAL, 'A/CN.9/245 – Report of the Working Group on International Contract Practices on the Work of Its Sixth Session (Vienna, 29 August-9 September 1983)'; 'A/CN.9/246 – Report of the Working Group on International Contract Practices on the Work of Its Seventh Session (New York, 6–17 February 1984)'.

453 See UNCITRAL, *Report of the Working Group on International Contract Practices on the Work of Its Third Session*, at 2–3.

454 See UNCITRAL, *Report of the Working Group on International Contract Practices on the Work of Its Third Session*, 3.

in governmental bureaucracy.[455] As the Hungarian representative, he did take part in the elaboration of the UNCITRAL Arbitration Rules.[456] Yet, at the time, he did not seem to be a leading voice in the process. His status in the field of arbitration would greatly change as an outcome of his chairmanship of the working group that elaborated the UNCITRAL Model Law. Indeed, when the 1984 ICCA Interim Meeting opened in Geneva, Peter Sanders, then ICCA's chairman, praised Szász as the "highly effective Chairman of the Working Group which elaborated the draft we are going to discuss these two days."[457] Furthermore, he was given the role of presenting the draft to the arbitral community.[458]

A similar phenomenon had already taken place in relation to Aron Broches, given that the role he performed in the creation of ICSID would then guarantee his future involvement in the production of the UNCITRAL Arbitration Rules and the UNCITRAL Model Law. His participation in these many codification projects granted him a permanent seat at that invisible college (or senate) overseeing the codification and circulation of arbitral technique. The same would hold true in the years to come regarding the staffers at the UNCITRAL Secretariat labouring on the codification of arbitration. This was the case, for instance, of Gerold Herrmann, who would become in a few years a leading arbitration practitioner and future president of ICCA.

Turning to the instrument itself, one must note that a fundamental dimension of the UNCITRAL Model Law was to define in more precise terms the division of labour between judges and arbitrators, detailing what had been broadly established in the New York Convention. A particular innovation was the introduction of an express rule defining that court intervention in arbitral proceedings was to take place only in the situations provided for in the model law.[459] In this regard, municipal courts could be called to oversee the

455 In 1972, in a document compiled by UNCITRAL to serve as a registry of experts in international trade law, Szász had been listed as the Head of the Legal Department of the Ministry of Foreign Trade and as a Professor of Law in the Hungarian College of Foreign Trade. In this regard, his field of interest was recorded as the international sales of goods. His professional experience was described as follows: "Practising lawyer from 1955; legal adviser of various foreign trade companies; first senior officer, later head of the Legal Department of the Ministry of Foreign Trade; member of drafting committee on several national and international legislations; significant experience in the practice of international commercial transactions and treaty practices." See UNCITRAL, 'A/CN.9/61 – Register of Experts and Scholars in International Trade Law, Supplement to the Register of Experts and Scholars in International Law', at 42.

456 See, for instance, UNGA, *1st Meeting of the Committee of the Whole II*.

457 See Sanders, *Opening Address*, at 24.

458 See Szász, *Introduction*.

459 Pursuant to Article 5 of the model law, it was established that "[i]n matters governed by this law, no court shall intervene except where so provided in this Law". See UN, *1985*

appointment and challenge of arbitrators,[460] the jurisdiction of the arbitral tribunal,[461] the recognition of the arbitration agreement,[462] the issuance of interim measures,[463] and the administration of evidence.[464] Furthermore, State judges were vested with the prerogative of controlling arbitral awards,[465] echoing the solutions laid out in the New York Convention. On the side of arbitral tribunals, the model law reinforced the arbitrator's prerogatives regarding competence-competence and the conduct of proceedings through the adoption of provisions copied, in slightly revised form, from the UNCITRAL Arbitration Rules.[466]

Evidently, the UNCITRAL Model Law on ICA greatly mirrors the New York Convention and the UNCITRAL Arbitration Rules. This was no accident, for there was an express intent to establish an integrated multi-tiered normative regime.[467] At the apex, one would find the New York Convention, a hard law instrument with few and very general provisions which could accommodate the diversity of municipal views on arbitration given its higher level of abstraction. Then, the model law would serve as transnational force fostering positive law reform at the municipal level. In other terms, the contribution of the model law would be to serve as a vector for the internalization of transnational uniform solutions into national law. Finally, the UNCITRAL Arbitration Rules would operate at the *inter partes* contractual level, furthering the uniform regulation of arbitral proceedings and arbitral authority.

The importance of the United Nations arbitration regime for the uniformization of arbitral authority is beyond questioning. This is true not just for the wide adoption of the New York Convention, the incontestable relevance achieved by the UNCITRAL Model Law or the popularity and influence of

UNCITRAL Model Law on International Commercial Arbitration (United Nations Publications 1994).

460 See Articles 11, 13 and 14 of the 1985 Model Law in UN, *1985 UNCITRAL Model Law on ICA*, 4–5.

461 See Article 16(3) of the 1985 Model Law in UN, *1985 UNCITRAL Model Law on ICA*, 7.

462 See Article 8 of the 1985 Model Law in UN, *1985 UNCITRAL Model Law on ICA*, 3–4.

463 See Article 9 of the 1985 Model Law in UN, *1985 UNCITRAL Model Law on ICA*, 4.

464 See Article 27 of the 1985 Model Law in UN, *1985 UNCITRAL Model Law on ICA*, 10.

465 See Articles 34–36 of the 1985 Model Law in UN, *1985 UNCITRAL Model Law on ICA*, 12–14.

466 See Articles 16, 18 and 19 of the 1985 Model Law in UN, *1985 UNCITRAL Model Law on ICA*, 6–7.

467 Ivan Szász notes the following: "The next step was that, in order to reduce the legal obstacles to arbitration, UNCITRAL decided to prepare a Model Law on arbitration procedure taking into account particularly the provisions of the 1958 Convention on the Recognition and Enforcement of Foreign Arbitral Awards and of the UNCITRAL Arbitration Rules. Harmonizing the Model Law with these documents and using, whenever possible, previously adopted solutions, was a very important guideline." See Szász, *Introduction*, 35–36.

the UNCITRAL Arbitration Rules. More importantly, the creation of a normative regime embedding hard and soft codification elements opened a new avenue for the uniformization of arbitral authority. In this context, it is no longer necessary to produce an overarching positive law instrument to codify the practice of arbitration. Rather, in such a hybrid and tiered regime, soft instruments with the vocation to be embedded in contracts can be plugged into the hard normative instruments structuring the field.

This strategy would gain popularity in the late 20th century, to the extent that contractual codification of arbitral procedure would become the preferred method in the transnational uniformization of arbitral authority sponsored by private professional bodies. Hence, when the IBA adopted its instrument on the administration of evidence in 1983, the so-called "IBA Rules of Evidence,"[468] it did so in furtherance of this strategy. Rather than advocating before States, or lobbying in an intergovernmental forum like UNCITRAL, the IBA deposited its hope of influencing the architecture of arbitral authority on an instrument to be given force at the contractual level. This private professional network of practicing lawyers would maintain the same approach when it adopted its IBA Rules on Ethics for international Arbitrators in 1987.[469]

As a testament to the success of the strategy, after many amendments, the two IBA instruments have reached the second decade of the 21st century exerting considerable influence over the practice of arbitration.[470] Still, it is doubtful whether this would have been possible without the transnational normative infrastructure implemented at the United Nations.

468 The full title of the instrument was Supplementary Rules Governing the Presentation and Reception of Evidence in International Commercial Arbitration. For the text of the rules and a brief commentary, see DW Shenton, 'An Introduction to the IBA Rules of Evidence' (1985) 1 Arbitration International 118.

469 See David J Branson, 'Ethics for International Arbitrators' (1987) 3 Arbitration International 72; David J. Branson, 'IBA Rules of Ethics for International Arbitrators' (1987) 15 International Business Lawyer 335. The IBA regulation was preceded by a soft code of ethics produced by the AAA in 1977. See John D Feerick, '1977 Code of Ethics for Arbitrators: An Outside Perspective, The Symposium: Ethics in a World of Mandatory Arbitration' (2002) 18 Georgia State University Law Review 907.

470 For the evolution of the IBA regulation on the taking of evidence, see Christoph Müller, 'Importance and Impact of the First PRT, the IBA Evidence Rules' in Daniele Favalli (ed), *Sense and Non-sense of Guidelines, Rules and Other Para-regulatory Texts in International Arbitration* (Juris Net LLC 2015). For a contemporary analysis of the professional regulation of ethics in arbitration, see Catherine Rogers, *Ethics in International Arbitration* (Oxford University Press 2014). See also IBA, *IBA Rules on the Taking of Evidence in International Arbitration: Adopted by a Resolution of the IBA Council on 17 December 2020* (International Bar Association 2020); IBA, *IBA Guidelines on Conflicts of Interest in International Arbitration: Adopted by Resolution of the IBA Council on Thursday 23 October 2014* (International Bar Association 2014).

CHAPTER 6

Conclusion

The codification of law can often explain the emergence of new boundaries within law itself, which takes place through the establishment of specialized binary dichotomies such as arbitrable/inarbitrable.[1] Some may see this ever-expanding process of specialization as a symptom of the fragmentation of globalized law.[2] Nevertheless, a main argument developed in this monograph turns the fragmentation narrative upside down. In the case of arbitration, what may seem like fragmentation at the surface level, can be read as a deep running process of progressive legal unification.

The proliferation of arbitral institutions with their corresponding procedural frameworks hardly disguises a confluence of epistemic assumptions and procedural features. This is most notable if one compares the current state of the art with early debates on the mandate of arbitrators (equitable *versus* jurisdictional), on the need for enforcement of awards (purely voluntary *versus* coercive), or on the organization of proceedings themselves (under the law of the seat *versus* at the discretion of the parties and tribunal). At the turn of 19th century, everything was to be constructed, from the most prosaic elements of arbitral procedure like the number of arbitrators seating in a tribunal or the title of the chairperson (often referred to as umpire instead of president), to more fundamental issues like the impartiality of adjudicators, the need to motivate awards or the arbitrators' ability to rule on its own jurisdiction. In less than a century, most of these issues were somewhat uniformly settled and codified, regardless of whether arbitral procedure was implemented to administer disputes under public or private international law.

It has been demonstrated in this monograph that the encoded form of arbitration currently in existence did not emerge in a vacuum or by accident.

1 See Niklas Luhmann, 'What Is Communication?' (1992) 2 Communication Theory 251; Niklas Luhmann, 'Operational Closure and Structural Coupling: The Differentiation of the Legal System' (1992) 13 Cardozo Law Review 1419; Niklas Luhmann, 'Law as a Social System' (1989) 83 Northwestern Law Review 136.

2 See Martti Koskenniemi, 'Fragmentation of International Law: Difficulties Arising from the Diversification and Expansion of International' (United Nations 2006) Report of the Study Group of the International Law Commission A/CN.4/L.682; Andreas Fischer-Lescano and Gunther Teubner, 'Regime-Collisions: The Vain Search for Legal Unity in the Fragmentation of Global Law' (2004) 25 Michigan Journal of International Law 999.

 | DOI:10.1163/9789004728998_007

Instead, the codification of arbitral practice was an intentional and coordinated project emerging of an ambition to create a uniform normative regime to govern international arbitration. Similarly, it was shown that the authority of arbitration procedure in the administration of transnational disputes was very much dependent first on its ambition to govern war and peace, and at a later stage, on geopolitical factors pertaining to the organisation of the global economy. While these contextual elements may explain the general conditions sustaining the transnational codification of arbitral authority, answering the question as to how arbitration came to be concretely codified and embedded in a globalized administration of justice requires looking into internal professional struggles within a broader movement labouring for the uniformization of international law.

In this monograph, the author asserts the existence of a gradual and progressive convergence of international arbitral forms, which starts at the late 19th century and continues to these days. This convergence was launched by an organized movement promoting the idea of the uniformization of arbitral practice through the codification of procedure. This took place first in relation to interstate disputes, then it was expanded to cross-border commercial disputes, and finally reached disputes involving States and private parties. In all stances, great cross-fertilization existed among the most diverse codification projects, which was not just a fortuitous situation. The intertextuality was intentional, often implemented by people circulating across the many fora labouring for the transnational codification of arbitration. In this regard, the findings of this monograph provide evidence that the transnational codification of international arbitration has always been firmly placed at the intersection of public and private international law, while also receiving a particularly important contribution from comparative lawyers working in the unification of commercial law.

An important finding of this monograph consists of the fact that even unsuccessful codification projects have contributed to increasing the convergence between public and private forms of arbitration governing disputes placed at the crossroads of national and international law. As can be seen throughout this monograph, every codification project is preceded by the compilation and analysis of fragments of legal technique. Scattered information emerging from national or scholarly legal traditions are brought together in various preparatory documents, which will ultimately be processed in order to make some sense out of this wealth of disorganized information. By reassembling chaotic data under an intelligible legal document (like a report or a draft instrument), a cognitive boundary is established and limited normative avenues for further codification emerge. From chaos comes form. This pattern appears time and again throughout the monograph, as was the case with the IDI Arbitration Rules, the UNIDROIT project of uniform arbitration law and its draft convention on arbitration involving governments and individuals, the ILC Model Rules on Arbitral Procedure or even Ion Nestor's report to UNCITRAL on the problems concerning the application and interpretation of existing multilateral conventions on international commercial arbitration.

Evidently, it is beyond questioning that successful codification projects would lay the terms of the division of labour in relation to adjacent dispute resolution mechanisms, embedding the authority of arbitration in a transnational administration of justice. Notably, these successful instruments have created a normative grammar guiding the actions not just of those within the field of arbitration itself, but also of agents operating in parallel to it – as is the case of municipal and international judges.

One knows that, at its most basic level, the practice of arbitration requires that two contending parties submit themselves to the judgment rendered by a third party in relation to their dispute. In abstract, the subject matter at stake could range from family relations to territorial disputes. Concretely, the transnational authority of arbitral procedure first emerged as a type of alternative mechanism for the settlement of interstate disputes with the aspiration to govern war and peace, gradually shifting its attention towards the administration of global economic flows.

It is not excessive to highlight that the transnational codification of arbitral authority was prompted by the long shadows of war. It was the desire to curb the use of force in international dispute settlement that would trigger the creation of the PCA in 1899. Similarly, amidst the Venezuelan blockade, it was the desire to move away from gunboat diplomacy that led to the adoption of the 1907 Drago-Porter Convention. This instrument, often forgotten in the arbitration literature, was a most important step towards the transnationalization of arbitration, for it placed arbitral authority, even if under the guise of diplomatic protection, at the core of the administration of contractual disputes involving governments and private parties. The ambition to govern war and peace would also lead to the embedment of arbitral procedure in the economic settlement of WWI, as well as to the push forward of the agenda of Arbitration, Security and Disarmament in the League of Nations.

In parallel, the transnational codification of arbitral procedure was also pursued under the auspices of the movement for the unification of private international law – a movement marked by an early transnational alliance of public and private actors. While talks about peace also influenced the codification of private international arbitral forms, which were presented as means of fostering peace,[3] this was rather a rhetorical device. The main drive at play here was to promote trade through legal uniformization. Notably, it was felt that the inclusion of arbitration in the agenda of the Economic Committee of the League of Nations would be of "great practical value" in avoiding litigation and as a means of promoting "commercial honesty."[4]

The adoption of the 1923 Geneva Protocol on Arbitration Clauses was the first product of the League's involvement with arbitration. This instrument must be understood as an essential element for the expansion of arbitral authority, for it would give a transnational effect to boilerplate arbitral clauses. As one knows, these clauses would become the main tool through which arbitral institutions would advance their control over arbitration proceedings. In addition, the 1923 Protocol stands as an example of an early codification of the principle of competence-competence,[5] providing that the courts of the contracting States should "refer the parties on the application of either of them to the decision of the arbitrators."[6] Another innovation of the treaty was the formalization of procedural autonomy, as it provided that the arbitral proceedings should be governed by the "will of the parties."[7]

For its part, the 1927 Geneva Convention on Execution of Foreign Arbitral Awards would stand as a most notable accomplishment in the unification of private international law. Until then, anything pertaining to the codification of procedure was seen as too controversial, for it touched upon enormous sovereign sensitivities. As previously discussed in this monograph, the enactment of this instrument followed a tortuous path, starting in the Hague and ending in Geneva. Notably, the often overlooked Fifth Hague Conference on Private

---

3 The founders of the International Chamber of Commerce portrayed themselves as merchants of peace. The idea that economic interdependence was a deterrent to war was clearly articulated by Norman Angell in a book originally published in 1909. In particular, he argued that a general European war would be unlikely as a result of the costs of war and of European economic interdependence. See Norman Angell, *The Great Illusion* (The Floating Press 2014).

4 M Wallenberg and MD Serruys, 'Provisional Economic and Financial Committee, Report on the Session of the Committee Held at Geneva in September 1922, and Submitted to the Council on September 16th, 1922, Annex 421a, A.73.1922.II.' (1922) 3 League of Nations Official Journal 1212, 1403–1404.

5 This priority is now referred to as the negative effect of competence-competence. See Emmanuel Gaillard and Yas Banifatemi, 'The Negative Effect of Competence-Competence: The Rule of Priority in Favour of the Arbitrators' in Emmanuel Gaillard and Domenico di Pietro (eds), *Enforcement of Arbitration Agreements and International Arbitral Awards: The New York Convention in Practice* (Cameron May 2008).

6 See Article 4 in League of Nations, Protocol on Arbitration Clauses [Treaty Series, 1923, vol.27], at 159.

7 Still, this autonomy was placed under the surveillance of the law of the seat. See Article 2 in League of Nations, *Protocol on Arbitration Clauses*, at 158.

International Law, held in 1925, served *de facto* as a preliminary instance for the preparation of the Geneva Convention.

After the adoption of these instruments at the League of Nations, many concerns remained over the unification of legislation governing private forms of arbitration. It was shown in this monograph that a project to complement the Geneva framework existed since the early 1930s, led by UNIDROIT, with the stewardship of René David and under the close watch of the ICC. Notwithstanding its initial support for the uniformization of arbitration laws, the ICC soon realized that uniformization would be too impractical of a task and the idea was put on hold. In essence, most stakeholders were aware that States had little appetite for engaging with the unification of their judicial prerogatives. Consequently, the uniformization of arbitration legislation was put on halt for decades, until UNCITRAL produced in 1985 a soft instrument for the codification of domestic legislation on international commercial arbitration.

This monograph has also found that the production process of the New York Convention was rather fuzzier than what is usually assumed, for the mainstream view places the ICC front and centre of this project. Certainly, there is truth to that, but there is also much more. Voices of members of the ICC network, like Pieter Sanders and René Arnaud, were not necessarily the most authoritative ones. In fact, the two were not even the plenipotentiaries for their delegations, acting as alternates. Instead, core contributions were given by other individuals, such as Gunnar de Sydow, B.A. Wortley and Mario Mateucci. The latter, due to his position at UNIDROIT, clearly performed the function of custodian of expert knowledge, taking an active and preeminent role in all discussions.

Also, this study has brought to light that socialist and capitalist countries worked together towards delineating the final contours of the United Nations arbitration regime. This had been the case at the United Nations Conference on International Commercial Arbitration, as well as in the development of the Arbitration Rules and the Model Law at UNCITRAL. Individuals like Ion Nestor and Sergei Lebdev are the most visible faces of this phenomenon, but the structural force sustaining it was the fact that economic cooperation seemed central to both sides of the Iron Curtain. Hence, the transnational codification of arbitral authority would emerge as an important element in the economic governance of East-West trading relations, allowing the cold war to be momentarily suspended. Evidently, the United Nations arbitration framework would enjoy a strengthened legitimacy as a result of this cooperation beyond the ideological divide – and also due to its broader constituency.

It was also seen in this monograph that the province of transnational arbitral authority was further enlarged in the 1960s with the creation of ICSID. This institution, an appendix of the World Bank, was forged using an instrument of positive law. Even still, the Washington Convention is a quite remarkable example of the influence of institutional bureaucracies over the transnational codification of arbitral authority. Indeed, the World Bank's staff were the protagonists of the drafting of the instrument – notably represented by the figure of the Bank's General Counsel at the time, Aron Broches. In this regard, albeit some believe that investment arbitration was moulded to the image of commercial arbitration, it was shown in this study that the conceptualization of the ICSID arbitration regime was decisively influenced by the PCA framework and the ILC Model Rules on Arbitral Procedure.

Besides producing a normative grammar that structured the practice of arbitration and the division of labour in a globalized administration of justice, the transnational codification of arbitral authority has also served as a measure for the quantification of legal knowledge and the creation of an identifiable epistemic community. It generated a commensurable technical expertise, setting a common measure of proficiency to be assessed in relation to one's command of encoded procedural technique. This in turn would produce disciplinary boundaries and internal hierarchies among different stakeholders, based on proficiency over transnationally codified arbitral procedure. Such proficiency would come to define membership and rank within the transnational arbitral community.

One must bear in mind that private or unprocessed records are oftentimes disclosed as part of a codification effort. Outstanding examples are the caseload of arbitral institutions, or the judicial records of a given country on a specific issue. Access to this knowledge was uneven and actors taking part in a codification project would enjoy a privileged entry point to this wealth of information. This elevates those "in" the process to the status of sources of arbitral knowledge, regardless of the status of the project itself. Obviously, being chosen to take part in one of these initiatives is already a marker of prestige, for it demonstrates that one holds the ability to amass and process a large amount of disconnected information and turn it into a systematic body of discernible technique.

All these features put together did vest certain individuals with professional gravitas within the field itself. Those individuals would emerge as sort of oracles of the law, acting both as custodians of practice and producers of knowledge. Indeed, authority is a notion very much related to the distribution of knowledge within social spaces,[8] manifesting particularly well a relation

8 See Barry Barnes, 'On Authority and Its Relationship to Power' (1984) 32 The Sociological Review 180, 184 ss.

of subordination between producers of knowledge and its recipients. Those who spearheaded codification endeavours would come to occupy positions of authority within the field, for they would be considered the masters of the art – as was the case, for instance, with individuals like Aron Broches, Pieter Sanders, Howard Holtzmann or Sergei Lebdev.

With regards to the impact of the transnational codification of arbitral authority on the cohort of individuals populating the field of arbitration, the monograph has produced another interesting finding. Indeed, the individuals and professional networks involved in transnational codification projects show that the craft of arbitration concerned a somewhat larger audience than what has usually been imagined. Indeed, it was not just the people gravitating around the ICC or a few "grand old men" who have driven the expansion of arbitral authority through the codification of procedure. Rather, one finds on the stage a multitude of state officials, international bureaucrats, law professionals and institutions.

Besides the ICC, bodies like the IDI, the Hague Conference on Private International Law, UNIDROIT, the ILA, and the United Nations have been of utmost importance to the history unfolding in the pages of this monograph. In addition, and despite a certain belief that arbitration would be seen "with scepticism by enthusiasts of central planning,"[9] it has been shown that the development of transnational arbitral procedure received great support on both sides of the Iron Curtain. Not by chance, a great many socialist jurists left their fingerprint at different stages of the transnational codification of arbitral procedure.

That said, this monograph has also found that the constituency of the arbitral field was never static. A notable dynamic has to do with an initial dominant presence of public international lawyers, which overlaps with the period in time when arbitral procedure was seen as the way forward to curb the use of force in international law. With the advent of permanent international courts, arbitral procedure would gradually shift its purview to the administration of economic flows. With this shift, came a change of guard. Indeed, the mechanism fell out of favour with public international lawyers, while gaining interest amongst private international lawyers. This dynamic continues in flux, for one observes a renewed interest amongst public international lawyers in relation to arbitral procedure due to the central role played by arbitral authority in the governance of international investments.

This brings this monograph to a close. However, prior to bidding the reader farewell, a final word should be said on the paradox of codification.

9 See Jan Paulsson, *The Idea of Arbitration* (Oxford University Press 2013), at 1.

Fragmentation may have been described as an illusion in this study, but there are certainly fragmentary forces at play in any codification process. As it has been often highlighted in the preceding pages, a codification instrument is not just the carrier of a unified normative meaning, but also a place of struggle and contestation. As a consequence, every new codification element, whether it is a hard or soft instrument, can also be an opportunity seized to re-shuffle the distribution of authority and the balance of power within the transnational administration of justice.

This dynamic seems to be at play when States try to regain control over transnational economic dispute settlement, both through the reform of investment arbitration and the creation of State sponsored international commercial courts. The same holds true in relation to the advocates of adjacent elements in the transnational administration of justice, which try to break through the ramparts of codified arbitral authority by emulating some of its development strategies. This is most evident with the adoption of the Singapore Convention on Mediation, which has been created with the ambition to replicate the success of the New York Convention. Yet, the fragmentary threats do not come only from outside of the field of arbitration. This can be easily illustrated with the recent clash between the IBA Rules on the Taking of Evidence and the Prague Rules on the Efficient Conduct of Proceedings.

A guessing game is always a risky one, for there is also a constellation of agents in place serving to guard against these fragmentary forces. Just as the years to come may see the rise of completely different mechanisms for the transnational administration of justice, it may also be the case that everything changes in order to continue the same. In all likelihood, codified arbitral authority will gradually and progressively evolve, being superimposed to new judicial and contractual dispute settlement mechanisms. What is almost certain is that all these changes, or lack thereof, will be inscribed and materialized in transnational codification documents.

Bibliography

Archival Materials

Anzilotti D, 'Draft Protocol on the Execution of Foreign Arbitral Awards, Report of the Committee of Legal Experts and Text of Its Draft, Annex 969, A.11.1927 II. [C.2341927 II.]' (1927) 8 League of Nations Official Journal 890

Anzilotti D, 'Meeting of Legal Experts to Consider the Execution of Arbitral Awards, Report by the Chairman, Appendix 2' (1927) 8 League of Nations Official Journal 582

Asian-African Conference, 'Final Communiqué of the Asian-African Conference of Bandung (24 April 1955)'. Available at: <http://www.cvce.eu/obj/final_communique_of_the_asian_african_conference_of_bandung_24_april_1955-en-676237bd-72f7-471f-949a-88b6ae513585.html>

Asher RE, 'The World BankI/IFC Archives, Oral History Program, Transcript of Interview with Aron Broches, 23 May 1984'. Available at: <https://oralhistory.worldbank.org/transcripts/transcript-oral-history-interview-aron-broches-held-april-18-and-may-23-1984-second>

Asser TMC, 'Questionnaire de Mars 1875' (1875) 7 Revue de droit international et de législation comparée 592

Asser TMC, 'Rapport de M. Asser sur la procédure civile' (1875) Revue de droit international et de législation comparée 37

Asser TMC, 'Rapport supplémentaire, par M. Asser: résumé des réponses au questionnaire de mars 1875' (1875) 7 Revue de droit international et de législation comparée 593

Bevans CI (ed), '1899 Convention for the Pacific Settlement of International Disputes', *Treaties and other international agreements of the United States of America, Multilateral 1776–1917*, vol 1 (Department of State Publication 1968)

Bomani M, 'SID/LC/48 (December 7, 1964) – Working Group IV: Report on Scope of Jurisdiction of the Centre (Articles 26 and 29)', *History of the ICSID Convention*, vol II–2 (*ICSID* Publication 2006)

Brocher C, 'Propositions de M. Ch. Brocher relatives à un questionnaire se rapportant aux conflits de législations en droit pénal' (1875) 7 Revue de droit international et de législation comparée 416

Broches A, 'R65-11 (January 19, 1965): Memorandum from the General Counsel and Draft Report of the Executive Directors to Accompany the Convention', *History of the ICSID Convention*, vols 2–II (ICSID Publication 2006)

Broches A, 'Report of the Chairman of the Legal Committee on Settlement of Investment Disputes', *History of the ICSID Convention*, vol II–2 (ICSID Publication 2006)

Broches A, 'R 62–1 (SD) (June 5, 1962): Working Paper in the Form of a Draft Convention Prepared by the General Counsel and Transmitted to the Executive Directors', *History of the ICSID Convention*, vol 2 (ICSID 2009)

Broches A, 'SecM 61–192 (August 28, 1961): Note by A. Broches, General Counsel; Transmitted to the Executive Directors: "Settlement of Disputes between Governments and Private Parties"', *History of ICSID the Convention*, vol 2 (ICSID Publication 2009)

Broches A, 'SecM 62–17 (January 19, 1962): Note by the General Counsel Transmitted to the Executive Directors', *History of ICSID the Convention*, vol 2 (ICSID Publication 2009)

Broches A, 'SID/63-2 (February 18, 1963): Paper Prepared by the General Counsel and Transmitted to the Members of the Committee of the Whole', *History of the ICSID Convention*, vol 2 (ICSID Publication 2009)

Broches A, 'SID/63-15 (August 9, 1963): First Preliminary Draft of a Convention on the Settlement of Investment Disputes between States and Nationals of Other States', *History of the ICSID Convention*, vol 2 (ICSID Publication 2009)

Brown Scott J (ed), *The Proceedings of The Hague Peace Conference: The Conference of 1899* (Oxford University Press 1920)

Brown Scott J (ed), *The Proceedings of The Hague Peace Conference: The Conference of 1907, Plenary Meetings of the Conference*, vol 1 (Oxford University Press 1920)

Brown Scott J (ed), *The Proceedings of The Hague Peace Conference: The Conference of 1907, Meetings of the First Commission*, vol 2 (Oxford University Press 1921)

Comité Permanent des Congrès, 'Compte rendu du Ie Congrès international des Chambres de commerce et des associations commerciales et industrielles (Liège – 7, 8 et 9 Septembre 1905)' (Imprimerie Dequesne-Masquillier & Fils 1905)

Comité Permanent des Congrès, 'Fifth International Congress of Chambers of Commerce and Commercial and Industrial Associations (Boston – 24, 25, 26 September 1912)' (Boston Chamber of Commerce 1912)

Comité Permanent des Congrès, 'Compte rendu du VIe Congrès international des chambres de commerce et des associations commerciales et industrielles (Paris – 8, 9 et 10 Juin)' (Chambre de commerce de Paris 1914) Bulletin de la Chambre de commerce de Paris

Canon-Legrand L and Jottrand E, *Letter from the Comité Permanent – Actes and Resolutions of the Congress of Milan and Prague* (Comité permanent des Congrès internationaux des Chambres de commerce et des Associations commerciales et industrielles 1908)

Canon-Legrand L and Jottrand E, *Letter from the Comité Permanent – Invitation to the 6th Congress, 20 December 1913* (Comité permanent des Congrès internationaux des Chambres de commerce et des Associations commerciales et industrielles 1913)

Conférence de la Haye de Droit International Privé, *Actes de la cinquième session, tenue du 12 octobre au 7 Novembre 1925* (Imprimerie Nationale 1926)

David R, *Rapport sur l'arbitrage conventionnel en droit privé: étude de droit comparé* (L'Universale – Tipografia Poliglotta 1932)

Delegation of Hungary, 'Steps to Be Taken for the Progressive Development of Private International Law with a View to Promoting International Trade', in *Yearbook of the United Nations Commission on International Trade Law* (United Nations Publications 1970)

Drago L, 'Letter from Señor Luis M. Drago, Minister of Foreign Relations of the Argentine Republic, to Señor Martin Garcia Mérou, Minister of the Argentine Republic to the United States' (29 December 1902). Available at: <https://history.state.gov/historicaldocuments/frus1903/d2> accessed 13 August 2020

Goldschmidt L, 'Projet de règlement pour tribunaux arbitraux internationaux présenté à l'Institut de droit international (Session de Genève 1874)' (1874) 6 Revue de droit international et de législation comparée 421

Hellners V, 'SID/LC/50 (December 8, 1964) – Working Group VI: Chairman Mr. Vidar Hellners (Sweden), Report on Article 57', *History of the ICSID Convention*, vol II–2 (ICSID Publication 2006)

Institut de Droit International, 'Procès verbal de la session de Genève, n. 1, séance du 31 août de 1874' (1874) 6 Revue de droit international et de législation comparée 585

Institut de Droit International, 'Procès verbal de la session de Genève, n. 2, séance du 1 septembre de 1874' (1874) 6 Revue de droit international et de législation comparée 589

Institut de Droit International, 'Procès verbal de la session de Genève, n. 3, séance du 2 septembre de 1874' (1874) 6 Revue de droit international et de législation comparée 591

Institut de Droit International, *Annuaire: Tome 1/1877* (Schmidt Periodicals 1994)

Institut de Droit International, *Annuaire: Tome 2/1878* (Schmidt Periodicals 1994)

International Chamber of Commerce, 'E/C.2/373 – Enforcement of International Arbitral Awards: Statement Submitted by the International Chamber of Commerce, a Non-Governmental Organization Having Consultative Status in Category A'

International Law Association, *Reports of the First Conference Held at Brussels, 1873 and of the Second Conference Held at Geneva, 1874* (West, Newman & Co 1903)

International Law Association, *Report of the Thirty-First Conference Held at the Palace of Justice, Buenos Aires, 24th August – 30th August, 1922* (Sweet & Maxwell 1923)

International Law Association, *Report of the Thirty-Third Conference Held at the Riddarhuset and the Riksdaghuset, Stockholm, September 8th to 13th, 1924* (Sweet & Maxwell 1925)

International Law Association, *Report of the Thirty-Fourth Conference Held at the Imperial Palace and the Chamber of Commerce, Vienna, August 5th to August 11th, 1926* (Sweet & Maxwell 1927)

International Law Association, *Report of the Thirty-Fifth Conference Held at Warsaw, August 9th to 16th, 1928* (Sweet & Maxwell 1929)

International Law Association, *Report of the Thirty-Sixth Conference Held at New York in the Hourse of the Association of the Bar, September 2nd to 9th, 1930* (Sweet & Maxwell 1931)

International Law Association, *Report of the Thirty-Seventh Conference Held at Oxford in the Hall of the Union Society, August 8th to 12th, 1932* (Eastern Press 1933)

International Law Association, *Report of the Thirty-Eighth Conference Held at Budapest in the Hungarian Academy of Science, September 6th to 10th, 1934* (Eastern Press 1935)

International Law Association, *Report of the Thirty-Ninth Conference Held at Paris in the Cour de Cassation, September 10th to 15th, 1936* (Richard Clay & Sons 1937)

International Law Association, *Report of the Fortieth Conference Held at Amsterdam in the Royal Colonial Institute, August 29 to September 2, 1938* (Richard Clay & Sons 1939)

Koskenniemi M, 'A/CN.4/L.682: Fragmentation of International Law: Difficulties arising from the Diversification and Expansion of International', Report of the Study Group of the International Law Commission (United Nations 2006)

League of Nations, 'Records of the Fifth Assembly – Text of the Debates – Twenty-Fifth to Twenty-Eight Plenary Meetings, October 1st and 2nd, 1924 – Arbitration, Security and Reduction of Armaments: Protocol for the Pacific Settlement of International Disputes: Reports of the First and Third Committees' (1924) 23 League of Nations Official Journal 192

League of Nations, 'Sub-Committee of Jurists to Study the Question of the Execution of Foreign Arbitral Awards, Annex 2b., A.II/14/1927' (1927) 56 League of Nations Official Journal, Special Supplement 88

Leitmaier M, 'Opening of a Convention Relating to the Execution of Foreign Arbitral Awards, Annex 2a., A.II/23/1927' (1927) 56 League of Nations Official Journal, Special Supplement 81

Lyon-Caen, Charles and others, *Unification de la législation sur la lettre de change et le billet à ordre – rapport général et rapports individuels* (Société des Nations 1923)

MacKinnon FD, 'Report of Committee on the Law of Arbitration' (1927) Cmd. Papers 2817, no. 43.

MacKinnon FD, 'Sub-Committee on Arbitration Clauses: Report on the Session Held in London, July 1922' (1922) 3 League of Nations Official Journal 1410

Nestor I, 'Problems Concerning the Application and Interpretation of Existing Multilateral Conventions on International Commercial Arbitration and Related Matters (A/CN.9/64)', *Yearbook of the United Nations Commission on International Trade Law*, vol III (United Nations Publications 1972)

Oliver H, 'The World BankI/IFC Archives, Oral History Program, Transcript of Interview with Aron Broches, July 11, 1961'. Available at: <https://oralhistory.worldbank.org/transcripts/transcript-oral-history-interview-aron-broches-held-july-11-1961-summary>

Oliver RW, 'A Conversation with Aron Broches, Washington D.C., November 7, 1985'. Available at: <https://oralhistory.worldbank.org/transcripts/transcript-oral-history-interview-aron-broches-held-november-7-1985-main-transcript>

Permanent Court of Arbitration, *Annual Report 2006* (PCA 2006)

Politis N, 'Records of the Ninth Ordinary Session of the Assembly – Meetings of the Committees – Minutes (Reduction of Armaments) – A. 86(1).1928.IX. – Annex 7. Pacific Settlement of International Disputes, Non-Aggression and Mutual Assistance – Report Submitted to the Assembly by M.N. Politis' (1928) 67 League of Nations Official Journal, Special Supplement 117

Politis N and Beneš E, 'Records of the Fifth Assembly – Text of the Debates – Annex 30, A.135(I).1924.IX – Arbitration, Security and Reduction of Armaments – General Report Submitted to the Assembly on Behalf of the First and Third Committees' (1924) 223 League of Nations Official Journal, Special Supplement 479

Pozzi R, 'Summary Notes on the Theme of Private International Arbitration' (International Congress of Chambers of Commerce and of the Industrial Associations 1914)

Rolin-Jaequemyns G, 'Procès verbal de la session de la Haye du 25 au 31 août' (1875) 7 Revue de droit international et de législation comparée 273

Sailly and Duché, 'Rapport en réponse à la 3e question de l'ordre du Jour du Congrès: "De l'unification des législation relatives à la procédure d'arbitrage pour régler les litiges entre citoyens de pays différents" – presenté au nom de la Chambre française de commerce et d'industrie de Bruxelles.' (Publications du VIe Congrès Internationaux des Chambres des Commerce et des Associations Commerciales et industriales 1914)

Scelle G, 'Procédure arbitrale: rapport de Georges Scelle, rapporteur spécial, A/CN.4/18', *Yearbook of the International Law Commission*, vol II (United Nations Publications 1950)

Secrétaire Général de la Commission des réparations, *Rapport sur les travaux de la Commission des réparations de 1920 à 1922, Tome 1* (F Alcan 1923)

Secrétaire Général de la Commission des réparations, *Rapport sur les travaux de la Commission des réparations de 1920 à 1922, Tome 2* (F Alcan 1923)

United Nations, 'Official Records of the Second Session of the General Assembly, Resolutions, 16 September-November 1947' (United Nations 1948) A/519

United Nations, 'Resolutions Adopted by the General Assembly at Its Eight Session during the Period from 15 September to 9 December 1953' (United Nations 1954) A/2640

United Nations, 'Resolutions Adopted by the General Assembly during Its Tenth Session from 20 September to 20 December 1955' (United Nations 1956) A/3116

United Nations, *Yearbook of the International Law Commission, 1949, Summary of Record and Documents of the First Session Including the Report of the Commission to the General Assembly* (United Nations Publications 1956)

United Nations, *Yearbook of the International Law Commission, 1957, Volume I, Summary Records of the Ninth Session, 23 April – 28 June 1957* (United Nations Publications 1957)

United Nations, *Yearbook of the International Law Commission, 1958, Volume I, Summary Records of the Tenth Session, 28 April-4 July 1958*, vol I (United Nations Publications 1958)

United Nations, *Yearbook of the International Law Commission, 1958, Volume II, Documents of the Tenth Session Including the Report of the Commission to the General Assembly*, vol II (United Nations Publications 1958)

United Nations, 'Resolutions Adopted by the General Assembly during Its Thirteenth Session, Volume II, 20 February – 13 March 1959' (United Nations) A/4090/Add.1

United Nations Commission on International Trade Law, 'Report of the United Nations Commission on International Trade Law on the Work of Its First Session, 29 January – 26 February 1968', *General Assembly, Official Records: Twenty-Third Session, Supplement No. 16 (A/7216)* (United Nations Publications 1968)

United Nations Commission on International Trade Law, 'Register of Experts and Scholars in International Trade Law, Supplement to the Register of Experts and Scholars in International Law' (United Nations Commission on International Trade Law 1972) A/CN.9/61.

United Nations Commission on International Trade Law, 'Report of the Secretary-General: Summary of Comments by Members of the Commission on the Proposals of the Special Rapporteur on International Commercial Arbitration (A/CN.9/79)', *Yearbook of the United Nations Commission on International Trade Law*, vol IV (United Nations Publications 1973)

United Nations Commission on International Trade Law, 'Report of the United Nations Commission on International Trade Law on the Work of Its Sixth Session, 2–13 April 1973', *General Assembly Official Records: Twenty-Eight Session, Supplement No. 17 (A/9017)* (United Nations Publications 1973)

United Nations Commission on International Trade Law, 'Provisional List of Participants' (United Nations Commission on International Trade Law 1975) A/CN9/(VIII)/Misc1

United Nations Commission on International Trade Law, 'Report of the United Nations Commission on International Trade Law on the Work of Its Eight Session, 1–17 April 1975', *General Assembly Official Records: Thirtieth Session, Supplement No. 17 (A/10017)* (United Nations Publications 1975)

United Nations Commission on International Trade Law, 'Report of the United Nations Commission on International Trade Law on the Work of Its Ninth Session, 12 April – 7 May 1976', *General Assembly Official Records: Thirty-First Session, Supplement No. 17 (A/31/17)* (United Nations Publications 1976)

United Nations Commission on International Trade Law, 'A/CN.9/216 – Report of the Working Group on International Contract Practices on the Work of Its Third Session (New York, 16–26 February 1982)'

United Nations Commission on International Trade Law, 'A/CN.9/232 – Report of the Working Group on International Contract Practices on the Work of Its Fourth Session (Vienna, 4–15 October 1982)'

United Nations Commission on International Trade Law, 'A/CN.9/233 – Report of the Working Group on International Contract Practices on the Work of Its Fifth Session (New York, 22 February-4 March 1983)'

United Nations Commission on International Trade Law, 'A/CN.9/245 – Report of the Working Group on International Contract Practices on the Work of Its Sixth Session (Vienna, 29 August-9 September 1983)'

United Nations Commission on International Trade Law, 'A/CN.9/246 – Report of the Working Group on International Contract Practices on the Work of Its Seventh Session (New York, 6–17 February 1984)'

United Nations Commission on International Trade Law, 'Report of the United Nations Commission on International Trade Law', *General Assembly Official Records: Fortieth Session, Supplement No. 17* (A/40/17) (United Nations Publications 1985)

United Nations Commission on International Trade Law, 'Report of the United Nations Commission on International Trade Law on the Work of Its Forty-First Session (16 June-3 July 2008)', *General Assembly Official Records, Sixty-third session, Supplement No. 17* (United Nations Publications 2008)

United Nations Commission on International Trade Law, 'Report on the Survey Relating to the Legislative Implementation of the Convention on the Recognition and Enforcement of Foreign Arbitral Awards' (United Nations Commission on International Trade Law 2008) A/CN.9/656

United Nations Commission on International Trade Law, 'Report of the United Nations Commission on International Trade Law on the Work of Its Fiftieth Session (3–21 July 2017)', *General Assembly Official Records, Seventy-second session, Supplement No. 17* (United Nations Publications 2017)

United Nations Conference on International Commercial Arbitration, '1st Meeting [E/CONF.26/SR.1 – Opening of the Conference, Adoption of the Agenda, Adoption of the Rules of Procedure]'

United Nations Conference on International Commercial Arbitration, '2nd Meeting [E/CONF.26/SR.2 – Adoption of the Rules of Procedure (Continued), Consideration of the Draft Convention on the Recognition and Enforcement of Foreign Arbitral Awards (E/2704 and Corr.1, E/2822 and Add. 1 to 6, E/CONF.26/2. 26/3 and Add.1, 26/4)]'

United Nations Conference on International Commercial Arbitration, '4th Meeting [E/CONF.26/SR.4 – E/2704 and Corr.1, E/CONF.26/2, E/CONF.26/3 and Add.1, E/CONF.26/7]'

United Nations Conference on International Commercial Arbitration, '5th Meeting [E/CONF.26/SR.5 – E/2704 and Corr.1, E/2822 and Add.1 to 6, E/CONF.26/2, 26/3 and Add.1, 26/4, 26/7, E/CONF.26/L.6 and L.9]'

United Nations Conference on International Commercial Arbitration, '7th Meeting [E/CONF.26/SR.7 – E/2704 and Corr.1, E/2822 and Add.1 to 6, E/CONF.26/2, 26/3 and Add.1, 26/4, 26/7, E/CONF.26/L.6 to 13]'

United Nations Conference on International Commercial Arbitration, '8th Meeting [E/CONF.26/SR.8 – E/2704 and Corr.1, E/CONF.26/L.10]'

United Nations Conference on International Commercial Arbitration, '9th Meeting [E/CONF.26/SR.9 – E/2704 and Corr. 1, E/2822 and Add.1 to 6, E/CONF.26/2, 26/3 and Add.1, 26/4, 26/7, E/CONF.26/L.7, L.8, L.12. L.14, L.16]'

United Nations Conference on International Commercial Arbitration, '11th Meeting [E/CONF.26/SR.11 – E/2704/Rev.1, E/2822 and Add.1-6, E/CONF.26/2, 6/3 and Add.1, 26/4, 26/7, E/CONF.26/L.6-L.31]'

United Nations Conference on International Commercial Arbitration, '12th Meeting [E/CONF.26/SR.12 – E/2704 and Corr.1, E/CONF.26/7, E/CONF.26/L.8 and Corr.1, L.15/Rev.1, L.16, L.19, L.22, L.31 to L.34]'

United Nations Conference on International Commercial Arbitration, '13th Meeting [E/CONF.26/SR.13 – E/2704 and Corr. 1, E/2822 and Add.1 to 6, E/CONF.26/2, 26/3 and Add.1, 26/4, 26/7, E/CONF.26/L.8 and Corr.1, L.15/Rev.1, L.16, L.17, L.22 to L.25, L.30 to L.36]'

United Nations Conference on International Commercial Arbitration, '14th Meeting [E/CONF.26/SR.14 – E/2704 and Corr.1, E/2822, E/CONF.26/L.17, L.31, L.33/Rev.1, L.34. L.38 and L.40]'

United Nations Conference on International Commercial Arbitration, '17th Meeting [E/CONF.26/SR.17 – E/2704 and Corr.1, E/CONF.26/L.31, L.37/Rev.1, L.43 and L.45]'

United Nations Conference on International Commercial Arbitration, '21st Meeting [E/CONF.26/SR.21 – E/2704 and Corr.1, E/2822 and Add.1 to 6, E/CONF.26/2, 3 and Add.1, E/CONF.26/4, 7, E/CONF.26/L.16, L.28, L.49, L.52, L.55, L.56]'

United Nations Conference on International Commercial Arbitration, '23rd Meeting [E/CONF.26/SR.23 – E/CONF.26/L.60; Adoption and Signature of the Final Act and Convention (E/CONF.26/8, 9, E/CONF.26/L.28, L.49, L.58, L.61)]'

United Nations Conference on International Commercial Arbitration, '24th Meeting [E/CONF.26/SR.24 – Adoption and Signature of the Final Act and Convention (E/CONF.26/8 and 9, E/CONF.26/L.63), Report of the Credentials Committee (E/CONF.26/10)]'

United Nations Conference on International Commercial Arbitration, 'E/CONF.26/7 – Poland: Amendments to the Title of the Convention and Articles 1, 3, 7, 8 10'

United Nations Conference on International Commercial Arbitration, 'E/CONF.26/8/Rev.1 – Final Act and Convention on the Recognition and Enforcement of Foreign Arbitral Awards'

United Nations Conference on International Commercial Arbitration, 'E/CONF.26/C.3/L.1 – Sweden: Draft Additional Protocol on Arbitration Agreements: Submitted for Consideration by Working Party II'

United Nations Conference on International Commercial Arbitration, 'E/CONF.26/INF.1/Rev.2 – List of Representatives and Observers.'

United Nations Conference on International Commercial Arbitration, 'E/CONF.26/L.17 – Netherlands: Amendments to Articles 3, 4, 5'

United Nations Conference on International Commercial Arbitration, 'E/CONF.26/L.33 – Amendments Proposed by the Netherlands, Sweden, the Committee, France, Pakistan and Israel'

United Nations Conference on International Commercial Arbitration, 'E/CONF.26/L.40 – France, Federal Republic of Germany and Netherlands: Amendment to Articles 3, 4 and 5'

United Nations Conference on International Commercial Arbitration, 'E/CONF.26/L.42 – Report on Article 1, Paragraph 1 and Article 2 of the Draft Convention (E/2704 and Corr.1)'

United Nations Conference on International Commercial Arbitration, 'E/CONF.26/L.43 – Text of Articles III, IV and V of the Draft Convention Proposed by Working Party III: 3 June 1958'

United Nations Conference on International Commercial Arbitration, 'E/CONF.26/L.52 – Text Additional Protocol on the Validity of Arbitral Agreements Submitted by the Working Party No. 2–5 June 1958'

United Nations Conference on International Commercial Arbitration, 'E/CONF.26/L.54 – Netherlands: Amendment to Proposal Made by Working Party No. 2 (E/CONF.26/L.52)'

United Nations Economic and Social Council, E/AC.42/4 – Report of the Committee on the Enforcement of International Arbitral Awards'

United Nations Economic and Social Council, 'Resolution 604 (XXI). Recognition and Enforcement of Foreign Arbitral Awards'. Available at: <https://treaties.un.org/doc/source/docs/E_RES_604_XXI-E.pdf>

UN ECOSOC, 'Report of the Committee on the Enforcement of International Arbitral Awards', (United Nations Economic and Social Council, ECOSOC 1955) UN Doc. E/2704

UN Secretariat, 'A/CN.9/113 – Working Paper Prepared by the Secretariat; Revised Draft Set of Arbitration Rules for Optional Use in Ad Hoc Arbitration Relating to International Trade (UNCITRAL Arbitration Rules); Alternative Draft Provisions for the Draft UNCITRAL Arbitration Rules', *Yearbook of the United Nations Commission on International Trade Law*, vol VII (United Nations Publications 1976)

UN Secretariat, 'A/CN.9/114 – Note by the Secretariat: Draft UNCITRAL Arbitration Rules; Schedule of Fees of Arbitrators', *Yearbook of the United Nations Commission on International Trade Law*, vol VII (United Nations Publications 1976)

UN Secretary-General, 'E/2822 – Report by the Secretary-General, Recognition and Enforcement of Foreign Arbitral Awards, 31 Jan 1956'

UN Secretary-General, 'Progressive Development of the Law of International Trade', *Yearbook of the United Nations Commission on International Trade Law*, vol I (United Nations Publications 1970)

UN Secretary-General, 'Unification of the Law of International Trade: Note by the Secretariat', *Yearbook of the United Nations Commission on International Trade Law*, vol I (United Nations Publications 1970)

UN Secretary-General, 'Report of the Secretary-General: Preliminary Draft Set of Arbitration Rules for Optional Use in Ad Hoc Arbitration Relating to International Trade (UNCITRAL Arbitration Rules) (A/CN.9/97)', *Yearbook of the United Nations Commission on International Trade Law*, vol IV (United Nations Publications 1975)

UN Secretary-General, 'A/CN.9/112 – Report of the Secretary-General: Revised Draft Set of Arbitration Rules for Optional Use in Ad Hoc Arbitration Relating to International Trade (UNCITRAL Arbitration Rules)', *Yearbook of the United Nations Commission on International Trade Law*, vol VII (United Nations Publications 1976)

United Nations General Assembly, 'United Nations Development Decade. A Programme for International Economic Co-Operation (I)' (United Nations Publications 1962) A/RES/1710(XVI)

United Nations General Assembly, 'Resolution 2005 (XXI): The Establishment of UNCITRAL, 17 December 1966', *Yearbook of the United Nations Commission on International Trade Law*, vol I (United Nations Publications 1970)

United Nations General Assembly, 'A/CN.9/9/C.2/SR.1 – UNCITRAL Ninth Session, Committee of the Whole II, Summary Records of the 1st Meeting'

UNIDROIT, 'Comité d'étude pour l'arbitrage. Chambre de Commerce Internationale : Discussion du Comité d'études de l'arbitrage commercial international sur l'avant-projet d'une loi internationale sur l'arbitrage en droit privé (Doc. 13) : I. – extrait du procès-verbal de la 12ème session, 19 Décembre 1935; II. – procès-verbal de la 13ème Session, 9 et 10 Janvier 1936' (1936) U.D.P 1936 – Etude III – Arbitrage – Doc. 17

UNIDROIT, 'Preliminary Draft of an International Law on Arbitration' (UNIDROIT 1936) S.D.N.-U.D.P. 1935–Études: III, Arbitrage Doc. 20

UNIDROIT, 'Amendements proposés par la Chambre de Commerce Internationale sur l'avant-projet d'une loi internationale sur l'arbitrage en droit privé' (1937) S.d.N. – U.D.P 1937 – Etude III – Arbitrage – Doc. 26

UNIDROIT, 'Procès-verbaux, sixième session, Stockholm, 30 septembre – 1er octobre 1937' (1938) S.d.N. – U.D.P 1938 – Etude III – Arbitrage – Doc. 28

UNIDROIT, 'Avant-projet d'une loi uniforme sur l'arbitrage dans les rapports internationaux en droit privé et rapport explicatif' (Institut International pour l'Unification du Droit Privé 1940) UDP 1940 – Projet III (I)

UNIDROIT, 'Première session du Comité de travail pour l'étude de l'arbitrage entre gouvernements et particuliers, procès-verbal, Rome, le 11 mai 1948' (UNIDROIT 1948) U.D.P. 1948–Études: XXV, Doc. 2

UNIDROIT, 'Arbitration between Governments and Individuals, Draft Report (Revised Edition)' (UNIDROIT 1948) U.P.L. 1948–Papers: XXV-Arbitration between Governments and Individuals-Doc. 1(1)

UNIDROIT, 'Avant projet d'une Convention internationale permettant de recourir à la Cour Permanent d'Arbitrage de la Haye, pour le règlement des différends nés des contracts commerciaux conclus entre États et particuliers' (UNIDROIT 1949) U.D.P. 1949–Études: XXV-Arbitrage entre Gouvernements et Particuliers-Doc.3

UNIDROIT, 'Comité de travail pour l'étude de l'arbitrage entre gouvernements et particuliers, procès-verbal, deuxième session, Paris, les 10 et 11 mars 1949' (UNIDROIT 1949) U.D.P. 1949–Études: XXV-Arbitrage entre Gouvernements et Particuliers-Doc. 5

UNIDROIT, 'Comité de travail pour l'étude de l'arbitrage entre gouvernements et particuliers, procès-verbal, troisième session, Rome, les 8 et 9 juin 1949' (UNIDROIT 1949) U.D.P. 1949–Études: XXV-Arbitrage entre Gouvernements et Particuliers-Doc. 6

UNIDROIT, 'Avant-Projet d'une Convention Internationale sur l'arbitrage entre gouvernements et particuliers' (UNIDROIT 1950) U.D.P. 1950–Études: XXV-Arbitrage entre Gouvermenement et Particuliers-Doc. 7

UNIDROIT, 'Comité de travail pour l'étude de l'arbitrage entre gouvernements et particuliers, procès-verbal, quatrième session, Rome, les 3, 4 et 10 mars 1950' (UNIDROIT 1951) U.D.P. 1951–Études: XXV-Arbitrage entre Gouvernements et Particuliers-Doc. 8

United States Department of State, 'Papers Relating to the Foreign Relations of the United States, with the Annual Message of the President Transmitted to Congress December 5, 1899' <http://digital.library.wisc.edu/1711.dl/FRUS.FRUS1899> accessed 3 April 2020

Vandervelde É, 'Work of the Economic Committee during Its Eighteenth Session, Annex 847' (1926) 7 League of Nations Official Journal 540

Vandervelde É, 'Work of the Economic Committee during Its Nineteenth and Twentieth Sessions, Annex 905, C.521(I).1926.II.' (1926) 7 League of Nations Official Journal 1358

Wallenberg M and Serruys MD, 'Provisional Economic and Financial Committee, Report on the Session of the Committee Held at Geneva in September 1922, and Submitted to the Council on September 16th, 1922, Annex 421a, A.73.1922.II.' (1922) 3 League of Nations Official Journal 1212

Woods G, 'SID/64-3 (June 10, 1964) Memorandum from the President to the Committee of the Whole', *History of the ICSID Convention*, vol II–1 (ICSID Publication 2009)

World Bank, 'SecM65-3 (January 4, 1965) Memorandum of the President to the Executive Directors', *History of the ICSID Convention*, vol II–2 (ICSID Publication 2006)

World Bank, 'SID/65-2 (February 17, 1965) Memorandum of the Meeting of the Committee of the Whole, February 16, 1965, Not an Approved Record. Discussion of Chapters I and II of the Draft Convention', *History of the ICSID Convention*, vol II–2 (ICSID Publication 2006)

World Bank, 'SID/65-6 (February 25, 1965) Memorandum of the Meeting of the Committee of the Whole, February 23, 1965, Afternoon, Not an Approved Record. Continuation of the Discussion of Chapter IV, and Discussion of Chapters V, VI, VIII, IX and X', vol II–2 (ICSID Publication 2006)

World Bank, 'SID/65-11 (March 11,1965) Memorandum of the Meeting of the Committee of the Whole, March 4, 1965, Not an Approved Record. Continuation of the Discussion of Article 26(2), and Discussion of Article 54 and of the Preamble', *History of the ICSID Convention*, vol II–2 (ICSID Publication 2006)

World Bank, 'SID/LC/1 (November 17, 1964) Legal Committee on Settlement of Investment Disputes', *History of the ICSID Convention*, vols 2–II (ICSID Publication 2006)

World Bank, 'SID/LC/SR/2 (December 17, 1964) Summary Proceedings of the Legal Committee Meeting, November 24, Morning', *History of the ICSID Convention*, vol II–2 (ICSID Publication 2006)

World Bank, 'SID/LC/SR/5 (December 21, 1964) Summary Proceedings of the Legal Committee Meeting, November 27, Morning', *History of the ICSID Convention*, vol II–2 (ICSID Publication 2006)

World Bank, 'SID/LC/SR/11 (December 29, 1964) Summary Proceedings of the Legal Committee Meeting, December 3, Morning', *History of the ICSID Convention*, vol II–2 (ICSID Publication 2006)

World Bank, 'SID/LC/SR/13 (December 30, 1964) Summary Proceedings of the Legal Committee Meeting, December 4, Afternoon', *History of the ICSID Convention*, vol II–2 (ICSID Publication 2006)

World Bank, 'SID/LC/SR/14 (December 30, 1964) Summary Proceedings of the Legal Committee Meeting, December 7, Morning', *History of the ICSID Convention*, vol II–2 (ICSID Publication 2006)

World Bank, 'SID/LC/SR/17 (December 30, 1964) Summary Proceedings of the Legal Committee Meeting, December 8, Afternoon', *History of the ICSID Convention*, vol II–2 (ICSID Publication 2006)

World Bank 'SID/LC/SR/22 (January 11, 1965) – Summary Proceedings of the Legal Committee Meeting, December 11, Morning', *History of the ICSID Convention*, vol II–2 (ICSID Publication 2006)

World Bank, 'Z-13 (December 11, 1964) Revised Draft of Convention on the Settlement of Investment Disputes between States and Nationals of Other States', *History of the ICSID Convention*, vol II–2 (ICSID Publication 2006)

World Bank, 'Memorandum of Meeting of Executive Directors on the Subject of "Settlement of Investment Disputes", Tuesday, March 13, 1962', vol II–1 (ICSID Publication 2009)

World Bank, 'Preliminary Draft of a Convention on the Settlement of Investment Disputes between States and Nationals of Other States. Working Paper for Consultative Meetings with Legal Experts Designated by Governments', *History of the ICSID Convention*, vol II–1 (ICSID Publication 2009)

World Bank, 'Settlement of Investment Disputes. Consultative Meeting of Legal Experts. Addis Ababa, December 16–20, 1963. Summary Record of Proceedings.', *History of the ICSID Convention*, vol II–1 (ICSID Publication 2009)

World Bank, 'Settlement of Investment Disputes. Consultative Meeting of Legal Experts. Bangkok, Thailand, April 27 – May 1, 1964. Summary Record of Proceedings.', *History of the ICSID Convention*, vol II–1 (ICSID Publication 2009)

World Bank, 'Settlement of Investment Disputes. Consultative Meeting of Legal Experts. Geneva, February 17–22, 1964. Summary Record of Proceedings.', *History of the ICSID Convention*, vol II–1 (ICSID Publication 2009)

World Bank, 'Settlement of Investment Disputes. Consultative Meeting of Legal Experts. Santiago, Chile, February 3–7, 1964. Summary Record of Proceedings.', *History of the ICSID Convention*, vol II–1 (ICSID Publication 2009)

World Bank, 'SID 62–1 (December 28, 1962) Memorandum of the Meeting of the Committee of the Whole; December 18, 1962', *History of the ICSID Convention*, vol II–1 (ICSID Publication 2009)

World Bank, 'SID/62-2 (January 7, 1963) Memorandum of the Meeting of the Committee of the Whole, December 27, 1962', *History of the ICSID Convention*, vol II–1 (ICSID Publication 2009)

World Bank, 'SID/63-8 (June 5, 1963) Memorandum of the Meeting of the Committee of the Whole, May 28, 1963.', *History of the ICSID Convention*, vol II–1 (ICSID Publication 2009)

World Bank, 'SID/63-10 (June 13, 1963) Memorandum of the Meeting of the Committee of the Whole, June 4, 1963', *History of the ICSID Convention*, vol II–1 (ICSID Publication 2009)

World Bank, 'SID/63-11 (June 19, 1963) Memorandum of the Meeting of the Committee of the Whole, June 6, 1963', *History of ICSID Convention*, vol II–1 (ICSID Publication 2009)

World Bank, 'SID/63-12 (June 21, 1963) Memorandum of the Meeting of the Committee of the Whole, June 11, 1963', *History of the ICSID Convention*, vol II–1 (ICSID Publication 2009)

World Bank, 'SID/63-16 (September 20, 1963) Memorandum of the Discussion by the Executive Directors, September 10, 1963', *History of the ICSID Convention*, vol II–1 (ICSID Publication 2009)

World Bank, 'Z 12 (September 11, 1964) Draft Convention: Working Paper for the Legal Committee', *History of the ICSID Convention*, vol II–1 (ICSID Publication 2009)

World Bank, 'IBRD Articles of Agreement' <https://www.worldbank.org/en/about/articles-of-agreement/ibrd-articles-of-agreement>

World Bank, 'Board of Directors'. Available at: <https://www.worldbank.org/en/about/leadership/directors>

World Bank, 'Eugene R. Black: 3rd President of the World Bank Group, July 1, 1949 – December 31, 1962' <worldbank.org/en/archive/history/past-presidents/eugene-robert-black>

Cases and Normative Instruments

Allied Governments and Germany, 'Agreement between the Allied Governments and the German Government Concerning the Agreement of August 9, 1924, between the German Government and the Reparation Commission' (1925) 19 American Journal of International Law, Supplement 36

Allied Powers, Associated Powers and Germany, 'Treaty of Peace with Germany (Treaty of Versailles)', *Treaties and other international agreements of the United States of America 1776–1949: Multilateral, 1918–1930*, vol 2 (Department of State Publication 1969)

Bevans CI (ed), '1899 Convention for the Pacific Settlement of International Disputes', *Treaties and other international agreements of the United States of America, Multilateral 1776–1917*, vol 1 (Department of State Publication 1968)

Bevans CI (ed), 'Convention Respecting the Limitation of Employment of Force for the Recovery of Contract Debts', *Treaties and other international agreements of the United States of America, Multilateral 1776–1917*, vol 1 (Department of State Publication 1968)

'Compagnie L'Alliance v. Prunier, Cour de Cassation (Chambre Civile), 10 July 1843' [1992] Revue de l'arbitrage 399

Dell Computer Corp v Union des Consommateurs 34 (Supreme Court of Canada)

International Bar Association, *IBA Guidelines on Conflicts of Interest in International Arbitration: Adopted by Resolution of the IBA Council on Thursday 23 October 2014* (International Bar Association 2014)

International Bar Association, *IBA Rules on the Taking of Evidence in International Arbitration: Adopted by a Resolution of the IBA Council on 17 December 2020* (International Bar Association 2020)

International Chamber of Commerce, 'Former Rules of the Court of Arbitration of the International Chamber of Commerce (1922)' in Arthur Nussbaum (ed), *International Yearbook on Civil and Commercial Arbitration* (Oxford University Press 1928)

International Chamber of Commerce, 'Rules of Conciliation and Arbitration of the International Chamber of Commerce (1928)' in Arthur Nussbaum (ed) (Oxford University Press 1928)

International Chamber of Commerce, *Arbitration Rules in Force as from 1 January 2021* (ICC 2021)

International Law Commission, 'Model Rules on Arbitral Procedure with a General Commentary, 1958', *Yearbook of the International Law Commission*, vol II (United Nations Publications 1958)

League of Nations, 'The Covenant of the League of Nations' (1920) 1 League of Nations Official Journal 3

League of Nations, 'Protocol on Arbitration Clauses, Note by the Secretary-General' (1924) 5 League of Nations Official Journal 235

League of Nations, Protocol on Arbitration Clauses [Treaty Series, 1923, vol.27] 158

League of Nations, 'Protocol for the Pacific Settlement of International Disputes' (1924) 21 League of Nations Official Journal, Special Supplement 21

League of Nations, 'Opening of a Convention Relating to the Execution of Foreign Arbitral Awards' (1927) 11 Resolutions and recommendations adopted by the Assembly during its Eight Ordinary Session – September 5th to 27th, 1927, League of Nations Official Journal, Supplement 15

League of Nations, Convention on Execution of Foreign Arbitral Awards, the League of Nations [Treaty Series, 1927, vol. 92] 301

League of Nations, 'Annex 1. General Act' (1928) 63 League of Nations Official Journal, Special Supplement 20

League of Nations, 'Annex 2. Three Model Bilateral Conventions in Regard to Conciliation, Arbitration and Judicial Settlement' (1928) 63 League of Nations Official Journal, Special Supplement 26

League of Nations, 'Opening for Signature of a Protocol Relating to the Execution of Foreign Arbitral Awards, Report of the Secretariat, Annex 2, A.11/3/1927' (1927) 56 League of Nations Official Journal, Special Supplement 70

Perkins TN and others, 'Award No. III, Delivered on May 29, 1928', *Reports of International Arbitral Awards/Recueil des Sentences Arbitrales* (United Nations 1928)

Perkins TN and others, 'Award No. II, Delivered on January 29, 1927', *Reports of International Arbitral Awards/Recueil des Sentences Arbitrales* (United Nations 2006)

Permanent Court of Arbitration, 'Island of Palmas (United States/The Netherlands)'. Available at: https://pca-cpa.org/en/cases/94/. Accessed 7 April 2022

Permanent Court of Arbitration, 'Rules of Arbitration and Conciliation for Settlement of International Disputes Between Two Parties of Which Only One Is a State. The Hague, February, 1962' (1963) 57 American Journal of International Law 500

Reparation Commission and Germany, 'Agreement between the Reparation Commission and the German Government, Signed at London, August 9, 1924' (1925) 19 American Journal of International Law, Supplement

United Nations, 'Charter of the United Nations' https://www.un.org/en/about-us/un-charter/full-text

United Nations, Convention on the Recognition and Enforcement of Foreign Arbitral Awards [Treaty Series, 1959, vol. 330]

United Nations Commission on International Trade Law, *1985 UNCITRAL Model Law on International Commercial Arbitration* (United Nations Publications 1994)

United States District Court for the Southern District of New York, 'United States Asphalt Refining Co. v. Trinidad Lake Petroleum Co. Limited, 222F 1006, Nos. 58–115, 58–121'

Bibliographical References

Abi-Saab G, 'Fragmentation or Unification: Concluding Remarks' (1999) 31 New York University Journal of International Law and Political Science 919

Angell N, *The Great Illusion* (The Floating Press 2014)

Anzilotti D, *Scritti di diritto internazionale privato* (CEDAM 1960)

Archambault M, 'La jurisprudence des Tribunaux Arbitraux Mixtes sur les comptes courants' (1924) 19 Revue de droit international privé 507

Arendt H, *Between Past and Future* (Viking Press 1961)

Arendt H, 'Les projets de convention de la Haye pour le droit international privé' (1901) 33 Revue de droit international et de législation comparée

Arendt H, 'Droit international privé et droit uniforme' (1880) 12 Revue de droit international et de législation comparée 5

Arendt H, 'Le droit commercial uniforme' (1886) 18 Revue de droit international et de législation comparée 5

Audi P, 'Sémantique de l'autorité' (2002) 50 La lettre de l'enfance et de l'adolescence 15

Audren F and Moreau de Bellaing C, 'Bruno Latour's Legal Anthropology' in Reza Banakar and Max Travers (eds), *Law and Social Theory* (Hart Publishing 2013)

Bacon M, *The Compleat Arbitrator, or, The Law of Awards and Arbitraments* (Printed by E and R Nutt, and R Goslin (Assigns of Edward Sayer, Efq;) for John Worrall, at the Dove in Bell-Tard, near Lincoln's Inn 1731)

Bagge A, 'International Chamber of Commerce and the Development of International Arbitration' (1939) 10 Nordisk Tidsskrift for International Ret 3

Balladore Pallieri G, 'L'arbitrage Privé Dans Les Rapports Internationaux', in *Collected Courses of the Hague Academy of International Law*, vol 51 (Brill 1935)

Banakar R and Travers M, *Theory and Method in Socio-Legal Research* (Hart Publishing 2005)

Baranov RS, 'Contract and Arbitration in Soviet State Economy' (1950) 1 Soviet Studies 383

Barclay T, 'The Antwerp Congress and the Assimilation of Mercantile Law' (1886) 2 Law Quarterly Review 66

Barcroft S, 'The Hague Peace Conference of 1899' 3 Irish Studies in International Affairs 55

Barnes B, 'On Authority and its Relationship to Power' (1984) 32 The Sociological Review 180

Basdevant J, 'Études sur quelques conflits de lois dans les arbitrages internationaux de la première moitié du XIXe siècle' (1906) 2 Revue de droit international privé et de droit pénal international 861

Basdevant J, 'Conflits de nationalité dans les arbitrages vénézuéliens de 1903–1905' (1909) 5 Revue de droit international privé et de droit pénal international 41

Beck U, *The Cosmopolitan Vision* (Polity 2006)

Beck U, 'Reframing Power in the Globalized World' (2008) 29 Organization Studies 793

Beck U, 'Varieties of Second Modernity and the Cosmopolitan Vision' (2016) 33 Theory, Culture & Society 257

Benjamin P, 'Soviet Treaty Practice on Commercial Arbitration Since 1940' (1959) 53 American Journal of International Law 882

Bentham J, Papers relative to Codification and Public Instructions, including correspondence with the Russian Emperor and the Divers Constituted Authorities in the American United States (J. M'Creery, 1817)

Bergmann C, *The History of Reparations* (E Benn 1927)

Berlia G, 'Le président Jules Basdevant' (1968) 33 Politique étrangère 5

Bernheimer CL, *International Arbitration of Individual Commercial Disputes: Tentative Plan Suggested by the Chamber of Commerce of the State of New York* (Chamber of Commerce of the State of New York 1914)

Bewes W, 'The Treaties of Montevideo' (1920) 6 Transactions of the Grotius Society 59

Binder P, *International Commercial Arbitration and Mediation in UNCITRAL Model Law Jurisdictions* (Kluwer law international 2019)

Blühdorn R, 'Le fonctionnement et la jurisprudence des Tribunaux Arbitraux Mixtes créés par les Traités de Paris', in *Collected Courses of the Hague Academy of International Law*, vol 41 (Brill 1932)

Bluntschli JK, *Le droit international codifié* (Guillaume et Cie, Éditeurs 1895)

Bobbio N, *De la structure à la fonction : nouveaux essais de théorie du droit* (Dalloz 2012)

Born GB, *International Commercial Arbitration* (Kluwer law international 2021)

Bouchard C, 'Le « plan américain » Shotwell-Bliss de 1924 : une initiative méconnue pour le renforcement de la paix' (2001) 202–203 Guerres mondiales et conflits contemporains 203

Boucher PB, *Manuel des arbitres, ou Traité complet de l'arbitrage, tant en matière de commerce qu'en matière civile* (Arthur-Bertrand 1807)

Bourdieu P, *Choses Dites* (Les Éditions de Minuit, 1987)

Bourdieu P, 'The Force of Law: Towards a Sociology of the Juridical Field' (1987) 38 The Hastings Law Journal 805

Bourdieu P, *Esquisse d'une théorie de la pratique: précédé de trois études d'ethnologie kabyle* (Librairie Droz 2015)

Bourgeois L, *Pour la Société des Nations* (Bibliothèque-Charpentier 1910)

Branson DJ, 'Ethics for International Arbitrators' (1987) 3 Arbitration International 72

Branson DJ, 'IBA Rules of Ethics for International Arbitrators' (1987) 15 International Business Lawyer 335

Braudel F, *Les ambitions de l'histoire* (Éditions de Fallois 1997)

Briggs HW, 'Reflections on the Codification of International Law by the International Law Commission and by Other Agencies' in *Collected Courses of the Hague Academy of International Law*, vol. 126 (Brill NV 1969)

Broches A, 'International Legal Aspects of the Operations of the World Bank' in *Collected Courses of the Hague Academy of International Law*, vol. 98 (Brill NV 1959)

Bruno P, 'La Saga Des Giscard' (1980) *Le Nouvel Observateur* 94

Bunni NG, *The FIDIC Forms of Contract: The Fourth Edition of the Red Book, 1992, the 1996 Supplement, the 1999 Red Book, the 1999 Yellow Book, the 1999 Silver Book* (3rd ed, Blackwell Pub 2005)

Burchard A, 'The Mixed Claims Commission and German Property in the United States of America' (1927) American Journal of International Law 472

Cafaggi F, 'New Foundations of Transnational Private Regulation' (2011) 38 Journal of Law and Society 20

Caflisch L, 'Cent ans de règlement pacifique des différends interétatiques' in *Collected Courses of the Hague Academy*, vol 288 (Brill NV 2001)

Calvo C, 'Examen des trois règles de droit international proposées dans le traité de Washington: mémoire présenté à l'Institut de droit international (Session de Genève 1874)' (1874) 6 Revue de droit international et de législation comparée 453

Canon-Legrand L and Jottrand E, *Letter from the Comité Permanent – Actes and Resolutions of the Congress of Milan and Prague* (Comité permanent des Congrès internationaux des Chambres de commerce et des Associations commerciales et industrielles 1908)

Carlston KS, 'Codification of International Arbitral Procedure' (1953) 47 American Journal of International Law 203

Carlston KS, 'Draft Convention on Arbitral Procedure of the International Law Commission' (1954) 48 American Journal of International Law 296

Champeil-Desplats V, *Méthodologies du droit et des sciences du droit* (Dalloz 2022)

Choudhury B, 'Democratic Implications Arising from the Intersection of Investment Arbitration and Human Rights' (2009) 46 Alberta Law Review 983

Cohendy G, 'La clause compromissoire au point de vue du droit interne' (1923) 52 Bulletin de la Société de Legislation Comparée 347

Cohn EJ, 'The Unification of the Law of Commercial Arbitration' (1938) 24 Transactions of the Grotius Society 1

Cook WP and others, 'Award Delivered on March 24, 1926', *Reports of International Arbitral Awards/Recueil des Sentences Arbitrales* (United Nations 2006)

Cordero-Moss G, 'Limitations on Party Autonomy in International Commercial Arbitration' in *Collected Courses of the Hague Academy of International Law*, vol 372 (Brill | Nijhoff 2014)

Cotterrell R, 'What Is Transnational Law?' (2012) 37 Law & Social Inquiry 500

Cutler AC, 'Reclaiming Sovereignty: Resistance to Transnational Authority and the Investor-State Regime' in Peer Zumbansen (ed), *The Oxford Handbook of Transnational Law* (Oxford University Press 2021)

Dasser F, '"Soft Law" in International Commercial Arbitration', in *Collected Courses of the Hague Academy of International Law*, vol 44 (Brill | Nijhoff 2019)

David R, 'Un projet de loi uniforme sur l'arbitrage', in *Introduction à l'étude du droit comparé: Recueil d'Études en l'honneur d'Edouard Lambert* (LGDJ 1938)

David R, 'The Methods of Unification' (1968) 16 American Journal of Comparative Law 13

David R, 'La Commission des Nations Unies pour le droit commercial international' (1970) 16 Annuaire français de droit international 435

Dawes RC, *The Dawes Plan in the Making* (The Bobbs-Merrill Company 1925)

De Auer P, 'The Competency of Mixed Arbitral Tribunals' (1927) 13 Transactions of the Grotius Society 17

De Baere G and Mills A, 'T.M.C. Asser and Public and Private International Law: The Life and Legacy of "a Practical Legal Statesman"' (2011) Netherlands Yearbook of International Law 3

De Chazournes LB, 'The International Law Commission in a Mirror—Forms, Impact and Authority' in United Nations (ed), *Seventy Years of the International Law Commission: Drawing a Balance for the Future* (Brill NV 2021)

De Courcy A, *Congrès international de droit commercial tenu à Anvers en 1885* (F Pichon, Successeur, Imprimeur – Éditeur 1885)

De la Rasilla I and Viñuales JE, *Experiments in International Adjudication: Historical Accounts* (Cambridge University Press 2019)

De Visscher C, 'La codification du droit international', in *Collected Courses of the Hague Academy of International Law*, vol 6 (Brill | Nijhoff 1925)

Delmas-Marty M, *Le pluralisme ordonné* (Seuil 2005)

Demogue R, *Traité des obligations en général*, vol 1 (Libraire Arthur Rousseau 1923)

Demogue R, *L'unification internationale du droit privé* (Rousseau & Co, Editeurs 1927)

Descamps É, *Essai sur l'organisation de l'arbitrage international: mémoire aux puissance* (E Guyot 1896)

Dezalay Y and Garth BG, *Dealing in Virtue: International Commercial Arbitration and the Construction of a Transnational Legal Order* (University of Chicago Press 1996)

Domke M, 'The United Nations Conference on International Commercial Arbitration' (1959) 53 American Journal of International Law 414

Domke M, 'Reviewed Work: Problems of Foreign Trade Arbitration in Socialist Countries of Europe, by Ion Nestor' (1964) 58 American Journal of International Law 228

Drago LM, 'State Loans in their Relation to International Policy' (1907) 1 The American Journal of International Law 692

Durkheim É, *Les règles de la méthode sociologique* (Champs Classiques 2010)

Erpelding M, Hess B and Ruiz Fabri H, *Peace Through Law: The Versailles Peace Treaty and Dispute Settlement After World War I* (Nomos Verlagsgesellschaft mbH & Co KG 2019)

Fahey JH, 'The International Chamber of Commerce' (1926) 94 The Annals of the American Academy of Political and Social Science 126

Feerick JD, '1977 Code of Ethics for Arbitrators: An Outside Perspective, The Symposium: Ethics in a World of Mandatory Arbitration' (2002) 18 Georgia State University Law Review 907

Fernández Arroyo DP, 'La codificación del derecho internacional privado en América Latina (Ambitos de Producción Jurídica y Orientaciones Metodológicas)' (Universidad Complutense de Madrid 1993)

Fernández Arroyo DP, 'Private Adjudication without Precedent?' in Horatia Muir Watt and Diego P Fernández Arroyo (eds), *Private International Law and Global Governance* (Oxford University Press 2014)

Fernández Arroyo DP, 'Arbitrator's Procedural Powers: The Last Frontier of Party Autonomy?' in Franco Ferrari (ed), *Limits to party autonomy in international commercial arbitration* (JurisNet 2016)

Fernández Arroyo DP, 'The Growing Significance of Sets of Principles to Govern Trans-Boundary Private Relationships' in UNIDROIT (ed), *Eppur si muove: The Agenda of Uniform Law – Essays in honour of Michael Joachim Bonell to celebrate his 70th birthday*, vol 1 (UNIDROIT 2016)

Finch GA, 'The London Conference on the Application of the Dawes Plan' (1924) 18 American Journal of International Law 707

Fischer-Lescano A and Teubner G, 'Regime-Collisions: The Vain Search for Legal Unity in the Fragmentation of Global Law' (2004) 25 Michigan Journal of International Law 999

Foelix JJG, 'Du conflit des lois de différentes nations, ou du droit international' (1840) 7 Revue étrangère et française de législation, de jurisprudence et d'économie politique 81

Foucault M, *L'archéologie du savoir* (Gallimard 1969)

Frank J, *Law and the Modern Mind* (Stevens & Sons Limited 1949)

Frendo R, 'The Archives of the International Law Association' (2017) 17 Legal Information Management 97

Freyer DH and Gharavi HG, 'Finality and Enforceability of Foreign Arbitral Awards: From "Double Exequatur" to the Enforcement of Annulled Awards: A Suggested Path to Uniformity Amidst Diversity' (1998) 13 ICSID Review 101

Gaillard E, 'Aspects philosophiques du droit de l'arbitrage international' in *Collected Courses of the Hague Academy of International Law*, vol. 329 (Brill | Nijhoff 2007)

Gaillard E, 'The Urgency of Not Revising the New York Convention' in Albert Jan Van den Berg (ed), *50 Years of the New York Convention: ICCA international Arbitration Conference* (Kluwer law international 2009)

Gaillard E, 'Sociology of International Arbitration' (2015) 31 Arbitration International 1

Gaillard E, 'The Myth of Harmony in International Arbitration' (2020) 34 ICSID Review 553

Gaillard E and Banifatemi Y, 'The Negative Effect of Competence-Competence: The Rule of Priority in Favour of the Arbitrators' in Emmanuel Gaillard and Domenico di Pietro (eds), *Enforcement of Arbitration Agreements and International Arbitral Awards: The New York Convention in Practice* (Cameron May 2008)

Gaillard J, *Procès verbal de la Conférence interparlementaire de juin 1889* (Imprimerie de G Balitout et Cie 1889)

Geertz C, 'Thick Description: Toward an Interpretive Theory of Culture', in Geertz (ed), *The interpretation of cultures: selected essays* (Basic Books 1973)

Genin V, 'Pasquale S. Mancini: Du laboratoire juridique national à la fabrique du droit international' (2018) 130(2) Mélanges de l'École française de Rome – Italie et Méditerranée modernes et contemporaines 323

Giorgetti C and Pollack M, *Beyond Fragmentation* (Cambridge University Press 2022)

Glasgow G, *From Dawes to Locarno* (Harper & Brothers Publishers 1926)

Goldman B, 'Les conflits de lois dans l'arbitrage international de droit privé' in *Collected Courses of the Hague Academy of International Law*, vol. 109 (Brill | Nijhoff 1963)

Goldman B, 'La lex mercatoria dans les contrats et l'arbitrage internationaux: réalité et perspectives' (1980) Droit international privé: travaux du Comité français de droit international privé 221

Gounot E, 'La clause compromissoire dans les relations commerciales internationales' (1923) 52 Bulletin de la Société de Legislation Comparée 354

Grieco G, 'A Legal Theory for the Nation State. Pasquale Stanislao Mancini, Hegelianism and Piedmontese Liberalism after 1848' (2019) 24 Journal of Modern Italian Studies 266

Grisel F, *L'arbitrage international ou le droit contre l'ordre juridique: application et création du droit en arbitrage international* (Fondation Varenne/LGDJ 2011)

Grisel F, 'Droit et non-droit dans les sentence arbitrales CCI: une perspective historique' (2014) 25 ICC International Court of Arbitration Bulletin 13

Grisel F, 'Treaty-Making between Public Authority and Private Interests: The Genealogy of the Convention on the Recognition and Enforcement of Foreign Arbitral Awards' (2017) 28(1) European Journal of International Law 73

Halpérin J-L, *Entre nationalisme juridique et communauté de droit* (PUF 1999)

Halpérin J-L, 'Article 231 of the Versailles Treaty and Reparations: The Reparation Commission as a Place for Dispute Settlement?' in Hélène Ruiz Fabri, Burkhard Hess and

Michel Erpelding (eds), *Peace Through Law: The Versailles Peace Treaty and Dispute Settlement After World War I* (Nomos Verlagsgesellschaft mbH & Co KG 2019)

Hamel J, 'La clause compromissoire dans le rapports de commerce internationaux' (1923) 18 Revue de Droit International Privé 721

Hamel J, 'La clause compromissoire dans les rapports de commerce internationaux' (1924) 19 Revue de Droit International Privé 15

Hart HLA, 'Positivism and the Separation of Law and Morals' (1958) 71 Harvard Law Review 593

Hathaway O and Shapiro SJ, *The Internationalists: How a Radical Plan to Outlaw War Remade the World* (Simon & Schuster Paperbacks 2017)

Herrmann G, 'The UNCITRAL Model Law – Its Background, Salient Features and Purposes' (1985) 1 Arbitration International 6

Herrmann G, 'UNCITRAL Adopts Model Law on International Commercial Arbitration: (A Brief Account of the Final Text)' (1986) 2 Arbitration International 2

Hoffher R, 'Discussion sur la validité de la clause compromissoire au groupe lyonnais de la Société de Législation Comparée' (1923) 52 Bulletin de la Société de Législation Comparée 345

Holtzmann HM and Neuhaus J, *A Guide to the UNCITRAL Model Law on International Commercial Arbitration: Legislative History and Commentary* (Kluwer Law International 1989)

Honnold J, 'The United Nations Commission on International Trade Law: Mission and Methods' (1979) 27 American Journal of Comparative Law 201

Hull W, *The Two Hague Conferences and Their Contribution to International Law* (Ginn & Company 1908)

International Chamber of Commerce, BROCHURE NO. 20: THE ORGANIZATION OF THE INTERNATIONAL CHAMBER OF COMMERCE (INTERNATIONAL HEADQUARTERS 1922)

Jackson P, *Beyond the Balance of Power: France and the Politics of National Security in the Era of the First World War* (Cambridge University Press 2013)

Jakubowski J, 'Some Legal Aspects of Industrial Co-Operation in East-West Relations', in Collected Courses of the Hague Academy of International Law, vol. 163 (Martinus Nijhoff Publishers 1979)

Jallamion C, 'La jurisprudence française et l'arbitrage de 1843 a 1958: De la defaveur a la faveur jusqu'à l'avenement de l'arbitrage international (Partie I)' (2015) Revue de l'arbitrage 739

Jarrosson Charles, *La notion d'arbitrage* (LGDJ 1987)

Jessup PC, 'Responsibility of States for Injuries to Individuals' (1946) 46(6) Columbia Law Review 903

Jessup PC, *Transnational Law* (Yale University Press 1956)

Jones NG, 'Bacon, Mathew (b. c. 1700, d. in or before 1757), Legal Writer'. Available at: <https://www.oxforddnb.com/view/10.1093/ref:odnb/9780198614128.001.0001/odnb-9780198614128-e-64033>

Kantorowicz H, 'Savigny and the Historical School of Law' (1937) 53 The Law Quarterly Review 326

Kalenský P, 'Le droit international privé comparé des états socialistes dans leur coopération économique', in *Collected Courses of the Hague Academy of International Law*, vol. 208 (Martinus Nijhoff Publishers 1988)

Kaufmann-Kohler G, 'Soft Law in International Arbitration: Codification and Normativity' (2010) 1 Journal of International Dispute Settlement 283

Kaufmann-Kohler G and Potestà M, 'Can the Mauritius Convention Serve as a Model for the Reform of Investor-State Arbitration in Connection with the Introduction of a Permanent Investment Tribunal or an Appeal Mechanism?' (2016) SSRN Electronic Journal <http://dx.doi.org/10.2139/ssrn.3455511>

Kellor F, *Code of Arbitration: Practice and Procedure of the American Arbitration Tribunal* (Commerce Clearing House Inc 1931)

Kellor F, *American Arbitration: Its History, Functions and Achievements* (Harper & Brothers Publishers 1948)

Kellor F and Domke M, *Arbitration in International Controversy* (Commission to Study the Organization of Peace and American Arbitration Association 1944)

Kelsen H, 'Théorie du droit international public' in *Collected Courses of the Hague Academy of International Law*, vol. 84 (Martinus Nijhoff Publishers 1953)

Kelsen H, 'Foundation of the Natural Law Doctrine' (1973) 2 Anglo-American Law Review 83

Kelsen H, *Pure Theory of Law* (The lawbook exchange 2005)

Kessedjian C, 'Codification du droit commercial international et droit international privé : de la gouvernance normative pour les relations économiques transnationales', in *Collected Courses of the Hague Academy of International Law*, vol. 300 (Martinus Nijhoff Publishers 2002)

Kingsbury B, Krisch N and Stewart RB, 'The Emergence of Global Administrative Law' (2005) 68 Law and Contemporary Problems 15

Kojève A, *La notion de l'autorité* (Gallimard 2004)

Koskenniemi M, *From apology to utopia the structure of international legal argument: reissue with a new epilogue* (Cambridge University Press 1980)

Koskenniemi M, *The Gentle Civilizer of Nations: The Rise and Fall of International Law 1870–1960* (Cambridge University Press 2001)

Koskenniemi M and Leino P, 'Fragmentation of International Law? Postmodern Anxieties' (2002) 15 Leiden Journal of International Law 553

Krisch N, 'Liquid Authority in Global Governance' (2017) 9 International Theory 237

Kronke H, 'The Role of Private International Law: UNIDROIT and the Geneva Conventions on Arbitration' in Hélène Ruiz Fabri, Burkhard Hess and Michel Erpelding (eds), *Peace Through Law: The Versailles Peace Treaty and Dispute Settlement After World War I* (Nomos Verlagsgesellschaft mbH & Co KG 2019)

Lalande A, 'Ch. Lyon-Caen' (1935) 89 Revue internationale de l'enseignement 235

Lauterpacht H, 'La théorie des différends non justiciables en droit international', in *Collected Courses of the Hague Academy of International Law*, vol. 34 (Martinus Nijhoff Publishers 1930)

Lauterpacht H, *The Function of Law in the International Community* (Oxford University Press 2011)

Latour B, *The Making of Law* (Polity Press 2010)

Lebedev SN, 'International Commercial Arbitration in the Socialist Countries Members of the CMEA', in *Collected Courses of the Hague Academy of International Law*, vol 158 (Martinus Nijhoff Publishers 1978)

Leclerc M, 'De l'unification des législations relatives à la procédure d'arbitrage pour régler les litiges entre citoyens de pays différents' (1914) Bulletin de la Chambre de commerce de Paris

Lemercier C and Sgard J, *Arbitrage privé international et globalisation(s)* (CNRS; Sciences Po 2015)

Les directeurs, 'Nécrologie: Max Leclerc 1864–1932' (1932) 41 Annales de Géographie 337

Lipstein K, 'One Hundred Years of Hague Conferences on Private International Law' (1993) 42 The International and Comparative Law Quarterly 553

Llewellyn KN, 'Law and the Social Sciences – Especially Sociology' (1949) 62 Harvard Law Review 1286

Lord Thomas of Cwmgiedd, 'Bailii Lecture 2016: Developing Commercial Law through the Courts: Rebalancing the Relationship between the Courts and Arbitration' (London, 9 March 2016). Available at: <https://www.judiciary.uk/announcements/speech-by-the-lord-chief-justice-the-bailii-lecture-2016/> accessed 24 October 2020

Llowenfeld A, 'The ICSID Convention: Origins and Transformations' (2009) 38 Georgia Journal of International and Comparative Law 37

Luhmann N, 'Law as a Social System' (1989) 83 Northwestern Law Review 136

Luhmann N, 'Operational Closure and Structural Coupling: The Differentiation of the Legal System' (1992) 13 Cardozo Law Review 1419

Luhmann N, 'What Is Communication?' (1992) 2 Communication Theory 251

Lyon-Caen C, 'Notice nécrologique sur M. Goldschmidt, décédé en 1897', in *Annuaire de l'Institut de Droit International*, vol. 17 (Imprimerie James Regame 1898)

MacCormick N, *Rhetoric and the Rule of Law: A Theory of Legal Reasoning* (Oxford University Press 2005)

Mancini P, *Della nazionalità come fondamento del diritto delle genti: prelezione al corso di diritto internazionale e marittimo pronunziata nella R. Università di Torino* (Tipografia Eredi Botta 1851)

Mancini P, 'De l'utilité de rendre obligatoires pour tous les États, sous la forme d'un ou de plusieurs traités internationaux, un certain nombre de règles générales du droit international privé pour assurer la décision uniforme des conflits entre les

différentes législations civiles et criminelles' (1874) 1 Journal de Droit International Privé 221
Mancini P, *Della vocazione del nostro secolo per la riforma e la codificazione del diritto delle genti, e per l'ordinamento di una giustizia internazionale : discorso per la inaugurazione degli studi nella Universitá dii Roma, pronunziato nel 2 Novembre 1874* (Stabilimento Civelli 1874)
Mangabeira Unger R, *Law in Modern Society* (The Free Press 1977)
Mangabeira Unger R, *False Necessity: Anti-Necessitarian Social Theory in the Service of Radical Democracy* (Verso 2004)
Mann FA, 'Lex Facit Arbitrum' (1986) 2 Arbitration International 241
Marks S, 'The Myths of Reparations' (1978) 11 Central European History 231
Marmor A, 'The Dilemma of Authority' (2011) 2 Jurisprudence 121
Marmor A, 'An Institutional Conception of Authority: An Institutional Conception of Authority' (2011) 39 Philosophy & Public Affairs 238
Martiny D, 'Hague Conference on Private International Law', in *Max Planck Encyclopedia of Public International Law* (Oxford University Press 2009)
Mattli W and Dietz T, *International Arbitration and Global Governance* (Oxford University Press 2014)
Mayer P, 'L' autonomie de l'arbitre international dans l'appréciation de sa propre compétence' in *Collected Courses of the Hague Academy of International Law*, vol. 217 (Martinus Nijhoff Publishers 1989)
Michaels R, 'Post-Critical Private International Law: From Politics to Technique' in Diego P Fernández Arroyo and Horatia Muir Watt (eds), *Private International Law and Global Governance* (Oxford University Press 2014)
Miles K, *The Origins of International Investment Law* (Cambridge University Press 2013)
Mills A, 'The Private History of International Law' (2006) 55 The international and comparative law quarterly 1
Mitchell N, 'The Height of the German Challenge: The Venezuela Blockade, 1902–03' (1996) 20 Diplomatic History 185
Moore JB, 'Pan-American Financial Conferences and the Inter-American High Commission' (1920) 14 The American Journal of International Law 343
Morse J, *The Law of Arbitration and Award* (Little, Brown, and Company 1872)
Müller C, 'Importance and Impact of the First PRT, the IBA Evidence Rules' in Daniele Favalli (ed), *Sense and Non-sense of Guidelines, Rules and Other Para-regulatory Texts in International Arbitration* (Juris Net LLC 2015)
Neves M, *Transconstitutionalism* (Hart Publishing 2013)
Niboyet JP, 'Les tribunaux arbitraux mixtes organisés en exécution des traités de paix' (1922) 7 Bulletin de l'Institut Intermediaire International 215
Niboyet JP, 'La Théorie de l'autonomie de La Volonté' in *Collected Courses of the Hague Academy of International Law*, vol. 16 (Martinus Nijhoff Publishers 1927)

Nussbaum A, 'Problems of International Arbitration' in Arthur Nussbaum (ed), *International Yearbook on Civil and Commecial Arbitration* (Oxford University Presss 1928)

Nussbaum A, 'Treaties on Commercial Arbitration: A Test of International Private-Law Legislation' (1942) 56 Columbia Law Review 219

Ogien R, 'Sanctions diffuses: carcasmes, rires, mépris' (1990) 31 Revue Française de Sociologie 591

Oppetit B, *Théorie de l'arbitrage* (Presses universitaires de France 1998)

Parra A, *The History of ICSID* (2nd edn, Oxford University Press 2017)

Partridge SK, 'Frances Kellor and the American Arbitration Association' (2012) 67 Dispute Resolution Journal 16

Paulsson J, *The Idea of Arbitration* (Oxford University Press 2013)

Paulsson M, *1958 New York Convention in Action* (Kluwer Law International 2016)

Pauwelyn J, 'At the Edge of Chaos? Foreign Investment Law as a Complex Adaptive System, How It Emerged and How It Can Be Reformed' (2014) 29 ICSID Review 372

Pellet A, 'Between Codification and Progressive Development of the Law: Some Reflections from the ILC' (2004) 6 International Law FORUM du droit international 15

Picard M, 'La clause compromissoire et l'arbitrage dans les rapports internationaux' (1923) 50 Journal du Droit International 508

Pound R, 'Law in Books and Law in Action' (1910) 44 American Law Review 12

Pound R, 'Sociology of Law and Sociological Jurisprudence' (1943) 5 The University of Toronto Law Journal 1

Radcliffe-Brown A, *Structure and Function in Primitive Society* (The Free Press 1952)

Rajagopal B, *International Law from below: Development, Social Movements, and Third World Resistance* (Cambridge University Press 2003)

Raz J, *Between Authority and Interpretation: On the Theory of Law and Practical Reason* (Oxford University Press 2009)

Requejo Isidro M and Hess B, 'International Adjudication of Private Rights: The Mixed Arbitral Tribunals in the Peace Treaties of 1919–1922', in Ruiz Fabri H, Hess B and Erpelding M (eds), *Peace Through Law: The Versailles Peace Treaty and Dispute Settlement After World War I* (Nomos Verlagsgesellschaft mbH & Co KG 2019)

Revault d'Allonnes M, *Le pouvoir des commencements: essai sur l'autorité* (Seuil 2012)

Ridgeway GL, *Merchants of Peace: Twenty Years of Business Diplomacy through the International Chamber of Commerce, 1919–1938* (Columbia University Press 1938)

Riles A, 'Models and Documents: Artefacts of International Legal Knowledge' (1999) 48 The International and Comparative Law Quarterly

Riles A, 'A New Agenda for the Cultural Study of Law: Taking on the Technicalities' (2005) 53 Buffalo Law Review 973

Rivier A, 'Notice: congrès international de droit commercial à Anvers' (1885) XVIII Revue de droit international et de législation comparée 161

Roberts A, 'Clash of Paradigms: Actors and Analogies Shaping the Investment Treaty System' (2013) 107 American Journal of International Law 45

Rolin-Jaequemyns G, 'De l'étude de la législation comparée et du droit international' (1869) 1 Revue de droit international et de législation comparée 1

Rolin-Jaequemyns G, 'Communications relatives à l'Institut de droit international' (1873) 5 Revue de droit international et de législation comparée 667

Rogers C, *Ethics in International Arbitration* (Oxford University Press 2014)

Romero ES, Jolivet E and Grisel F, 'Aux origines de l'arbitrage commercial contemporain : l'émergence de l'arbitrage CCI (1920–1958)' (2016) Revue de l'arbitrage 403

Roosevelt N, 'The Ruhr Occupation' (1925) 4 Foreign Affairs 112

Root E, 'The Basis of Protection to Citizens Residing Abroad' (1910) 4 American Journal of International Law 517

Rovine A, 'In memoriam: Howard_Holtzmann' (2014) 108 American Society of International Law Proceedings 506

Rubellin-Devichi J, *L'arbitrage: nature juridique, droit Interne et droit international privé* (LGDJ 1964)

Rudstein S, 'L'arbitrage international en matière privée', in *Collected Courses of the Hague Academy of International Law*, vol. 23 (Brill NV 1926)

Ruiz Fabri H, Hess B and Erpelding M, *Peace Through Law: The Versailles Peace Treaty and Dispute Settlement After World War I* (Nomos Verlagsgesellschaft mbH & Co KG 2019)

Ruiz Fabri H and Paine J, 'The Procedural Cross-Fertilization Pull' in Giorgetti C and Pollack M (eds) *Beyond Fragmentation* (Cambridge University Press 2022)

Russell F, *A Treatise on the power and duty of an arbitrator, and the law of submissions and awards; with an Appendix of forms, and of the statutes relating to arbitration* (T & J W Johnson 1849)

Samuel G, *Epistemology and Method in Law* (Routledge 2003)

Sanders P, 'Opening Address Professor Pieter Sanders', in *UNCITRAL's Project for a Model Law on International Commercial Arbitration* (Kluwer Law International 1984)

Sanders P, 'The Making of the Convention', in *Enforcing arbitration awards under the New York Convention: Experience and Prospect* (United Nations 1999)

Santos M, *A natureza do espaço: técnica e tempo, razão e emoção* (Edusp 2009)

Santos M, *Técnica, Espaço, Tempo* (Edusp 2013)

Savigny CV, *Traité de droit romain*, vol. 8 (2nd edn, Librairie de Firmin Didot Frères, Fils et Cie 1860)

Savigny C, *Les droits des obligations*, vol. 1 (Auguste Durand Libraire-Editeur 1863)

Schiavone A, *The Invention of Law in the West* (Harvard University Press 2012)

Schill SW, 'Reforming Investor–State Dispute Settlement: A (Comparative and International) Constitutional Law Framework' (2017) 20 Journal of International Economic Law 649

Schinazi M, 'The Three Ages of International Commercial Arbitration: Between Renewal and Anxiety' (Sciences Po 2019)

Schinazi M, *The Three Ages of International Commercial Arbitration* (Cambridge University Press 2022)

Schuster E, 'The Question as to the Legality of the Ruhr Occupation' (1924) 18 American Journal of International Law 407

Schultz T, *Transnational Legality* (Oxford University Press 2014)

Sending OJ, 'Recognition and Liquid Authority' (2017) 9 International Theory 311

Sgard J, 'A Tale of Three Cities: The Construction of International Commercial Arbitration' in Grégoire Mallard and Jérôme Sgard (eds), *Contractual Knowledge* (Cambridge University Press 2016)

Shenton DW, 'An Introduction to the IBA Rules of Evidence' (1985) 1 Arbitration International 118

Shotwell JT, 'The "American Plan" and the Protocol' (1924) 10 International Conciliation 527

Spiermann O, '"Who Attempts Too Much Does Nothing Well": The 1920 Advisory Committee of Jurists and the Statute of the Permanent Court of International Justice' (2002) 73 British Yearbook of International Law 187

Spiermann O, *International Legal Argument in the Permanent Court of International Justice: The Rise of the International Judiciary* (Cambridge University Press 2004)

Straznicky M, 'Les conferences de droit international privé depuis la fin de la Guerre Mondiale', in *Collected Courses of the Hague Academy of International Law*, vol. 44 (Brill 1933)

Strupp K, 'The Competence of the Mixed Arbitral Courts of the Treaty of Versailles' (1923) 17 The American Journal of International Law 661

Sturges WA, 'Commercial Arbitration in the United States of America' in Arthur Nussbaum (ed), *International Yearbook on Civil and Commercial Arbitration* (Oxford University Press 1928)

Sutton D, Gill J and Gearing M, *Russell on Arbitration* (24th edn, Sweet & Maxwell 2015)

Szász I, 'Introduction to the Model Law of UNCITRAL on International Commercial Arbitration', in *UNCITRAL's Project for a Model Law on International Commercial Arbitration* (Kluwer law international 1984)

Tanca A, 'Dionisio Anzilotti (1867–1950): Biographical Note with Bibliography' (1992) 3 European Journal of International Law 156

Tomashot SR, 'Selling Peace: The History of the International Chamber of Commerce, 1919–1925' (Georgia State University 2015)

Ustor E, 'Le développement progressif du droit commercial international. Un nouveau programme juridique de l'ONU' (1967) 13 Annuaire Français de Droit International 289

Vaïsse M, 'La Société des Nations et le désarmement', in *The League of Nations in Retrospect: Proceedings of the Symposium* (Walter de Gruyter 1983)

Valladão H, 'Le droit international privé des états américains', in *Collected Courses of the Hague Academy of International Law*, vol. 81 (Martinus Nijhoff Publishers 1952)

Veeder V, 'Procedural Soft Law in International Arbitration', in *Max Planck Encyclopedia of International Law* (Oxford University Press 2019)

Venzke I, 'Between Power and Persuasion: On International Institutions' Authority in Making Law' (2013) 4 Transnational Legal Theory 354

Waibel M, 'Opening Pandora's Box: Sovereign Bonds in International Arbitration' (2007) 101 The American Journal of International Law 711

Waibel M and others, *The Backlash against Investment Arbitration* (Kluwer Law International 2010)

Weber M, *Economy and Society* (University of California Press 1978)

Weber M, *Sociologie du droit* (Presses Universitaires de France 2013)

Westlake J, *A Treatise on Private International Law* (William Maxwell & Son 1880)

Westlake J, 'Introduction au droit international privé' (1880) 12 Revue de droit international et de législation comparée 23

Wilgus C, 'The Third International American Conference at Rio de Janeiro, 1906' (1932) 12 The Hispanic American Historical Review 420

Williams JF, 'The Geneva Protocol of 1924 for the Pacific Settlement of International Disputes' (1924) 3 International Affairs 288

Williams JF, 'The Tribunal for the Interpretation of the Dawes Plan' (1928) 22 American Journal of International Law 797

Winfield Scott G, 'Hague Convention Restricting the Use of Force to Recover on Contract Claims' (1908) 2 The American Journal of International Law 78

Witenberg J-C, 'Les jugements des tribunaux arbitraux mixtes et le plan Dawes' (1927) 54 Journal du Droit International 307

Wortley BA, 'Problèmes soulevés en droit international privé par la législation sur l'expropriation', in *Collected Courses of the Hague Academy of International Law*, vol. 67 (Martinus Nijhoff Publishers 1939)

Wortley BA, 'The Interaction of Public and Private International Law Today', in *Collected Courses of the Hague Academy of International Law*, vol. 85 (Martinus Nijhoff Publishers 1954)

Wortley BA, 'The General Principles of Private International Law', in *Collected Courses of the Hague Academy of International Law*, vol. 194 (Martinus Nijhoff Publishers 1958)

Wright Q, 'The General Act for the Pacific Settlement of International Disputes' (1930) 24 American Journal of International Law 582

Yotis Ch, 'De l'influence de la notion de justice et d'équité sur l'application des traités de paix par les tribunaux arbitraux mixtes' (1923) 50 Journal du Droit International 249

Zimmermann R, 'Codification' (2012) 8 European Review of Contract Law

Index

www.ingramcontent.com/pod-product-compliance
Lightning Source LLC
LaVergne TN
LVHW020653300926
849161LV00004B/930